Shakespeare and the Japanese Stage

Shakespeare has been performed in Japan since shortly before the re-opening of the country to the West in the Meiji period (1868–1912). This book breaks new ground by studying the interaction of Japanese and Western conceptions of Shakespeare, and the assimilation of Shakespeare into a richly traditional theatre practice.

The book is a collaboration between leading Shakespeare scholars from Japan and the West. The first part deals with key twentieth-century moments in the assimilation of Shakespeare, including the work of world-famous Japanese directors such as Ninagawa, Suzuki and Noda; the second part considers parallels and differences between Japanese and Western theatre over a longer timespan, focusing on the relationship of Shakespeare to traditional Japanese Noh, Kabuki, Bunraku and Kyogen.

Additional features include black and white and full-colour illustrations of Shakespearean and traditional Japanese productions, a comprehensive chronology of Shakespeare performances in Japan from 1866 to 1994 and the English text of Yasunari Takahashi's celebrated Kyogen adaptation of *The Merry Wives of Windsor*.

Takashi Sasayama is Professor in the Department of English at Kwansei Gakuin University, Kobe, Japan. He is one of Japan's leading Shakespearean scholars and an expert on Japanese theatre. He has written studies in Japanese and English on Elizabethan, Jacobean and Caroline drama.

J. R. Mulryne is Professor in the Department of English at the University of Warwick. Professor Mulryne was until 1997 Chairman of the British Council Drama and Dance Advisory Committee. He is General Editor of the Revels Plays, author of studies of Shakespeare, Yeats and Jacobean Drama and the co-editor, with Margaret Shewring, of seven collections, including *Theatre and Government under the Early Stuarts* and *Shakespeare's Globe Rebuilt*.

Margaret Shewring is a Senior Lecturer in the School of Theatre Studies at the University of Warwick. She is author of a study of Shakespeare's *Richard II* and of articles on Shakespearean and modern performance as well as co-editor, with J. R. Mulryne, of seven collections, including *Theatre and Government under the Early Stuarts* and *Shakespeare's Globe Rebuilt*.

Shakespeare and the Japanese Stage

edited by

Takashi Sasayama
J. R. Mulryne
Margaret Shewring

CAMBRIDGE
UNIVERSITY PRESS

PUBLISHED BY THE PRESS SYNDICATE OF THE UNIVERSITY OF CAMBRIDGE
The Pitt Building, Trumpington Street, Cambridge CB2 1RP, United Kingdom

CAMBRIDGE UNIVERSITY PRESS
The Edinburgh Building, Cambridge CB2 2RU, UK http://www.cup.cam.ac.uk
40 West 20th Street, New York, NY 10011-4211, USA http://www.cup.org
10 Stamford Road, Oakleigh, Melbourne 3166, Australia

First published 1998

Printed in the United Kingdom at the University Press, Cambridge

Typeset in Plantin 10/12   [SE]

A catalogue record for this book is available from the British Library

ISBN 0 521 47043 9 hardback

Contents

Illustrations

Colour plates

Plate 1 Scene from Barry Kyle's production of *The Two Noble Kinsmen*, Swan Theatre, Stratford-upon-Avon (1986).

Plate 2 Toshifumi Suematsu's production of Harue Tsutsumi's *Kanadehon Hamlet* (1994). Katsuya Kobayashi as theatre manager Kan'ya Morita.

Plate 3 A poster for Senda's *Hamlet* (1964), with Nakadai's image superimposed.

Plate 4 The shipwreck scene from Yukio Ninagawa's production of *The Tempest*.

Plate 5 Caliban (foreground centre) with Stephano and Trinculo watched by Ariel (above right) in Ninagawa's production of *The Tempest*.

Plate 6 Caliban and Prospero in Ninagawa's production of *The Tempest*.

Plate 7 Miranda and Prospero.

Plate 8 Ferdinand's attempt to resist Prospero's power in *The Tempest*. The photograph shows the use of the 'spider' device.

Plate 9 Banquo and Macbeth 'on horseback' behind the Butsudan screen which separated an inner stage area from the forestage in Ninagawa's production of *Macbeth*.

Plate 10 Komaki Kurihara as Lady Macbeth in Ninagawa's production of *Macbeth*.

Plate 11 Samisen player and narrator on the Bunraku stage, National Bunraku Theatre, Osaka.

Plate 12 Puppets and manipulators on the Bunraku stage, National Bunraku Theatre, Osaka.

Plate 13 Publicity photograph of puppets and manipulators for the Bunraku stage, National Bunraku Theatre, Osaka.

Plate 14 A scene from Chikamatsu's *The Love Suicides at Sonezaki*, National Bunraku Theatre, Osaka.

Plate 15 Tamao Yoshida manipulating the puppet of Prospero and Minosuke Yoshida that of Miranda in the 1992 Bunraku adaptation of *The Tempest*.

The illustrations are reproduced by kind permission of the following:

Colour plates

1 Shakespeare Birthplace Trust; 2 Asahi Shimbun Co. Ltd; 4–10 Yukio
Ninagawa and the Point Tokyo Company Ltd; 11–15 The National
Bunraku Theatre, Osaka; 16 Mansaku Nomura and the Mansaku-no-
kai.

Black and white illustrations

1, 4, 5, 6, 7–9 and 10 Akihiko Senda and the Asahi Shimbun Co. Ltd; 2
John Haynes; 3 Yukio Ninagawa and the Asahi Shimbun Co. Ltd; 6, 7
and 8 [Credit to come]; 11 and 12 Tetsuo Anzai and Theatre Group En;
13 and 14 The National Bunraku Theatre, Osaka; 15 and 16 Minoru
Fujita and the National Bunraku Theatre, Osaka

Contributors

Tetsuo Anzai, Sophia University, Tokyo
Minoru Fujita, Kansai University, Osaka
Stephen Greenblatt, University of California, Berkeley
Robert Hapgood, University of New Hampshire
Dennis Kennedy, Trinity College, University of Dublin
Tetsuo Kishi, Kyoto University
Ryuta Minami, Kobe City University of Foreign Studies
Izumi Momose, Chuo University, Tokyo
J. R. Mulryne, University of Warwick
Brian Powell, Keble College, University of Oxford
J. Thomas Rimer, University of Pittsburgh
Takashi Sasayama, Kwansei Gakuin University, Kobe
Akihiko Senda, Asahi Shimbun (Newspaper), Tokyo
Margaret Shewring, University of Warwick
Yasunari Takahashi, University of Tokyo
Yuko Takakuwa, Chuo University and Kanda University of International
    Studies, Tokyo
Gerry Yokota-Murakami, Osaka University

Preface

The experience of editing this book has been made a great deal more pleasant by the genial co-operation of all our contributors, both Japanese and Western.

We have incurred many debts. Principal among them is the debt we owe to the Saison Foundation, Tokyo, for its generous grant-in-aid for research towards, and publication of, this book. Kwansei Gakuin University, Kobe, and the University of Warwick generously made it possible for two of the editors to undertake a research trip to Japan. Professor Yasunari Takahashi not only helped in securing the support of the Foundation but has been repeatedly active on our behalf in making contacts, suggesting directions our work might take and generally stimulating the progress of the enterprise. Mr Akihiko Senda, theatre critic of the *Asahi* newspaper, Tokyo, put at our disposal his vast knowledge of theatre performance, and was instrumental in securing valuable photographs. Ms Kazuko Matsuoka helped us again and again by sharing her extraordinary knowledge of Shakespeare performance in Japan, and by discussing with us the insights garnered from her experience as one of the theatre's most expert and sensitive translators. Many other friends and scholars assisted us with advice, commentary and practical help. These included Sue Henny, formerly of the Japan Foundation, Charmaine Witherall, formerly of the Centre for the Study of the Renaissance, University of Warwick, Carole McFadden and Jenny White of the British Council, and staff of the Cultural Section of the Japanese Embassy in London. Ian Carruthers, Ted Motohashi, Ryuta Minami and John Gillies of the Japanese Shakespeare seminar at the Shakespeare World Congress in Los Angeles commented helpfully on our work, and generously allowed us access to valuable interview material. We are very grateful for untiring practical help and guidance from Sarah Stanton, Teresa Sheppard and Karl Howe of Cambridge University Press.

We have had opportunities to discuss Japanese Shakespeare with theatre practitioners in Britain and Japan. We should like to thank especially Sir Ian McKellen, Sir Richard Eyre, Mr Declan Donnellan, Mr Adrian Noble, Mr Simon Russell Beale, Mr Roger Chapman and, in

Japan, Master Mansaku Nomura, Living National Treasure, the distinguished Kyogen actor. We are grateful to Professor Takahashi, Ms Matsuoka and the General Manager and Staff of the Panasonic Globe Theatre, Tokyo, for opportunities to see Shakespeare performances.

We owe a debt of gratitude to past and present students of the Centre for the Study of the Renaissance, the Department of English and the School of Theatre Studies at the University of Warwick for their perceptive comments on Japanese Shakespeare in the theatre and on video. We owe a particular debt to Ryuta Minami and Tomoko Ohtani, who not only helped us in many practical and scholarly ways in England, but also acted as generous and genial hosts in Japan. Mr Minami, as a doctoral student of the Centre for the Study of the Renaissance, was tireless in translating for us, providing us with videotapes, and putting at our disposal his detailed knowledge of Shakespeare performance in Japan. Nobuko Kawashima of the School of Theatre Studies at Warwick has also been very helpful in translating Japanese texts.

We are grateful to the staffs of a number of libraries. We should particularly like to thank the librarians of the Birmingham Shakespeare Library, the Nuffield Library of Shakespeare's Birthplace Trust, Stratford-upon-Avon, and the Library of the Oriental Institute, University of Oxford. We are indebted to the National Bunraku Theatre, Osaka, the *Asahi* newspaper, Tokyo, and the Japan Foundation for assistance in obtaining photographs. We have received expert typing and other secretarial assistance from Mrs Pauline Wilson, Ms Kate Brennan and Mrs Alison Cressey of the University of Warwick.

The increasing significance of Japanese Shakespeare on the world stage is evidenced not only by extensive international touring by professional companies but by the notice given to Japanese theatre performances and Japanese directors by reviewers and scholars in Europe, America and Australia. Dennis Kennedy's *Looking at Shakespeare* and his edited collection *Foreign Shakespeare* devote considerable attention to Japan. Plans are in hand to publish a volume on Tadashi Suzuki in the Cambridge University Press series Directors in Perspective. Several sessions of the World Shakespeare Congress in Tokyo in 1991 dealt with Japanese Shakespeare, and the subsequent World Congress in Los Angeles in 1996 included a highly successful seminar wholly devoted to this topic, plus a Forum on Intercultural Shakespeare with a particular emphasis on Japan and China. These are no more perhaps than straws in the wind, but our hope is that alongside the present book they signify a recognition that Japanese Shakespeare has an illuminating contribution to make not only to the wider aspects of Shakespeare study but to the study and practice of world theatre generally.

Note on text

The macron sometimes used in Japanese printed texts to indicate a long vowel (ō, ū etc.) has been omitted throughout this book, with the exception of the Chronological Table. With the same exception, we have used the Western word order in citing personal names, that is given name followed by family name.

T. S., J. R. M., M. S.

1 Introduction

J. R. Mulryne

The origins of this book go back, for two of its editors, to the Edinburgh Festival of 1988 and a performance of Yukio Ninagawa's *The Tempest*. At the end of the evening, the huge audience in the cavernous Playhouse Theatre sat for a few moments in silence, profoundly moved, before bursting into applause. Our own response paralleled that of other audience members, and the newspaper critics confirmed in the next few days that in their judgement too something of remarkable power had been staged. 'The "rough magic" of Ninagawa's *Tempest*', wrote Michael Ratcliffe in *The Observer* (19 August 1988), 'is so sinister it scares you half to death, and so beautiful it brings tears to your eyes.' Reservations were voiced, but the overwhelming balance of opinion placed Ninagawa's interpretation among the most moving of the multitude of stagings of Shakespeare's play. Years later, Jude Kelly, artistic director of the West Yorkshire Playhouse, asked by the *Guardian* newspaper (15 November 1995) to recall the highlights of her theatre-going life, wrote of the production as 'one of the most emotional evenings I can remember'. 'Ninagawa', she asserted,

combined the theatricality and magic of the play with a fearsomely psychologically-based central character . . . Prospero, a magnificent and frightening man, was wracked both with the moral burden of total power and the terror of relinquishing it . . . Finally, he broke his staff across his knee and the sadness and relief was overwhelming. Prospero dealt with his own hubris through an act of astonishing moral courage – and so Ninagawa revealed the play.

It was precisely this sense of Ninagawa 'revealing the play' that struck us as so remarkable and so open to question. We were aware of the success his productions of *Medea* and *Macbeth* had enjoyed at previous Festivals. No doubt expectation and advertising hype had played their part in the positive audience response on the evening we attended. No doubt, too, the sheer scale of the production, the crowded stage, the richly colourful costumes and settings, the mix of traditional and modern music, the precisely choreographed movement, and the exotic glamour of the Eastern references had appealed to the expectant sensibilities of an ethnically very varied festival-going audience. Yet the sense remained of something more deeply ingrained and significant, something that went to the heart of contemporary Shakespeare performance. What was the relationship of this exotic theatricality to Shakespeare? 'Shakespeare', we fully realised, is a construct responsive to political, social, economic and cultural influences, and to theatrical preoccupations and resources. Did the accessibility and the power of Ninagawa's *The Tempest* mean that in the so-called global village a Japanese Shakespeare speaks our language? And if so, whose language is that? Problems of a verbal kind were obvious, superficially coped with in the Playhouse by electronic surtitles. Yet the language was heard or the translation read by so diverse an audience that understanding must have varied even more widely than in the case of a non-festival performance. And the production, while using a remarkably full and (so far as this is ever the case) literal translation, employed a language of theatre that transformed the script into an experience at once profoundly appealing and undeniably strange. How far were the Japanese theatrical traditions so overtly on display in this *Tempest* essential to its meaning, and who could read that meaning? How far was the readable meaning of the acting techniques and stage strategies influenced by the actors' and the director's practised knowledge of Noh and Kabuki and Kyogen, all of them directly alluded to in the performance? Was our own limited acquaintance with these theatre-forms a barrier to understanding? It could scarcely be a bridge. Was our enjoyment coloured, perhaps deeply coloured, by an unconscious orientalism of the kind Edward Said had so notably exposed? Could we be more than *voyeurs* at a spectacle that flaunted its debt to the unbroken inheritance of Japanese theatre since Zeami, and that meanwhile vividly evoked the peculiar mix of past and present that characterises Japanese society today? Could this Shakespeare ever be *our* contemporary? What had happened to Shakespeare when his work had slipped across a linguistic and cultural divide far wider than the fissures that separate England's culture, of the seventeenth century or the twentieth, from the cultures that inform the theatre practice of Giorgio Strehler or Ariane Mnouchkine, Peter Zadek or Robert Lepage? How much light would a thorough understanding of Ninagawa's work throw on the Japanese mind of the late twentieth century, and on our own minds? Was it somehow incumbent on us as students of Shakespeare to attempt by further study to understand the evident power of the Edinburgh theatre experience by way of a more developed knowledge of Japanese Shakespeare?

This book offers an attempt to provide answers to some of these questions, implicitly and overtly, through our own inquiries and through the participation of colleagues both in Japan and the West. Study of the teasing and compelling relationships between East and West, specifically in regard to theatre, and in regard to culture more generally, has been in train in the West for a century or more (and has roots, as Said and others have shown, much deeper than that). The implicit framework for our inquiries, from a Western perspective, had to be the subtle presence-and-absence of Japanese life and art in the cultural life of the West. Theatre, like the other arts, has picked up for a long time the echoes of Japanese artistic practice. The craze for 'things Chinese' and 'things Japanese' that marked the 1870s and after made its way into the world of high art through its influence on painters such as Whistler, Manet, Pissarro and Klimt, and on composers such as Saint-Saëns. Dancers including Loie Fuller and Isadora Duncan drew inspiration from oriental performers, and in the theatre theorists and practitioners of the stature of Artaud, Craig and Yeats have been in various ways impressed and influenced by what they learned of Eastern stages. The theatre culture of Europe and America had therefore well before mid-century absorbed and re-created a series of impressions of Eastern theatre, including the Japanese. Since then, the pace of knowledge and response has only accelerated, due in part to increasing ease of travel. The few Asian touring troupes of the 1920s and 30s have been replaced by frequent visits in both directions by companies large and small. In part it has been due to increased study (one estimate, probably an under-estimate, puts the number of institutions studying Eastern theatre in Europe and America at fifty to sixty) and increased attention in the broadcast and other media. In film, the Shakespeare adaptations of Kurosawa and Kosintsev have reached and influenced a wide audience. In theatre itself, it is only necessary to mention Brecht's 'Chinese plays', the music theatre of Britten, and the theatrical experiments of Brook, Grotowski, Mnouchkine, Barba and Lepage to recognise how widespread in Western performance the knowledge and assimilation of Eastern theatre practice has become. The same names evoke also how hybrid and perhaps questionable a form this development has taken, as the controversies between theorists such as Richard Schechner and Rustom Bharucha, in books and in the pages of specialist journals such as the *Asian Theatre Review* and *TDR*, amply demonstrate (see chapter 5 below). An understanding of the cultural meanings of Ninagawa's *The Tempest* could not be achieved, we can see, without some awareness of the qualifying context of its staging, from a Western point of view at least, including the conscious and unconscious memories of its audience.

From an Eastern perspective, the performance of *The Tempest* is bound to look rather different. As essays in this volume show in detail, the story of the assimilation of Shakespeare in Japan stretches back to the Meiji

Restoration, the moment (in 1868) when Japan turned once more towards the outside world. This is a span of 100 years or so that parallels, but with marked differences, the period of absorption of Japanese theatre in the West. Perhaps it is too gross a simplification, but it could be claimed that while the West's assimilation of Japanese theatre may be marked by hints, at the least, of orientalism, Japan's absorption of Shakespeare (and Ibsen and Gorky) has been the product of a cultural stance characterised by deference and a sense, however misplaced, of inferiority. At the end of the nineteenth century, in a kind of inverse colonialism, Japanese scholars and writers, the product of a civilisation emerging from centuries of cultural isolation, thought of Western theatre, and of Shakespeare in particular, as representing a privileged sector of cultural knowledge. Thus the translation of Shakespeare's texts, and the performance of the plays, carried the implication of homage, of offering a kind of service, an approach likely to be inhibiting to genuine creativity. Imitation of Western styles and performance techniques marked much of the theatrical output. The *Shingeki* movement in particular (see chapter 2 below) represented a form of deference towards the West, rather than the discovery of a culturally relevant idiom. The claims of the academy also hung heavily on the reception of Shakespeare, more heavily even than they have sometimes hung in the West. At the same time, the traditional theatre arts of Japan, Noh, Kyogen, Kabuki and Bunraku, embodying the distinctive experience of the culture, had forfeited any significant role in contemporary theatre. By a poignant irony, it was not until Japan had become an economic power of international stature (a fact not unconnected with its ability to fund international touring) that its theatre gained once more the confidence to embrace and incorporate its traditional arts.

All of this may be 'read' in Ninagawa's *The Tempest*, a production that hybridises Shakespeare with traditional theatre, and splices both of them with allusions to current popular culture. But the implications, and the ironies, run wider. Ninagawa learned his theatre craft on the experimental stages of the *Shogekijo Undo*, the radical 'little theatre movement' of the 1960s and early 70s. *The Tempest* at Edinburgh drew, by contrast, on the resources of the wealthy Toho company and filled the vast stage of the Playhouse with a cast including celebrated actors and media personalities. How was a Japanese spectator, implicated in the history of modern Japan and the history of its theatre, to interpret this Shakespearean performance? Did Ninagawa's internationalisation of the Japanese stage offer a genuine image of his cultural moment? How far was Shakespeare fully assimilated, technically and emotionally, and how far was his work merely the occasion for soliciting international attention? Even if this latter were the case, did the monied representation of a Western writer, more lavishly presented and more vigorously performed than in his own country, stand for the appropriate Japanese contribution to an emergent 'world culture'? Was the traditional theatre of Japan genuinely incorporated, or used merely for effect? Was the audience witnessing a culturally fragmented or culturally integrated work of art? What had all this to say to Japanese audiences in Tokyo or Osaka or Kyoto, as compared with audiences in the Edinburgh Playhouse? It became evident that Ninagawa's *The Tempest* raised numerous questions of a socio-cultural kind, for the Eastern observer as much as for the Western.

The moment seemed propitious for embarking on a book of the present kind. Cultural exchange between Japan and the West was quite evidently on the increase, fuelled by the electronic media, by more frequent international travel and (in the late 1980s and early 90s at any rate) by rising economic prosperity, especially in Japan. People exchanges between America and Japan and Europe and Japan, at both student and instructor levels, as well as between businesses and in leisure travel, were becoming more numerous. Strong socio-political as well as cultural links were developing between the countries of the Pacific Rim, with a marked increase in awareness of the Japanese arts in, especially, Australia. All of this was accompanied by much greater frequency in theatrical touring in both directions, with a significant number of theatre professionals now making the journey to observe Japanese performances and to study under Japanese masters (a considerable volume of similar traffic had moved in the opposite direction for some decades). From our own perspective in Britain, a particular effort was in place, especially through the British Council, to raise awareness of British culture in Japan. The UK90 initiative, which ran for three months of 1990 in Tokyo and thirty-five other Japanese cities, and comprised 120 different events, was 'the largest festival of British culture ever mounted in Japan, and possibly the largest cultural festival in Japan which has been staged by any country.'[1] Among the events were performances by the English Shakespeare Company, Cheek by Jowl and the Royal National Theatre. The costs of the Festival were largely met by Japanese business, and there were considerable commercial and goodwill spin-offs. In the day-to-day work of the Drama and Dance Advisory Committee of the Council, Japan became a frequent destination for touring by British companies large and small. Plainly, the days were coming to an end when the popular media could regard Japan and its arts as belonging to an Eastern world where an exotic civilisation lived out its life in cultural isolation. The overlap of cultures, ensured by the American occupation of Japan after the Second World War, and by subsequent Japanese economic successes, was turning into a cultural mingling. In the Shakespearean theatre, the visits to Japan of leading British companies were having their effect, as chapters of this book indicate, not only on audience attitudes to Shakespeare but on the techniques of Japanese performance. The frequency in Japan of home-bred and visiting Shakespeare productions increased. In 1990, to take an exceptional but telling instance, seventeen different productions of *Hamlet* were staged in Tokyo, many of them at the Tokyo Globe, itself erected in 1988 as a monument to Japanese Shakespeare, thus anticipating by almost a decade the opening of Shakespeare's Globe in London.[2] Of the seventeen, six were foreign, including outstanding interpretations such as those of Yuri Lyubimov from Russia and Andrei Wajda from Poland. Any account of Shakespeare and the Japanese stage would have to be written in an awareness of this multifarious cultural interchange, social, commercial and theatrical, both as a relevant context for practical matters of theatre performance, and as conditioning the imaginative awareness of audiences, directors and performers.

Several theatre events of 1991 further illustrate the growing complexity of the cultural matrix within which Japanese Shakespeare needs to be understood. The Japan Festival, beginning in August 1991 and running for six months, brought to London and other centres throughout Britain 'a sample of the many different strands that make up life in Japan'.[3] For most observers, however, the Festival offered principally a glimpse of Japanese culture as expressed through its creative arts, from the 'Visions of Japan' exhibition of artefacts at the Victoria and Albert Museum to the 'Japanesque' version (to use the word of the show's translator and director Keita Asari) of *Jesus Christ Superstar*. Among the diverse offerings carried on the powerful tides of diplomatic and financial interest that motivated the Festival – the UK 'Committee of Honour' included John Major, Neil Kinnock, Douglas Hurd and Margaret Thatcher and the parallel Japanese Committee included the then Prime Minister Toshiki Kaifu and his Minister of Foreign Affairs Taro Nakayama – there came to Britain a series of Japanese theatre events, traditional and contemporary, that provided for many British audiences their first (and certainly their most concentrated) opportunity to experience a range of Japanese performance, including Shakespeare. Contemporary plays such as the Chijinkai Theatre's *Orin*, directed by Koichi Kimura, and Yukio Ninagawa's production of Kunio Shimizu's *Tango at the End of Winter* (played by a British cast, including Alan Rickman) combined with showings of Bunraku puppets, Noh plays and Grand Kabuki to offer a wide if necessarily unrepresentative and displaced (and in that sense inaccurate) survey of the Japanese theatre scene. Shakespeare performances included a Kabuki

Hamlet, Yasunari Takahashi's *The Braggart Samurai* (an adaptation of *The Merry Wives of Windsor*; see chapter 16 of this book) and the Tokyo Globe Theatre Company's *King Lear*. The *Hamlet*, centred on the exquisite talents of Somegoro, an eighteen-year old idol who played both Hamlet and Ophelia, raised even more acutely for many in its audiences the same questions that intrigued and troubled observers of the Ninagawa *Tempest*. Here was a delicate and technically brilliant art that bore a singularly problematic relationship to Shakespeare, both in terms of its performance styles and its highly uncertain cultural placing. (The adaptation was by the Kabuki author Robun Kanagaki. A century old, it had never been played.) As Peter Lewis reported in the *Sunday Times* (22 September 1991), 'one soon accepts the white mask-like faces, the painted screens that serve as scenery, the metallic twanging of the *samisen* from the musicians' booths on stage, even the beating of the wooden clappers to intensify moments of excitement', though within this willing adjustment he found it more difficult to relate to 'the stylised chanting and dialogue in a deep "belly voice" which sounds as if it was forced out of actors straining in agony'. Others present were disconcerted by the invitation to mimic Japanese audiences by greeting particularly striking moments by crying out the performer's name. Plainly the theatre culture offered here was foreign in ways that represented not cultural mingling but cultural divorce, even if by a sympathetic effort of imagination the gulf could be temporarily crossed. The question of how this performance fitted into the paradigm 'Shakespeare' was scarcely broached, at least in the press. Banyu Inryoku's experimental *King Lear* construed this same conundrum in almost diametrically opposite ways. Here was an updated version, drawing on rock music, current references and big sound, though also incorporating allusions to traditional Japanese theatre. The show set its actors physical challenges that ranged from the naked one-man mime with which the performance opened to the athleticism of rapid scaling of networks of ropes and an engagement in choric ensemble-playing that cut short its stampedes, especially in the confined spaces of the Other Place in Stratford, within milliseconds of collision with the audience. Kenneth Rea found the production one that 'reflected both a distrust of simplicity and a pressure to feed the audience . . . an unremitting barrage of sensation.'[4] This might have been Western Shakespeare except for the choreographic discipline and athletic skill of the performers, which owed its intensity and refinement to the severe regime of Japanese theatre training.

Yet the most culturally informative experience of the Festival for students of Japanese Shakespeare was perhaps not one of the Shakespeare productions but the powerful theatricality of Grand Kabuki at the Royal National Theatre. Here one gathered a sense of the artistry of the

Shochiku Company as an ensemble – the absolute integrity of the performance, in sound, costume, colour, setting, gesture and choreography – and of Tamasaburo Bando V and Kankuro Nakamura V as individual performers. Tamasaburo's utter refinement as *onnagata* (male performer of female roles), his control of every facial expression, every nuance of sound, every expressive posture, every conscious movement of head or body or feet, not only validated his international fame in Australia and America as well as Japan but allowed the audience to glimpse the ideal theatricality towards which this Kabuki performance gestured. For the student of Japanese Shakespeare the question arose whether this magnificent and fragile theatre could ever be successfully married to the robust expressiveness of a Shakespearean script. This is not a matter of the Kabuki performance being 'fixed' while Shakespeare undergoes a process of continuous renewal. As Sir Richard Eyre has written, 'the fact that Kabuki, for all its formality, takes the stage with such freshness, is a challenge to our ideas of tradition, of theatre and of human emotion'.[5] When Tamasaburo Bando, with his supreme and practised artistry, inhabits his role in *Narukami* or *Sagi-Musume* he *renews* it, making it current for today's audience. The interaction of past and present is as strong and active as in stagings of Shakespeare. The problematic issue is whether the marriage of Shakespeare and Kabuki can ever breed other than a bastard theatre. The question is an important one, since Kabuki represents the Japanese sensibility as expressed in theatre terms, taking Kabuki as the characterising form that draws on the essence of Noh, Kyogen and Bunraku. The success of Ninagawa's *The Tempest*, measured in terms of audience response and drawing as it does on all these forms, becomes yet more puzzling. A less puzzling matter, one might think, is the failure of an enterprise such as Shunkan, which came to Saddler's Wells in London in July 1994, with its company seeking to stage on a single occasion Noh, Bunraku and Kabuki versions of the same famous story, with interwoven commentary and explanation. Despite the skills and experience of the performers, the occasion succumbed to the dead hand of instruction (or even 'education') and the undermining pressures of inappropriate theatre-space, wrong audience and (one might argue) perversely inappropriate cultural assumptions.

It is difficult to assess with any certainty the effect of Japanese performance on contemporary British Shakespeare, a topic not taken up at any length in this book. There have been a number of pastiche imitations, betraying mainly the performers' lack of knowledge and skill. Occasionally, as in the Shakespeare and Fletcher *Two Noble Kinsmen* that opened the Swan theatre in Stratford in 1986, a more serious attempt was made to annex Japanese motifs in the interest of exploring the play's meanings. Barry Kyle's careful and conscious use of samurai allusions was felt by some observers to be valid and revealing, and by others no more than colourful. Adrian Noble's *Cymbeline* for the Royal Shakespeare Company (Stratford-on-Avon, 1997), designed by Anthony Ward, incorporated allusions to Japanese costuming and theatre-space, including a mock-up *hanamichi* (entrance walkway through the audience) that consorted with other features of the production to acknowledge by reference and pastiche the presence of Japanese theatre within the vocabulary of the Western stage. More extensive attempts to use Japanese techniques have been undertaken in the United States and Canada, both at college level and on the professional stage. The work of such leading directors as Robert Wilson and Robert Lepage has been influenced in ways that reach into the smallest details of their craft, even if not so conspicuously in relation to their Shakespeare (though Lepage's *A Midsummer Night's Dream*, *Coriolanus* and *The Tempest* could be fruitfully studied in relation to Japanese theatre forms).[6] Ariane Mnouchkine in France is an obvious case where the relationship to Japanese theatre is overt, even if also open to debate (see chapter 6 below). Tracing influence in the other direction, the work of the Royal Shakespeare Company in particular has had its effect on Japanese performance. Peter Brook's *A Midsummer Night's Dream* and Trevor Nunn's *The Winter's Tale* are repeatedly mentioned by Japanese theatre professionals as having provided stimulus for their own work. Other Western theatre pieces have taken their place in the Japanese repertoire. Britten's *Curlew River*, once resisted by Noh troupes, has been assimilated into the practice of more than one company. Noh masters have been influenced in their own theatre practice by observing new approaches to staging Shakespeare in the West.[7] The trend towards appointing Western directors for productions of Shakespeare in Japan has contributed in its own fashion (not I think a very positive one) to the overlapping of Western and Japanese Shakespeare. An instance might be the interpretation of *Macbeth* directed by the English director David Leveaux at the Ginza Saison theatre in Tokyo in September 1996. Even with a noted Kabuki actor, Koshiro Matsumoto IX, in the title role, this was an 'English' production with Japanese actors, and only in the most superficial sense intercultural. The production, strong and visually compelling as it was,[8] and with a supple and playable new translation by Kazuko Matsuoka, might even be characterised as representative of a new phase of *Shingeki*, so markedly indebted was it to Western perceptions and practices. Pressed to comment further, an unsympathetic observer might even ponder whether the Leveaux production fell within Richard Schechner's icy remarks about unconscious colonialism: 'I think that this is one of the deepest leftovers of colonialism: that we think colonized people can master Western forms . . . That's a residue of colonialism; the native can "step up", but the Western "developed" person ought not to "step down". It's a kind of reverse patriarchalism'.[9] The impulse behind *Shingeki* reverence for Western culture has not quite faded, perhaps, in the Japanese Shakespeare theatre.

Leveaux's *Macbeth* might be seen as indicative in another respect. The boundaries between cultures are being eroded, for the most obvious reasons, and with this erosion the vigour of cultural translation is itself in danger of being lost. The tension of political distance that characterised the production of Shakespeare under Communist regimes was one important source of strength that withered away when communism fell. It may be that a similar attrition awaits intercultural Shakespeare as differences between cultures, still so considerable at present, gradually fade. Or is there some truth in the assertion by current commentators that, while business grows ever more international, politics (and with politics culture) becomes increasingly national? The forces of nationalism, in both Britain and Japan, are by no means exhausted, and there are many examples of the resurgence of national and indeed intra-national loyalties across the world. Japanese Shakespeare lies at the point of intersection between traditional theatre forms and the internationalism of a significant sector of contemporary performance. The striking success of Ninagawa's *The Tempest*, it could be argued, among many other examples, shows such an interaction to be theatrically viable – an interaction that justifies exploration from the various perspectives represented in this book.

We have arranged the book's chapters in four parts. The first deals in a broadly chronological fashion with the 'discovery' of Shakespeare in Japan this century, following Akihiko Senda's account of Japanese Shakespeare today. The essays here identify some of the key moments and key persons in the assimilation of Shakespeare, and, in Kishi's essay in particular, ponder the barriers of misunderstanding and lack of knowledge that may compromise the reception of Japanese Shakespeare abroad. The book's second part focuses on the relationship of Shakespeare to the traditional forms of Japanese theatre, Noh, Kabuki, Bunraku and Kyogen. Some chapters in this section consider the questions raised by Western texts for the interpreter of Japanese traditional theatre. Are there clues in *Antony and Cleopatra* to the meanings assumed by the *onnagata* (male performer of female roles) in Noh and Kabuki? How do Shakespeare and Zeami, the acknowledged masters of Western and Japanese theatre, illuminate each other's place as cultural icons? We have included here too both an interpretive essay on, and the text of, Yasunari Takahashi's *The Braggart Samurai*, a Kyogen adaptation of Shakespeare's *The Merry Wives of Windsor*. In part III Robert Hapgood rounds out the volume by giving an account of the reflections of one experienced Western theatre-goer exposed to the cultural novelty of the theatre of Japan. Part IV offers a chronology of Japanese Shakespeare from 1886 to 1994, compiled by Ryuta Minami. Thus the interaction of Shakespeare and the Japanese stage, a lively instance of the cultural chemistry of the modern world, is viewed by writers and scholars of differing cultural backgrounds from diverse but related perspectives. While the outcome can never be an overview of so rich a topic, the student of Shakespeare and modern theatre may gain here, we hope, a sense of the fertility of Shakespeare's scripts and the hospitable adaptability of the traditional Japanese stage.

Part 1

Japanese Shakespeare in performance

2 The rebirth of Shakespeare in Japan: from the 1960s to the 1990s

Akihiko Senda
Translated by Ryuta Minami

I

Imagine that Shakespeare came back to life and visited today's Japan. It is almost certain that he would be greatly surprised to find himself playing an important role in the world of theatre in a country which, though far removed from his fatherland geographically as well as culturally, is possessed of theatrical traditions as long and variegated as those at home. Expert at making free use of sources to create his plays, he would be greatly delighted rather than displeased to see Japanese playwrights and directors transforming his plays *à la japonaise*. This does not simply mean that every year in Japan a surprisingly large number of Shakespeare's plays are staged in translation and favourably received by the audience. It also implies that in modern Japanese theatre, uniquely Japanese interpretations of Shakespeare have produced many adaptations as well as new Japanese plays inspired by the bard's work.

In 1994 Hideki Noda, one of the leading dramatists in Japan, published three of his Shakespearean adaptations gathered together under the title, *Mawashi wo shimeta Shakespeare* (Shakespeare Wearing a *Mawashi*).[1] The title, in which Shakespeare is likened to a sumo wrestler wearing a *mawashi* band, symbolically represents the recent cultural phenomenon of the Japanisation of Shakespeare. The belt-wrapper of the book says, 'Shakespeare has come to Japan from London in the guise of a sumo wrestler'.

In the 1970s Hisashi Inoue, a popular writer of comedies, published *Tempo Juninen no Shakespeare* (Shakespeare in the Twelfth Year of the Tempo Era), a black comedy, dealing with the world of *Yakuza*, or the Japanese Mafia, in 1841 (the twelfth year of the Tempo Era in the Edo Period). Inoue managed to weave into this comedy fragments of all thirty-seven plays of Shakespeare. In this play appears a song that ridicules Japanese theatrical troupes which have a penchant for leaning on Shakespeare for their repertoire. The song goes:

> Shakespeare is a rice chest, a source of income.
> As long as he exists, we will never starve.

Shakespeare is a rice granary, a substantial food source.
As long as he exists, we will never die.
Shakespeare has no alternate.
There is no substitute for him.[2]

In the 1990s more and more theatres and theatrical troupes seem inclined to present Shakespeare each in its own way on the Japanese stage.

From ancient times the Japanese have introduced and assimilated with ardent curiosity entirely different cultures of alien lands such as China, America and various European countries. Whatever could be converted to the native style took root in Japanese soil, enriching in a somewhat chaotic manner the culture there, which has come to be characterised by a hybrid nature.[3] An aspect of the cultural history of this sort can be recognised in the reception of Shakespeare's plays that have been translated, adapted and staged in various manners to the benefit of Japanese theatre since the Meiji Era, the time of rapid modernisation of the country from 1868 to 1912.

Particularly important is the rise in the 1960s and early 70s of a New Wave called *Shogekijo Undo* (literally, 'Little Theatre Movement') among young theatre professionals. This experimental movement, from which were born a great many talented dramatists, directors and actors, changed the course of modern Japanese theatre by rebelling against the traditions of the established *Shingeki* companies. Thus *Shogekijo Undo* can be seen as a contemporary Japanese counterpart to Off-Off Broadway in New York or the Fringe in London. It also initiated radical changes in the mode of reception as well as staging of Shakespeare in Japan. Many theatrical troupes started producing Shakespeare's plays with distinctively Japanese colourings associated with their own history and culture, instead of imitating traditional English styles.

The present chapter is intended to trace Shakespeare's metamorphoses in Japan in the three decades from the 1960s to the early 1990s. Jan Kott saw Shakespeare from the viewpoint of a modern Pole living under an oppressive Communist regime, and wrote *Shakespeare Our Contemporary*. (This book, which was translated into Japanese in 1968, exerted great influence upon Japanese concepts of Shakespeare.) But the bard is now different from that portrayed by Kott.

II

From the end of World War II to the 1960s, Shakespeare's plays were staged chiefly by *Shingeki* companies such as Bungaku-za (The Literary Company) and Haiyu-za (The Actors' Company). *Shingeki* (literally, 'New Theatre') was born at the beginning of our century with the intention of establishing a modern theatre separable from the traditional theatres such as Noh and Kabuki. It is still active today with quite a number of companies that are mostly engaged in non-profit activities. It has staged contemporary Japanese plays as well as works by European dramatists such as Shakespeare, Ibsen, Strindberg, Gorky, Chekhov and Brecht. These companies, until the 1960s, had a pronounced tendency to regard European theatre as their model.

Naturally, in presenting Shakespeare in translation, *Shingeki* companies followed English and other European examples. The players tried to look like Europeans on stage by wearing Renaissance-style clothes, dying their hair red or blond, or even using artificial noses. What was happening at that time was not limited to the world of theatre: people at large were endeavouring to imitate their Western counterparts. Thus *Shingeki*, in a sense, epitomised the ethos of the age when the whole nation was making strenuous efforts to overtake advanced Western nations.

The 1960s saw changes in these trends. By this time, Japan's economic growth had enabled her to make a complete recovery from the damages suffered during and after World War II. In 1968 Japan surpassed West Germany in gross national product, becoming second only to the United States. This economic growth inspired confidence in Japanese bureaucrats and entrepreneurs, and prompted them to lead the nation to a place where they were no longer to follow in the footsteps of Europe and America. The whole nation appeared invigorated with newly acquired confidence.

This economic development, which raised the standard of living, resulted, on the other hand, in the appearance of a strictly controlled society. The youth who were discontented with control aspired for liberation from it, and went into action encouraged by the May Revolt in France in 1968, the Anti-Vietnam War Movement throughout Japan and the Cultural Revolution in China which declared 'There is no rebel without good reason'. University and high school students throughout Japan raised violent protests against government control in the late 1960s and early 1970s. The energy that sustained the economic growth on the part of the Establishment also gave vigour to anti-Establishment activist groups of radical students and young artists. It was in this tumultuous atmosphere that many avant-garde theatrical troupes were formed by young theatre professionals who criticised *Shingeki* and aimed at creating a truly new Japanese theatre fit for their age. Operating with insufficient funds, these companies held performances in small theatres and open-air tents. Under these circumstances, audiences usually numbered less than 200, and their movement was called *Shogekijo Undo*, or Little Theatre Movement.

Many leaders of today's Japanese theatre are the artists who took active parts in the *Shogekijo Undo*: Juro Kara, playwright and leader of the Jokyo Gekijo (the Situation Theatre, now known as Kara Gumi); Tadashi Suzuki, director and leader of the Waseda Shogekijo (the Waseda Little Theatre, now known as SCOT);[4] Shuji Terayama (d. 1983), playwright and leader of the Engeki Jikkenshitsu 'Tenjo Sajiki' (the Theatre Laboratory 'the Gallery'); Makoto Sato, playwright and leader of the 68/71 Kokushoku Tento (the 68/71 Black Tent Theatre, now known as Kuro Tento); Shogo Ohta, playwright and leader of the Tenkei Gekijo (the Theatre of Transformation, now disbanded); and Yukio Ninagawa, director and leader of the Gendaijin Gekijo (the Theatre of Modern Men) and the Sakurasha (the Cherry Blossom Company). Such dramatists as Kunio Shimizu and Minoru Betsuyaku also began their careers in this theatre movement.

The second and third generations in the *Shogekijo Undo* appeared in the 1970s and 80s. Dramatists and directors originating from this movement have come to constitute the most important part of today's Japanese theatre, which is so rich in creative energy and resources. Hideki Noda is one of these third-generation playwrights.

Unlike the *Shingeki* companies, the *Shogekijo* troupes staged very few Western plays in translation. Instead, each of them tried to put on stage original experimental plays written and directed by its leaders. There were, indeed, some exceptional playwrights such as Minoru Betsuyaku who was inspired by Samuel Beckett, and Makoto Sato who wrote under the influence of Bertolt Brecht. Yet, generally speaking, the *Shogekijo* troupes refused to follow the models of Western theatre and addressed themselves to developing a new theatre that had its roots in Japanese soil. Even when they presented foreign plays, these troupes usually adapted them radically in a Japanese style. In this sense, the *Shogekijo* movement had an aspect of the revivalism of Japanese identity in contemporary theatre. Such was also the case with their Shakespeare productions.

The 1970s witnessed two important events which served to accelerate this tendency to review Shakespeare's plays from a Japanese point of view. One is the new Shakespeare translation by Yushi Odashima, a man of acute contemporary sensibility. The other is the Royal Shakespeare Company's three visits to Japan.

The first translator of the whole corpus of Shakespeare into Japanese was Shoyo Tsubouchi. His one-man translation was completed in 1927. In 1935 he revised and published the *Shinshu Shakespeare Zenshu* (The Newly Revised Translation of Shakespeare's Complete Works). His phraseology was somewhat reminiscent of Kabuki styles. After World War II Tsuneari Fukuda, a dramatist as well as literary critic, translated nine-

1. Takahide Tashiro as Henry VI (third from left) and Yasunori Kawakami as the Duke of York (second from right) in Norio Deguchi's *King Henry VI, Part III*, Shakespeare Theatre, Tokyo (1981).

teen plays of Shakespeare into contemporary Japanese. He made much of the characteristics of Shakespeare's work as poetic drama. His was a translation in an exalted, dignified style, without vulgar or slangy expressions.

Fukuda was followed in the 1970s by Yushi Odashima who is a scholar of English drama and a popular theatre critic. (He completed the translation of all Shakespeare's plays in 1980.) His crisp and plain style made the translated texts as readable as contemporary plays in the native language. Unlike other translators, Odashima made frequent use of puns to generate humorous tones in his translation. 'I attempted to make the distance between the translation and the Japanese audience comparable to the distance between Shakespeare's work and the Elizabethan audience', explained Odashima.[5] It was, as he put it, Shakespeare rendered into Japanese as though it were contemporary Japanese drama. His translation, it is true, had to face the criticism that it was monotonous and tedious because it lacked the poetic quality necessary for classical drama.

But since the language he used is easy to speak for actors and easy to understand for the audience, his translation has generally been received favourably in the theatre world. Yukio Ninagawa and other directors have used Odashima's texts extensively since the 1970s.

In parallel with this translation by Odashima, a young theatrical troupe in Tokyo named the 'Shakespeare Theatre' performed all Shakespeare's plays one by one consecutively in six years between 1975 and 1981. The troupe accomplished this 'Shakespeare Marathon' at a small theatre under the direction of Norio Deguchi, with nothing but jeans and casual wear for costume, using very simple sets and rock music. They were the first in Japan to present the whole canon of the bard on the stage. In fact, ten plays, including the three parts of *King Henry VI* were performed in Japan for the first time by this troupe. Although the level of acting of the young actors and actresses was not very high, their Shakespeare presented in jeans appeared to the audience very novel and fresh. The achievement of the Shakespeare Theatre is also important in that they made Shakespeare familiar to the Japanese audience. But it should be noted that it is Odashima's translation that enabled this troupe successfully to undertake this prodigious task.

The Royal Shakespeare Company's visits to Japan also gave great stimulus to Japanese theatre professionals. The company presented *The Winter's Tale* and *The Merry Wives of Windsor* on their first visit in 1970; *Othello, Twelfth Night* and *King Henry V* in 1972; *A Midsummer Night's Dream* in 1973. Among these productions Trevor Nunn's *The Winter's Tale* and Peter Brook's *A Midsummer Night's Dream* had particularly strong impact on the Japanese theatre.

While aiming at a production with grace and dignity, Trevor Nunn, in his *The Winter's Tale*, exerted his ingenuity in various ways such as representing the shepherds' festival as a wild, hippies' party. This performance, which created a great sensation among Japanese theatre professionals, proved epoch-making in that its novelties in stagecraft shattered the fixed ideas of a Shakespearean stage cherished among them. Seen against this background, it can be said that this production took on a meaning in Japan that was not intended by Nunn himself at home: it showed Japanese theatre people a way to liberate themselves from Western models and stage Shakespeare on the basis of their own interpretations.

While *The Winter's Tale* was running at the Nissei Theatre, a conversation took place between Trevor Nunn, then thirty years old, and Tadashi Suzuki, an avant-garde director in Japan of the same age. The remarks Suzuki made during this conversation fully illustrate the reaction this talented young Japanese had to the British production. Suzuki says:

Now that I have seen your *The Winter's Tale*, all Shakespeare plays that are put on the stage by *shingeki* companies here seem to me nothing but dull and shoddy imitations of Western productions. Since such imitations can never surpass the originals, I think we have no choice but to start tackling Shakespeare with our uniquely Japanese sense of theatre.[6]

Suzuki put his words into practice in 1975 by staging *Night and Clock*, an adaptation of *Macbeth*. All subsequent Shakespearean adaptations directed by him demonstrate the 'uniquely Japanese sense of theatre.'

Peter Brook's *A Midsummer Night's Dream*, performed in a white 'empty space' in 1973, also affected the theatre world of Japan to a great extent. Ninagawa was one of those who were greatly impressed by this production. In answer to a question I put to him, he gave his impression of Brook's masterpiece:

Brook's directorial *tour de force* in his *A Midsummer Night's Dream* exercised a decisive influence upon my career as director. I wondered, with astonishment, if one could put on Shakespeare as freely as this – as freely as our contemporary plays. I felt released to realise that I could do anything I liked in staging Shakespeare.

III

Peter Brook's *A Midsummer Night's Dream* prompted Ninagawa to his first attempt to direct Shakespeare. His *Romeo and Juliet*, with Koshiro Matsumoto IX, then called Somegoro Ichikawa, a Kabuki star, in the title role, was presented in 1974 at Nissei in Tokyo, the same theatre where Brook's *A Midsummer Night's Dream* was performed the year before. This production which marked Ninagawa's debut in a commercial theatre was full of vigour and passion, inviting both favourable and unfavourable reviews. It must be noted that Ninagawa introduced to the conservative world of commercial theatre in Japan a new spirit of daring experimentalism that he had been fostering in the Little Theatre Movement.

In contrast to Brook, Ninagawa gave keen attention to visual effects, developing a spectacular method for directing *Romeo and Juliet*. A huge three-layered set that looked like a citadel was placed on the stage, which was thronged by a crowd of more than sixty people in Renaissance-style costume. Ninagawa said: 'I sought to emphasise raunchiness and vulgarity in Shakespeare instead of the sophistication Brook displayed in his *A Midsummer Night's Dream*. I thought too much refinement in directing could result in a decline of theatre as was the case with Beckett's plays.'

Ninagawa consulted Mikhail Bakhtin's *Rabelais and his World* (1965) which had recently been translated into Japanese. He established in the play a plebeian point of view to give it a conceptual frame. In this production, the romantic affair of the star-crossed lovers who, driven by blind love, make their way to death, is being witnessed with mixed feelings of sympathy and hostility by common people who, living at the bottom level of society, cannot but lead dull monotonous lives totally different from the stormy and colourful lives that are lived by the hero and heroine. Ninagawa stressed the contrast between the young noblemen and the plebeians throughout the play. His depiction of youths who consume themselves in the flames of burning passion was somewhat reminiscent of Franco Zeffirelli's film of 1968.

Ninagawa next staged *King Lear*, again with Koshiro Matsumoto in the title role, using Western-style costume. It was in his *Hamlet* in 1978 that interesting changes first appeared in his directing style.

What was most noteworthy about this *Hamlet* is that Ninagawa introduced into the play-within-the-play scene some elements of the Dolls' Festival. This March festival is still celebrated by many families in Japan concerned for their girls' healthy growth and happiness. On a red-carpeted, tiered platform are placed a set of dolls representing the emperor, the empress, ministers, court ladies and others. Ninagawa seated living actors and actresses on large tiers of the platform to produce a beautiful tableau, realising visually in the drama the old aristocratic society of Japan. These kinds of devices served effectively to form a bridge between Europe and Asia and make the play world familiar to the Japanese audience.

Thus, Ninagawa furnishes Shakespeare's plays with Japanese frameworks, yet he never makes any alterations in the playscripts; he does not change names of characters or places. He says: 'When I direct a Shakespeare play, I basically present it as it was originally written by the author. However, as far as what is not written is concerned, I think I am free to behave in whatever way I like. It is for this reason that I put into the production more than is actually written in the original text.'[7] In *Ninagawa Macbeth* (first staged in 1980) and all other Shakespearean productions in the following years, Ninagawa continued to encase the whole Shakespearean drama in a Japanese frame. As Kazuko Matsuoka, a drama critic, pointed out, it shows a process in which the uniquely Japanese device of the tiered platform, used only partially in the play-within-the-play scene in *Hamlet*, has expanded to occupy the whole stage.[8]

The originator of this kind of Shakespeare *à la japonaise* is considered to be Akira Kurosawa in his monumental film *Throne of Blood* released in 1957. This film, in which *Macbeth* is translated to the samurai world in the period of the Japanese Civil War, created a world-wide sensation with its ingenious scenario and vivid images. Ninagawa is among ardent admirers of Kurosawa. The intensity of theatrical expression that characterises

2. Masane Tsukayama as Macbeth and Komaki Kurihara as Lady Macbeth in Yukio Ninagawa's *Macbeth* at the Lyttleton, the Royal National Theatre (1987).

Ninagawa's directing indicates the influence of Kurosawa's cinematography upon him.

In Ninagawa's *Macbeth* the whole stage was occupied by a huge Buddhist altar (*butsudan*), designed by Kappa Seno. A *butsudan* is a small cabinet which contains an image of Buddha as well as the family's mortuary ancestral tablets (*ihai*). Many Japanese families still have such Buddhist altars at home to appease the spirits of the dead. As a prelude to *Macbeth* proper, two old women appear in front of the altar and sit down on the floor in a Japanese fashion to offer prayers. After the prayers they open the sliding doors of the altar and go to opposite sides of the stage. As Fauré's *Requiem* softly comes up, *Macbeth* starts as a play-within-the-play taking place inside the altar. Ninagawa presents the internal play *Macbeth* as set in the Japan of the Azuchi-Momoyama Period (1568–1600), with kimonos and customs peculiar to that period. Ninagawa writes about how the idea of using a *butsudan* occurred to him:

One day, at my parents' home, I opened the doors of a Buddhist altar to offer sticks of incense for prayer. While praying with my hands folded before the altar, I recalled my dead father and elder brother and found myself conversing with them. At that moment the idea crossed my mind that *Macbeth* could be a story of my ancestors or even of myself, if it originated as a fantasy from my dialogues with the dead. The warriors who repeatedly committed carnage could be our ancestors or even what I might possibly have been.[9]

This statement reveals what Ninagawa meant to achieve by framing the whole stage with a Buddhist altar.

The Japanese flavour in Ninagawa's production was accentuated by the three witches played by *onnagatas* (female impersonators) in a Kabuki style. Also characteristic of this production were cherry trees in full blossom whose petals floated gorgeously down to the ground when Macbeth made his first appearance on the stage as well as when Birnam Wood advanced to Dunsinane. This *Macbeth* which was visually dominated by Japanese aesthetics was favourably welcomed at the Edinburgh Festival in 1985 and at the Royal National Theatre in London in 1987.

More important than Japanese aesthetics, however, were modern Japanese political motifs incorporated into this production. Ninagawa directed *Macbeth* so as to make it a surreptitious *requiescat* for the radical groups of the New Left Movement, baffled and defeated in the 1970s. In the late 1960s and early 70s, Ninagawa had headed the avant-garde theatrical troupe, the *Gendaijin Gekijo* (The Theatre of the Modern), which was to be transformed later on into the *Sakura-sha* (The Cherry Blossom Company). Many of the members of his troupe had participated in New Left political activities, towards which he himself felt sympathy.

Among many New Left political groups at that time, the United Red Army was the most radical, advocating Communist world revolution through armed violence. In 1972 the leading members of the United Red Army were arrested after gunfights with riot police. Soon after, it was revealed that they had lynched twelve of their comrades at a secret location in the mountains of Gunma Prefecture. The cruel and ironical fact that young people aspiring to human liberation and social revolution liquidated so many of their fellow 'soldiers', an action which reminded us of the terrors of Stalinism, caused a great sensation throughout Japanese society.

This horrible event haunted Ninagawa's mind ever after. His wish to summarise the process of the collapse of the Japanese New Left Movement in the 1970s became a covert motif running through his *Macbeth*. He frankly admits that the dead he saw inside the Buddhist altar were called up in his mind as illusions of the dead soldiers of the United Red Army.[10]

To the Japanese, cherry blossoms are laden with ambivalent images: they symbolise both magnificent beauty and the pathos of evanescence, with associations of death and the repose of the soul. 'A dead body is buried under a cherry tree in full blossom.'[11] This well-known phrase by

Motojiro Kajii fully conveys the sense of mortality hidden beneath the image of cherry blossom. The phrase "One thousand cherry trees" in the title of a representative Bunraku play, *Yoshitsune Sembon Zakura* (The Thousand Cherry Trees of Yoshitsune), connotes grave markers for the dead.[12] The cherry trees in full bloom in *Ninagawa Macbeth* are none other than those cherry trees under which dead bodies are buried, cherry trees that pacify the souls of the young revolutionaries who died in so tragic a way.

This is why the figure of Macbeth presented by Ninagawa assumes the appearance of a gloomy revolutionary who comes to power in a period of social upheaval and murders his comrades. In the scene towards the end of the play in which Macbeth is besieged by his enemies, Ninagawa used for sound effects the recorded explosions of tear-gas canisters fired by riot police at the students holed-up behind barricades in the auditorium of Tokyo University during the campus disturbance in 1969.

Another important production of Shakespeare by Ninagawa is *The Tempest* with a subtitle 'A Rehearsal of a Noh Play on the Island of Sado'. It was first performed in Tokyo in 1987 and then at the Edinburgh Festival in 1988. This time again Ninagawa created a Japanese framework for the drama with his usual virtuosity. However, unlike any of his previous stagings, *The Tempest* was presented as a multi-layered, meta-theatrical event.

The action is set on Sado Island in the Sea of Japan, an island which was formerly a penal settlement. In the fifteenth century, Zeami, a genius who established the tradition of Noh theatre, was also exiled to this offshore island; many old outdoor Noh stages still remain there. Ninagawa linked such historical associations of Sado Island with Prospero's island in the Mediterranean Sea. He thought that 'Sado Island and a Noh stage could serve to organise the memories shared by all Japanese, thus transforming the whole play into a force field where those memories would intersect'.[13] Ninagawa staged the play as a dress-rehearsal being mounted by modern Japanese actors and stagehands on a dilapidated outdoor Noh stage on Sado Island. The actor in the role of the director and lead-performer in this dress-rehearsal played Prospero in the play-within-the-play, which is *The Tempest* proper. The director, a character who in some respects is reminiscent of Zeami, bore a close parallel to Prospero, who controls the action of *The Tempest* like a stage-manager. Instead of the book of magic the director-Prospero threw away the prompt book at the end of the play.

Ninagawa's *The Tempest* has a meta-theatrical structure of four concentric circles. At the innermost centre of the play-cosmos is the masque staged as a play within the play in the original *The Tempest*, which in its turn is encircled by the world of modern Japanese actors rehearsing it.

And this "rehearsal" takes place in an environment fraught with ancient memories of Zeami's exile to Sado Island, which is a historical fact of Japanese theatre. Thus a meditation on the nature of theatre permeates all of the meta-theatrical levels of this production and forms its *leitmotif*. *The Tempest* exhibits the most intricate structure of all Ninagawa's productions of Shakespeare.

In 1994 Ninagawa presented *A Midsummer Night's Dream*, bringing onto the stage a stone garden modelled upon the one at Ryojanji Temple in Kyoto, built in the fifteenth century. The stage design, consisting of five stones scattered on a bed of fine white gravel subtly textured with a wave pattern, reminds the audience of five islands or continents in the sea. This stone garden, which produces a condensed image of the earth, is transformed into a deep forest at night. The fairies as well as Titania (excellently performed by Kayoko Shiraishi) are dressed in kimonos and make their appearance as spirits of the earth, rising from under the expanse of sand. Each of the mechanicals enters on a scooter or a bicycle, or by car from the street, through large sliding doors at the end of the stage which, when opened, connect the stage to the real outside world. Also remarkable is Puck played by a Peking Opera actor performing acrobatic feats. Devices such as the simple white set and an acrobatic Puck were somewhat reminiscent of Peter Brook's *A Midsummer Night's Dream*, a production which had a significant impact upon Ninagawa. With this *A Midsummer Night's Dream*, Ninagawa can be seen as answering as a director to Brook whose monumental production of twenty years previously revealed to Ninagawa infinite possibilities for the creative staging of Shakespeare's drama.

IV

Tadashi Suzuki makes a marked contrast to Yukio Ninagawa with his own Shakespeare *à la japonaise*. Ninagawa creates a theatre rich in spectacle, overflowing with exuberant emotions. Suzuki, on the other hand, attaches great importance to a strict, stoic order. By means of a performance style uniquely his own, he fashions a stage dominated by critical consciousness. Ninagawa basically makes no change in Shakespeare's texts, while Suzuki radically alters the texts and, more often than not, presents theatrical pastiches made from fragments of various other plays.

Suzuki's work in the theatre always has a substructure similar to that of Gorky's *The Lower Depths* or of Beckett's *Waiting for Godot*. The stage seems to be haunted by destitutes and social drop-outs. Waiting for salvation that will never come, men and women with pathetic enthusiasm go on performing fragments of plays and novels they have seen or read in the

3. Yukio Ninagawa's *A Midsummer Night's Dream* set in a Zen-style rock garden in Kyoto (1994). Kayoko Shiraishi as Titania (left) and Goro Daimon as Bottom (centre).

past, in a futile attempt to gratify some of the wishes and desires that have been frustrated in real life. This is the essential *mise-en-scène* Suzuki creates on stage. Naturally the texts are abridged and transformed.

Suzuki's first Shakespearean production, *Night and Clock*, in 1975, was a *Macbeth* modified and transferred to the world of *The Lower Depths*. The action takes place at a mental hospital where a wall clock remains stopped with its hands pointing to two o'clock. An old man who has been in hospital for more than thirty years invites other patients to join him in nocturnal rites, performing *Macbeth*, narrating a Kabuki play, *Chushingura* (The Treasury of Loyal Retainers), and singing Japanese popular songs. The structure of *Night and Clock* is indeed reminiscent of Peter Weiss's *Marat/Sade*, but there is no hope for liberation in the play. Through this production of *Macbeth* Suzuki offers his own intellectual view of Japan and her people. The old man says, 'Alas, poor country, / Almost afraid to know itself! It cannot / Be call'd our mother, but our grave'. These words sounded like a scathing criticism of contemporary Japan.

In the late 1970s Tadashi Suzuki developed a method of training actors which was to become known as the 'Suzuki Method of Actor Training'. For this method, he incorporated the essence of Japanese traditional acting styles into modern acting techniques. While Western acting styles stress an actor's erect posture and a turning upwards towards heaven, in Japan's traditional performing arts such as Noh and Kabuki much is made of the actor's footwork with his centre of gravity at the hip, thus directing the energy of the body downwards towards the earth. Suzuki introduced this kind of physical movement, rooted in agricultural civilisation in Asia, into his method of actor training. It resulted in giving birth to highly stylised acting techniques that can be regarded as a modern counterpart of Noh acting. An actor in this style looks like a sculptured body in motion. In the 1970s Suzuki employed his method in directing two Greek tragedies, *The Trojan Women* (1974) and *The Bacchae* (1978), both of which scored international successes.

The marriage of the Suzuki Method of Actor Training and his technique of creating a stage imbued with critical consciousness brought forth in 1988 *The Tale of Lear*, adapted and directed by Suzuki himself. This was a co-production by four American Regional Theatres – Arena Stage, Milwaukee Repertory Theater, Stage West and Berkeley Repertory Theater – and was taken on tour to various American cities and then performed at the Toga Festival in Japan. The lively staging of *The Tale of Lear*, in which twelve American actors in Japanese costume acted in the Suzuki Method with plenty of verve, was in itself an exciting instance of interculturalism.

The action of the play, which deals with a solitary old man in the last hours of his life, proceeds in the form of a fantasy of *King Lear* as imagined by the old man, who identifies himself as Lear. A cheerful nurse who, laughing all the time, remains at the old man's side, reads the play *King Lear* as a comedy, and plays the role of the fool.

Suzuki's stage always centres on a group of people who cannot but seek for 'stories' at every moment of their lives of frustration and discontent. 'Stories' do not mean the favourite dramas or fictions of these people alone. They could also mean gods who may redeem them, hopes for their salvation, or ideologies of progress or of liberation; in short, they are morbid fantasies that haunt men in society. Suzuki draws in a critical perspective a tragicomic picture of men who are content to live hollow lives day by day, wandering from one fantasy to another.

Juliet, which Suzuki directed for his troupe SCOT in 1994, is another typical play of this kind in which criticism of 'stories' equates with criticism of man. The play begins with a passage frequently quoted by Suzuki from Beckett's *Cascando*: 'story . . . if you could finish it . . . you could rest . . . you could sleep . . .' The heroine of Suzuki's *Juliet*, who is actually a man in female attire, constantly makes efforts to break off from the 'stories' as well as from 'memories', yet she never succeeds in finding relief from them. Though Prokofiev's *Romeo and Juliet* is played during the performance, there is no stage business which comes close to Shakespeare's original at all. Here Juliet is only treated as a symbol of the bright young days that have passed. To express associations with past days, there are quotations from Masha and Vershinin's conversation in Chekhov's *Three Sisters*, in which they lament the passing of the spring-time of life. Also inserted are fragments from Beckett's *Endgame*, which describes men and women living in a doomsday-like world.

In most of his works Suzuki consistently tries to reveal the structure of Japanese mentality by depicting characters living with strong obsessions in a world where God is absent. To achieve this purpose, he fragments and transforms Shakespeare's texts as materials for his drama. In this sense, Suzuki is far from being a director who serves the Shakespeare canon.

As in *The Tale of Lear* and *Juliet*, Suzuki very often puts on stage the double act of a mad master and his servant. Such a duo is apparently a variant of King Lear and the Fool, yet it reminds us of the relationship between the obsessed Japanese elite, the power-holders, and the general public who serve them faithfully. The coolness and cynicism with which Suzuki casts his eyes upon men and society in Japan always characterise his stage.

V

In the 1980s and 90s, far more Shakespearean productions were seen in Japan. This is not only because Shakespearean stagings in adaptation as well as in translation rapidly increased in this period, but also because more foreign theatre companies than ever visited Japan from England and other countries to perform Shakespeare. For example, 1990 saw as many as seventeen productions of *Hamlet* presented by Japanese or foreign theatre companies. An overheated '*Hamlet* boom' was reported by many newspapers and magazines.

One of the factors which contributed to such great popularity of Shakespeare was the opening of the Tokyo Globe in 1988, the first Japanese theatre built for the exclusive purpose of staging Shakespeare. This indoor amphitheatre with a capacity of 700 was designed by Arata Isozaki under the sponsorship of National Panasonic, one of Japan's leading manufacturers of electrical and electronic appliances. It was based on the same structural plan as that of the Globe in London at Shakespeare's time, though fully equipped with today's latest lighting and acoustic facilities.

Since its opening, the Tokyo Globe has invited many theatre companies from abroad, among which were the English Shakespeare Company, the Royal National Theatre, the Royal Shakespeare Company, Cheek by

Jowl, Tara Arts, The Royal Dramatic Theatre Company from Sweden, Théâtre Reper from Canada, and Theatrul Bulandra from Romania. At the same time the theatre has established itself as a new centre of Shakespeare stagings in Japan by actively sponsoring Shakespearean productions in translation by young and mid-career actors.

One more reason for the increase in the number of Shakespeare performances in this period can be found in the recent sea change of Japanese theatre. Since the 1960s most theatrical troupes in the *Shogekijo* movement have refused to stage existing playscripts and tried to present only those plays written by the playwrights associated with them. However, the energy for experiment on their stages began to fail in the late 1980s. From their desperate attempts to find a way out of this blockage arose a marked tendency to direct their attention to classics. By borrowing solid dramatic structure as well as large-scale stories from Shakespeare's plays, they intended to charge their stages once again with dramatic energy. Especially remarkable among these troupes at this period was the technique with which they tried to project upon Shakespearean texts the mental climate of contemporary Japan, or the social situation of Asia, in order to create a new drama.

However, such an art of playwriting is nothing novel in the Japanese theatre. As indicated in *Kezairoku*, a book on drama in the Edo period, playwrights of Kabuki and *Ningyo Joruri* at that time were expert in creating a new play by incorporating their newly invented ideas and devices into the established patterns embedded in well-known history or stories. The traditional art of playwriting since the Edo period is echoed in the *Shogekijo's* practice of interweaving into the world of Shakespeare scenes and situations from the Japanese or Asian milieu as a new device.

Broken Hamlet by Shozo Uesugi offers a good example.[14] The play, based on *Hamlet*, presents a caricature of a contemporary Japanese youngster who never becomes mature, nor can he take any positive action.[15] Although the prince of Denmark is changed into a Japanese prince in the Asuka period (the late sixth century and early seventh), the play unfolds itself as a thoroughly modern play freighted with cheerful puns and jokes. In this play, Hamlet symbolises a youth who, though born in the 'age of flying birds',[16] can do nothing but talk garrulously, having like a garden fowl no wings to fly with. The stage was filled with frantic energy, which reflected the social situation of Japan economically overheated with the bubble of rapid expansion in the 1980s. With all this vigour, *Broken Hamlet* brought to light in a tragicomic perspective the helplessness of contemporary Japanese youths who cannot 'fly' in mental terms.

In contrast to Uesugi, it is Sho Ryuzanji who as director looks outside

4. Seisuke Yamasaki as King (front) and Shozo Uesugi as Hamlet in
Shozo Uesugi's *Broken Hamlet* (1990).

rather than inside Japan to create a series of plays in which the chaotic
situation of today's Asia is projected upon Shakespeare. His first
Shakespearean adaptation, *Ryuzanji Macbeth* (1988), directed by himself,
is set in a jungle in a Southeast Asia torn by war, a setting which is reminiscent of the Vietnam War. In this performance, Macbeth makes his
appearance on stage coming down a ladder from a helicopter with a

machine gun in his hand, and the witches are presented as homeless women who frequent the battle-field carrying shopping bags. In short, this is an Asian *Macbeth* in which Shakespeare's play is translated to the world of Francis Ford Coppola's *Apocalypse Now* (1979) featuring the Vietnam War. Unlike the original, Ryuzanji's *Macbeth* concludes with no order restored to the kingdom, suggesting unending struggles for power.

Ryuzanji's second work, *Ryuzanji Hamlet* (1990), is set in the under-world of Hong Kong which is shortly to be returned to China. The scene in which the ruler has the rebels shot to death with machine guns offered a vivid representation of the massacre at Tiananmen Square in Beijing of the previous year (1989). Here Hamlet is an Asian youth who dies while struggling to set right a time that is out of joint. In 1994 Ryuzanji also adapted and directed *Richard III* under the title of *Akkan Richard* (Richard the Villain) with the gifted actress Hideko Yoshida in its title role. The action takes place in an Asian country which reminds us of today's Philippines.

Among all these adaptations of Shakespeare, Hideki Noda's work surpasses others in the original creativity with which Shakespeare is so radically metamorphosed. Noda, a dramatist-director-actor, was the leader from 1976 to 1992 of Yume no Yuminsha,[17] one of Japan's leading young companies that attracted an enormous audience. Noda's plays, which abound in novel ideas, large-scale lyricism and speedy movement, were favourably received abroad as well as in Japan; *Descent of the Brutes* and *Half Gods* were presented at the Edinburgh Festival, and *Comet Messenger Siegfried* was shown at BAM in New York.

Noda created his unique adaptations by transposing the Shakespearean world into Japanese society, in most cases into certain specific business circles. For example, his *Much Ado About Nothing* (1990) is set in the sumo world, while the action of *A Midsummer Night's Dream* (1992) takes place in the community of Japanese cooks, with the woods transposed from the vicinity of Athens to the foot of Mt Fuji.[18]

With uniquely unconventional images that are far from realistic, Noda depicts the poignant gap between a primordial Edenic state before the growth and divergence of men, or periods such as the beginning of life or the founding of a nation, and the present state dominated by a sense of loss after specialisation and differentiation. Many of Noda's plays which evolve in pursuit of insoluble mysteries have a common structure in which the climax is reached when the story goes temporally backwards through a complex maze to a primordial time when no conflict or confusion has yet been born.

This penchant in Noda for avoiding maturation and returning to the inception of things prompted him to add a unique ending to his *Twelfth*

5. Sho Ryuzanji's *Ryuzanji Macbeth* set in modern South-East Asia (1988). Masayuki Shionoya as Macbeth (centre in front).

Night (1986). In this production the roles of both twins, Sebastian and Viola, were played by Mao Daichi, an actress who used to be a leading male-role player in *Takarazuka Kagekidan*, a popular all-female revue company. Viola who has been performing as Cesario in male costume returns to her own sex in the final scene when she meets her brother again. Noda seems to feel a strong sympathy with Cesario who, being undifferentiated as male or female, radiantly oscillates between both sexes, and sorely deplores the loss of him/her at the denouement. Therefore, he concludes the play with an epilogue in which Cesario appears in an intense spotlight as a beautiful androgyne with long silver hair swaying like seaweed against the sea of Chance.

The case is nearly the same with Noda's *Richard the Third* (1990). Inspired by the image of flowers in the Wars of the Roses that forms a motif in the original play, Noda laid the setting of his play in the world of Japanese flower arrangement. Here the protagonist Richard is a man who rises to be the third headmaster of the *Shirobana* (White Flowers) School of flower arrangement. The play takes the form of a law-court trial at which Richard the accused and Shakespeare the prosecutor dispute as to whether the former is guilty or not. Moreover, through the process of the trial, a quite unexpected deduction is made to enter the audience's mind: that Shakespeare's hatred for his crippled brother Richard may have driven him to write *Richard III*. Shakespeare reconciles himself with his brother in the end, and, as if they were back in the old days of childhood, they both climb bamboos to escape to the fantastic 'kingdom above the grove'.

Noda's play seems to have been written under the influence of Josephine Tey's *The Daughter of Time*, in which Richard is proved inno-cent, and of Anthony Burgess's *Nothing Like the Sun*, which portrays the young Shakespeare. Yet the genius shown here in transforming Shakespeare into a unique drama that points to a primordial Edenic time stands out in the theatre world in Japan.

From the 1980s to mid-90s, many other plays projecting Japanese history and society on to Shakespearean texts were mounted on the stage under inventive direction as well as in original adaptations. Takeshi Kawamura, for example, adapted and directed *Macbeth* as *A Man Named Macbeth* for his company 'Daisan [Third] Erotica'. Here he has translated the Scottish background of the original into the world of *Yakuza*, the Japanese Mafia. (This play was toured to Germany, Canada, America and Australia.)

The Theatre Cocoon in Tokyo produced *A Midsummer Night's Dream* every year from 1990 to 1995 with a different director each year, thus giving birth to a variety of interpretations of the play, such as Indian and

Balinese versions. Among these works, Norio Deguchi's production in 1990 and Kazuyoshi Kushida's in 1994 were particularly interesting.

Deguchi places the play in a frame in which a middle-aged Japanese director, undergoing a crisis in his relationship with his wife, thinks of his childhood while working out directorial plans for his *A Midsummer Night's Dream*. Here the comedy unfolds itself nostalgically as part of his illusion, set in a deserted primary school in his home village, and thus relieves the director of an anticlimax at the end. In this production, the original *A Midsummer Night's Dream* is made to come closer to the Japanese people's memories of the days immediately after World War II by presenting Puck as a primary schoolboy with a satchel on his back, or Bottom in the figure of a Japanese ex-soldier. Unlike Ninagawa who makes much of the 'traditional' Japan in his Shakespearean productions, Deguchi here links the world of Shakespeare to 'today's Japan'. Kazuyoshi Kushida, in contrast to Deguchi, set *A Midsummer Night's Dream* in a city in the near future, a city devastated probably by a nuclear war. No trees or grasses are to be seen on the stage, the floor and walls of which are all covered by lead. The play develops as a melancholic illusion cherished by a man who is trying to plant a nursery tree in the soil of this desolate city. Very little use is made of Japanese costumes or customs. However, the sense of crisis on the part of a director who cannot be optimistic about the future lent an uncanny reality to this *A Midsummer Night's Dream*.

It was, however, Juichiro Takeuchi who connected Shakespeare to the collapse of a family in *Himawari* (Sunflower) in 1988.[19] In this comedy, three sisters and a father (who has abandoned the role of father and has himself called 'Mum') hire a part-timer as their 'father' in an attempt to restore life by theatrical means to a family that is on the verge of breakdown. Here Takeuchi achieves an intellectual *tour de force*, incorporating into the comedy many extracts from *King Lear* and Chekhov's *Three Sisters* on the theme of family collapse.

Particularly noteworthy among these Shakespeares *à la japonaise* is *Kanadehon Hamlet* written by Harue Tsutsumi and produced by Kiyama Jimusho in 1992 and 1994.[20] Tsutsumi, a specialist on Kabuki in the Meiji period, is a woman playwright now living in Indiana, in the United States. A broad view of comparative culture that has enabled her to see Japanese culture from the outside has brought forth this outstanding Japanese play based on Shakespeare.

The play is set in Tokyo in 1897. A stage rehearsal of *Hamlet* is now going on at the Shintomi-za, an actual Kabuki theatre, for the next day's opening. This is to be Japan's first production of *Hamlet* in translation, planned by Kan'ya Morita, the owner of the theatre.[21] However, knowing nothing about Western drama, the Kabuki actors are at a loss with *Hamlet* and try to put it on the stage in the familiar style of *Kanadehon Chushingura* (a popular Kabuki play first staged in 1748). This infuriates the Japanese director, who has recently come back from America and is a rabid enthusiast for things Western, and the rehearsal falls into a comical confusion. Morita, the producer, facing a large deficit, dies during the rehearsal, and the curtain of the première of *Hamlet* remains unraised as the play continues.

What is thrilling about *Kanadehon Hamlet* is the way in which a number of quite unexpected common factors between *Hamlet* and *Kanadehon Chushingura* are brought to notice through conflicts and arguments among the actors during the rehearsal. There are indeed many similarities between these two popular classical tragedies of the East and the West: they are both revenge plays in which the protagonists take vengeance for the death of their lords; both protagonists are forced to act a play in order to deceive their enemies; the chief retainers (Polonius in *Hamlet* and Ono Kyudaiu in *Kanadehon Chushingura*) who took the enemies' side after their master's death are killed by the protagonists while hiding behind cover. This is why two of the Kabuki actors exchange speeches such as these: 'This is quite an achievement. I suppose the English playwright called Shakespeare read *Kanadehon Chushingura* and wrote *Hamlet*.' 'Then, Shakespeare must have been able to read Japanese.' Such comic dialogue appeals to an audience.

Kanadehon Chushingura dramatises an actual revenge accomplished by forty-seven samurais in Tokyo (or Edo) in 1702, and the play, needless to say, exists independently of *Hamlet*. However, the point suggested in Tsutsumi's play that these two popular pieces, representing the Japanese and the European drama respectively, share common elements to an unexpectedly great extent seems to give us hints regarding what is shared by dramatic masterpieces that have been favoured by audiences for centuries. The reason *Hamlet* has been loved by a Japanese audience, and been staged so many times, may possibly be that *Kanadehon Chushingura* had prepared, for a Japanese sensibility, the mental set for receiving *Hamlet*. Harue Tsutsumi's *Kanadehon Hamlet* has proved more than an interesting fictional episode in the history of the reception of Shakespeare in the Meiji period. It is indeed epoch-making in that it describes in a broad perspective the ways in which foreign cultures including Shakespeare can be assimilated in Japan.

A culture cannot establish itself where it cannot strike root. It will not be amiss to think that Shakespearean drama has established itself in Japan because, as seen in the relationship between *Hamlet* and *Kanadehon Chushingura,* there is a receptive soil for it in Japanese life and customs.

When theatre professionals find a ready responsiveness in their own imaginations and create attractive and well-founded compounds of Shakespeare and the Japanese mind, it is to be expected that Shakespeare will come closer to us to become 'our Japanese contemporary'.

One man's *Hamlet* in 1911 Japan: The Bungei
Kyokai production in the Imperial Theatre

Brian Powell

The director of a famous production of *Hamlet* in the Imperial Theatre,
Tokyo, in May 1911 expressed the hope that one day Westerners would be
prepared to take Japanese productions of Shakespeare seriously. It proba-
bly never occurred to him that more than seventy years would pass before
this hope would be realised with the Shakespeare productions of Yukio
Ninagawa in Britain and Tadashi Suzuki in the United States. It was more
than fifty years before there were even performances of Shakespeare in
Tokyo that drew the attention of foreigners who happened to be there.
Hamlet in 1964 and the 1966 *Richard III* with a Kabuki actor playing
Richard were probably the first strong indications that there could be
Japanese Shakespeare just as there were German and French
Shakespeares.

Why it took so long is the underlying theme of this chapter. Other contributors to this book are considering Shakespeare translation and chart-
ing the development of Shakespeare production in Japan from the 1920s
to the present day. This chapter will focus on the 1911 *Hamlet* to try to
identify the obstacles that lay in the path of subsequent Shakespearean
actors and directors. The 1911 *Hamlet* pointed up the dilemmas faced by
those who were trying to modernise Japanese theatre after it had been isolated from the rest of world, and particularly from European theatre, for
more than two and a half centuries during Japan's feudal period from
roughly the time of the première of *Hamlet* in England to the last quarter
of the nineteenth century. What follows, therefore, is an excursion into
Japanese theatre history at the beginning of the twentieth century and a
consideration of Shakespeare's place in it.

The company that performed *Hamlet* in 1911 had the name Bungei
Kyokai (Literary Arts Association). It had mounted a less ambitious production of *Hamlet* four years earlier, and the two productions together
represent significant steps in the development of modern theatre and
Shakespeare performance in Japan. They were the first productions true
to the text, in a theatre culture that traditionally had treated texts with
disdain. The 1911 *Hamlet* was the first modern production to use

actresses in the female parts, in a culture where actresses had been officially banned from the theatre between 1629 and the 1870s. Another mark of the modernity of the 1911 *Hamlet* is that commentators noted how few geisha there were in the audience. These seemingly frivolous observations add up to theatrical advances of epochal (the Japanese word appears often in the sources) proportions.

Early productions of *Hamlet* in Japan

As Toshio Kawatake points out in his monograph-length study of *Hamlet* in Japan, to which frequent reference will be made here, the introduction of Shakespeare to Japan differed from that of the other Western playwrights who figure prominently in the history of modern Japanese theatre.[1] In contrast to, for example, Ibsen, who first became known to Japan through full translations (more strictly, re-translations from English) of his plays, Shakespeare had to go through a long period of summaries, partial translations and adaptations before full versions of the plays were available. *Hamlet* is an extreme example of this. The first full translation was produced for the 1907 Bungei Kyokai production. Long before that, in 1882, a Japanese version of the fourth Soliloquy had appeared in a collection of Western poetry intended to stimulate Japan's new poets. As a revenge story it had tickled the interest of writers close to the Kabuki theatre from the 1870s onwards. Versions of the Lambs' *Hamlet* started appearing in the late 1880s. *Hamlet* was introduced as poetry, a dramatic plot and a good story decades before it became known as a play.

Before the Bungei Kyokai production of 1907, the Japanese theatre-going public had been introduced to a number of staged adaptations. There had been thirteen in all: five in Tokyo, four in Osaka, two in Kyoto and the others in Kobe and Hakata.[2] The adaptations used had been done by a young novelist named Kayo Yamagishi (1878–1945), with help for some productions from Shunsho Doi, who was later to play Hamlet in both Bungei Kyokai stagings. Essentially these were scripts for a genre of theatre referred to generically as *Shimpa*. The word *Shimpa* literally means 'new school' and was a term that had only been in use in Japan since the 1880s. The significance that this word was intended to convey was that this theatre would be very different from the 'old school' of Kabuki. In effect it was not, especially in its acting style, but it had broken the monopoly of the Kabuki acting families, had introduced a modicum of realism, not least by allowing actresses on the stage alongside the traditional female impersonators, and in other ways had opened up Japanese theatre to new ideas. Its public – and there have always been many

'theatre-going publics' in modern Japan, as theatre-going has been seg-
mented in a way unknown in the West – consisted partly of traditional
Kabuki fans tasting something new, a new class of spectators which
hoped it was participating in the new Japanese culture, and a few intellectuals, who lost interest later.

Seven of the pre-Bungei Kyokai *Hamlet* adaptations had been directed
and performed by Otojiro Kawakami (1864–1911) and his company.
Kawakami had been the most famous, notorious and colourful practitioner of *Shimpa* in the last decade of the nineteenth century. By the early
years of the twentieth century he had renounced the term *Shimpa*, pro-
claiming that he wished to take Japanese theatre a stage further towards
realism. There is not a little irony in Meyerhold being inspired by
Kawakami's anti-realistic 'Kabuki' during a performance in Moscow in
1901.[3] In Japan Kabuki was still the only theatrical referent Kawakami
and others like him had.

Kawakami's *Hamlet* was in the line of other Japanese Shakespeare
adaptations up to that time. The names of the characters were changed to
approximations which would not grate on Japanese ears. It was, however,
set in nineteenth-century Japan, thus qualifying it to be described as a
Hamlet in modern dress. Perhaps crucially, however, the soliloquies were
omitted. Until Bungei Kyokai, Japanese actors seemed to have particular
difficulty with this aspect of *Hamlet* and this is something that I will come
back to later. Earlier adaptations for the stage, including the one by
Robun Kanagaki which was used for the 1991 Japan Festival Kabuki
Hamlet in London, did not include the soliloquies. The adaptation by
Yamagishi that Kawakami used did provide versions for the actors, but
they were not spoken from the stage. Kawakami's *Hamlet* was a great
commercial success. He was generally despised by intellectuals who knew
anything about Shakespeare, but at least one Japanese theatre historian
credits him with creating a momentum for Shakespeare production that
culminated in the performances of Bungei Kyokai.

Shoyo Tsubouchi

Both Bungei Kyokai productions of *Hamlet* were directed by Shoyo
Tsubouchi (1859–1935) and used his translations. Tsubouchi was the first
and arguably the greatest Japanese translator of Shakespeare and
information about him appears in several chapters of this book. Here I am
looking at him specifically as a man of the theatre, as the person who provided a text of *Hamlet* for actors to act and helped them act it. This side of
Tsubouchi's life is less well known in the West and is indeed so extensive
that no brief summary can do justice to it. He was always keen to put his

theories, which he was developing all the time, into practice, and in the theatre this resulted in productions of many kinds, from a student performance of a Kabuki play, through a series of dance dramas, the *Hamlet* that we are considering here, to large-scale pageants in the 1920s.

Tsubouchi, like many of his intellectual and theatrical contemporaries, wanted Japan to have a new theatre worthy of a modern nation. 'Art should reflect the essence of the ideals of its age, but theatre does not', he told his students in 1911.[4] The problem was how to communicate that essential spirit from the stage and it was a problem with which Tsubouchi wrestled all his life.

Tsubouchi had a good voice and apparently liked using it. While at school he was taught by two American teachers who believed that making their pupils read a text aloud was useful pedagogical practice, and Tsubouchi would stand at the window of his dormitory declaiming in a loud voice. This interest stayed with him as he went to Tokyo to study at university (1878) and when he became a lecturer at Tokyo Senmon Gakko (1883; the name was changed to Waseda University in 1902). In 1890 with two other lecturers Tsubouchi founded the *Rodoku-kai* (a 'reading aloud club' – in effect, it was a playreading club).[5] From this time on Tsubouchi held many playreading sessions with interested students, among whom were Shunsho Doi and Biyo Mizuguchi, his Hamlet and Gertrude in 1907. The main texts used were recent historical plays written for the Kabuki stage.

Tsubouchi believed strongly that reading aloud held the key to the emergence of a new drama. In this we can see something of a parallel with Junji Kinoshita (1914–), a later translator of Shakespeare, who in the 1970s similarly experimented with words as sounds, especially as spoken chorally, in his own search for a new dramatic medium. In Tsubouchi's case it may with hindsight appear unfortunate that the only Japanese texts available to him in the 1890s were written against the background of traditional theatre. By the time Tsubouchi was ready to engage with Shakespeare as a practical playwright, the *Rodoku* that he was teaching his student-actors had developed into a declamatory style of delivery using full body gestures that retained many features redolent of Kabuki technique.[6]

Tsubouchi was a scholar prepared to dedicate himself to the theatre, and this was a difficult destiny for a teacher at a prestigious new university. Tsubouchi contributed fully to academic debate on drama, engaging in a notable exchange of views with the novelist Ogai Mori and publishing his own theory of historical drama in the 1890s. In 1896 he was appointed head of the newly founded Waseda Middle School and took his responsibilities very seriously, publishing a series of books on practical morals that were estimated highly. But from his mother he seems to have inherited a love of theatre; during his boyhood she took him often to see (Kabuki) plays, and as a student in Tokyo he saw as much theatre as he could. He was passionate about it – he could not help it and in spite of all criticism from respectable quarters of the frivolousness of what he was doing, he persisted in believing that practical theatre must contribute to the evolving modern Japan.

His early playreadings (which had to be moved to his house because of opposition within the university) led to a student production in a gymnasium in 1894.[7] In 1905 the successor to the playreading club staged a performance of a classical play adapted and directed by Tsubouchi. And its successor again, Bungei Kyokai, performed in a professional theatre in 1906 and 1907. Tsubouchi increasingly felt that his students were trying to rush ahead too fast, but he was always eager to carry out practical experiments.

Bungei Kyokai and its 1907 *Hamlet*

Bungei Kyokai was founded in February 1906, at the urging of Tsubouchi's students. It was planned to be primarily an extra-curricular study association which would engage in a wide range of cultural activities.[8] The main interest of its core members, however, was in drama, and three of them had been studying *Rodoku* with Tsubouchi for several years. As an organisation it did not last very long, and apart from publishing a journal and mounting two productions twelve months apart its initial loudly proclaimed promise remained largely unfulfilled at the end of its three-year life.

Bungei Kyokai did, however, mount a production of *Hamlet* in a professional theatre in November 1907. Assessing the significance of this production is difficult. It has been referred to as 'literati drama' (*Bunshigeki*), implying strongly that the company was not serious about the play it was performing nor any good at acting it, and as being not far from an amateur show for families and friends. But it was the first Shakespeare production to use the names of the characters as they were, instead of trying to make them sound Japanese, and for all its internal contradictions it can be seen as the point where theatrical adaptation of Shakespeare stories and literary study of the plays begin to come together.[9]

There are a number of aspects of this production which suggest, particularly when compared to the *Hamlet* of 1911, that it was not prepared as thoroughly as it might have been. The establishment of the text was itself strange. The first drafts were not done by Tsubouchi but by a pupil and budding playwright, who had one of his plays performed on the same bill as *Hamlet*.[10] The drafts came rather slowly, and Tsubouchi had to finish the translation himself hurriedly to have it ready for his actors. This did not mean that he had not considered carefully the principles he would follow, but an article written at about that time seems to indicate that his ideas were still evolving.

Tsubouchi goes into considerable detail in trying to locate a period in Japanese history from which to take language that would adequately convey the play's meaning to a Japanese audience. He searches into Japanese classical theatre to try to discover whether hints of Japan's own classical stage language might be appropriate. The Mousetrap becomes a Noh play at one stage, but this does not work. What on earth is he to do about the Danish court? It would be laughable to suggest the Japanese Imperial court in the language given to it. One would have to come some way down the Japanese aristocratic scale to find someone who slept alone, without any attendants, on the ground in an orchard.[11] Tsubouchi is primarily concerned with credibility, preventing the translation becoming a barrier between the play and the audiences.

He was also anxious to answer his critics, who had condemned the language, with its admixture of archaisms, that he had used for the performance of the trial scene from *The Merchant of Venice* the previous year. *Shimpa* had developed a stage language which mainly used the contemporary colloquial even for plays that were not set in contemporary Japan. It had many supporters among regular theatre-goers who wanted to think of themselves as modern, but Tsubouchi could not accept that he should use this type of language. Shakespeare is 70 per cent poetry, he protests, and ignoring this in translation will destroy the balance between form and content.[12] Tsubouchi persisted in his ideas, even though no less an adversary than Lafcadio Hearn is reported as having espoused the cause of translation into contemporary Japanese.

The original translator of the text omitted the fourth soliloquy. He did not consider it very important, and it was a burden on the actor to have to deliver it so soon after the curtain had risen on the third act. Tsubouchi restored it. Kawatake attaches some importance to this incident, as it is a neat contrast with the *Hamlet* adaptations of the same period. They had 'To be or not to be' in their scripts but omitted it in performance; Bungei Kyokai did the opposite, thus showing a modern regard for drama's rightful status as literature as well as playtext.[13]

It is interesting to speculate why adaptations of *Hamlet* by theatre companies which were traditional or semi-traditional in their presentations should have had difficulties with the soliloquies. Soliloquies, in the basic sense of one character alone on the stage talking to him/herself, are not uncommon in Kabuki and Bunraku, or indeed in Noh, although relatively few people had seen Noh since the rise of popular theatre in the early seventeenth century. Functionally, however, Japanese soliloquies are different from their Shakespearean counterparts, as Toshio Kawatake points out.[14] Often the character speaking them comments on the scenery or the general surroundings of the place where he is standing. Or he may use the opportunity to announce who he is. Sometimes such soliloquies may well give an indirect indication of the character's feelings at that point in the play. In plays involving love-suicides one of the couple may state the reasons for dying. In the latter cases, however, this is in terms of the external pressures forcing suicide upon them, and Kawatake detects a matter-of-fact quality that contrasts sharply with the soliloquies in *Hamlet*. Hamlet's musing on his own individual inner being and his metaphysical linking of this with the workings of an active godhead were strikingly modern to nineteenth- and early twentieth-century Japanese, and Kabuki was only superficially being modernised during this period.

Casting Bungei Kyokai's 1907 *Hamlet* was very difficult. Tsubouchi had three students who had been studying *Rodoku* with him for some years, and they were clearly going to be the core of the cast. Shunsho Doi was cast as Hamlet, Biyo Mizuguchi as Gertrude and Tetteki Togi as Claudius. They were all men, and by casting one of them in a female part Tsubouchi was continuing a Kabuki tradition that the modern Japanese theatre was trying to abandon. There may have been more than an echo of Kabuki tradition in Doi's Hamlet too. Reviews refer to him as handsome and graceful and as having a beautiful voice, and he had played Portia in *The Merchant of Venice*. Princes were regularly played in a rather effeminate way in Kabuki, often by *onnagata*, the actors who specialised in female roles. Ophelia, however, was played by a female student, who gained no favour with the critics. Doi commented that she was so bad at singing that her song was mimed while an expert sang offstage. It was, however, Tsubouchi's declared policy to use actresses – but not professional *Shimpa* actresses – as much as possible, and this too set the tone for this and future productions of Shakespeare.

All in all the Bungei Kyokai *Hamlet* of 1907 was an ambitious venture which revealed the extent of the problems facing Tsubouchi. It was greeted enthusiastically by its audiences, who have been described as being very serious and earnest – quite unlike the audiences traditional actors were used to. The reviews, however, reveal some confusion over what the production was trying to achieve. In most cases judgements, favourable or not, were not substantiated in any way, but whereas this was acceptable in Kabuki, where the assumed referent was past productions of the same play, it made no sense here. The coherence that Tsubouchi was aiming at, where text, actors, scenery and direction were broadly unified, was lost on them.

Bungei Kyokai and Jiyu Gekijo

Bungei Kyokai's activities after the *Hamlet* production were rather desultory and in 1909 it was reorganised to give it a sharper theatrical focus. It is usual in Japanese sources to refer to the 'early period Bungei Kyokai' and the 'later period Bungei Kyokai'. In English these are cumbersome terms and I will use Bungei Kyokai I and II from now on. At about the same time that Bungei Kyokai II came into being, another company appeared that offered a different approach to performing translated drama. The name given to this company was Jiyu Gekijo (Free Theatre). Together Jiyu Gekijo and Bungei Kyokai II are usually credited with having laid the foundations of modern drama in Japan. Their first studio productions were in November 1909 and March 1910 respectively. Jiyu Gekijo performed Ibsen's *John Gabriel Borkman* and Bungei Kyokai II a new production of *Hamlet*.

The preoccupation with foreign plays in building up a modern Japanese drama may seem strange to us in the 1990s when Japanese traditional theatre, especially Kabuki, is being perceived in the West as embodying a vital theatricality that we have lost. The situation looked very different, however, to Japanese intellectuals of the 1890s and early 1900s. The fact that Kabuki was totally actor-centred, to the extent that (self) positioning on stage depended on the seniority of the actor, was anathema to them. The fact that actors, if sufficiently senior, could instruct the playwright to alter lines that did not suit them for apparently frivolous reasons, was unacceptable. How could one admire a theatre where the great eighteenth-century classics of Kabuki were performed piecemeal, a famous act in this programme, a spectacular scene in that? Now we, and even they, might say that Kabuki actors were such consummate professionals that they naturally dominated communication with the audience; and that the quality of experience enjoyed by the audiences was not less when watching just a purple passage because they knew the story anyway and the physicality of the acting style expressed intensely to them the accumulation of the emotions suffered by the character up to that point.

This was not, however, how Tsubouchi or Kaoru Osanai (1881–1928), one of the two leaders of Jiyu Gekijo, saw it. In the West, as had only recently been appreciated in Japan, there were plays that could stand on their own as artistic wholes. Plot complexity was recognised in Kabuki, but here there was added to it levels of emotional response that were developed by the playwright in a controlled way. Verbal complexity to enrich the surface meaning was one of the hallmarks of Chikamatsu, Japan's greatest classic playwright, but Western playwrights, especially Shakespeare, integrated their use of language with the development of plot and character. Stage characters in the West talked about their states of mind, whereas the Kabuki spectator had to use his imagination much more. The fundamental revelation that in the West stage-scripts could be literature convinced both Tsubouchi and Osanai that full-scale performances of translated Western plays were what Japan needed.

Around this time there was much debate about the course modern Japanese theatre should take: whether it would be enough to encourage new playwriting, whether the whole edifice of Japanese theatre as it existed at the time should be demolished and a fresh start made, or whether there was some less drastic solution. It was left to Osanai and Tsubouchi, however, to lead the way in practical performances using what facilities were available to them, and they approached the problem in different ways. Both agreed that in their repertory of plays, Western translated drama should be given priority. They differed in their use of actors. Osanai teamed up with a progressive Kabuki actor named Sadanji Ichikawa II (1880–1940), who co-founded Jiyu Gekijo with him, and their opening Ibsen production was acted by Kabuki actors in Sadanji's company. In other words Osanai, willingly or perforce, recognised the professionalism of the Kabuki actors and expected them to be able to adjust their acting technique radically to suit modern western drama. Tsubouchi, on the other hand, was determined to train up the student members of Bungei Kyokai II, who with one or two exceptions had had no experience of the professional stage. This policy in the case of the 1907 *Hamlet* had led to a hybrid production with a disastrous Ophelia and a male Gertrude. But Tsubouchi was convinced he was right and could do better for the second production.

Hamlet in the Imperial Theatre, 1911

The theatre building in which Bungei Kyokai II was to perform its *Hamlet* was the most magnificent in Japan. Opened in March 1911 the Imperial Theatre was the first large-scale theatre in the Western style. Its architecture was described as Renaissance and French and it was consciously modelled on the Comédie Française. It had one of the best sites in Tokyo, standing across from the Imperial Palace. According to one spectator who saw *Hamlet* there in 1911, one could look out of the windows at the willows along the bank of the palace moat. It could hold 1,700 people. Most of its shows were highly commercial, but it had considerable significance in the development of modern Japanese theatre. It set up a production system of starting each show on the first of the month and finishing on about the 25th and then allowed modern theatre groups to use its facilities between the 26th and the start of the next month's show. Bungei Kyokai II performed its *Hamlet* at the end of May by invitation of the Imperial Theatre management.

Casting did not present Tsubouchi with as many problems this time. He was able to cast all the female parts with student actresses. He did believe that there was not a single professional actor in Japan who could bring all the facets of Hamlet's character together, but he was confident that Doi could at least speak the lines naturally and with conviction.[15] Doi played Hamlet again, and his considerable experience with Hamlet itself, with *Rodoku* and with the theatre in general, made him the personality round which the whole production revolved. Tsubouchi appeared to have little confidence in his Ophelia. He described her (without once using her name) as a complete amateur who could not sing and he begged his audences in print to watch her in an indulgent frame of mind.[16] Ophelia was played by Sumako Matsui, a Bungei Kyokai II student of awesome dedication to acting and a disconcerting disregard for the *amour propre* of the male actors. Sumako went on to perform Nora in Ibsen's *A Doll's House* and Magda in Sudermann's *Heimat* to great acclaim and some controversy, and is known as Japan's first modern actress. *Hamlet* introduced her to the Japanese stage.[17]

Tsubouchi rehearsed his cast fiercely for three months. He had appeared quite late in the rehearsal process for the Bungei Kyokai I *Hamlet*, but this time he directed his actors and actresses in a sustained and comprehensive way. This meant that the production was going to bear very clearly the stamp of his own theories on stage movement and delivery and would therefore be a valid test of the acceptability of those theories. Tsubouchi had watched foreigners acting at a theatre in Yokohama that put on plays for the foreign community and had decided that foreign modes of expression and gesture were not suitable for Japanese actors playing to Japanese audiences.[18] An American woman with experience in the theatre had helped the Bungei Kyokai I actors, but Tsubouchi had forced the actors to abandon the Western gestures she had taught them. She helped with this second *Hamlet* too and Tsubouchi was apparently less inflexible towards the results of her instruction, but overall the production was one which was designed not to alienate Japanese spectators. *Hamlet* at the Imperial Theatre was a great commercial success. It achieved 91 per cent capacity audiences over its seven-day run, better than any previous production at the theatre.[19] The Tokyo *Nichinichi Shinbun* (newspaper) critic noticed how serious the audience was in its attitude to the play.[20] Theatre had been a place where typically a male theatre-goer would spend some hours with a geisha companion. The absence of geisha was taken to mean that more attention would be paid to the play. One of a group of student spectators described how deeply moved the audience had been on the night they saw the production: spontaneous and loud applause, virtually unknown in traditional theatre, greeted Hamlet's acting after The Mousetrap and the audience left the theatre looking as if they had seen a dream that they longed to see again.[21] Artistically and culturally, however, controversy surrounded the production, as many contemporary impressions and later memories show.

The choice of play for this first public production of Bungei Kyokai II was criticised widely. While Kawakami's wild adaptations may have prepared the theatre-going public for Shakespeare, many young intellectuals, including a sizeable group within Bungei Kyokai II itself, were more interested in contemporary Western drama. By the time this *Hamlet* was performed, Jiyu Gekijo had already put on plays by Ibsen, Chekhov, Wedekind and Gorky. Tsubouchi intended *Hamlet* to be the first of a series of Shakespeare productions, but in the event he had to bow to pressure for more up-to-date plays, and Ibsen, Shaw and Sudermann followed.

The translation was generally not liked. Tsubouchi's quest for a communicative language seems to have failed. There are several contemporary complaints that it was hard to understand. He had mixed elegant and vulgar speech levels, as indeed Shakespeare does, but the audiences found this confusing. Not only that, but the deliberate use of archaisms from a variety of different historical periods compounded the problem.[22] One review recognised what Tsubouchi was trying to achieve but still pronounced the effect on the ear as harsh. There were doubts about the translation even among the actors. The theatre historian Shigetoshi Kawatake who acted Voltimand in this production remembered the language as too elegant, too remote from what the audiences could have been expecting.[23]

The main source of the problem was variously located, but there are several references to the use of language from Noh and Kyogen. One newspaper review actually cited watching Noh as analogous to seeing this Shakespeare. You had to prepare ahead of time; read the play before seeing it. This was a theme in a number of contemporary comments, and it was reinforced by a piece that Tsubouchi wrote at the time to the effect that this indeed was what he expected of his audiences. He was clear that he had a right to expect his audiences not only to read the play beforehand but to come to the theatre in a studious frame of mind.[24] The translation had aimed high, at those with the intelligence and cultural refinement to appreciate it.

Against this was a body of opinion that urged the use of contemporary language. From the newly emergent left came an assault on the elitist, privileged principles on which Tsubouchi's comments were premised. Others felt that the language of *Hamlet* was in fact a barrier to understanding. An audience could adjust to an unfamiliar cultural context if the language was their own. At least then the feelings and emotions of the characters would come across and the audiences had a chance of being drawn into the atmosphere of the play.

The unhappy, but it must be said defiant, Tsubouchi was assailed from all sides, by young intellectuals and established writers. Tetsuro Watsuji (1889–1960), later to become a well-known philosopher and cultural historian, bewailed the lack of a European feel to the translation. The novelist Soseki Natsume, by contrast, stated bluntly that Tsubouchi had been too faithful to Shakespeare and in doing so had ignored the requirements of the Japanese psychology.[25]

Tsubouchi was vigorous in his own defence, or rather he was concerned that his point of view should be clearly understood. His high profile in the media around the time of *Hamlet* is remarkable considering how busy he must have been with the production himself. He published articles, on occasion rather repetitive, it must be said, in a number of magazines, not only specialist theatre journals but general interest monthlies as well. Perhaps his own solution to the immense problems of translating *Hamlet* was the wrong one, but he seemed to want to prove that he had at least pondered them more intensively than his critics. At bottom he did not believe that any translation could locate the play fully in any one cultural context and had not attempted to do so.

The *Hamlet* actors and actresses clearly did the best they could. They were praised generally for their enthusiasm and dedication. Apart from the difficulties of the play, most of them had to risk considerable social and familial opprobrium at appearing at all, such was the low esteem in which acting, even highbrow acting of this kind, was still held in society at large. Hence the prevailing use of stage names to conceal real identities. Tsubouchi had to spend some time pacifying irate or anxious parents. As slight compensation for this, each actor's name on the programmes was graced by the suffix -shi, an honorific word corresponding to the English Mr/Miss/Mrs in English programmes of the same period.

The influence of Tsubouchi's *Rodoku* training was generally detected and decried. One reviewer praised the actresses for having broken through this constriction, as it was seen. Perhaps Tsubouchi, whose writings do not reveal much enthusiasm for female actors, had developed *Rodoku* primarily with male actors in mind. Certainly the leading actors – Doi and Togi – were so well schooled in it that they must have drawn the attention of critics. It was also felt that the cast had been drilled too thoroughly by Tsubouchi and that this had imparted an unfortunate stiffness to their performance.

There is little in contemporary sources to guide us in forming an impression of the interpretations that the actors and actresses gave to their roles. In the manner of the time there is a minute by minute description of one performance in the leading theatrical journal, but this is mainly concerned with telling the plot and informing us about basic movements.[26] During the fourth soliloquy, for example, Hamlet is described as 'muttering painfully', then sitting down 'in a chair with arms' after ''Tis a consummation'. He curses himself and his indecisiveness. Doi himself tells us that he played this soliloquy with much less movement in this production than he had in 1907, putting more emphasis on Hamlet's reflective melancholy, but he does not say why apart from the observation that his previous performance had been too showy and ostentatious.[27]

In this respect the reviews were disappointing. According to one contemporary academic observer of the theatre scene, 1911 was the year in which newspapers realised their responsibilities to provide serious reviews, but the general standard was very low.[28] The reviewers were not academics, however, and still by this time had had virtually no experience of assessing a production like Tsubouchi's *Hamlet*. Traditional theatre criticism depended largely on precedent, and a knowledge of past productions of the same play enabled judgements to be made without supporting arguments. The reviews of *Hamlet* read like a string of *ex cathedra* pronouncements on individual scenes or episodes. Occasionally there is an attempt to see individual performances as wholes: for example, that making Claudius melancholy early in the play lessened the credibility of his self-doubt later, but this was written by the actor who had played Gertrude in 1907;[29] and that 'Ophelia made us think that it was natural she should go mad with grief for Hamlet, who had lost his heart, and her father, who had lost his life',[30] but this was also not the comment of a professional critic but a student who knew or may even have been taught by Tsubouchi.

Most realised, however, even if they were unable to comment on it, that here was the first significant example of a unified production of a type previously unknown in Japan. A director had had overall control. The actors were co-operatively engaged in performing a complete dramatic text. The scenery was appropriate. The music had been chosen to enhance the production. Coherence on this scale had always been practically unattainable (though sometimes inadvertently attained) on the Kabuki stage because of competing vested interests, but there was unmistakable conscious coherence in this production.

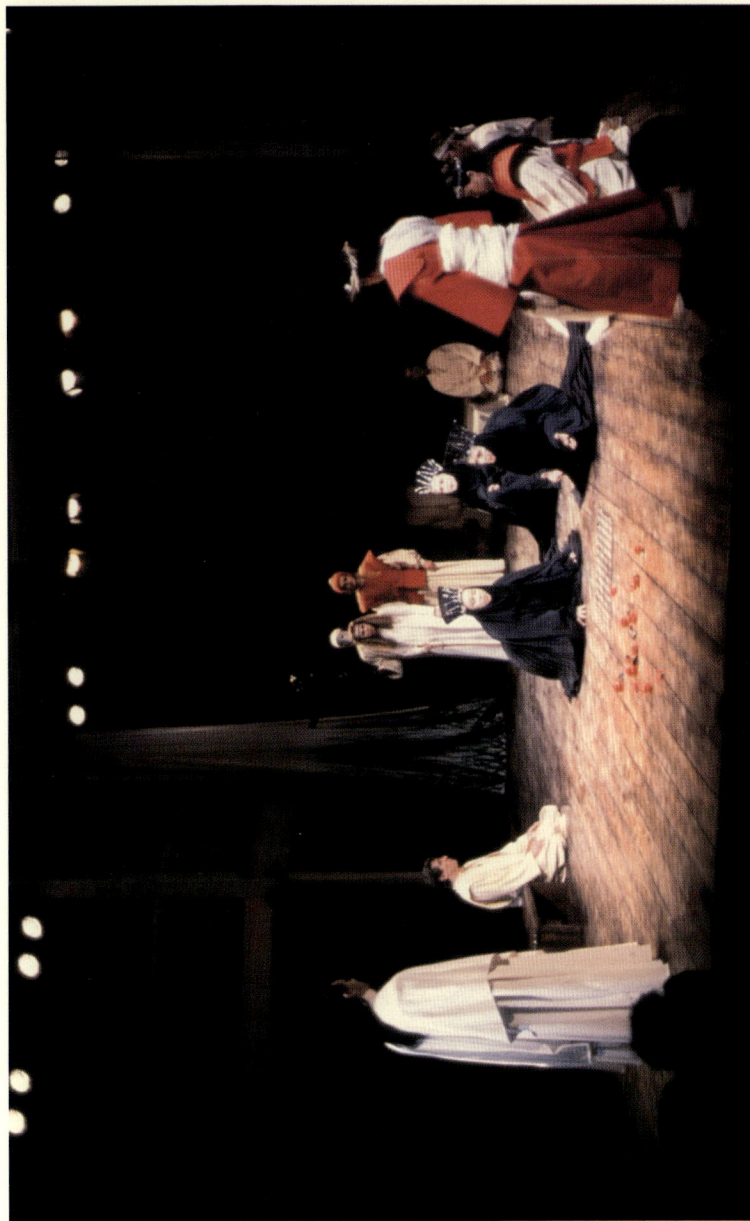

Plate 1 Scene from Barry Kyle's production of *The Two Noble Kinsmen*, Swan Theatre, Stratford-upon-Avon (1986).

Plate 2 Toshifumi Suematsu's production of Harue Tsutsumi's *Kanadehon Hamlet* (1994). Katsuya Kobayashi as theatre manager Kan'ya Morita.

Plate 3 A poster for Senda's *Hamlet* (1964), with Nakadai's image
superimposed.

Plate 4 The shipwreck scene from Yukio Ninagawa's production of *The Tempest*.

In some respects *Hamlet* was a rattling good story for the Japanese stage. Revenge and intra-family feuds had been the stuff of Kabuki and Bunraku for centuries. Even feigning madness in the cause of revenge would have had a familiar ring to it. Had not Kuranosuke Oishi, the hero of Japan's most famous revenge story, feigned dissoluteness, 'madness for women', in his quest to avenge the dishonourable death of his lord? It is not surprising that *Hamlet* attracted the attention of Kabuki and *Shimpa* playwrights and actors.

Hamlet is of course much more than a good story. Why was not *Hamlet* a contemporary of the Japanese in 1911, as it was to Kott and the citizens of Cracow in 1956? This is not as fanciful a question as it seems. Tsubouchi's first translation of Shakespeare had been *Julius Caesar*, translated in 1884 at a time of political ferment, and given a title in Japanese that included the phrase 'a swordstroke for freedom'. The Japanese authorities had been well aware of the subversive power of theatre for two centuries, and literature with a distinct and oppositional political message was common in the 1880s. Soon after *Hamlet* conservative forces in and around the government objected violently to Nora and Magda, as characters subversive to the kind of society that suited their political policies. *Hamlet*, however, was not a play with an overt social or political message and escaped all such unwanted attention.

There are large areas of the plot that would have been largely unintelligible to Japanese audiences. The lack of comment on the religious dimension of the play may be significant. Hamlet hesitating to kill himself because he does not know what is waiting for him after death would only have meant something to those few who had had some contact with a Christian movement only newly allowed to be active. Refraining from killing Claudius because he was at prayer and therefore in a state of grace would surely have been lost on even them, although the text is explicit on this point – if, that is, the audience was understanding the translation.

What one misses in comment on the 1911 *Hamlet* is comment on Hamlet's battle with himself. 'To be or not to be' had inspired Japanese poets in the 1880s, but the full range of his probing of his inner being appears not to have been appreciated by audiences a quarter of a century later. Probably, in the context of Japanese theatre at the time, there was simply too much for audiences to cope with in this production. Tsubouchi himself told his students in 1911 that what they were attempting in putting on *Hamlet* was much more difficult than an Antarctic expedition (there was considerable media interest in Scott and Amundsen at the time), which had finite goals. They were merely fighting a first battle in a war that would continue for many years.[31] Changing the metaphor, when Tsubouchi paid his respects to the audience on the night when our perceptive student was there, he described the company as newborn babies; it would take another ten years to achieve true reform of the theatre.[32]

Tsubouchi was ahead of his time. He knew it, but he also knew that someone had to be. Ironically, he was criticised from all sides for his choice of play, translation, his voice training and his direction. He was too old-fashioned. The play was not modern like Ibsen; the translation was archaic; his actors' delivery suggested Kabuki too much; they had acquired in their acting a distinctive Bungei Kyokai mannerism that would never leave them in their later careers. But if anything, these criticisms can be seen to vindicate Tsubouchi. In spite of having in some eyes not gone far enough, he had gone too far. Nothing like the Bungei Kyokai II *Hamlet* had ever been seen before and the range of reform, viewed in the context of theatre history, may have kept the audiences at some distance from the play.

4   Koreya Senda and political Shakespeare

Dennis Kennedy and J. Thomas Rimer

Overview

For Western observers there appears to be a gap in the development of the appreciation of Shakespeare in twentieth-century Japan. The initial enthusiasms of Shoyo Tsubouchi and his colleagues, chronicled elsewhere in this volume, brought prototypes of translations and productions; by the 1920s Japanese versions of much of the Shakespeare canon were available to a large public in inexpensive paperback editions, and the study of Shakespeare became an important element in the humanistic culture of many Japanese universities. By the 1970s the theatre had caught up, and there was no shortage of popular and well-appreciated stagings of most of the tragedies and many of the comedies. But what came in between?

The answer lies not in the academy but in the professional theatre itself. And no Japanese theatre artist kept Shakespeare before the public more than Koreya Senda, the professional name taken by Kunio Ito, whose long career extended from the mid-1920s to 1994. (He died in December of that year as this essay was being written; at the age of 90 he was still active in rehearsals and in the running of his company, the Actor's Theatre.) In many ways the *Hamlet* he directed in 1964 represented the culmination of his efforts to produce Shakespeare in an enlightening political context, though it was only one important step in a number of similar experiments he conducted as an actor or director since the 1930s. Because he regarded Shakespeare both as a contemporary playwright and a political thinker, his career points most clearly to the intercultural complexities of Shakespeare on the Japanese stage. In this essay we propose to outline Senda's importance by contextualising his work with international socialism and international Shakespeare performance.

Senda was born in 1904 into a well-educated business family and received a bourgeois education himself. His father had been to America as a young man, and three of his brothers became active in the theatre. His oldest brother was Michio Ito, born in 1893, who studied the Dalcroze method at Hellerau, just outside Dresden. His dancing inspired

Yeats and prompted the interest in Asian theatre that culminated in the poet's *Three Plays for Dancers*. Eventually Michio performed in the première of the Yeats' Noh play *At the Hawk's Well* in London in 1916, before going to the United States for a successful career as a dancer and choreographer. Senda's second brother, Kisaku Ito, born in 1899, showed a great talent for drawing and became Japan's leading set designer during the early postwar years. Osuke Ito, Senda's younger brother, became a composer and musical pedagogue. Given this intellectual and artistic background, Senda was a very much a child of his time.

With the opening of Japan in 1868 under the aegis of the Emperor Meiji, new ideas began to flood the country. By the turn of the century, Japanese higher education had moved away from the neo-Confucian sureties and severities that had formed the curriculum for virtually 300 years. These were now replaced by a variety of influences from nineteenth-century Europe, particularly in the form of German philosophy; instructors such as the legendary Raphael von Koeber (1848–1923) taught Kant, Hegel, and Schopenhauer at Tokyo Imperial University.

What was new about German thought was its emphasis on the sanctity and high purpose of the individual. This brought a new kind of psychic stress to young Japanese men of the time, perhaps best captured in the famous farewell note of a brilliant student, Misao Fujimori, who committed the most celebrated suicide of the period by jumping into the Kegon waterfall at Nikko, north of Tokyo, in 1903. The text reads in part:

> Ensconced in the vastness of space and time,
> I, with my meagre body, have tried to fathom the enormity of this universe.
> But what authority can be attributed to Horatio's philosophy?
> There is, after all, only one word for truth: 'incomprehensible'.[1]

As the mention of Horatio's words suggests, the range of texts read by eager students had now become dominated by Western classics. And, after all, Shakespeare himself had long since been appropriated as a 'German' classic. For Japanese students in this period, however, since all the ideas expressed in these works were new to them, their reading often evoked a spiritual response rare in the West. It should be no real surprise, then, that Shakespeare became for many both a vital source and point of repair; this generation felt that he spoke to their immediate concerns and was a thoroughly contemporary figure. For the elite university students in the first decade of the century, Western writers and thinkers made possible the creation of the individual self. Yet the purposes of that liberation remained fearsomely unclear.

By the time that Senda became a college student himself, a decade or more later, a vision of purpose for the individual soul had emerged. With the continuing prestige of German studies in so many circles, it was almost inevitable that an interest in Hegel and Schopenhauer would be followed by a fascination with Marx and Nietzsche. Marx's analysis of social ills struck a particularly strong chord, since the development of an urban working force, and the attendant sharp division into classes of the rich and the poor, brought about the same social rifts in Japan that had plagued Europe during its similar phase of economic development in the nineteenth century. Thus to a study of philosophic Marxism were added the practical activities of socialists, anarchists, and communists, which eventually resulted in the official establishment of the Japan Communist Party in 1922. From the start, leftist elements in Japanese society drew the ire of the government, and the movement was to acquire important martyrs even in its early days. Among them was the anarchist Sakae Osugi, murdered by the police in 1923, whose writings Senda remembers reading as a young man.

Senda took up the study of German literature at Waseda University (where Tsubouchi continued to teach and translate Shakespeare). Given the example of his older brothers, it is not surprising that he abandoned his studies midway through in order the join the Tsukiji Little Theatre. Founded in 1924, the Tsukiji was the first theatre built after the devastating Tokyo earthquake of 1923 that was exclusively dedicated to *Shingeki*, the Japanese term for the new theatre movement, a modern Japanese theatre inspired by Western models. Its triumvirate of directors based the repertory of the Tsukiji on a range that ran from Chekhov and Ibsen to German Expressionist drama. Senda was given the status of a research student, but managed to land a small role in the first Expressionist production, Reinhardt Goering's *The Sea Battle*. He continued to work with the company in a variety of functions until he left Japan in 1927, shortly before the troupe was disbanded after the death of the most important of its founders, Kaoru Osanai (1881–1928). It was at this point that Senda came of age, politically and artistically.

The German movement

Senda was fond of noting that he was born on 15 July 1904, the day Chekhov died, almost as if he were some form of reincarnation. His dramatic and political sympathies, however, had little reference to pre-revolutionary Russia and much to Weimar Germany; it was not Osanai's idol Anton Chekhov who formed Senda's thinking, but Bertolt Brecht. Indeed in order to understand Senda's unique contribution to Shakespeare in Japan, it is necessary to see how he was affected by internationalist ideals formulated in the playhouses and meeting rooms of Berlin in the 1920s.

To be involved in *Shingeki* from 1920 to 1970 meant, for most of those interested in anything more than simple entertainment, to be a member of the left wing, and perhaps a Communist. Even before he went to Germany, Senda was a committed theatre socialist. While at the Tsukiji he was already reading *Das Kapital* as well as Rosa Luxemburg, Trotsky, and Bukahin. He joined the Proletarian Literary Federation (Proletaria Bungei Renmei) in Tokyo, became an editor of its journal, and founded its drama section. In an interview in 1970 he recalled that while Tsukiji in 1925–6 was still performing the late nineteenth-century works of Ibsen, Chekhov, and Maeterlinck, 'I thought that we ought to consistently be doing proletarian plays'.[2] Soon he started a workers' theatre group called the Vanguard Theatre (Zen'eiza), the first professional revolutionary theatre in Japan. It later became the Tokyo Left Theatre, an important arm of PROT, the Japanese Proletarian Theatre League. Its first production was Anatoli Lunacharsky's *Don Quixote Liberated*, with Senda in the major role of the revolutionary Drigo Pass, acting in a manner which was, according to a socialist journal of the era, 'full of energy, force and militancy.'[3]

Senda arrived in Berlin in 1927 just after Erwin Piscator had been expelled from the Volksbühne and had started the Piscatorbühne. Accepted into his research institute, Senda soon felt that Piscator's experiments 'were being conducted on a scale too large for Japanese proletarian theatre', and left to join an amateur group run by workers. 'I didn't really study much theatre', he said. 'It would be more appropriate to say that I had gone to Germany to get involved in the German movement.' (Yamamoto-Goodman, pp. 57–8). He was deeply absorbed in Communist activities, publishing placards, arranging exhibitions for workers, and issuing the paper *Arbeiter Bühne und Film*. He was a delegate to the First International Congress of the Anti-Imperialist League and to the Eighth World Congress of the Workers' International Relief.

The Berlin of the Weimar Republic seemed to Senda enormously cosmopolitan and free, as it did to many other artists, of course. That freedom, which was political as well as artistic, encouraged Senda to work in both spheres:

There was a certain balance struck, I thought, between the right and the left. And Berlin was really the centre of world theatre at the time. In Berlin, you could see the most important theatre from all parts of the world being performed: Russian theatre, French or Italian. These were the years of relative economic stability for the Weimar Republic, but when Germany was swallowed up by the Great Depression, the Nazis began to gain power. I remember the Nazis coming by in a truck and firing their pistols into the headquarters of the German Communist Party where I was drawing pictures for posters and handbills. (Yamamoto-Goodman p. 58)

In addition to his political activity, he acted at the Volksbühne under the direction of Karl Heinz Martin, in agitprop street theatre, and in films. He also spent a few months in the Soviet Union, where he continued to study both revolutionary theatre and film.

So Senda's time abroad solidified his belief in the primacy of politics in the theatre. In clear contrast to the dominant tradition in Japan – which tended to consider art, especially Western art, as existing only in an aesthetic and introspective realm – Senda aligned himself with the radical left of Berlin and Moscow. 'I can't conceive of dealing with theatre as something that is, in itself, an end', he said years later. 'I consider theatre a means to communicate with people, to change them; it is something more than a means to self-expression or self-realisation. It is a way of influencing people in certain directions with dramatic technique' (Yamamoto-Goodman, p. 59) This is, of course, a 'Brechtian' statement, proposing that social and aesthetic impulses can be conjoined into a single, coherent, and political experience.

Though Senda never met Brecht, he did see the original productions of *The Threepenny Opera* (1928) and the most politically radical of Brecht's *Lehrstücke*, *The Measures Taken* (1930). It can be argued that those two productions were the most important events in the making of a political theatre in the twentieth century; from them Brecht and his numerous followers developed and refined strategies that have vastly affected playwriting and performance techniques throughout the world. Those strategies came to affect Senda as well, but like others in the worker's movement he had reservations about Brecht during the Weimar period itself. Though Brecht was gradually moving towards Marxism and experimenting with a dialectical dramaturgy, 'most proletarian theatre artists were not very enthusiastic about him,' Senda remembered. 'Of course, they changed their opinions later, but at the time you could see in them a very strong sense of distrust in professional theatre artists and intellectual revolutionaries' (Yamamoto-Goodman, p. 59).

For his own part, Senda was convinced that the most important lesson of his travels abroad was not theatrical. 'The finest thing I gained during my stay in Germany was the experience of living and working with German labourers', he insisted (Yamamoto-Goodman, p. 59). Such an idealistic and utopian conviction was characteristic of the international socialist movement in 1930. But Senda made that statement forty years later, at the age of sixty-six, long after the clash between communism and fascism had faded and the turmoils of the war, in Europe and in Japan, were over. It is clear that the movement held life-long importance for him.

Senda returned to Japan just after the Manchurian invasion of September 1931, and was immediately arrested: the irony of leaving a fascist Germany for a fascist Japan must have been severe. He was soon set free, though he would be arrested numerous times again in the years before the war – at meetings, at conferences, at home, and more than once on the stage. In a single period of eighteen months, he was imprisoned by Tokyo authorities five separate times. None of this stopped his continued work in political theatre, however; his opposition to the militaristic government grew as its militarism grew, and he found ways to express that opposition through performance.

Senda's first action on return was to establish a broad-based company to protest against the repressive regime. The Tokyo Theatre Group (Tokyo Engeki Shudan) was made up of theatre artists from all segments of the profession, from the avant-garde to vaudeville entertainers, from art-for-art's-sake dramatists to members of PROT. Its initial production was the Japanese première of *The Threepenny Opera* in March of 1932, an almost obvious choice for Senda. The trouble was that the script was not available in Japan. The Pabst film had been shown, and Weill's music had been published there, so Senda made up a version from the music, the film, Gay's *The Beggar's Opera*, and from his memory of the Berlin stage production. Since few Japanese had seen a Western opera, Senda thought that audiences could not understand the irony of Brecht's title. He therefore called it *Kojiki Shibai*, or *The Beggars' Play*. A movie star, Tsukigata Ryunosuke, known only for his samurai films, asked for a part, so Senda wrote a scene especially for him. The performers had trouble with the sophisticated music, Senda notes. As a result he was forced to make the production more like a music hall event, a carnivalesque entertainment that lost most of its political bite.[4] 'In terms of introducing Brecht to Japan by faithfully producing his plays', Senda admitted, 'our production was a total failure, but our social and political circumstances demanded the approach we took' (Yamamoto-Goodman, p. 60).

Senda's strategies were apparent in key performance details. Though Brecht set his play on the day of Victoria's coronation, the original production dressed Macheath and his henchmen in costumes evoking Chicago gangsters of the 1920s. Seeking a cultural equivalent, Senda placed his version in the years just after the Meiji Restoration: Peacham was in a traditional Japanese costume with samurai hairdo, while Macheath (played by Senda himself) and his gang were in the newly fashionable Western clothes of the 1870s.

The declining years of the 1930s were as difficult for Senda as they were for the leftist movement. The leaders of PROT were all arrested, and

Senda had to run the organisation by himself for a time. As the war approached and the government became more repressive, the Japanese Communist Party became inflexible and demanded that the Tokyo Theatre Group operate within what Senda called 'their very rigid political line' (Yamamoto-Goodman, p. 60). Since the troupe had been formed specifically to appeal to a wide spectrum of political (and apolitical) artists, many members were quickly uncertain or afraid; after a short time it disbanded entirely. Senda had been a party member in Berlin, but had not joined in Japan; none the less he was constantly harassed by the police for aiding and abetting the Communist cause. Eventually he spent 1940 to 1942 in jail, though he was never sentenced; he 'recanted' in 1942, like many other artists, by agreeing to work for the national cause. Senda claimed that he signed his recantation solely to see if it were still possible to continue his political movement, even in wartime; 'I was not concerned with whether Japan won or lost the war. It was not important to me', he said (Yamamoto-Goodman, p. 63).

Despite isolation and hardship, the leftist theatres represented one important public source of political opposition in Japan in the late 1930s. They often relied on coded messages to speak to their audiences, as theatres in the Stalinist countries of Eastern Europe did after the war. Since all plays were censored by the authorities in advance, it was difficult for the police to close approved productions down, and it is always difficult – though not impossible – for the police to monitor what actually happens on every stage night after night. One example will serve to make the point, and to indicate Senda's implacable persistence in his political cause. Speaking of the trials of making proletarian theatre in a repressive environment, he noted:

Generally, my attitude is to always keep doing things. When the police said to us before the war that we weren't to be allowed to use red lights, we used pink ones. And when pink light was banned, we used amber. The audience always applauded because they understood what we were trying to say. (Yamamoto-Goodman, p. 64).

Socialist Shakespeare

Senda's connection with Shakespeare began with his work as an actor at Tsukiji before his German excursion. In 1925 he performed the role of Antony in *Julius Caesar* to good reviews, and took Antonio in the 1926 production of *The Merchant of Venice*, the last part he played for the company before leaving for Germany. After his return he assumed the title role in a 1938 production of *Hamlet* for the New Tsukiji Theatre Company (Shin-Tsukijiza), which had been formed in 1929 by Yoshi

Hijikata, a leftist colleague of Osanai's, after the original troupe was disbanded in 1927. The production was mounted shortly after the start of Japan's war with China, however, and the censor demanded that all textual references to royalty be removed. In Osaka it was banned entirely because 'depravity was shown within the imperial chambers'.[5] The story of *Hamlet*, with its three political rebellions and corrupt king, has often struck oppressive governments as threatening; Stalin, for example, banned it during the Second World War and it was not seen again in the Soviet Union until 1954, after his death. Senda's own performance of the role in 1938 was attuned to the rough and violent times. 'He disdained the romantic melancholic Hamlet of the elder Tsubouchi', wrote Akimasa Minamitani, 'and wanted to recreate him as active and brisk.'[6]

A similar force lay behind Senda's own production of the play in 1964. At the very end of the war, Senda and a group of colleagues founded the company which was to provide the base to carry on the development of the quest for a truly contemporary theatre in postwar Japan. The 1944 manifestos for the Haiyuza (Actor's Theatre), as the name suggests, called for the creation of a troupe that would provide an opportunity for performers and audiences alike to experience the emotional power of the theatre. The group felt that the curtailment of theatrical activity during the war years had virtually destroyed the New Theatre movement, and they were determined to move forward and build audiences. Senda's views and proclivities were certainly more to the left than those of some of his colleagues, but all agreed that the first task before them was to keep alive the development of a modern theatre which was professionally skilled and authentically Japanese. A few early and tentative productions were staged just before the end of the war, and a wide variety of plays, both European and Japanese, were mounted during the American occupation. All of these were performed in commercial, rented halls. By 1954 the company was sufficiently strong and financially well supported to construct their own theatre in Tokyo's (now) fashionable Roppongi district, the only New Theatre troupe with the funds to do so.

The repertory of the company was varied, yet the European classics chosen for production were marked by politically progressive themes, like the plays of Gogol and Beaumarchais. Not surprisingly, the company staged two works by Brecht. *The Good Person of Szechuan* was first performed in 1960 and was so successful that it was revived in 1962 and 1963. In 1962, Senda had the opportunity to renew his interest in *The Threepenny Opera*; he translated Brecht's original text himself and supervised a visually sophisticated production which toured the country and which was revived at the Actor's Theatre in 1963.

Shakespeare, however, came to occupy an increasingly central role in

6. Hamlet (Tatsuya Nakadai) and Laertes (Tetsuo Hasegawa) in the final scene of Senda's production of *Hamlet*, Nissei Theatre, Tokyo (1964). The illustration suggests some of the vigorous movement that characterized the acting.

the fortunes of the company. In an important essay on Shakespeare and the modern actor written in 1951, Senda spoke with considerable eloquence of his lasting attraction to Shakespeare. 'As actors, with our practical sense of the theatre', he wrote, 'we know that Shakespeare is the one who brought the drama as we know it to perfection'; it is he who created the modern art of the actor, and 'to him all respect and thanks are owed'. Then follow some striking remarks on Shakespeare which prefigure the ideas of Jan Kott:

We have undertaken many efforts in our own country to create, in the real sense of the word, a modern drama. All of them can be considered as an extension of the road first opened up by Shakespeare. And so it is that this playwright, born in Stratford, England, feels closer to us in our own work than the great men of our own tradition: Zeami, Chikamatsu, Mokuami. This is in no way related to the fact that our New Theatre itself appears Western in style. Rather, it truly feels to us that Shakespeare is our own contemporary.[7]

It was in such a context that the company mounted *Othello* in 1951 and a well-received version of *The Merry Wives of Windsor* in 1952, which was redubbed *Falstaff*. The production was remounted in 1957. *Twelfth Night* was first produced in 1959. Senda was involved in all these productions as an actor; although he did not direct them, he wrote persuasive essays on their meaning and importance.

Senda's *Hamlet*, however, was another matter. After *The Threepenny Opera*, this was the most important of his postwar productions and the one to which he gave the greatest thought. He wrote a number of essays on his conception of the play, on his own experiences in playing the role in 1938, and showed in the variety of European writers he quoted a considerable knowledge of the scholarship of the play and of its twenti-eth-century mountings. When the run was over, he wrote again on the results of his directing. It seems clear from the thrust of his remarks throughout that he was generally offering this production as a test case: was it possible to transfer his socialist concerns to a swiftly changing postwar Japan?

Around the time of Senda's *Hamlet*, global Shakespeare production had been greatly affected by two postwar influences: the Marxist ideals of Brecht and his theatre company, the Berliner Ensemble, sponsored by the German Democratic Republic; and the darker, Beckettian vision of the Polish critic Jan Kott. The first saw Shakespeare and other classic drama as the means to a realistic analysis of class and power struggles in history and in the present. For Brecht and his actors, Shakespeare was material for appropriation. His exemplary status meant that audiences were pre-disposed to listen, but the messages they would hear from the Berliner Ensemble would be those born of the great socialist project – the struggle to defeat fascism and to establish a new people's democracy in war-torn Europe – not some complicit notion of 'timeless' humanism character-istic of liberal capitalism.

Kott, on the other hand, saw in Shakespeare's plays examples of the absurdist universe. Lost amid the great void that surrounds us, Shakespeare presents characters who are marked as alienated and alone, free to define themselves and to fail grandly. In his book *Shakespeare Our Contemporary* (published in Polish and French in 1962 and in English in 1964), Kott outlined a world of cruelty and pain, drawing upon the Stalinist nightmares of Eastern Europe after the war. As Peter Brook wrote, 'Kott is undoubtedly the only writer on Elizabethan matters who assumes without question that every one of his readers will at some point or other have been woken by the police in the middle of the night'.[8] The tragedies showed the fragility and meaninglessness of life, the history plays showed horror and bloodshed as an unending cycle of absurd sav-agery, while the comedies provided examples of bestial sexuality and nightmarish sex changes.

7. Nakadai dying in Horatio's arms, with Fortinbras in the background.

The social concerns of Brecht and the existential *angst* of Kott came together powerfully in 1961 when Peter Hall formed the Royal Shakespeare Company in Stratford. Hall had been much impressed by the visit of the Berliner Ensemble to London in 1956, and established his new company in its organisational and social wake. His announced intention was to produce a Shakespeare that was relevant to the time, one that avoided the glossy, star-laden traditions of high culture and showed instead a gritty, hard-headed vision appropriate to a world being redefined by the Cold War. Hall's productions of the history plays between 1963 and 1964, generically called 'The Wars of the Roses', accented the Brechtian mode to reveal the power struggles of the middle ages, outfitting those struggles with leather, metal, and grunting actors wielding heavy broadswords. At the same time Kott also became a major presence in Stratford through the work of Brook, who was an associate director at the RSC. Already a leading Shakespearean director, Brook had met Kott in Warsaw in 1957 and the two began a series of discussions on *King Lear* that eventually led to Brook's production in 1962. Brook read an early version in French of Kott's famous essay on the play, ultimately published in *Shakespeare Our Contemporary* as 'King Lear or Endgame'. Kott's comparison of Shakespeare's cruellest tragedy to Beckett's tragicomedy of nuclear devastation prompted Brook to direct *Lear* as a play about the meaninglessness of the postwar condition.

In a sense, then, the RSC, which rapidly became the most important producer of Shakespeare in the world, combined European social and philosophical resources. By the time the quadricentenary of Shakespeare's birth arrived in 1964, the RSC had already demonstrated how contemporary issues could share the stage with a 400-year-old text. Other European theatre companies used the celebration year for similar projects, often with a socialist twist: Roger Planchon's *Troilus and Cressida* in Lyons, Leopold Lindtberg's histories in Vienna, Wolfgang Heinz's *Hamlet* in East Berlin, side by side with the Berliner Ensemble's *Coriolanus*.

Senda's choice of *Hamlet* for 1964 fitted into this international pattern. It is unclear if he knew about the recent work of the RSC, and he probably had not read Kott's book, which did not appear in Japanese until 1968.[9] But there is no doubt about the influence of Brecht. Senda wrote an essay on Brecht and Shakespeare while he was working on his production of *Hamlet*, in which he notes that from the start Brecht used Shakespeare to react to contemporary political events. Brecht's revision of *Coriolanus* (the basis of the Berliner Ensemble production in 1964, eight years after Brecht's death) used a materialist strategy 'to examine in the mirror held up by Shakespeare the character of the autocrat Coriolanus in terms of the cruel experiences which occurred when the Nazis seized power', as Senda put it. Brecht did this chiefly by stressing how great and heroic characters are usually bad news for the working class. His position on *Hamlet* was similar. Referring to Brecht's rehearsal scenes, intended to help actors build up their roles by filling out the social issues and class divisions missing from the text, Senda noted that the urge was to remove the heroic aspects of the play and to take the accent off of Romantic interiority.[10]

Senda's production proceeded from this point. In his essay on directing *Hamlet*, originally published as a pamphlet accompanying the performance, he emphasised that the play takes place when Shakespeare wrote it, at the end of the sixteenth century, and not in a mythical medieval world: 'the ideas and interior life of the characters belong to the Renaissance, not the Middle Ages'. Such a setting permits the director to situate the economic era at a time when England already had early capitalist structures in place, such as manufacturing and trade. The nobility had adopted bourgeois ideas, Senda wrote, and, as some had strengthened ties to Queen Elizabeth, they made some of their projects part of state policy. In the play itself, Senda insisted, Polonius and the King's council reveal the values of the new, mercantilised nobility:

8. Tatsuya Nakadai in an overtly European Renaissance costume, in keeping with Senda's Marxist insistence on the importance of early capitalism to the play.

'Polonius' speech of advice, and his prescriptions for his son going to Paris, show a kind of bourgeois morality, which is the very pattern of capitalist thinking'.[11] Modern-dress productions often try to stress 'universals', he noted in another place; but the play cannot be universal, since it is of necessity linked to its own time. Any universality it may have must exist 'on top' of its specific circumstance. Thus what Senda strove for was the complex and ambiguous changeover from the medieval world to the Renaissance. He made this noticeably apparent in the visual choices: not medieval gloom in the castle but 'a certain baroque quality in its elegance . . . not a castle made for warfare but for watching ships sailing on business for the country'.[12]

Relying on Bacon's essay on revenge, published at about the same time as *Hamlet* was staged, Senda concludes that there are two attitudes in conflict in the play. Laertes exhibits the feudal notion of revenge, based in unthinking family honour. Hamlet, Senda observes, in his hesitation to avenge his father's ghost, questioning, applying reason and logic and worrying over consequences, leans toward the new bourgeois thinking.[13] But Hamlet is also caught in the vice of history. Not only does he act in a 'feudal' manner at the end when he kills Claudius, he does so when he mistakenly stabs Polonius. In that scene, Senda's production emphasised the brutality and ugliness in Hamlet's character by following the stage directions that require him to drag the body away ('I'll lug the guts into the neighbour room', III.iv). 'Hamlet is to pull the body ruthlessly; this seems "unlike" him and so this gesture is often cut.' On the walls of the palace, Senda had placed portraits representing the former kings of Norway, who had 'calmly killed their own parents, older brothers, and their own subjects'. As Hamlet dragged the body off, the portraits were lit, as if the past rulers were observing the scene.[14]

It is hardly necessary to note that Senda's analysis and production choices were vastly different from the standard, romanticised interpretation of *Hamlet* common in 1964. In Japan especially the view of the play was dominated by the nineteenth-century notion of Hamlet as the 'sweet prince', a man out of place, an artist *manqué* whose sensitive soul could not endure the burden of the harsh world. 'There has been too much emphasis placed on the analysis of Hamlet's character', Senda said. 'People think they know what a "Hamlet-like" character is even if they have never read or seen the play.' In place of this the director wanted a rougher, harder character, whose own contradictions would show and whose political attributes would be apparent. 'I have started from the action of the play and then gone to Hamlet's character, not the other way around.'[15]

Accordingly, what most characterised Tatsuya Nakadai's performance as the prince was a kind of restless movement. The idea was to show Hamlet's contradictions through physical expression that implied nervousness and uncertainty rather than reflective inaction and indecision. The tradition of playing the character as a vacillator would be countered in this production by showing him as an active participant in his own fate. According to Senda, Hamlet thinks it is his destiny to become king and believes he is working toward this end, making mistakes along the way; most productions ignore what Hamlet's future might be had he lived. When Nakadai realised he had stabbed Polonius in error, for example, he reacted physically by giving a 'laugh of horror'.[16] At other moments he shifted on his feet or made jerky and violent gestures. Thus interiority was de-emphasised in favour of a Brechtian gestural acting designed to point out Hamlet's complicity in his political fate.

Assessment

There is no question that the production represented an important moment for Japanese Shakespeare. Senda was invited to co-produce the

play at the newest and most prestigious theatre in Tokyo, the Nissei
Theatre, near the Imperial Hotel in the centre of the city. The potential
size of the audience was thereby increased some three-fold, as the Actor's
Theatre seats only 400. When the run was finished, the play was taken on
tour to Osaka, Kyoto, Kobe, Nagoya, and Yokohama. In that sense alone,
Senda's *Hamlet* probably reached a larger audience than any previous
Shakespearean production staged in Japan.

Yet it fell considerably short of the director's desires. The reviewers in
the three major national papers, the *Asahi*, the *Yomiuri*, and the *Mainichi*,
were generally respectful but somewhat baffled by what they saw.[17] All
three found Tatsuya Nakadai's performance in the title role refreshing in
its youthful energy yet remained puzzled by the relative lack of introspection he showed in this part so famous for its 'interior' qualities. Thus they
missed Senda's point entirely. Nevertheless, the *Mainichi* reviewer
remarked that Nakadai provided a strong and convincing portrayal of a
Hamlet of action, rather than of introspection, and that, 'in his black
tights which suit him well,' he was 'the very picture of a prince'. Etsuko
Ichihara was uniformly praised for her portrayal of Ophelia. The translation of Isao Mikami, a leading Shakespearean scholar, teacher, and translator (who did his graduate work in the United States), was judged
refreshingly colloquial, particularly since, as the *Yomiuri* reviewer mentioned with relief, the lines could be clearly understood in the theatre.

As for Senda's direction, all three reviewers noted that the production
exuded none of the customary medieval gloom, but they were confused
by what they took to be merely a pleasant Renaissance opulence, created
perhaps to take advantage of the formidable technical facilities of the
Nissei Theatre. Nothing was said about the class divisions and social
issues, or the Marxist historicising of the setting, which had loomed so
large in Senda's plans for the production. In this sense, at least as far as
the written record can tell us, the production did not succeed in convey-
ing the director's most central concerns.

This response – or rather, this lack of response – leads to a series of
other questions. Leaving aside the skills of the reviewers, who were
perhaps poorly prepared to interpret such a production ('they have no
idea of what's going on', Senda said of postwar critics) (Yamamoto-
Goodman, p. 75), we might begin with the actors themselves. Were they
capable of suggesting Senda's purpose to their audiences?

Nakadai, a performer subsequently known in the West from his appear-
ances in several famous films (notably Masaki Kobayashi's *Kwaidan* and
Akira Kurosawa's *Ran*), wrote an article for the leading scholarly magazine on modern theatre about his experience in learning the part. For
him, he said, a role is like a lover, and Hamlet was difficult to embrace.

Senda had asked him to think about playing the role, and it was only because he was ill and had to cancel other work that he found the requisite time to read the play with sufficient care, and to study the various ideas about the part that Senda and others had set down and that the director insisted he read. His greatest challenge was to face up to the text itself, which seemed to contain more meanings at each reading. Perhaps, he concluded, the text is almost too thick with meaning for performance; in Japanese culture where 'reticence is thought of as a virtue', the text thus poses problems of rhetoric, diction, and speed of delivery. He found the play literally fatiguing to read, although, he added, it never lost its fascination.[18]

Perhaps Senda could not bring his concepts to fruition on the stage itself; perhaps his abilities as an analytical, Marxist intellectual exceeded those of a practical, skilful director. The written reviews suggest that a number of his concepts did come across to his audiences, however: the energetic pace, the Renaissance brilliance, a certain sense of politics and history. Therefore, a case might be made – at least we would like to make it – that the slippage lay less with the quality of the performance than with the nature of the audiences themselves. This is another way of saying that Senda, despite his political and artistic sophistication, had lost touch with contemporary Japanese culture.

Although Senda began and remained a leftist, by the time of the establishment of the Actor's Theatre company in 1944 he committed himself to the position that developing new performance skills for *Shingeki* was the central task for his generation. By 1964, his audiences had increased considerably; but the newcomers to the ranks of those long devoted to the New Theatre were younger and, on the whole, far less ideologically committed than the older generation. These spectators came for entertainment and an opportunity to experience a classic of world high culture. Most of them, of course, had never seen *Hamlet* before and so had no point of comparison for Senda's changes and refinements. Increasing the size of his audience merely diluted their former commitment and understanding.

That is not to say that there was no interest shown in the theatre by the young and radical intelligentsia of the time. The left in Japan in 1964 was reacting to a number of troubling international situations, notably the beginnings of worry over the war in Vietnam and the failure to block the renewal of the Security Treaty with the United States, both of which caused considerable social ferment. These younger radicals turned not to Western theatre to express a sense of outrage, however, but to work done by their own contemporaries, young playwrights and directors (some just finishing their college years) such as Minoru Betsuyaku, Juro Kara, and

Tadashi Suzuki. True enough, Senda's company itself had staged plays by the slightly older left-leaning absurdist playwright and novelist Kobo Abe, but within a larger context of dramas within the proscenium tradition. Kara, Betsuyaku and others, however, performed their plays in tiny halls, in tents, in coffee shops, in the streets. The socialist revolution was still alive, but it had moved on to the next generation, and that generation used its own means of expression. Shakespeare might occasionally be used as well, he might become 'our contemporary' again, but younger artists were to use him in their own way and for their own ends. Senda had, suddenly, become a member of the old left.

In the end, Senda's public, now increasingly bourgeois, had failed to understand his deepest level of commitment. The skills he and his colleagues had spent a lifetime in preparing were no longer sought out by the young, who doubtless looked on his *Hamlet* as a relatively empty exercise in importing high culture. But from a larger perspective Senda's work set standards for accomplishment in the Japanese theatre. Even the new generation of radical playwrights, as they grew older and moved more into the mainstream of Japanese theatrical culture, sometimes found themselves produced at the Actor's Theatre, had their plays sent out on tour and their reputations generally polished by the association. During his long career, Senda managed to take the plays of Shakespeare out of the study and away from those who would see them as genteel contributions to Japan's increasingly international civilisation. Senda made the plays real, real in social meanings and real in the theatre. Even though the next generation operated with different standards, and with other ends in mind, it was Senda, with his relentless and inquiring commitment, who made it possible for the next generation to take the theatre seriously as a means of political and intellectual expression. In this light, Senda's *Hamlet* had a considerable role to play.

The great irony of Shakespeare in Japanese theatre is its placement as part of the modern movement. In the West, and particularly in the Anglophone countries, Shakespeare is the major international theatre classic. His work, whether accepted or rejected, imposed as high culture or used subversively, comes with centuries of accumulated tradition, clearly established as great, irrefutable, permanent. But in Japan, because Shakespeare's plays are foreign, they are *Shingeki*: they may be classics, but they are somebody else's classics.

This climate has freed the Japanese theatre from an over-reliance on any Shakespeare tradition or from obligations of subservience, and in the contemporary period directors like Yukio Ninagawa and Tadashi Suzuki have profited as a result. At the same time, however, during much of Senda's career Japanese producers of Shakespeare have tended to feel

inferior to the West. Assuming a subaltern status, the *Shingeki* movement
has worried about getting productions and interpretations 'right', concerned that they will never equal the insight of British and European
companies into the world's most visible playwright. More than any other
artist of the century, Senda managed to unite these two sides of the
Japanese cultural coin. By bridging the prewar and postwar periods, and
by transforming Marxist and Brechtian issues into Japanese methods, he
also bridged the gap between *Shingeki* and the European past from which
it derived.

5   The perils and profits of interculturalism and the theatre art of Tadashi Suzuki

J. R. Mulryne

Writing in a collection of essays published in English in 1992, Patrice Pavis, the French cultural theorist, sets out to define what he takes to be the present situation of world theatre 'at the crossroads of culture'. 'Never before', he asserts, 'has the western stage contemplated and manipulated the various cultures of the world to such a degree, but never before has it been at such a loss as to what to make of their inexhaustible babble, their explosive mix, the inextricable collage of their languages'.[1] From the perspective of the ordinary theatre-goer in London or on Broadway, or even in Berlin or Paris, such a view must seem extravagant. The insular conservatism, some might say the torpor, of so much in Western theatre-practice makes it seem largely untroubled by the excitements Pavis associates with cultural exchange. Yet it is certainly true that the British stage (and in this it is, with adjustment, representative of Western theatre generally) has in recent years played host to the theatre of the world on a scale that while not unprecedented has nevertheless made an increasing and increasingly influential contribution to theatre experience in this country. The LIFT (London International Festival of Theatre) seasons, the seasons of international theatre organised by Thelma Holt, the World Theatre contributions to successive Edinburgh Festivals, the international visiting companies hosted by the Royal National Theatre, the Nottingham Playhouse and the Royal Shakespeare Company (the Everyman's Shakespeare season of October/November 1994, for example) are all representative of the truism that for British playgoers theatre has become international in ways it scarcely was before. Much of this widening experience has been supplied by companies from the United States and Western Europe, and from the countries of the former Soviet Union and the Communist bloc, Romania and Poland especially. But it has come also from further east, and in particular from Japan (though also from India, China and Indonesia). As the Introduction to this book points out, the Japan Festival of 1991 brought to Britain a six-months' sample (to quote the official brochure) 'of the many different strands that make up life in Japan' including, prominently, the visual and applied arts and traditional and contemporary theatre. Nor has this international theatre traffic been merely one way. In the preceding year an arts festival entitled UK90, including theatre performances by leading British companies, was held in Japan under the auspices of the British Council, with generous financial support from Japanese sources. British theatre companies, from the 'flagship' Royal National Theatre and Royal Shakespeare Company to the smallest experimental groups, now tour the world to a multiplicity of venues, including the increasing number of international Festivals, with backing from the British Council or through the services of burgeoning networks of international promoters and festival organisers. On this evidence, there is an appetite, whether at official level or among theatre practitioners and audiences (though box-office results do not always bear this out), for international or, to make no distinction at this point, intercultural theatre. It is also the case, as Pavis notes, that many of the most admired and influential theorists and practitioners of the contemporary stage have laid emphasis on cultural mingling. Pavis offers a roll-call 'from Artaud to Wilson, from Brook to Barba, from Heiner Müller to Ariane Mnouchkine',[2] but might equally have added, with greater chronological consistency, Robert Lepage, Peter Zadek, Giorgio Strehler and Tadashi Suzuki. Theatre seems committed to the international arena, both in terms of practice and of theory. Why, then, does Pavis discern impending crisis, invoking cultural stress and fracture that make this theatre seem a veritable Tower of Babel?

A distinction may be drawn between 'touring' theatre, where the theatre performance remains essentially the same whether in home or foreign venues, and 'intercultural' theatre which actively seeks in its composition and presentation to incorporate the theatre languages (textual, gestural, costumed, choreographed) of a foreign culture. Yet the distinction is not absolute. The presentation of a theatre piece before a culturally distant audience entails for that audience a process of imaginative decoding that is inevitably intercultural in nature, requiring the negotiation of cultural divides no less real, though possibly less evident, than the distances crossed by the author, director and acting company of a piece that makes overt use of culturally foreign material and techniques. The phenomenon known as 'Festival Theatre' is avowedly intercultural, at its most complex when (as with, say, Ninagawa's *Macbeth* at the Edinburgh Festival, or Suzuki's *The Tale of Lear* in America or Australia) the theatre piece is already the result of cultural translation, including, but going beyond, verbal translation, and is now re-presented before an audience of mixed cultural origin, some members of which may well belong to the source culture itself (insofar as that culture is continuous from the time of the play's composition). The international commerce in theatre is not therefore merely a matter of commerce, though it *is* that, and distortions arise from its commercial orientation, but deriving from its audience's experience also one of considerable intercultural interest. Rustom Bharucha has written pungently of the need for theatre to acknowledge the immediate social and political circumstances of its audience even, indeed especially, when translating foreign works, and so provide 'a conscious resistance not only to the cultural monoliths of New Delhi [he is writing specifically of the Indian situation] but to the larger "system of power" that promotes cultures on the basis of political exigencies, fashion, and the demands of the international market'.[3] Bharucha deplores therefore the internationalisation of theatre practice, at least where this trend fails to acknowledge the foreignness of the chosen text in all its cultural specificity. And Bharucha's voice is only one among many to deplore what have come to seem, in these terms, the exploitative tendencies of intercultural theatre, mired in commercialism, colonialism, orientalism and other politically impermissible stances. In common with business and media, the theatre has become increasingly international, but it has also become more acutely aware, at least among reflective practitioners and theorists, of the implications of this internationalism for a culturally diverse and unequally privileged world. By its very nature, theatre deals with sensitive issues of a political as well as a personal kind. It is scarcely surprising, therefore, that over recent years it has been troubled, as business scarcely has, by a kind of intercultural *angst* that has qualified and perhaps undermined the satisfactions of international exchange.

Intercultural angst

One of the most fascinating documents among recent discussions of interculturalism is Richard Schechner's *The Future of Ritual: Writings on Culture and Performance*. The book has much to offer the student of interculturalism in its analyses of the work of Artaud, Grotowski, Barba, Brook and very much else. But I call it a document because it situates so precisely the *angst* that has gripped intercultural study over the last fifteen years, and probably more. It may be helpful to sketch in the broad outlines of this *angst* as a way of entering on the territory mentioned in the title of this paper.

Schechner begins his book with a highly sanguine statement about the benefits, personal, social, political, and cultural of theatre practice:

The best way to . . . understand, enliven, investigate, get in touch with, outwit, contend with, defend oneself against, love . . . others, other cultures, the elusive and intimate 'I-thou', the other in oneself, the other opposed to oneself, the feared, hated, envied, different other . . . is to perform and to study performances and performative behaviours in all their various genres, contexts, expressions, and historical processes.[4]

It is a clarion call in support of theatre's cultural role. The cumulating verbs testify to the excitement that underlies a lifetime's commitment to, and achievement in, theatre. Yet as the chapter goes on, the tone changes when Schechner describes his 'conversion' to Hinduism, the better to explore and recreate the theatrical achievements normally closed to those outside the Hindu faith. Schechner courageously and candidly (so far as one can tell) records the deep uneasiness he felt in compromising his Jewishness and accepting initiation, in July 1976, as the Hindu novice Jayaganesh. 'After my initiation', he writes, 'I felt easier in the temples, though wicked in my heart.' The self-emptying offered a new identity, but a qualified one: 'Threaded in my new Hindu identity, I was "authentic", almost.'[5] He was released into a new self-consciousness that carried with it, with a kind of inevitability, the burden of a duplicitous performance: 'What [he asks himself] was this Jayaganesh doing, if not performing himself performing his Hinduism?'[6] Schechner's commitment to Hinduism issued in creative achievement, but entailed also personal cost in self-division. One remembers Yeats's poetic credo, 'It is myself that I remake'. Interculturalism, while it seeks to heal divisions, may equally bring about – seems bound to bring about – fractures that are personal, socio-political and ultimately cultural.

If I choose Schechner's experience and self-examination as parable, it is partly because Schechner is himself at the cutting edge of the inter-cultural debate. His analysis in *The Future of Ritual* and elsewhere of the work of practitioners such as Eugenio Barba and Jerzy Grotowski is marked by deep and practical knowledge. It is also marked by what I take to be a healthy scepticism towards some of the mystifications that may attend intercultural or multicultural practice in the theatre and outside. The commercially profitable satisfactions offered to naive youth through access to the 'ancient wisdom' of the East draws particular mockery, but even Grotowski's theatre work, distinguished as it is and of unexampled seriousness, merits some sceptical reporting. In so much theatre work, Schechner notes, today's experience seems to call for support from the imagery of "old" cultures: 'There is a wish for validation and mutual con-firmation'.[7] Schechner declares himself 'uncomfortable' with Grotowski's work and with that of the theorist Victor Turner:

I am uncomfortable with Grotowski's Performer and with wisdom that exists before or behind genres, in the "original" times, in the "old cultures". These anthologies of cultures, or the wish for globalism, strike me as premature because they are unavoidably expressions of Western hegemony, attempts to cull and harvest the world's cultures. Maybe later in history, if there is more equality of power, more actual multiculturalism, but not now.[8]

These are almost the book's last words on a topic that has preoccupied its author not only for the length of the volume, but for much of his working life. While overtly critical of one distinguished practitioner, Grotowski, and one distinguished theorist, Turner, they revert to a discomfort (at best an Augustinian 'save me, Lord, but not yet') with the entire multi-cultural project. One does not have to point out the oxymoronic contradictions between 'cull' and 'harvest', or the resonances of these words with the suppressed image embedded in 'cultures', to appreciate the profound conflict between such sentiments and the up-beat hopes incorporated in the book's opening claims for theatre. It seems as though interculturalism can do little, at least as yet, to give expression to the global wish for cultural wholeness.

There is one phrase in Schechner's culminating statement that leads to my other reason for highlighting his contribution to the intercultural debate. The phrase, 'they are unavoidably expressions of Western hegemony' raises the spectre that has for many years haunted commentators on matters intercultural. If it is true that *everything* is political, that truth seems to have particular force, perhaps unsurprisingly, in discussions of the cultural relationships of societies old and new, north and south, east and west. The guilt-ridden sense that the history of Western hegemony is indeed 'unavoidable' is everywhere present. The geo-political tensions that have become so prominent, acute and newsworthy since communications have spectacularly improved could scarcely do other than leave their imprint on the discussion and the reception, by real-world audiences, of intercultural theatre. The modernist readiness to read sub-text rather than text has only accentuated the tendency. Even more specifically the impact of conceptions of Orientalism, of which Edward Said's work is both source and symptom, has had its effect on the inter-pretation of the political and politico-cultural meanings of intercultural theatre, in part because so much of the work has elected an East–West axis. Schechner was himself embroiled, directly and by allusion, in just such a politico-cultural controversy with the Indian-American scholar Rustom Bharucha, running through issues of the *Asian Theatre Journal*, and spilling over into subsequent writing by Schechner and into Bharucha's *Theatre and the World*. The Schechner/Bharucha disagree-ment, briefly summarised, offers a further and I think clarifying instance of the tensions that underlie intercultural theatre practice.

It could be said, without significant exaggeration, that Bharucha con-sistently views interculturalism as irremediably tainted by the impure ethics of capitalism, imperialism and orientalism, an intertissued web of ideologies within which we are all caught, at least in the West (though Eastern power-structures are not exempt). Within such a deterministic framework, the outlook for intercultural practice is gloomy, indeed in ethical terms, for the Western or advanced society, doomed:

I think it should be acknowledged that the implications of interculturalism are very different for people in impoverished, 'developing' countries like India, and for their counterparts in technologically advanced, capitalist societies like America, where interculturalism has been more strongly promoted both as a philosophy and a business . . . Colonialism, one might say, does not operate through principles of 'exchange'. Rather, it appropriates, decontextualises, and represents the 'other' culture, often with the complicity of its colonised subjects. It legitimates its authority only by asserting its cultural superiority.[9]

If the practice of interculturalism is, for the developed West at least, ethically untenable, it is also in aesthetic terms questionable. The separation of ethics from aesthetics is for Bharucha almost a matter of indifference. 'Whether one views this fascination for predominantly non-western cultures as part of a general curiosity for the exotic, or as a perpetuation and consolidation of "orientalism", would depend on one's political position and place in history.'[10] The 'general curiosity for the exotic' becomes indeed the nub of Bharucha's critique of what he takes to be the superficialities of Western theatrical interculturalism, an interculturalism blamable, not only politically but morally and artistically. Peter Brook's *Mahabharata* becomes the focus of especially pointed criticism: 'Not only does the production, in my view, blatantly trivialise Indian culture in its nine-hour encapsulation of the epic, and its reduction of Hindu philosophy to platitudes, it upholds a Eurocentric structure of action and performance that has been specifically designed for international audiences.'[11] The critique expands, in Bharucha's reading of Brook (and others), to take in the economics of theatrical internationalism, a topic associated with the injustices of global distribution of wealth, but one even more calculated to inflame vituperative comment among the haves and the have-nots. It is only a small step from here to the castigation of 'festival culture' more generally, as symptom and product of an unequally divided and shrinking world: 'Today, "Indian culture" is being reduced to a commodity by our own government and a new brand of bureaucrats, who have shaped, marketed and transported this "culture" to different parts of the world.'[12] If these are the outward and visible signs of a perverse interculturalism, the inward and spiritual state is a kind of cultural tourism that annexes legends, epics and rituals without paying the price (in any case an impossibly exorbitant one) of a lifetime's rootedness in the beliefs and practices of those for whom they are 'a way of life'. Bharucha partially exonerates the notable practitioner and theorist

Eugenio Barba from the charge of superficiality, on the grounds of his 'insight and tenacity', but even Barba's committed Eurasian experiments suffer, according to Bharucha, from a lack of specificity, a tendency towards universalising 'that diffuses the historical differences permeating forms', and that condemns his work, ultimately, to 'a heightened and essentially lifeless state of virtuosity'.[13] In the end, Bharucha finds us and our theatre in an historical *cul-de-sac*. Intercultural theatre, he argues, cannot be successfully undertaken if one separates 'a reflection of its modalities from the particular contradictions of the historical context in which the work is placed'[14] and yet that context is virtually inaccessible to anyone who is not born into it. Bharucha quotes with approval Patrice Pavis' admission that 'our western culture, be it modern or postmodern, is certainly tired'[15] but rather strongly doubts whether intercultural attempts to refresh it have been or can be successful. Ariane Mnouchkine is accused, for example, of a *Twelfth Night* characterised by Indian images 'so contrived and dated that it [the production] embodies the worst indulgences of "orientalism"'. By Bharucha's account, while there may be successful experiments of a limited kind, such as the 'exemplary cultural organisation called Ninasam' based in the village of Heggodu in Karnataka (exemplary because of 'its decentralised, assertively "small" structure' and its 'concrete embodiment of an essentially socialist vision'[16]), international interculturalism is at best premature and at worst politically, morally and aesthetically irresponsible.

It would be wrong to ignore or underestimate Bharucha's criticism of global interculturalism.[17] It is not only that he is acute in specifying the laziness, the condescension and the greed that can underlie intercultural practice, but he also asks difficult questions about the artistic motivations and goals of intercultural borrowings and transfers. Schechner's reply to Bharucha in the *Asian Theatre Journal* takes off from some corrections of dates and influences, but reaches its centre in a discussion of the artistic availability of culturally distant forms. He concedes (indeed asserts) that 'to perform someone else's culture . . . takes a knowledge, a "translation" that is different, more viscerally experimental, than translating a book' and goes on to quote an earlier report (itself quoting director Mohan Agasha of Pune) to the effect that 'a certain metabolisis is necessary – the work to be taken from has to be ingested and digested, truly metabolised and made part of the performer's body (and soul) before being re-expressed in possibly a totally new and unrecognizable way'.[18] Such a cultural assimilation, scarcely an appropriation, takes time ('years of training'), and demands respect for the 'specific concrete cultural contexts' of the original work. Yet Schechner is led to propose a self-division that may come to seem crucial in the intercultural debate. 'As an artist', he writes, 'my imagination is stimulated by my experiences, and my work responds to this stimulation' while as a *scholar* he tries 'to be sensitive to the different meanings that actions – ritual, aesthetic, and ordinary – have in their various social/cultural contexts'. The tug between artist and scholar, between the appropriating imagination and the scrupulous intellect, is one that is far from unfamiliar in the history of aesthetic modernism, and indeed before. It is not inappropriate to refer again to Yeats, magpie intellectual and amateur scholar, building his imaginative universe out of the ruins of civilisations old and new, north and south. But if the lingering Victorian ethic forgave Yeats his plunder, the same generosity is not available to the current interculturalist, caught among today's anxieties and guilts. Schechner quotes his own address (1983) to a conference on the Indian Dance Tradition, as a way of balancing anxiety and hope:

I know many people fear 'cultural imperialism' – the subjugation of one tradition by another. But there is an alternative to exploitation: the necessary and fruitful exchange among cultures and traditions. For in learning about the Other we also deepen our grasp of who we ourselves are: the Other is another and a mirror at the same time.[19]

'The *necessary* . . . exchange' derives from a sense that the only way to assuage our modern guilt comes from submission to the Other, the artist as, precisely, interculturalist. Yet the sheer difficulty if not impossibility of such submission has been borne in on the modern artist simultaneously with the necessity. The outcome is the significant *angst* that attaches to intercultural creativity, the fracture between the conscious artist and his task, a variant perhaps of the modernist theme of the dissociated creator. One of the age-old ironies, of course, is that the creator of *theatrical* interculturalism must confront by the very nature of his craft the common guilts and anxieties in so much more public a way than other creators, a reality that leads on the one hand to the 'secret' theatre of Grotowski and on the other to the cultural multiplicity of international festival.

It would be false to represent Schechner's immense contribution to thinking about interculturalism by drawing only on this minor piece. It would be false also to represent his work in isolation from that of other leading practitioners and theorists. Eugenio Barba, for example, has superbly defended his claim that the history of modern writing for the theatre is the history of 'that *movement* between East and West which I now call Eurasian theatre'.[20] Barba's emphasis is on the body of the performer, on what he calls 'a scenic *bios*'. 'When we speak of "Eurasian theatre"', he writes, 'we are recognizing the existence of a unity sanctioned by our cultural history. . . . For all those who in the twentieth century have reflected in a competent way on the performer, the borders between "European theatre" and "Asian theatre" do not exist.'[21] Barba's appreciation of the physical competencies of Japanese Noh actors, and his meticulously accurate evocation of their craft, is only one feature of his comprehensive sense that theatre *craft* is a currency *sans frontiers*. As such it plays its part in what he sees as the culturally desirable, indeed obligatory, recognition that the boundaries of nation states do not confer on these states an internal cultural unity: 'There is no *genius loci*, genie of the place, either in theatre or culture. Everything drifts away from its original context, and is transplanted. There are no traditions which are inseparably connected to a particular geographical location, language or profession.'[22] It is a radical view, rooted in the universal propriety of gesture, movement, posture, as well as in the sense of a common past and the tendencies of current international history. It is also one with which Schechner's intercultural outlook shares some common ground. Schechner's *The End of Humanism: Writings in Performance* is nostalgic for the days before about 1975 when 'there was something simply celebratory about discovering how diverse the world was, how many performance genres there were, and how we could enrich our own experience by borrowing, stealing, exchanging'.[23] Such Edenic innocence no longer obtains, after the entry through the gates of colonial guilt and orientalism. Yet, as Schechner argues, a wider transhistorical picture urges experimental theatre to forsake its virtuosic emptiness and confront issues of the *polis* and the people, in oppositional parallel with the multinational corporations, and in the faith that 'if nations defend their boundaries, cultures have always been promiscuous, and happily so'.[24] Schechner's more recent *The Future of Ritual* emphasises the need for a strong and confident theatre to address the *differences* between cultures, 'engaging intercultural fractures, philosophical difficulties, ideological contradictions, and crumbling national myths'.[25] Brook's *Mahabharata*, to take the familiar case, could be described in a revealing distinction as intercultural, seeking as it does to elide the differences between cultures, but not genuinely avant-garde, in that it 'does not interrogate the [originating] epic or subvert it'.[26] It is a sign of our times that 'interrogate' and 'subvert' have now become the necessary terms of approval. It is also a sign of these times that the intercultural artist, if his work is to be valid, has to recognise and convey a sense of cultural isolation and deracination, in awareness of, but distant from, the other and current cultures that press upon him. The discourse of postmodernism has substituted pastiche and allusion for the unity of culture. The intercultural project could scarcely separate itself with integrity from the prevailing mindset or, it is tautologous to say, from prevailing history, so that cultural allusion must it now seems do duty for cultural assimilation. Such are the cross-currents of perception and opinion that disturb the choppy seas of *angst* within which intercultural performance, from the creator's perspective and the audience's, now takes place.

Perhaps at this precise moment the spirit of the nineties has relieved some of the pressure on international theatre, due to a habit of mind, broadly postmodern in character, that nourishes awareness while dissolving guilt. The common if undeclared theme of Patrice Pavis's recently published collection, *The Intercultural Performance Reader,* is the recovery of those writers and directors whose work has been most heavily criticised by intercultural theorists.[27] Pavis quotes, for example, T. Burzynski and Z. Osinski to the effect that 'in his [Grotowski's] production of *Shakuntala* . . . he wanted to "create a performance which gave an image of Oriental theatre – not an authentic one, but as Europeans imagined it".'[28] Pavis is able simply to slide past the apology that would have been required for such a stance no more than a year or two ago. The elaborate refinement of Roland Barthes's self-exculpation in *The Empire of Signs* as he emphasises and excuses the fictionality of his 'Japan' has come to seem by Pavis's account nothing more than an unnecessary defence of such intercultural appropriation as is evident in Grotowski's work.[29] In the same way, Peter Brook's controversial *Mahabharata* begins to look not controversial at all amidst talk in the Pavis collection of artists as *bricoleurs,* and claims that stealing from other cultures is simply 'what they do'. Pavis acutely remarks that often 'the interests of the individual artist run counter to the political interests of larger cultural groups', without apparently feeling a need to consider and take on board the 'interests' of those larger groups that are the artists' audiences. At another point he remarks that 'both Brook and Mnouchkine have resolved that their work on the representation of the Other is primarily of a formal and professional kind, rather than being driven by an ethnological respect for an authenticity of reproductions'.[30] This separation of the professional from the culturally engaged surfaces repeatedly throughout the book, modified for example in Richard Schechner's emphasis in one of the essays on the necessary parity of cultural exchanges,[31] or in Clive Barker's generous and experienced account of intercultural negotiation.[32] Yet it could be argued that the very selection of the book's materials, together with Pavis's framing commentaries, represent rather accurately the climate of nineties theatre, adroit, allusive and technically and visually brilliant but politically and morally disengaged. Robert Lepage's *The Seven Streams of the River Ota,* in gestation since 1994 and overtly indebted to Japanese life and theatre, may be considered typical in making technical surprise and spatial manipulation more evident than grief or anger, even though the subject-matter includes Hiroshima, Aids and the Holocaust.[33] In such a

theatrical, and by implication cultural, climate, the pressures of intercultural *angst* have unquestionably eased, though that easing has brought
loss at least equally with gain.

The ethnologist James Clifford has written that 'the world's societies
are too systematically interconnected to permit any easy isolation of
separate or independently functioning systems . . . Twentieth-century
identities no longer presuppose continuous cultures or traditions.'[34] It is
within the matrix proposed by this inescapable interconnection yet
deracination that theatrical art in today's world has to honour its intercultural obligations. One response to the challenge is radical detachment
in the postmodernist vein. Another is the extraordinarily demanding
attempt to respond to intercultural existence by creating a theatre which
embraces divergent impulses generously. Perhaps the most remarkable
instance of such an attempt may be found, I wish to argue, in the work of
the Japanese theatre artist and director Tadashi Suzuki.

The theatre paradoxes of Tadashi Suzuki

It is evident that the above discussion of intercultural anxiety adopts a
perspective that is predominantly Western (or Western and Anglo-
Indian) in its terms and field of reference. Yet it is true, and telling, that
the theorists and practitioners cited, whatever their immediate preoccupations, are each of them in their writings conscious and admiring of
the theatres and theatre practices of Japan. This consciousness is from
one angle an implicit acknowledgment of the profound and persistent
influence that Japanese theatre and Japanese performers have exercised
on Western theatre tradition, from Yeats and Artaud to Stanislavski,
Brecht, Grotowski and Beckett, or in specific reference to the USA from
Michio Ito, Nam June Paik and Yoko Ono to Martha Graham, Allan
Kaprow, Lee Breuer, Peter Sellars and Robert Wilson. From another
angle it honours the widespread sense that Japanese theatre represents
the Other that Western theatre needs for its full realisation, in physical
authority, in movement and dance, in music, mask and mime. One recalls
Ariane Mnouchkine's resonant admission that 'when we decided to
perform Shakespeare a recourse to Asia became a necessity'. But it is furthermore the case that the same currents of anxiety that have disturbed
the Western theatre have also, differently construed, disturbed the
Japanese. The intercultural project, conditioned as it always is by particular histories, has assumed in Japan almost a mirror-image of the parallel
project in the West. The history of Japanese Shakespeare (or, in a modified way, of Japanese Ibsen or Brecht) can be read as an adjustment to an
evolving world as vexed and crossed by contradictions as the nervous

adjustments of the West outlined above. The opening up of the country after the Meiji Restoration in 1868 was characterised by the simultaneous goals of modernisation and Westernisation, a pairing fraught in cultural terms with conflict. Where the West had reason in recent times to feel anxiety about imperialism, Japanese cultural forms had to deal with a kind of reverse imperialism (in the respect for Western culture and cultural artefacts) associated nevertheless with a powerful and enduring commitment to tradition.[35] The results are manifest in the unsteady history of Kabuki in this century, veering from attempts at modernisation to the restoration as far as practical of a fully traditional performance style. Neither reform was artistically successful, at least for long. Equally, the omnivorous *Shingeki* (new theatre) movement swallowed Western theatre material wholesale in an attempt to distance itself from traditional forms, a cultural fracture that issued in an eventual sense of the unrooted superficiality of this movement's work.[36]

Such artistic failures as these have merely reflected (how could they not?) the enduring ideological divide that has vexed and preoccupied the country in its search for a permanent and persuasive self-image. As J. Thomas Rimer remarks, 'the question as to whether the "modernisation" of Japan also requires its "westernisation", and indeed the question concerning the extent to which the two terms may or may not be synonymous, has been an important intellectual and spiritual issue in Japan' for more than a century.[37] The Japanese playwright in particular, though the same applies, with adjustment, to other artists, has had to craft his work in the space between these two over-arching terms, and in response to the pervasive if ill-defined claims of tradition, tugged this way and that by the influence of them all, and responsive too (in the Little Theatre movement for example) to the more immediate claims of current micropolitics, those of the left especially. Tadashi Suzuki, I wish to argue, offers a remarkable example of navigating the awkward artistic waters of the recent past, in terms of practice and theory, reconciling as he does the opposing claims on his artistic integrity through the elaboration of a series of artistic and practical paradoxes.

Suzuki has been recognised as one of the leading theatre directors of the world, a notable presence on the stages of France, Britain, Australia and the United States as well as Japan. His work, always strongly personal and Japanese, has nevertheless reached out to embrace the cultural archetypes of the Western theatre tradition, most notably the Greeks, Chekhov and Shakespeare. His home base at Toga, a countryside refuge from cosmopolitan Tokyo, has played host to the outstanding names in international performance, including in the first ten years such practitioners as Robert Wilson, Meredith Monk, Tadeusz Kantor, Lee Breuer, Maguy

Plate 5 Caliban (foreground centre) with Stephano and Trinculo watched by Ariel (above right) in Ninagawa's production of *The Tempest*.

Plate 6 Caliban and Prospero in Ninagawa's production of *The Tempest*.

Plate 7 Miranda and Prospero.

Plate 8 Ferdinand's attempt to resist Prospero's power in *The Tempest*. The photograph shows the use of the 'spider' device.

Marin. His acting companies, bred up at Toga by a training discipline of extraordinary rigour and scale, have also drawn in performers from other lands and other traditions, imparting both philosophy and skills. Suzuki has undertaken residencies abroad, exploring and adapting the classical texts and acting traditions of other cultures. On these grounds and others, his intercultural credentials can scarcely be questioned. In the paradoxes embedded in his personal odyssey of centre and periphery lie some of the signs of, and some of the palliatives for, the *angst* of today's intercultural theory and practice.

Suzuki's work is rooted in the Little Theatre movement of the 1960s, stemming from the formation in 1966, in collaboration with the playwright Minoru Betsuyaku and the actor Seki Ono, of the Waseda Shogekijo (Little Theatre). A 'child of the tumultuous 60s', beholden to the left-wing ideologies of the time, Suzuki's first notable success came none the less with *On the Dramatic Passions II*, a performance distanced from current preoccupations through the device of an isolated madwoman recalling and performing selected scraps from the theatre repertoire of the past. Thus were established in embryo the contours of Suzuki's theatre practice. The stratagem of what might be named the decentred hero is one that recurs repeatedly in subsequent performances. In *The Chekhov: A Paradise Lost*, in *Clytemnestra*, in *The Chronicle of Macbeth* and notably in *The Tale of Lear*, the central figure becomes the victim of the narrative rather than its protagonist or initiator. In this perspective, the interculturalism of the work maps its anxieties on to the narratology of the performance. The cultural borrowings are acknowledged, not apologised for, through their assault on the consciousness of the 'hero', a surrogate everyman for the audience's cultural experience. Working by way of the stratagem of the decentred hero, Suzuki as playwright/adapter/director garners the wealth of the culturally distant text without invasive appropriation and without sacrifice of his own cultural identity. Thus he seeks to pass over one of the fractures of contemporary interculturalism, avoiding the Scylla of a false localism and the Charybdis of unrooted internationalism. (See also pp. 26–29 above.)

It has to be said that Suzuki has drawn detractors as well as admirers, and in almost equal numbers, both in his homeland and abroad. No one can be blind to the distinctive, almost defiant, personality of his work. Robert Brustein has written of Suzuki, Robert Wilson and Andrei Serban as being 'among the most visionary theatre artists in the *auteur* tradition'.[38] Suzuki's authoring of the theatre experience, it has to be agreed, is all-encompassing. From adaptation of the text to choreography of movement his theatre work represents an egotistical sublime. 'It is true that in *The Tale of Lear*', he has said, 'I have made many cuts and simplifications.

But the first responsibility of a director is to define what interests him the most, what resonates with his current concerns.'[39] Yet by a familiar though daunting paradox, the authoring creator (writer, adapter, director) *disappears* into the authored work, most evidently in theatre. The grammar of Suzuki's stage is the physicality of the actor, its lexicon the composite relationship of the actor's presence and the kinetic possibilities of theatre space. Stamping on the ground, Suzuki's notorious regimen of actor training, 'is a gesture that can lead to the creation of a fictional space, perhaps even a ritual space, in which the actor's body can achieve a transformation from the personal to the universal'.[40] Eugenio Barba, it could be said, is the master theorist of the symbolic realism of the actor's body,[41] but Suzuki is able to follow the symbolism of actorly presence even more securely than Barba into a theatrical tradition he posseses because it is his own. Kabuki, and especially Noh, provide a bodily discipline that may be transmuted by the modern artist into a *current*, not merely a 'traditional', theatre language. Suzuki's 'grammar of the feet' avoids the empty virtuosity of an adopted ritual because it is rooted in a theatre practice that is aesthetically real and available, and so immune to the intercultural anxiety of an adopted and false ritualism. By his preoccupation with the actor's bodily presence, Suzuki's personal domination of the theatrical artefact is transmuted into an impersonal stylisation.

Suzuki's dramaturgy is not simply however a matter of the symbolic presence of the moving, gesturing body, but of a ritual composed out of the complex dynamics of the body in space. Suzuki explains his reasons for valuing Noh as exemplar and mentor:

Our work in the theatre is not only spiritual; our task requires the use of our bodies as well. Thus there must be available to us a theatrical space that the body can remember. In this regard, I learned a great deal from studying the *no* stage. At the very instant an actor enters the performing space on a traditional *no* stage, his body transforms itself.[42]

This transformation takes on through the actor's instinctual memory a spiritual significance, one which an audience by its attentive presence confirms as ritual. Within Noh, and by extension within Suzuki's Noh-influenced theatre, there comes to exist a sacral reality that derives from a visual, or visual-dynamic, inherence of actor in space and space in actor:

Because *no* actors have a fixed space available to them which they have internalised into their very bodies, they instinctively move on any stage as though it were a *no* stage. The actor's body and the space reveal a mutual connection. I call a space which is thus connected to the actor's body *a sacred space*.[43]

'There already exists within the body of the *no* actor', Suzuki adds, 'the kind of space that can force a rent in the flow of worldly time'.[44] The formal (including *active*) configurations of Suzuki's stage pictures are not precisely aesthetic, not precisely spiritual, but a kind of existentialist affirmation that derives its authority, as in certain kinds of dance, from the delimited freedoms of the performing body. The credos Suzuki summons in confirmation of his enacted truths may sometimes be banal: 'We are a part of the ground. Our very beings will return to the ground when we die.'[45] But they also go deep into the spiritual thematics of Japanese philosophy. Suzuki explains how the performance practices of Noh share with surviving and ancient rituals an attentive respect for the bodied force of physical presence in contact with the earth. The appealing paradox of Suzuki's multi-dimensional existentialism is that within it the universality of bodied action consorts with the lived experience (in Noh performance) of a traditional wisdom – thus healing one of the sources of intercultural *angst*.

The ultimate paradox of Suzuki's theatre may be seen as a refinement of the common paradox of all performance (perhaps of all art) poised between message and style. 'Performances', Suzuki tells us 'deal with issues that cannot be dealt with in daily life. Religion, war, sex, family – things that an individual cannot solve . . . theatre illuminates situations in which human beings find themselves. It deals with problems without an answer.' 'Shakespeare', he adds, 'incorporates so many of these problems'.[46] Yet the leading impression of a Suzuki performance (of *The Tale of Lear* for example) may not be the exploration of an insoluble problem, but a demonstration of style. Robert Brustein, most perceptive of critics, reports that 'If *The Tale of Lear* sometimes seems less a dramatic experience than an inspired acting demonstration, it is nevertheless a stunning transcultural achievement'.[47] William A Henry III is driven unlike Brustein to protest: 'Surely this is auteurist direction run riot, the sort of conceptual staging of Shakespeare that makes theatergoers yearn for the days of the director as traffic cop.'[48] Remembering a London performance of *The Tale of Lear*, one recalls the extreme rigour of the choreographed movement, the insistent geometry (in the London performances) of the rank of stage doors (like the starting stalls of a terrible horse race), the wide shallow stage that construed action as instance rather than experience, and the alienating ironies of decor and stage properties (the hospital cart and bedpan-crown, for example). One reads in these perhaps the modalities of postmodern theatre, as practised by Robert Lepage in *The Seven Streams of the River Ota* (an intercultural piece to be read as an instance of Western japonism), or in Lepage's *A Midsummer Night's Dream* or *Coriolanus* or *The Tempest*, all of them manipulating visual perspectives in the service of a dominant aesthetic, and all of them, the Shakespearean pieces certainly, employing text as

9. Tadashi Suzuki's bilingual production of *The Tale of Lear* with Japanese and American actors (1989).

counterpoint not as companion to sight. The point could be extended to Peter Brook's *L' Homme Qui* (another use, like Suzuki's, of the mentally unstable protagonist) and may have been prepared for in the strategies of Brook's *La Tempête*. It could be applied to recent Shakespeares in Stratford and London, including Sam Mendes's *The Tempest* and Adrian Noble's *A Midsummer Night's Dream*. But through the distancing stage devices and grotesquerie one recalls experiencing also in *The Tale of Lear*, with the solidity of fact, the anguish of the play's protagonist (or victim). The achieved interculturalism of which Brustein writes issues from a paradoxical unity of prompting text (Shakespeare's *King Lear* that is) and rigorous style, personal to the director and his company but reaching out also into their cultural inheritance, theatrical and other. Suzuki himself has been candid about this:

First comes style. I create a certain style of staging intentionally (Kabuki does the same; so do Noh and Takarazuka) . . . In my opinion, the Noh, Kabuki,

Takarazuka and Suzuki styles are the only solid styles! . . . How could one present the unconscious, which cannot be verbalised? I thought maybe I could do that using the forms of stylised theatre.[49]

Style is a name for the composing vision that embraces the deepest levels of personality, cultural inheritance, training (the 'second nature' of the disciplined body) and theatre practice. In its modesty and access, as the idiom, verbal, visual, aural and kinetic of the performance itself, it defines the intercultural statement, but is also paradoxically, like Yeats's great rooted blossomer, profoundly allusive and permanent.

To look briefly, but a little more closely, at the practice of Suzuki's Shakespeareanism, we may turn our attention to two productions, *The Tale of Lear* and *Greetings from the Edge of the Earth, Part One*. Suzuki's Shakespeare chronology takes in (thus far) six performance texts, with variations brought about by touring schedules and by changes of company (with American or Australian actors in place of his own) and adaptation (*The Chronicle of Macbeth*, for example, as performed by an Australian company, is distantly related to *Greetings from the Edge of the Earth, Part One*). The first was *Don Hamlet: A Pathetic Play* (1972), produced in a tiny upstairs theatre by actors of the Waseda Little Theatre, followed in 1975 by *Night and the Clock*, a collage drawing freely on material from *Macbeth*. *King Lear* was first performed at Suzuki's purpose-built theatre in Toga in 1984, toured to many locations in Japan, and revived in a new production in English (when it was known as *The Tale of Lear*) for a North American tour in 1988. A London visit, playing in Japanese, took place at the Barbican in 1994. *Greetings from the Edge of the Earth, Part One*, incorporating scenes from *Macbeth*, was first played at Toga in 1991 and revived in 1993. *The Chronicle of Macbeth* was staged in Melbourne, Adelaide, Geelong and Hobart in 1992, before closing at the Tokyo Mitsui Festival. *Greetings from the Edge of the Earth Part Three* (also known as *Waiting for Romeo*) draws something like one third of its text from *Romeo and Juliet*, and was staged in 1994.

If *Greetings from the Edge of the Earth, Part One* acknowledges wryly in its title the distances, difficulties and prejudices of the intercultural project, the kaleidoscopic surrealism of its staging offers in its theatrical style and temper a superbly crafted, and buoyant, artistic solution. With direct quotation from Act V scenes 3 and 5 of *Macbeth* at its core (in Yushi Odashima's translation) the performance interprets recent Japanese cultural history by referring to Suzuki's own art, to European theatrical masterpieces (*The Bacchae, Macbeth, Ivanov, Endgame*), and to the Second World War, social health policy, pop culture, patriotic sentiment and food. Proceeding with the logical illogic of Ionesco or Pinter, the narrative follows a profile that takes it from mocking caricature to despair. At stage centre sits almost throughout an Old Man, a Beckettian figure who is Everyman (as well as Cadmus, Ivanov, Hamm and Macbeth) attended by an unnamed Servant who recollects Hamm but is also Macbeth's psychologically anonymous servant, Seyton. Around them swirl, dance and propel themselves across the stage an assortment of creatures, Wheelchair People, Monks, Maenads (from *The Bacchae*) Women in Wedding Dresses (*Ivanov*) a Servant with a Telescope (*Endgame*), always choreographed but with distinctive motions and intents ranging from sentiment to menace. Particularly expressive are the Wheelchair People, dressed in an odd assortment of casual clothes, chanting in strangulated voices, and propelling their wheelchairs bare-legged in quick little motions that parody Suzuki's notorious discipline of physical stage-movement. The stage picture is in perpetual motion, abundantly colour-ful, richly detailed, fluid and shapely. The outdoor setting, natural and man-made, of Toga's lake, its buildings and forest, scale up the drama till it carries like the Noh intimations of eternity, yet parodied and undercut by the mundane contemporaneousness of the Old Man's lunch trolley and chopsticks (which he petulantly throws away), the saccharine emo-tions of pop song and the hollow patriotism of Oka Kiyoshi's propaganda. Other of Suzuki's shows take their meaning from their performance at Toga, but here, more spectacularly, the natural setting frames and com-ments on, for example, the visual extravagance of exploding fireworks, like a metonymic paradigm for excessive and self-destroying consump-tion. The fireworks are employed for purposes of dramatic punctuation, to evoke the sky-drenching firepower of the American invasion, and as extraordinary climax, when cascades of white light rain down behind (on the video) the Old Man's superimposed, bleakly transfixed, face. These visual signifiers complement the aural signals, from the wildly comic opening scene, where Monks in basket costume dance trippingly to the *Pizzicato Polka*, through Perez Prado's menacing *Voodoo Suite* to the schmalzy song *Karatachi Diary* and a hummed chorus of multiple male voices swelling behind the action. This patchwork of reminiscence, allusion, quotation and parody is suspended in typically postmodern fashion between hilarity and fear. The Shakespearean quotations are defamiliarised not only by their context, but by the insertion of stylistic and referential impertinences:

MONK 5: There is ten thousand –
OLD MAN: Geese, villain?
MONK 5: Soldiers, sir.
OLD MAN: Go prick thy face and over-red thy fear,
    Thou lily-livered boy. Whose soldiers, patch? (*Throws down his chopsticks.*)

MONK 5: *The Allied force*, so please you.
OLD MAN: Take thy face hence.
                                        Seyton! Pick that up! (*Seyton retrieves the*
        chopsticks)
    I am sick at heart.
                            (*Translation by Kayoko Hashimoto and Ian Carruthers.*)

But above the momentary laughter provoked by the impertinent verbal additions, and by the ridiculous visual and aural contextualising, the Old Man's words communicate feelings that lie on the edge of despair. Western, or indeed Japanese, bardolatry is appropriately quenched by this high-spirited eclecticism. What does survive is a powerful expressiveness that derives from Suzuki's disciplined skill across all the theatrical arts, and that of his company. Together they find a language rooted in Japanese perceptions of selfhood, one that exists within an international culture that is fractured and imperilled but emphatically real and present.

Greetings from the Edge of the Earth, Part One is characteristic of Suzuki's work in forming part of a more comprehensive project certifying the commitment of his theatre art to the exploration of contemporary consciousness. The so-called *Farewell Cult Trilogy* examines the cult's rise to power (in *The Bacchae*), its overreaching (in *Macbeth*) and its disintegration (in *Ivanov*). *Greetings Part One* offers what Suzuki calls a Grand Review, drawing on the three previous plays as allusive sources, a stratagem made artistically possible, as Ian Carruthers points out, by Tsutamori Kosuke having played the leading role in all three of the previous productions. Thus the Everyman figure of *Greetings Part One* becomes the gateway for allusion to the revelatory art of the earlier plays (an art of theatrical expression as much as text), and through the same gateway to the European culture to which the adopted texts have in their own era and circumstances given expression, and which live on in the received awareness of the culturally literate, in Japan as elsewhere. But the allusiveness is not restricted to the artistic record of Suzuki's company, though a notable reference *is* made through a whispered voice-over from the great Kayoko Shiraishi, Suzuki's former leading actress, as the absent Lady Macbeth. Nor is the allusiveness restricted to European theatre, or to the contemporary circumstances cited above. It also takes in current events such as the death of Emperor Hirohito, an occurrence evoking acute self-enquiry among Japanese people, and the time and place of its own performance at the summer festival, with the associated fireworks and the disparate audience of local people, sophisticated pilgrims from the towns and foreign visitors. Allusion is made, moreover, to the rural location and its pastoral references and enticements. As Carruthers points out, 'In such a location at such a time Suzuki could more easily get his audience to negotiate the gap between agricultural and urban, traditional and modern, indigenous and imported values'.[50] Suzuki's postmodern art draws its sustenance from allusions such as these, most overtly in the direct and extended quotation of pre-existent and culturally significant texts, including Shakespeare, but in so doing binds those texts and allusions into the living texture of everyday consciousness, everyday performance art and everyday occasions – the chilling accuracy with which he anticipates the deadly work of contemporary religious cults is only one instance.

If *Greetings from the Edge of the Earth, Part One* is Suzuki's masterpiece of the comic grotesque, by common consent *The Tale of Lear* is his most remarkable attempt to refashion Shakespeare in the idiom of contemporary tragedy. Other Shakespearean adaptations were attempted with varying success. *The Chronicle of Macbeth*, a version of the play written initially for an Australian theatre-group, was based on Shakespeare's text, somewhat cut and with various transpositions, within a framework supplied by an excerpt from Beckett's *Cascando*. As Suzuki's programme note explains, the *Chronicle*

is neither a Japanese nor English nor Australian play. It is a new meeting of elements that have up to now been unrelated, coming together inside the theatre to form a previously unseen spectacle of time and space . . . We take what we know and construct the unknown. This is, I believe, the calling and duty of today's theatre.[51]

Suzuki's adaptation, in characteristic fashion, offers a personal deconstruction of Shakespeare's text, interpreting it as

the tale of a man who is afflicted with a spiritual ailment called 'Macbeth'. In an attempt to cure himself, he attaches himself to a fake religious organisation called the 'Farewell Cult'. Macbeth is not an actual person or even a literary character. Macbeth is a symbol for the state in which one loses touch with one's own identity, and slips into an alienated anthropophobic condition in which there is no awareness of 'self' or 'other'.[52]

The *Chronicle* attracted divided responses. On video, the intense focus of Peter Curtin as Macbeth and Ellen Lauren as Lady Macbeth comes across powerfully, but Suzuki's hesitations over working with an acting company other than his own are borne out in the manifest ways in which the theatre experience diverges from the legendary consciousness of a Toga production, composed, anonymous, sculpted, offering instead the urgent expressiveness of a production that measures its achievements largely in terms of psychological insight and expression. The inheritance from Noh remains evident in the choreography of movement, in the formality of the disposition of stage space, in the pacing of the production, but the experienced instinct of almost all the players as represented in the detail of their playing remains specifically Western: in facial expression, in posture, in (most evidently) the occupation of personal space. Much the same judgement could be made of the Anglophone *Tale of Lear* made for an American tour in 1988. Robert Brustein has written of how the performance 'comes to you in a rush', with 'Lear's final cries over Cordelia's dead body wrenching at your heart'. 'This is a triumphant, noble and beautifully controlled performance', he asserts, 'which demonstrates that the Western actor is perfectly capable of subduing ego and vanity to an Eastern discipline.'[53] Yet the *personality* of each actor's performance makes itself apparent at every turn. Despite, once again, the fastidiousness of the choreography, the slow pace, and the careful composition of the stage picture, the supreme moments of the performance are those in which physical pain (the blinding of Gloucester) or mental anguish (Lear's torment on the heath) are expressed through the distractingly detailed facial and bodily gestures of the actor. One notices also the attention paid to narrative in a theatre unaccustomed to the inconsequence of the Noh. By way of contrast, *Waiting for Romeo* (*Greetings from the Edge of the World, Part Three*), employing text primarily from Shakespeare's *Romeo and Juliet* (in English and Japanese) but splicing it with material from Chekhov's *Three Sisters* and Beckett's *Endgame*, configures its transformation of Shakespeare in an idiom reminiscent of *Greetings Part One*, even if here less culturally and socially wide-ranging. The Wheelchair People, in white garments and bowler hats and carrying parasols, once again set the note of bitter-flavoured surrealism as they criss-cross the stage in a kind of parody ballet, with bent knees, angular arms and torsos, 'stomping' bare legs, sturdy red shoes, each with one arm shrivelled and uttering menacing guttural cries. Sometimes the tone is lightened, as for instance with the goose-stepping Nurse, or the choreographed wheelchair dance to military music, but pathos and anxiety are never far away. Romeo is absent, save for a brief transit of the stage, unnoticed by Juliet. Shakespeare's passionate words of longing and fulfilment are juxtaposed with the crippled figures and the mental atrophy, and blend into the reminiscence and the fantasy of Chekhov's Marsha and the existential despair of Beckett's Hamm. When the wheelchair chorus is temporarily replaced by a second chorus of wheelchair-bound nurses, we experience again the creative cross-referencing by means of which Suzuki's theatre elaborates its own expressiveness. In *Waiting for Romeo* the intercultural transformation we associate with Suzuki's Japanese pieces, mediated through the theatre art of his company, makes itself once more apparent, even if on a limited scale.

The Tale of Lear, according to Yasunari Takahashi, was received on its first performances (Toga, 1984) with reservations.[54] Audiences and critics, accustomed to the surreal experimentalism of Suzuki's theatre, and particularly its interweaving of motifs from the Japanese and European present and past, found *The Tale of Lear* disappointingly faithful to the words and structure of its Shakespearean original. Severe textual editing had, it is true, taken place. Kent is absent, so is the reconciliation between Lear and Cordelia and their subsequent capture. The final scene is drastically foreshortened. There are other adjustments. For example, Gloucester and not the anonymous servant stabs Cornwall to death. The total performance is moreover set within the sketchily-provided framework of a geriatric hospital. Lear is attended throughout by a Nurse who reads a text (the play-text?) and from time to time laughs horribly. In the first performances, this role was played by the Fool; the later decision to substitute the Nurse has the effect of demarcating the frame yet more sharply. The nursing-home motif surfaces in various production devices such as the hospital cart in which Lear is at one point wheeled on stage, and in the chipped enamel bedpan he uses as crown. These are obvious and indeed obtrusive changes. Yet in the context of Suzuki's theatre-practice, *The Tale of Lear* offers a notably respectful acculturation of a major text. Takahashi plausibly situates Suzuki's *Lear* along a mainstream interpretive line that takes in and goes beyond Peter Brook's absurdist, Kott-influenced, production of 1962.[55] When the Suzuki production was staged in London with an all-male cast of Japanese actors (Barbican, 1994), a significant strand in the critical response, in contrast to that at Toga ten years earlier, can be summarised by Michael Billington's complaint that 'all the turbulent contradictions that make Shakespeare a great dramatist get ironed out', reducing 'the multidimensionality of Shakespeare' and leaving 'no room for the emotional ambiguity and moral paradox that lies at the very heart' of his theatre.[56] To charges such as these, Suzuki responds with unrepentant directness, as a 1995 interview shows: 'My position is very clear. I have responsibly presented the aspects I'm interested in. It is tiring to cope with the rest. I think it is better to present the part that moves and interests me. In other words, I want to present a point of agreement with the text. That is my consistent attitude.'[57] *The Tale of Lear* represents an *auteur*ist reading of Shakespeare's play that rigorously transforms words and action through the disciplines of the Suzuki 'style'. The intense focus on the mental derangement of Lear is conveyed by means of a performance manner that offers the purest example in Suzuki's work of that revitalisation of Noh that forms the basis of his modern, and Japanese, theatre practice. None of the actors at the Barbican had had less than ten years of Suzuki training. Their extreme physical focus, the product of an intensely realised equilibrium between tension and relaxation, recalled the utterly disciplined stillness, and the superbly articulated movement-skills, of the Noh actor (the actors, perhaps as a sign of this, were in this production wearing the cotton 'slippers' used by Noh players). At the same time, the production style incorporated features responsive to the surrealism embedded in the textual strategies of Shakespeare's *Lear*, and characteristic also of much of today's postmodernist theatre – not only in the absurdist nature of the performance's frame, but in repeated instances of visual reference: Lear, for example, balanced precariously but through the actor's physical skills *securely* on the edge of the hospital cart, tussling with the Nurse for possession of the book/script.[58] Such incongruous appropriateness was offered too in the aural inconsequence, in support of a tragic script, of Handel's over-solemn *Largo* and Tchaikovsky's flamboyant *Danse Espagnol*. Suzuki transformed Shakespeare's text into a legended art characteristic of the Noh, a transformation underlined as well as lightly questioned in the 1993 NHK videotape by setting the performance against the shrubberies and pinewoods of a traditional *ryokan*, seen across a lake that reflected on its wind-blown surface a distorted mirror-image of the action. But Suzuki has also maintained for a contemporary audience the disturbing oddity of Shakespeare's vision, and made it ours, by the pervasive techniques of his style – a transcultural achievement of notable significance.

The paradoxes of Suzuki's theatre art offer a range and an incisiveness that permit it to be both culturally inclusive and culturally specific. The paradoxes of its reception veer from delight to indifference and outrage, within, often, the same audience. Intercultural boundaries are crossed, though in the diverse and unstable conditions of current theatre practice the crossing-points may well be more widely spaced and less secure than in an age of more established and consistent theatrical genres. Yet if the *angst* of interculturalism is to give way in time to cultural advance (in the way of mutual recognition across the cultural divides) some such art as Suzuki's is very likely to prove a necessary vehicle of progress.

Note

I am deeply grateful to Ian Carruthers for making available to me unpublished articles by himself and Yasunari Takahashi, together with videos of Suzuki's work and his and Kayoko Hashimoto's translation of *Greeting from the Edge of the World*.

                                                                    JRM

6   Hideki Noda's Shakespeare: the languages of performance

Margaret Shewring

Introduction

In 1986 a large-format 'photo collection' was published in Japan to celebrate the tenth anniversary of Yume no Yuminsha, a highly acclaimed experimental theatre company based in Tokyo.[1] The lavish publication offers a collage of text and visual illustration which records the extraordinary success of this innovative young group. The publication itself is an embodiment of the Company's performance style, dependent as it is on the vivid juxtaposition of rehearsal photographs with images of performances, narrative descriptions with graphically ingenious headlines and inserts, and full to overflowing with people taking on numerous roles, 'costumed' and 'everyday', past and present. A brief history of Yume no Yuminsha and its director, Hideki Noda, will set the subsequent discussion in context.

Yume no Yuminsha was established by Hideki Noda in 1976 while he was a law student at Tokyo University. By 1981 the Company had left its University environment to perform at the new, 400–seat Honda Theatre in Shimo-Kitazawa, Tokyo, 'the home of a number of small theatre groups and the nucleus of a new youth culture, with jazz clubs, boutiques and tiny art galleries, especially attractive to the young, fashionable Tokyoites who flock to see Noda's productions'.[2] In 1983 Noda won the Best Play Award (Kishida Drama Grand Prix) for *Descent of the Brutes*, in 1985 he won the Nokia Theatre Award for *The Stonehenge Trilogy* and in 1986 his company, Yume no Yuminsha, won the Kinokuniya Grand Prix. From their early, small-scale venues the Company graduated through medium-scale theatres to arenas. To celebrate the Kinokuniya award and Yuminsha's tenth anniversary, Noda staged all three parts of the *Trilogy* in the Yoyugi National Stadium, a huge athletics arena. The tickets were sold out in a matter of hours, one month in advance of the performance.[3]

Yume no Yuminsha has an international as well as a Japanese performance record. In 1987, Yume no Yuminsha performed for the first time outside Japan when they revived their 1983 production of *Descent of the Brutes* for the Edinburgh International Festival. In 1988 *Comet-*

Messenger Siegfried, the second part of *The Stonehenge Trilogy* (devised in 1985), played at the First New York International Festival (at the Majestic Theater of the Brooklyn Academy of Music) as part of a tour of the United States. Yume no Yuminsha returned to Edinburgh in 1990 with *Hanshin* (*Half-Gods*) first performed in Tokyo in 1986. The productions were well received in both Edinburgh and New York and yet the Company's achievements have been largely ignored in the West. So, for example, when Samuel Leiter published his record of the work of *100 Great Directors* (1992) he did not include Noda.[4] It is tempting to believe that this neglect in the West is, at least in part, due to the fact that Noda did not turn his attention to Shakespeare until 1985/86 and that none of his four Shakespearean productions, more or less closely based on the original scripts, has been performed outside Japan.

My purpose here is to explore the connections between Noda's theatrical development and his experiments, from 1986, with the staging of Shakespearean plays. I shall begin with some discussion of the work of Noda in the context of Yume no Yuminsha before turning to an analysis of his *Twelfth Night* in 1985/86. My perspective is not one of literary analysis (I neither read nor speak Japanese) but rather a response to the full range of performance languages. My discussion of *Twelfth Night* is influenced by seeing performances of Yume no Yuminsha's *Descent of the Brutes* and *Half Gods* at the Edinburgh Festival, in 1987 and 1990 respectively, and, more recently, by seeing a video-taped version of *Comet-Messenger Siegfried*. I have based my interpretation of *Twelfth Night* on a videotape.[5]

Yume no Yuminsha

The outstanding success of Yume no Yuminsha in Japan is not derived from the casting of star performers but from a collective involvement which allows the Company to develop productions through the physical aspects of performance. Nor are their scripts conventional. Rather, they have the zany logic suggested by the Company's name: the Dreaming Wanderers. Noda has written and directed numerous plays, each one replete with ideas, myths, symbols, puns and physical tricks of all kinds. His plots are complex, often juxtaposing different lands and times within a single scene. Jeanette Amano concludes in *The Tokyo Journal* that Noda 'approaches theatre like a circus-ring', creating a zany, autotelic world.[6] Complemented by the acrobatic energy of the youthful performers (fostered by their regular choreographer, Tamae Sha), the scripts juxtapose a series of visual images creating an effect that is comparable to that of channel-hopping on television, flipping through comic books, or even surfing the internet.[7] The overall effect is of a surreal kaleidoscope of colour and movement which, like surrealism, draws on both illusion and a deeply rooted reality.

In 1987, in the programme notes for Yume no Yuminsha's first performance outside Japan, their distinctive approach was acclaimed as having 'proved that there is no longer any confirmed style in Japanese theatre'. This fact, it was said, is illustrated by 'Yuminsha's appeal to all audiences and the breaking down of any perceived generation gap'. In the same programme the Company's work was described as 'the very antithesis of theatre'.[8] Certainly their fast-paced performances, executed with precision, seem a far cry from the verbal and physical skills necessary to bring out the richness of poetic language that is the great strength of Shakespeare's scripts. Yet the emergence and success of Yume no Yuminsha has, it could be argued, echoes of that of Shakespeare's own company, the Chamberlain's Men/King's Men and, indeed, of Shakespeare's place in it. Noda was not only the founder member of Yume no Yuminsha, he is a performer and, above all, a playwright whose work was devised with the troupe in mind. Noda is himself, like Shakespeare, not only a playwright but a poet. His genius with language derives, however, from distinctly modern sources including the rapid, almost 'telegrammese' juxtaposition of fragments culled from the great works of world literature coupled with the debased clichés of the twentieth-century mass-media-led global village. It is a language rooted in the immediacy and unpredictability of bizarre action, not the considered lexicon of poetic analysis and psychological self-scrutiny.

Sue Henny has described *The Stonehenge Trilogy* as 'a crazy surreal amalgam of themes inspired by Wagner's *Ring Cycle* . . . the discoveries of Galileo and the prognostications of Nostradamus, combined with the manifestation of Mark Twain's Tom Sawyer, Halley's Comet and Jules Verne's *Around the World in Eighty Days*'.[9] D. J. R. Bruckner, writing in response to the 1988 performance of *Comet-Messenger Siegfried*, at the Majestic Theater, Brooklyn, explains to the readers of *The New York Times* that in thirty scenes the play embraces 'religion, archaeology, mythology and astronomy; the samurai tradition and kabuki theater; Western music from the 19th-century Romantics to rock, and movies from "Around the World in Eighty Days" to "Superman" . . . The number of recognisable allusions to Western literary classics alone is staggering'.[10] Bruckner is stunned by the skill and sheer energy but, like so many Western critics brought up in a theatre tradition which privileges the word over the full range of non-verbal performance languages, he concludes: 'You would not want to sit through this thing twice, but once is a spectacular lot of fun if you don't think about it too much.'[11]

Like *The Stonehenge Trilogy*, the script of *Descent of the Brutes* is highly allusive. In common with all Noda's scripts, the play combines old and new tales of quests and adventures. In this case the stories include Thor Heyerdahl and the Kon-Tiki expedition, Jules Verne's narrative of a group of boys adrift on a raft, America's first Apollo moon-landing and the ancient Japanese legend of the Rabbit in the Moon. For this rich tapestry of allusions Setsu Asakura designed a set which consisted of several divisions or compartments ranged round the rear of the stage with a series of interconnecting upper levels. The central stage area moved and tilted. With extraordinary energy and dexterity the Company switched from myth to myth, from identity to identity, from past to present, pushing each narrative or anecdotal fragment through to its illogical conclusion with the surreal skill of Cocteau's *The Wedding on the Eiffel Tower*.[12] The costumes ranged from contemporary to traditional, from pantomime-style tunics and a 'bunny-girl' outfit, space-suits, smart western office-wear and clinical white coats (or overalls) to elaborate Kabuki-style dress for Princess Twelve-Layers and her Imperial court ladies from tenth-century Japan.[13] Similarly, the performance styles ranged from circus and zany 'sit-com' to the skilful manipulation of Bunraku puppets.

The programme for the Edinburgh staging of *The Descent of the Brutes* offered a synopsis of the plot, annotated (in italics) by Noda in a series of satirical, laconic 'asides' to members of the audience. In this way the programme became part of the two-way process between stage and auditorium. Setsu Asakura's set offered locations for on-stage audiences to see or spy on the action as well as extending the playing, and watching, spaces from the stage into the side boxes. From one of these boxes a narrator/commentator, wearing the traditional kimono of a samurai warrior, spoke an occasional brief, dry aside in English. This blurring of on-stage and off-stage served to make on-and-off-stage audiences complicit in the guilty aspirations embodied in the play's relentless quests for achievement (a parody of the pressures of human society). A similar blurring of realities is achieved in *Half-Gods* by Noda's decision to create a Pirandellian framing device of a rehearsal in which Yume no Yuminsha are rehearsing a performance of *Half-Gods*.[14] This, too, allows Noda to draw attention to the absurdities of human emotions and foibles.

The Yume no Yuminsha shows of the 1980s were not only hugely successful, they also offered Noda the opportunity to explore his personal obsessions, both through themes and performance-styles. So, for example, *Descent of the Brutes* contains frequent allusions to contemporary 'media-hype' set against myths and folk tales. Each is seen to defy logical explanation. This, in turn, makes them vulnerable to the Legendary Disease. A programme note for *Half-Gods* looks back at the narrative and the linguistic punning of *Descent of the Brutes,* and recalls the 'veiled criticism of the evils of contemporary society where the effects of contagious disease were manifested in humans possessed by animals who then, poor things, behaved as humans'.[15] A similar technique occurs in *Hanshin (Half-Gods)*. This piece, based on a narrative about Siamese twins by the cartoonist Moto Hagio, premièred in Tokyo in 1986 and was revived at the Edinburgh Festival in 1990.

As Noda developed it, the narrative of *Half Gods* foregrounded both his fascination with the punning use of numerical and verbal language and his equally powerful fascination with human origin and identity. All his plays draw on a fascination with stories of creation both Christian and mythological as well as those dependent on scientific explanation or even on the genetic engineering made possible through medical advances. Like Tolkien's *Lord of the Rings* Noda's narratives range through different 'areas' of life – space and the universe, the sky, the earth, below the earth's crust, the sea, beneath the sea – and their inhabitants – gods, mythic figures, monsters, half-beasts, half-gods. Stories of quest and adventure combine with the dream logic of *Alice in Wonderland* to explore human aspirations and dilemmas in the context of the blurring of the sane and the insane. Only the use of language, the ability to 'translate' the riddles concealed within the puns, allows for the transition between states giving the individual the power to control what is happening – as a writer can construct and control narratives by harnessing the power of language. The need to complete the physical, emotional and spiritual self, acute in the context of Siamese twins, crosses chronological and gender barriers both in a performance context and in philosophical, anatomical and ethical ones.

A leitmotif running through much of Noda's work is the move away from a sense of original order, perfection and harmony to what he sees as the 'contaminated', fragmented state of modern society which both results from, and leads to, split personalities and confused, blurred identities. Just as the stories that make up Noda's narratives shift and interrelate, so the characters seem to metamorphose in front of our eyes. In scene ii of *Descent of the Brutes* 'the Rabbit in the Moon (the Japanese don't see a Man in the Moon but a Rabbit), who looks like a Bunny Girl, magically transforms into the Earth Boy Brian (the hero of *Deux ans de Vacances* by Jules Verne)', while by scene vi the tenth-century Imperial Princess Twelve-Layers 'has changed into Thor Heyerdahl and together with the boy Brian is afloat on a raft. Heyerdahl is the boy's grown up alter-ego but actually he is just an ordinary middle-aged man'.[16] In a similar way the characters in *The Stonehenge Trilogy*, itself loosely based on Wagner's *Ring of the Niebelung*, transform before our eyes. Shozo Uesugi plays Galileo, Professor Ikigami and God, sometimes shifting identity within the space of a single scene. The three sisters whose fates are central to the narrative are both Val, Ky and Rie and, with the disconcerting intrusiveness of the Cardinals of the Spanish Inquisition in *Monty Python*, are also 'Enigmatic Nun One', 'Enigmatic Nun Two' and 'Enigmatic Nun Three'.[17]

'With uniquely unconventional images that are far from realistic', Noda depicts the discrepancy between a happy primeval state before men or things mature or grow specialised and the present state full of the 'sense of loss after specialisation'.[18] Much of Noda's theatrical creativity displays a deep-seated fascination with an un-corrupted state of being, when male and female were harmoniously united in one exquisite androgyne reminiscent of Plato's. The casting of crucial roles often depends on cross-dressing, whether it is Noda himself as Princess Twelve-Layers or an actress playing the Boy Brian (Akiko Takeshita). It is as if the *onnagata* tradition and the boy players of Elizabethan England are, consciously or unconsciously, understood to be a legacy of a perfect original harmony between male and female.

Noda's *Twelfth Night*

It was in Shakespeare's work that Noda was to find the source material for further explorations of human fantasies, dreams and aspirations. After ten successful years with his own theatre company, enjoying increasing popularity among young Japanese audiences, it may be somewhat surprising that Noda should turn his attention to the works of Shakespeare. It may be even more surprising that three of his four Shakespeare-inspired productions to date have been mounted under the auspices of the Toho Company using groups brought together for the individual shows rather than his own troupe. Noda staged *Twelfth Night* in 1985/86, *Much Ado About Nothing* in July 1990, *Richard III* in December 1990 and *A Midsummer Night's Dream* in 1992. Of these, only *Richard III* was with Yume no Yuminsha.

It is not, I believe, psychological realism or rhetorical elaboration that Noda finds in Shakespeare. His attention is focused, rather, on the scenic form of the plays.[19] He understands the Elizabethan emphasis both on continuity between scenes and on the juxtaposition of contrasting episodes. He celebrates the emblematic use of a limited range of props and costumes in an open space filled with performers. Above all he seeks a direct communication with his audience – a communication rooted in the identification of topical preoccupations and shared obsessions – encapsulated in a kaleidoscope of scenic moments timed to perfection.

Invited by the Toho Company to mount a production of his own choice in 1985, Noda's first concern was to find an appropriate vehicle for the talents of Mao Daichi, the leading lady already approached by Toho. By his own account he thought first of a spectacular musical before considering *Twelfth Night*.[20] Several other well-known performers were to join the cast including Junko Sakurado, a popular singer of the 1970s who had turned to acting and was cast as Olivia, Isao Hashizume as Malvolio and Takashi Sasano as Feste. Another famous actor, Hakutaro Honda, took on several 'cameo' parts including the Sea Captain and Fabian.

In *Twelfth Night* Noda found an Elizabethan script that shared his interest in the origin and nature of identity and that, at the same time, offered a scenic structure to suit the pace, continuity and juxtaposition of images that allowed Noda to develop, spatially and stylistically, a performance style appropriate to playing Shakespeare in the mass-media-dominated world of the late twentieth century. Unlike Ariane Mnouchkine's *Twelfth Night* (*La Nuit des rois*) that premièred in Avignon in 1982, Noda's production was not part of a pre-announced intention to stage a range of Shakespeare's plays. Nor is Noda's use of oriental references a conscious imposition on Shakespeare's play (as, it has been argued, Mnouchkine's fascination with Asian theatre was superimposed on her *Twelfth Night*)[21] – rather, Noda's staging depended on the same fluidity exploited in his own plays, mixing Eastern and Western costumes, styles, music and allusions and combining them into a larger vocabulary rooted in the business of performance itself. In *Half-Gods* Noda had used an Elizabethan-inspired performance space, designed by Masahiro Iwai. The stage was essentially bare, with a gallery or upper level running round the rear of the performance space and, by implication, extending outwards to embrace the auditorium. Within this space, theological, political, anatomical, social and familial issues are given dynamic expression that is at once intricate and zany, satirical and intensely emotional. A similar set of considerations governed his stage practice in *Twelfth Night*.

Noda's staging of *Twelfth Night* adopts a scenic structure similar to that in Shakespeare's script. He devised a set which, as for *Half-Gods,* allowed maximum flexibility and fluidity. As Noda himself has explained, he made a set-model from clay which he passed to Ichito Takada to develop.[22] This design is dominated by a single, striking concept: two huge, mobile masks (each ten to twelve feet in height and around eight feet in diameter) occupy the rear of the stage. These are flanked by two, low, equally mobile structures serving as steps or walls. These scenic elements are of a white-grey, stone-like appearance. The faces are unblemished and sculpted with simplicity, leaving holes for the mouths and eyes. The masks can stand side by side, move to stand at an angle to each other, or slide across each other completely, merging into one. The actors can both play in front of

them and climb over them, peering out through the cavities, even loung-
ing along the lower rim of the eye or lips. The structures are at once traditional and modern, legacies from ancient Western or Oriental cultures
and appropriate to a modern Mediterranean-island holiday resort. The
faces have the serenity and simplicity of Noh masks but do not directly
replicate these. Above all, they have an uncanny ability to convince the
audience that even the stone walls are responding (laughing, mocking,
sympathising) as they watch the trivial struggles of individuals in the face
of their destinies. The illusion is further enhanced in the final act as
mirror panels multiply the confusions on the stage.

One feature which makes this *Twelfth Night* distinctively Noda's is the
decision to frame the story with a dumb show that forges a connection
between Shakespeare's story and Noda's personal preoccupation with
androgyny. The performance opens with a choreographed entrance, from
the centre back of the stage, of a strangely androgynous dancer surrounded by billowing silken cloths. The sequence may be interpreted as
referring to the primeval state in Plato's *Symposium* in which male and
female were united in one perfect form. The voice of a narrator explains
that the sea is wild and the sea-dragons (sea-horses) are being driven
crazy. The androgynous creature is identified as Venus who, the narrator
explains, is bisexual, having both male and female characteristics. As the
dancer struggles amidst the silken waves two sea-horses move towards the
ambiguously-gendered creature. Before the audience's eyes a second
creature emerges from the waves, a mirror image of the first, and each is
seen to 'swim' off stage with one of the sea-horses as the narrator tells of
the fate of twins separated in a shipwreck. In this sequence Noda locates
Viola's separation from her twin brother, Sebastian, and her subsequent
decision to disguise herself to look like him, taking the name Cesario, in
the wider context of that blurring of identity between twins that
approaches the essence of androgyny. This blurring is further emphasised
by Noda in his decision to double the parts of Viola and Sebastian and,
thus, to take advantage of the opportunity to cast, in both roles, Mao
Daichi, an actress famous for playing leading male roles in Takarazuka
(the all-female review company).[23] Her performance retains the disturbing ambiguity in both roles that allows the world of Illyria to embrace
both dream and nightmare, triggered by intense spiritual and emotional
relationships. The theme of androgyny returns, memorably, in Noda's
inserted coda in which Cesario (the character who directly unites male
and female identity) appears 'in an intense spotlight as a beautiful
androgyne with long silver hair swaying like seaweed' against the sea of
origination.[24] Meanwhile, myths associated with birth and identity from
a wide range of periods and cultures are repeatedly recalled during a

performance which makes use of folk-traditional, carnivalesque figures (linked with the sea, with creation, with birth) with long-standing popular and archetypal associations.

Throughout the production Noda's framing device, with its emphasis on split identity, is allowed to intrude into the development of Shakespeare's narrative. This is achieved partly through visual, musical and verbal echoes of the opening scenes and partly through the inclusion of brief moments which seem to freeze the action as the characters glimpse their true selves. Noda's Cesario tells Orsino about the complete beings (*andorogyunusu*) who used to inhabit the sea. These perfect forms are said to have grown arrogant and defied the gods who then divided them into two bodies, one male, one female, as punishment. So the male will continue to seek out the female, and vice-versa, in order to return to a state of perfection. Cesario's sudden realisation that her twin may have survived the shipwreck is also made explicit, in contrast to Shakespeare's text. At the moment when Antonio risks his own life and freedom to protect Cesario (whom he takes to be Sebastian) he calls out Sebastian's name as he is led away. Viola/Cesario suddenly understands his confusion and, in a piece of stage-business far more explicit than is usual in Shakespearean productions, she runs out from between the two masks at the rear of the stage, her movement echoing the opening of the play when she emerges out of the billowing 'waves'. As she looks around her the scene changes to the maze-like streets of Illyria, suggested on stage by the movements of supernumeraries closing in on Sebastian, offering him only limited choices of direction and preventing him from seeing into the distance as Antonio is led away and Viola/Cesario is being swept along by a parallel 'crowd'. The confusion is emphasised by lighting effects when, for example, Sebastian's disorientation is made to seem more than coincidence as a bright light in one of the eye sockets of the ever-present masks appears to be spying on his movements.

As is evident from this description of the way in which the physical and psychological effect of Illyria is given life on stage, one of the great strengths of the staging is group work. The legacy of his years with Yume no Yuminsha is evident in Noda's skilful choreography of movement in *Twelfth Night*. Alongside the popular, well-known casting, appropriate to the commercial sector, Noda employs groups of supernumeraries to fill the stage repeatedly, sometimes providing human scenery, sometimes accompanying the principal players. This group-work, echoing both the skills of *commedia dell' arte* and Elizabethan playing companies, is a product of actor-led improvisations gradually orchestrated during the rehearsal process. In *Twelfth Night* it includes the formation of a carnival-style dragon/sea-horse which serves as an interlude linking the scenes, sometimes sweeping characters along with it onto or off the stage. Feste is frequently accompanied by a troupe clad in white tunic tops and trousers, performing with acrobatic skill and circus-style energy, at once part of the entertainment offered by Feste and also providing human scenic elements including seats, steps and tables. This constant influx of energy is not merely decorative or incidental. Noda uses it as a natural extension of ideas in Shakespeare's script in which Illyria is full of surprising illusions interwoven with the illogicality of dreams. He uses these performers to animate the scenery within a space in which everyone is watched, overheard, mimicked and teased while not always recognising the intruder-tormentor. So the human scenery moves forward to peer over shoulders or to 'crowd' confused individuals. It is the principle of Craig's 'kinetic scenery' in human rather than plastic form, making the space infinitely flexible without interrupting continuity and in full view of the audience.

The costumes for Noda's *Twelfth Night* are timeless. Sometimes, as in the context of the silken fabrics for Orsino and his courtiers, the costumes suggest Oriental luxury, sometimes the tunics and trousers simultaneously convey Western Renaissance dress and contemporary circus or even rehearsal clothes. With the exception of Olivia's ceremonial Kabuki costume in the finale, there is little in the costume to convey a specifically Japanese location. Instead, the costumes typically offer a witty allusiveness drawing on world-wide codes of dress. For example, when Malvolio is disturbed from his sleep by the drunken behaviour of Sir Toby and his friends, he enters in a loose kimono-style jacket, a floppy night-cap and large, furry, animal-paw slippers, clutching a teddy bear. The costumes also allow for a flexibility in cross-dressing, in keeping with Noda's interpretation of the narrative and beyond that suggested in Shakespeare's play. So, for example, Maria is not dressed as a lady's companion or maid but as a tom boy, thus echoing Viola/Cesario.

The music, composed by the leading rock musician Yukihide Takekawa, also ranges across styles and periods according to its theatrical function. Sometimes it is atmospheric (suggesting a threatening environment), sometimes romantic, sometimes celebratory and carnivalesque, sometimes orchestral, sometimes the pure lone sound of Feste's flute. And, with varying degrees of obtrusiveness, the sound effects echo the opening sequences, evoking the sea, sea-gulls, even dreamy, hallucinatory breezes. Occasionally the music serves as a deliberate counterpoint to the action, as when the strains of the 'William Tell' overture accompany Cesario's fight with Sir Andrew.

Towards the end of the production the musical score is used to underline the play's themes of love and separation. In a spectacular finale, Orsino and Viola (now in female attire) are carried forward on litters

supported by masked, androgynous creatures. Their exchange woven
through the lyrics of a hauntingly romantic, Western-style, popular song,
carries the audience along with its rhythm as the phrases echo key
moments from the play as a whole (supplemented, as ever, by Noda's irre-
pressible love of witty interjections):

VIOLA: I have a sister who loved a man. This love was deep.
ORSINO: And what became of this love?
VIOLA: Love was the creation of the gods.
           Hate is the invention of mankind.
ORSINO: The gramophone was invented by Eddison.
BOTH: Music. Oh, music.
           Love, oh, love.
VIOLA: I am finding memories inside myself . . .
           I can't hold them. They are as a tidal wave.

Olivia comes forward to join in the song, elaborating further on the
lyrics:

> When the sea breathes blue breath,
> My lover is born.
> Love was born from the sea.
> When the sea was very white,
> I parted from my lover.
> When the sea breathed black as night
> I remembered my lover.[25]

These lines are punctuated by a refrain, in which all the Company join,
echoing the words 'born', 'sea', 'love', 'memories', 'tidal wave'. As the
Company sways with the rhythm the mirror panels seem to multiply their
movements, swaying back and forth like the sea itself. Large cardboard
banners, cut to resemble Viola in her disguise as Cesario, and with a white
mask for a face, are raised up and drawn back into the swaying mass.
Gradually the music is replaced by the sounds of the sea.

Translation or adaptation?

One of the most interesting aspects of Noda's work is the way in which his
scripts relate to his sources. Even for a non-Japanese speaker it is apparent
that his *Twelfth Night* bears a much closer resemblance to Shakespeare's
play than his later Shakespeare-based shows or, indeed, than earlier
pieces like *Comet-Messenger Siegfried* does to *The Ring Cycle*. In any discussion of adaptation of Shakespeare it is important to remember that
Shakespeare himself was engaged in a comparable creative process in his
use of a variety of literary and historical sources. Equally, in any instance
in which a text is used outside its native country there arises a question as

to whether the resulting communication is a translation or an adaptation. Even these categories become blurred in the context of theatre-texts, for performance is inevitably a translation of the author's words on the page into a fully realised piece of theatre drawing on a full range of performance languages. This is as true for a Shakespeare script played in the 1990s in Stratford-upon-Avon as for a Shakespeare script performed by the Théâtre du Soleil, the Berliner Ensemble or a Japanese Company. David Johnston, in the introduction to a collection of essays on this topic, *Stages of Translation*, discusses what he describes as the 'immediacy of reception' of a text in the theatre, an 'immediacy' dependent upon the dynamics of the performer, stage and audience relationship. In the stage context, he argues, some of the choices made by a translator 'are genuinely akin to those taken by a creative writer'.[26]

As Hideki Noda is a prolific creative writer, of novels as well as theatre pieces, it is perhaps not surprising that his engagement with his sources goes beyond literal translation. Joseph Farrel shares a sense of creative transformation when he writes: 'A play is of course more than language, and the essential distinction between translation and adaptation lies in the respect not for the language but for the non-linguistic elements of the drama. As a rule of thumb, a translation becomes an adaptation when the transformation involved is more than linguistic.'[27] Andrea Nouryeh takes this further: 'Unlike European translations which can draw from common Christian symbols, climate and topography, and have linguistic correlatives, Japanese translations must be adaptations in which much of the verse, imagery, humour and cultural context of the original plays is lost.'[28]

Noda's *Twelfth Night* is an indication of the extent to which his understanding of Elizabethan staging and his interest in some of the thematic preoccupations of Shakespeare's play, which had already featured in his work with Yume no Yuminsha, informed his first engagement with a Shakespearean script. During the 1990s Noda continued to be attracted to the staging of plays by Shakespeare. Increasingly he chose to move away from the original scripts in favour of adaptations in which the imaginative worlds evoked by Shakespeare were given visual embodiment in terms of contemporary Japan. So, for example, Noda's adaptation of *Much Ado About Nothing* (at the Nissei Theatre, 5–28 July 1990) was transposed into the familiar Japanese world of Sumo wrestling, changing the names of some of the characters, omitting others, and incorporating some lines from *Othello* and *Romeo and Juliet* along the way. Even so, according to Professor Yushi Odashima, who translated all of Shakespeare's plays into Japanese, in Noda's *Twelfth Night* and *Much Ado* Odashima's own translation 'made up 70 – 80% of the whole script for each play'.[29]

Odashima's implicit acknowledgement that even Noda's *Twelfth Night* and *Much Ado* go beyond linguistic translation is instructive. Even if *Twelfth Night* bears the closest resemblance of all Noda's Shakespearean productions to Shakespeare's script it, too, has undergone a series of changes as a direct result of Noda's creative engagement with the process of performance. As Noda himself has commented: 'You see, my basic difference from a director like Mr. Ninagawa is that I write. Mr. Ninagawa makes it a rule never to deviate from the original texts, and he gets his energy from such self restraints. I approach Shakespeare from the opposite way.'[30] This 'opposite way' is rooted in Noda's innovative work, developed first with Yume no Yuminsha, in response to the perceived needs of the contemporary Japanese stage.

In the first article in a new journal, *Concerned Theatre Japan*, Tsuno Kaitaro writes of the ways in which the conventions of contemporary drama can result in 'dead theatre'.[31] He argues: 'Modern theatre has long since discarded that which once bound drama to the greater world beyond, that which simultaneously presided over both theatrical and non-theatrical worlds, the collective imagination'. What is needed is a 'carnival madness' that will 'explode out of the proscenium'.[32] For Kaitaro, even the RSC in their 1968/70 productions of *The Winter's Tale* and *The Merry Wives of Windsor* at the Nissei Theatre in Tokyo, 'had been trapped within the frame-work of modern drama'. Whilst recording his admiration for the flawless skills in the productions, Kaitaro goes on:

I was disappointed to realise that the Royal Shakespeare Company seemed to have so easily and so well forgotten – especially in producing Shakespeare – that the real question we must answer to-day is not how best to use the potentials inherent in modern theatre but rather how we might best use the productions of the pre-modern collective imagination and our image of those productions to transcend and destroy the walls of modern theatre fast closing in upon us.[33]

Kaitaro seems to be identifying the same sense of loss expressed by Peter Brook in *The Empty Space*: 'We do not know how to celebrate because we do not know what to celebrate'.[34] Noda's best work goes a long way towards answering that need for 'carnival madness' and 'celebration' in its ability to transcend the purely verbal and to use the full range of performance languages to trigger a 'collective popular imagination'. It is rooted in the youth culture of a generation brought up in a global village in which everything is instantly accessible through modern technology and channel-hopping can lead to the rapid juxtaposition of the comic and the tragic, the grotesque and the bizarre. Noda found in *Twelfth Night* an invitation to step into a world of carnival madness. Shakespeare's Illyria offers a freedom of location in a strange land where reality and identity become confused and blurred. Noda's Illyria shares this freedom. The voice-over at the opening of the video-recording of Noda's production states that it is 'carnival time' and indeed the atmosphere of carnival, at once confusing and celebratory, pervades the performance.[35] It is this ability to tap into 'the collective popular imagination' that gives Noda's theatre-pieces their compelling vigour, transforming them into 'living' theatre.

Noda's Shakespeares

Looking back on his work on *Twelfth Night* Noda has commented : 'I was still afraid to alter his [Shakespeare's] text. I was not sure how far I should go . . . After the production I thought I hadn't worked enough on it. I thought I should have drawn the play much closer to my side.'[36] If by 'to my side' Noda meant that he should have adapted the piece to assimilate it more fully into his own creative writing process, then it could be argued that he was to work much more fully on the script of Shakespeare's *Richard III* for a production with Yume no Yuminsha in December 1990. Certainly his *Sandaime Richard* 'is *written* and directed rather than adapted and directed by Hideki Noda'.[37] His script, taking its cue from the heraldic rose-emblems of the houses of York and Lancaster, transposes the struggle for power to a school of flower arranging with all its intensely competitive instinct for rivalry and success. Moreover Shakespeare's *Richard III* is only one of the major sources for *Sandaime Richard*. Others include Josephine Tay's *The Daughter of Time* and Anthony Burgess's *Nothing Like the Sun* as well as historical material about Shakespeare's life including references to his crippled brother, Richard.[38] In Noda's script, Shakespeare and others prosecute Richard III while barristers defend him – each side producing episodes from Richard's life in evidence. These episodes are mingled with Shakespeare's 'wild fancies' about his brother.[39] All of this distances the script, and its audience, from the historical struggles of fifteenth-century England. It also allows for a concentration on the infinite absurdities of human passions as revealed with all of Yume no Yuminsha's performance skills.

In 1992 Noda staged *A Midsummer Night's Dream* for the Toho Company at the Nissei Theatre (2–25 August). Like *Richard III* it was written, rather than adapted, by Noda. In it Noda draws not just on Shakespeare but on Lewis Carroll as well as on the story of Faustus (from which he borrows the spirit who is the embodiment of hell, Mephistopheles). The fast-moving plot is transposed from the Athenian court of Theseus to a Japanese restaurant (and kitchens) and from a 'wood near Athens' to the forests and amusement park at the base of Mt Fuji. Demetrius and Lysander are cooks, Helena the daughter of a cook and Hermia the only daughter of a restaurant-owner. In Shakespeare's play 'love is projected upon appetite, and love is talked about in the metaphor of food'.[40] In Noda's version the imagery is given a literal visual realisation, transformed through the fantastic world of *Alice in Wonderland*. Indeed, the play-within-the-play that is being rehearsed threatens to take over the whole stage world into *Wonderland*.[41]

It is, I believe, the play-within-the play that provides the key to understanding Noda's staging. *Alice in Wonderland* is, on one level, a classic fairy-tale, the staple reading-diet for hundreds of thousands of children. In its enchanted world humans talk to animals, size is far from constant and inanimate objects become animate. Noda's *Dream* has many of the qualities of a children's story. Childhood games and rhymes echo throughout. The set includes a steeply raked hill, bushes sprouting huge culinary utensils instead of flowers and a fairground merry-go-round complete with a giant tea-cup and saucer and a big fish in place of the traditional wooden horses. Hermia and Helena dress in bizarre costumes and stamp their feet like petulant children. In this zany world characters rush across the stage on bicycles or on roller-skates while Titania appears to fall in love with a children's-book character that is a cross between a starfish and an octopus. All the energy and story-telling skills of Noda's years with Yume no Yuminsha are evident here. The plot has its own crazy, Monty-Python-style logic. For a non-Japanese speaker the parallels with Shakespeare have none of the clarity of those in *Twelfth Night*. But Noda's adaptation undoubtedly captures the confusions and frustrations, aspirations and desires of midsummer night.

Indeed, as in *Alice in Wonderland,* desire threatens to turn the magic of dream into the dangerous absurdity of nightmare. The obviously harmless knife and fork that 'grow' on the bushes are paralleled by the real kitchen knives with which Lysander and Demetrius threaten each other. The fairies are partly natural spirits, with petals on their costumes, and partly a troupe of black-and-silver-clad sprites who, as in *Twelfth Night*, serve as human scenery as well as fairies and assistants. In this more sinister world Puck, whom Noda chooses to cast as female, is balanced by the devilish male energy of a spitefully malicious Mephistopheles. As the darker impulses of the sub-conscious threaten to tip the balance of the play into confusion the fairground music and Broadway-style production numbers pull it back from the brink into the relative safety of a game of make-believe.

To Western eyes and ears this is Shakespeare liberated from all its traditional theatrical heritage. The verbal skills are merely one element in the overall experience. As Sue Henny wrote in 1987, 'Noda believes that although language is important in his work in Japan, the very physical

10. Hideki Noda as Richard III (centre) in Hideki Noda's *Sandaime Richard*, Yume no Yuminsha (1990).

nature of his plays, the frenetic activity and visual imagery, will transcend dialogue. The puns may not be easily translatable, but the way he presents the jokes and images is universal'.[42] In his *A Midsummer Night's Dream* Noda develops a series of visual and verbal juxtapositions that belongs as much to the language of surreality as to a post-modern vocabulary. His adaptation moves beyond 'poetry in the theatre' to what Cocteau described as 'poetry of theatre'.[43] The outrageousness of the richly allusive, fast-moving production is rooted in a heightened sense of recognition, inviting response on a sub-conscious and instinctive level as well as on a conscious, rational plane. Noda's *Dream* is a disconcertingly zany, genuinely intercultural piece of theatre that is as 'beautiful as the chance meeting, on a dissection table, of a sewing machine and an umbrella'.[44]

7   Japanese Shakespeare and English reviewers

Tetsuo Kishi

Yukio Ninagawa's production of *Macbeth* was a sellout as well as a critical success at the 1985 Edinburgh Festival. Three years later the same director captivated the English audience again with his production of *The Tempest*, which turned out to be so successful that it was revived in London in 1992. It is not at all difficult to explain the reception these productions were blessed with. They were visually impressive and they were full of 'Japanese' elements, especially those elements which seemed to have made use of conventions of the traditional Japanese theatre. But the relation between the traditional Japanese theatre and these productions of Shakespeare's plays is actually much more complicated than Ninagawa's admiring critics appear to realise.

I will begin with an ostensibly simple example. Ninagawa's production of *The Tempest* is supposed to be enacted as a rehearsal of a Noh version of the play. There is indeed what looks like a Noh theatre towards the back of the stage, and one expects the rehearsal to take place in that theatre. This expectation, however, is betrayed as soon as the performance begins. The opening scene of the play takes place on a ship in a storm. In Ninagawa's production an enormous prow of a ship is thrust toward the front of the stage – that is, the main stage itself and not the smaller Noh stage built on this stage – and the storm is represented with fluttering of the sails and deafening sound effects. Even to a relatively careless audience it would be clear that this is against the basic premise of the whole production for two reasons.

If the play is indeed conceived as a rehearsal of a Noh play, it would be natural to expect it to be performed on the Noh stage, but the action is not confined to that space. It is spread all over the main stage and the areas outside the Noh theatre are regularly used throughout the production. It seems that the Noh stage is there to produce a vaguely 'Japanese' atmosphere rather than as a space with a coherent nature. This is not hard to accept, because limiting the action within the Noh theatre, thus using it as a kind of 'inner stage' (and it is used that way in some scenes), would somewhat alienate the performance from the audience.

Probably the director tried to avoid this remoteness at the expense of coherence.

Some people might accept this incoherence as something that is not unlike the flexible way Shakespeare himself used the acting space. It is true that the stage in Shakespeare's plays is not clearly defined, and it can represent a large variety of places as the action unfolds itself. There is, however, an important difference between Shakespeare and Ninagawa. Shakespearean theatre or rather Elizabethan theatre had virtually no scenery, while Ninagawa's productions of Shakespeare usually make use of a very prominent scenery which more or less dominates and clearly defines the nature of the whole space, as the Noh stage in his production of *The Tempest* does.

Of course one should bear in mind that the opening scene of *The Tempest* is notoriously difficult to stage. Peter Brook, who has himself directed the play several times, aptly explained the difficulty in his recent book:

Every designer and every director of *The Tempest* is forced right at the opening to face a major difficulty. The play has a unity of place, the island, except for the first scene, which takes place on a ship at sea during a storm. Is it necessary to violate this unity by making a complicated realistic stage picture for the first moments of the play? The better this is done, the more it destroys the possibility of evoking the island subsequently in a nonnaturalistic convention and the harder it makes the playing of the second long quiet scene of exposition, when Prospero tells his life to his daughter. If the convention chosen is one of elaborate pictorial scenery, the solution is easy: one makes an impressive shipwreck, then one slides into place a desert island. But if one rejects this approach, one must discover what can effortlessly convey at one moment sea and at the next, dry land.[1]

I do not know if Ninagawa was aware of the 'major difficulty', but he 'solved' it by making an impressive shipwreck outside the area of the ensuing action. (I must repeat, however, that the ensuing action is not limited within the Noh theatre either.) Whether or not this solution works, one cannot but admit that there is a violation of unity.

The second reason why the opening scene is against the premise of staging the whole play as a rehearsal of a Noh version is, in my opinion, rather more crucial. There are a number of Noh plays in which a storm is depicted, but it is never depicted with a large realistic ship and realistic sound effects. Let me take *Funa-Benkei* (Benkei in the Boat) part of which takes place on a ship at sea during a storm. The play deals with an aftermath of the twelfth-century feud between two powerful samurai clans, Minamoto and Taira, which ended with the decisive victory of the former. In the play Yoshitsune, one of the warlords belonging to this clan, and his followers leave a certain port in a ship. Suddenly the ship is plunged into a storm which turns out to have been caused by the ghost of Tomomori, a warlord belonging to the Taira clan. How then is the storm represented? It is true that a very simple ship is used in the performance so that the storm is represented to some extent by its movement, but it is never the kind of large realistic ship Ninagawa used in his production. The storm is primarily represented by actors' speeches and bodily movement to the accompaniment of some music which enhances the whole action and symbolically functions as sound effect. The waves and the wind are described verbally and not visually. If this is so, one can see how fundamentally different from the aesthetics of Noh theatre Ninagawa's approach is.

Thus the opening scene is against the premise of staging the whole production as a rehearsal of a Noh play. But some of the English reviewers thought they were really watching a rehearsal of a Noh play. This response, frankly speaking, was rather puzzling, and suggested, I am afraid, the reviewers' ignorance of those conventions and practices they professed to admire in Noh. Michael Billington, for instance, thought that 'a Noh version' of the play was being mounted, and described the opening scene as 'a majestically thrilling storm complete with riven galleon and flying mariners' (*The Guardian*, 19 August 1988). It seems he did not realise he was contradicting himself, because, even if the scene is majestically thrilling, a storm in a Noh play is never represented with a riven galleon. Billington is often an astute critic but, judging from this review, one cannot help wondering how much one can trust his knowledge and understanding of the semiotics of Noh drama. In other words, he seems to be thinking of a cosmopolitan artillery of exciting effects, and not of the aesthetics and semiotics of Noh drama, where the effects are constituents of a more sustained poetic-dramatic meaning.

According to Paul Taylor, the storm 'is spectacularly evoked with violently fluttering sheets, and the thundering prow of a galleon' (*The Independent*, 5 December 1992). It is not quite clear what he meant by 'spectacularly evoked', but a production of a Noh play is never 'spectacular' in the way violently fluttering sheets and a thundering prow of a galleon are. Benedict Nightingale even compared Ninagawa's storm with Shakespeare's. He said, 'Suddenly a prow emerges from the roughly timbered hut in which Prospero lives, followed by a shaken quilt and a falling blue cloth; and there, simply yet powerfully, is Shakespeare's very own shipwreck' (*The Times*, 5 December 1992). How does he think a storm and shipwreck were represented in Shakespeare's theatre? No doubt some sound effect was used, but a quick look at the text will show us that they were represented first and foremost by actors – that is, by their speeches and bodily movement. To put it differently, a storm in

Shakespearean theatre was acted rather than shown with visual means. Here we notice a striking and very interesting affinity with Noh, but neither Ninagawa nor English reviewers seemed to have paid any attention to it.

Whether or not one likes Ninagawa's Shakespearean productions, one should never forget that their connection with traditional Japanese theatre is hardly more than flimsy. The conventions of traditional Japanese theatre are used very loosely and sometimes quite whimsically, and their central purpose seems to be to evoke various emotional associations from the audience. In other words their use is rhapsodic rather than logical.

I will mention another example of the way a device of Noh is used out of context in Ninagawa's production of *The Tempest*. In Act I scene ii of the play, Ferdinand draws a sword to attack Prospero but he is 'charmed from moving'. Prospero 'charms' Ferdinand with his magical power. In the Ninagawa version Prospero throws a bunch of white threads toward Ferdinand. These white threads have a very clear meaning to anyone with some knowledge of Noh, because they derive from one particular Noh play *Tsuchigumo* (Earth Spider).

This play is about a warlord named Minamoto Raiko who is suffering from an illness. One midnight he is visited by a priest. Raiko is bemused. The priest throws a bunch of white threads to entrap him and kill him, thus revealing his true identity as a demon of a spider. Raiko draws his sword and attacks the spider which gets injured and flees. A samurai serving Raiko chases the spider, finds its abode, and after a lengthy fight during which the spider throws bunches of threads at the samurai over and over again (the scene is really spectacular), he finally kills it.

So the white threads are not at all like a kind of magic wand which any magician can use. They are inseparable from the identity of the demon as a spider. They are used twice in the play, and each time the spider tries to kill someone. The second time he is in a desperate situation. None of this applies to Prospero. He is not a spider. He does not want to kill Ferdinand. He is never in a desperate situation, although I admit that he is anxious about his magic, which apparently depends on particular conditions and will work at one time but not another. I do not deny that the white threads are visually impressive, and so I am not surprised if some directors are tempted to use them even at the risk of arbitrariness. When *Return to the Forbidden Planet*, a rock musical loosely based on *The Tempest* (and on *Forbidden Planet*, a film also based on *The Tempest*), was performed in Japan, a robot who is an equivalent to Ariel in the original play used the same white threads against the Stephano character. While I loved the whole production as a lively fusion of Shakespearean blank verse and rock-and-roll (I think the crucial point is that the creators were well aware of the incongruity and absurdity of their work), this particular stage business made no sense whatsoever to me and anyone who knew the original context. What happened here and in Ninagawa's production is that the director totally ignored this context, and those members of the audience who do not know it mistook the device for a rather general type of magic. In other words, we were presented with a signifier without the signified.

I do not mean to say that this is necessarily wrong, because something like this tends to happen whenever a work of art is deprived of the original context. Codes and icons which have a very particular significance to Westerners – a cross, for instance – can be used simply for ornamental puposes by people belonging to a different culture or a different, predominantly unchristian and secular, phase of the same culture. Still the fact remains that they retain more of the original significance to people who are aware of the original context, and so it would be awkward to praise something for what it is not, as some of the English reviewers did when they saw Ninagawa's productions of Shakespeare in which distortion of the devices of traditional Japanese theatre occurs constantly.

Another example is the way the masque in Act IV scene i is staged. A group of actors wearing Noh costume and Noh masks appear on a *hashigakari*, a walkway leading to the main stage of the Noh theatre, slowly approach the main stage, enter the main stage, and then descend the staircase toward the main stage. So the large part of the masque is performed on the floor of the main stage of the theatre, which in relation to the Noh theatre should represent the auditorium. As in the opening scene of the play, it may not be sensible to confine the action within the Noh theatre, but at the same time one should not forget that Noh actors never perform their dance in the middle of the audience.

Thus Ninagawa's use of the Noh theatre-like building in his production is sometimes very unorthodox, if inventive. In one scene Ariel perches on the top of the roof of the theatre. Of course this sort of thing never happens in a performance of a Noh play. One should also remember that the structure of the 'Noh theatre' in Ninagawa's production is remarkably different from that of a regular Noh theatre. In some of the scenes the stage is hidden from the audience's view with a set of doors which function like the curtain of a proscenium arch stage. The truth of course is that a Noh stage has no door. In some scenes the back wall of the stage is removed, and the sea beyond the island is revealed. It did have a breathtaking effect, but the back wall of a Noh stage with a pine tree painted on it is part of the permanent structure and has a very special ritualistic meaning. I realise of course that Ninagawa is not attempting to present an authentic Noh play, and so one should never for a moment mistake his production for one – as some English reviewers hastily did.

Occasionally elements of Kabuki also appear in this production of *The Tempest*. For instance Caliban wears Kabuki-like make-up (it has nothing to do with Kyogen, because Kyogen actors never put on make-up) and Kabuki-like costume. He makes his entrance from under the staircase which connects the Noh stage and the main stage. The staircase flies open and Caliban is thrown out on the ground. This kind of gimmicky staging is often used in Kabuki but never in Noh or Kyogen. It is true that Kabuki and Noh are closely related, and a large number of Noh plays were later adapted for Kabuki, but there is a distinct difference between the visual and aural practices of the two genres. To mix them in a single production is rather like composing an opera using the styles of both Wagner and Cole Porter. Both Kabuki and Noh are types of traditional Japanese theatre, and a non-Japanese audience may not notice the difference, but saying that they both belong to the Japanese theatrical tradition means as much (or as little) as saying that both Wagner and Cole Porter belong to the 'Western' musical tradition. It is highly unlikely that Ninagawa did not realise all this, and I am certain he knew what he was doing when he mixed Noh and Kabuki. No doubt he pursued visual effect at the expense of any deeper logic or dramatic coherence.

A similar incongruity was apparent in his production of *Macbeth*. Most English reviewers were enthusiastic about it and one of them, Stewart Conn, called it 'Kabuki ritual' (*The Listener*, 29 August 1985). This time the link with traditional theatre was even flimsier, and I suppose it was not Ninagawa's intention at all to shape the whole production in the style of Kabuki. So this criticism is quite pointless, and perhaps there is no need to bother with it. But the reason why such misunderstanding occurred even though the production in question did not adhere to the style of Kabuki deserves, I think, some consideration.

Ninagawa set the production in sixteenth-century Japan, and the characters wore the costume from that period. The entire stage was transformed into a huge Buddhist altar, complete with a set of double doors. When the performance starts, two old women appear at the rear of the auditorium, slowly walk toward the stage, reach the stage, and then open the double doors. This marks the beginning of the play proper. Throughout the performance the women remain crouched on each side of the fore-stage, and when the play of *Macbeth* is over, they stand up and close the double doors. In other words, Shakespeare's *Macbeth* is made into a play-within-a-play, or more specifically, into a pseudo-religious experience of the old women which the audience seems to be expected to share. The action is confined within the Buddhist altar, and technically speaking the double doors function as a kind of 'fourth wall' in modern realistic theatre, which, for once, is not transparent but visible.

I am not certain if confining Shakespeare's play within the fourth wall as if it were a play by Ibsen is a creative decision, because Shakespeare wrote for an open stage and not for a proscenium arch stage. Unlike language in modern realistic drama, Shakespeare's language contains a strong choric element. Many speeches are delivered directly to the audience, and I do not mean just soliloquies and asides. Would not the fourth wall make it somewhat difficult for actors to deliver such speeches? In Shakespeare's plays actors are often required to play to the audience. Building a proscenium arch stage on the stage can work as an obstacle to such acting.

Interestingly enough, this 'openness' is quite prominent in Kabuki, too. Unlike an Elizabethan stage a Kabuki stage has a curtain, but it also has a *hanamichi*, a long elevated passageway running from the main stage to the rear of the auditorium on which some of the most impressive scenes are played. As in Shakespeare, many speeches are delivered as a direct address to the audience. In other words, although Stewart Conn was far from accurate when he called Ninagawa's production 'Kabuki ritual', he referred, however naively, to a real convergence between Shakespeare and Kabuki. But although Ninagawa could have profited from this similarity, he treated *Macbeth* like a play belonging to the school of modern realism.

One is hardly surprised, however, when this basic premise of confining the action within 'the fourth wall' is ignored. In a scene toward the end of the play, Malcolm's soldiers enter the auditorium from the rear, just as the two old women did at the beginning of the performance, and rush to the stage with a loud war cry. If the play is supposed to be confined within the Buddhist altar and watched by the old women (who so to speak represent us the audience), then how can the performance extend itself over the auditorium? Where are we supposed to be when this happens?

Thus Ninagawa is extremely flexible as to the definition of the acting space on one hand, and on the other the space in his productions tends to be rigorously defined by some visual object – a Buddhist altar in *Macbeth* and a Noh theatre in *The Tempest*. While I admire this director's talent to materialise striking stage pictures, I suspect his preoccupation with a visual framing-device is based on a fatal and exploitative misunderstanding of the nature of Shakespearean language. In December 1988 he was interviewed by Kazuko Matsuoka, a dramatic critic and Shakespearean scholar. He was asked about this particular aspect in his approach to Shakespeare, and said, 'It is difficult to convey the true meaning of Shakespeare's language because of the difference of rhetoric . . . So I thought of Japanising visual elements.'[2] I am quoting from a summarised version of the interview, and what Ninagawa said may have been somewhat different – anyway the interview was conducted in Japanese – yet it is clear enough that Ninagawa thinks that making a production visually Japanese will make it more accessible to a modern Japanese audience. Perhaps. But there is a problem. To erect a kind of visually impressive edifice that dominates the stage makes the whole production totally un-Shakespearean, because – one cannot emphasise this point too much – Shakespeare wrote for an open stage with virtually no scenery. Impressive scenery can make language redundant.

In the same interview the director said, referring to his preoccupation with visual elements of a production, 'There is an expression "to see a play", but nobody says "to hear a play"'. This is very odd because people do say 'to hear a play'. For instance, in Act II scene ii of *Hamlet* the prince says, 'We'll hear a play tomorrow'. In the Japanese translation of the play Ninagawa used when he staged it in Japan, the speech reads 'We'll see a play tomorrow'. This is understandable because the expression 'to hear a play' is not congenial to a Japanese audience, but it does not in any way change Shakespeare's view of dramatic language.

What 1 hope is clear by now is that we are actually confronting two questions. One has to do with transposing a given play geographically and/or temporally, and the other has to do with assimilating practices and conventions which belong to a different theatrical tradition. Basically I am not against the former. It has always been done, albeit with varying degrees of success. In any case there would not be much point in trying to reproduce 'Elizabethan' productions of Shakespeare for a contemporary audience whether it is Japanese or English, and by every account it seems that Elizabethan productions did not try to adhere to historical accuracy in the first place. In other words there is nothing intrinsically wrong about Ninagawa's idea of setting *Macbeth* in sixteenth-century Japan and *The Tempest* on the island of Sado.

The trouble began when he tried to adopt practices and conventions – and perhaps styles as well – which belong to non-Shakespearean theatrical traditions. I always find it amazing that so many artists and critics talk about 'style' very casually. Dramatic style is inseparable from dramatic content, and the way an actor walks, whether or not an actor directly addresses the audience, the way the acting space is used and so forth are all components of an integral system. This applies to Shakespeare as well, who after all wrote for a particular type of theatre with a number of peculiarities. In this sense I think Shakespearean drama is more like cast iron than water, and it simply refuses to be put into certain types of moulds. It is perfectly acceptable to dress Shakespearean characters in nineteenth-century costume, but producing *Othello* as a domestic 'tragedy' like *Hedda Gabler* or *Much Ado About Nothing* as a drawing room comedy like *The Importance of Being Earnest*, complete with elaborate scenery, would result in something uninteresting, if not altogether ludicrous.

The serious reservation I have about Ninagawa's production of *Macbeth* is that he adopted the style of modern realistic theatre – not Kabuki, as some critics thought. For *The Tempest* he tried to use various fragments of practices and conventions of Noh and Kabuki more consciously, and I do not think they worked either, because the director was almost exclusively concerned with their visual appeal.

Having said this, I must hasten to add that I am not categorically opposed to using practices and conventions of non-Shakespearean theatrical traditions in producing Shakespeare. In my opinion there are perhaps three ways to do it successfully. One is to adapt Shakespeare and produce an indigenous work, whether it is Noh or Kabuki, which will fully utilise the practices and conventions of these forms. I think a Kabuki adaptation is likely to be more successful since Noh will not easily accommodate the complexity (and sometimes secularity) of Shakespearean plots. The second possibility is to cast actors who have been trained in other schools. I have seen Japanese productions of Shakespeare in which leading roles were played by Kabuki actors, and some of them were highly successful. They did not demonstrate Kabuki-like movement or Kabuki-like delivery – to do so would have been damaging – but since they are used to handling choric language and playing to the audience, the result was often more satisfactory than those Shakespearean productions in which Stanislavsky-trained actors played major roles.

The third possibility is to find a style which is not incompatible with the nature of Shakespearean language and Shakespeare's idea of the acting space. I think of Peter Brook's production of *A Midsummer Night's Dream* as one of the most impressive examples. Since traditional Japanese theatre shares so much with Shakespeare in the way of 'openness', it is a great pity that Ninagawa paid little attention to this aspect, and missed a chance to produce something genuinely stimulating.

Hence it is doubly puzzling that the English reviewers responded to the production in the way they did. I will quote from some of the reviews of *The Tempest* again. Robert Gore-Langton felt that 'The uncanny aptness of Noh theatre . . . calls for Noh characters and spirits to populate Prospero's island. Corn-dollies, a Kabuki Ariel, a fish-spirit Caliban, and so on, duly parade in front of a cabin flanked by giant pines, with a craggy, coastal backdrop beyond' (*The Sunday Telegraph*, 1 September 1988). This, to say the least, is baffling. I do not know how or why Noh theatre is uncannily apt, but it is certainly not populated with a Kabuki Ariel, and in any case the Ariel in Ninagawa's production had very little to do with Kabuki either.

According to another reviewer Jack Tinker, 'A strangely bi-sexual Ariel floats balletically above in changing skies that owe everything to the traditions of the Noh theatre' (*The Daily Mail*, 18 August 1988). Again I cannot understand what he means. Why do 'changing skies' owe everything to the traditions of the Noh theatre? Ninagawa's production used rather realistic lighting, but Noh, being an essentially nonrealistic and nonrepresentational type of theatre, never depends on lighting. To put it very bluntly, the sky never changes in the Noh theatre – at least not visibly.

Benedict Nightingale thought 'the style veers from something not unakin to Elizabethan-realistic to Noh itself' (*The Times*, 5 December 1992). What did he mean by 'Elizabethan-realistic'? Is Shakespeare 'realistic' in the way Ibsen and Chekhov are? If not, what is the point? Why does he think, as he clearly does, that the co-existence of different styles is a good thing?

Jack Tinker saw the production again in 1992. This time he felt that it was a 'vast, teeming production of light, sound and visual sensation' and that it married 'all the impressive theatricality of the Noh tradition with daring experimental ideas' (*The Daily Mail*, 4 December 1992). It is absolutely true that Noh theatre has 'impressive theatricality', but it is not the kind of theatricality which depends on elaborate lighting. When one reads this review together with his review of the 1988 production, one suspects that his understanding of the Noh tradition is not particularly profound.

Nicholas de Jongh seemed to have been impressed by Caliban in this production who, he thought, seemed just like an exotic clown (*The Evening Standard*, 4 December 1992). He went on to say, '[Caliban's] interchanges with a bare-buttocked Stephano in leotard are low, Noh comedy'. Again this is extremely odd, for Noh is notoriously lacking in comedy. It may be that he meant Kyogen, which is comic, but I know of no Kyogen play in which a barebuttocked character appears. Ninagawa's Stephano could belong to Kabuki, although I am not very certain about it either. What really worries me about these reviews is that the critics' idea of style seems to be primarily – and perhaps exclusively – concerned with the visual aspects of a production.

Of course style in drama is not confined to visual elements. This is true of Noh and Kabuki as well as Shakespeare, and what I find really interesting and even exciting is that there is a lot of affinity between traditional Japanese theatre and Shakespeare, that is, the kind of affinity which Ninagawa does not seem to have paid much attention to and which most English reviewers do not seem to have been aware of.

First, both Noh and Kabuki, on the one hand, and Shakespeare, on the other, are meant to be performed on an open stage. We all know that Elizabethan theatre, whether public or private, had virtually no scenery and used no lighting to produce an illusion of reality. This is certainly the case with Noh. Kabuki sometimes uses elaborate scenery, but it is often changed in full view of the audience. Kabuki is different from Noh and Shakespeare in that its stage is equipped with a curtain, but this curtain never functions as 'the fourth wall' as a curtain in a proscenium arch stage does. I have already mentioned the *hanamichi* in a Kabuki theatre, and its existence drastically changes the relation between the performance and the audience, which without it would be rather similar to that in a modern theatre. The Noh stage on the other hand is half surrounded by audience, and of course the stage in the Elizabethan theatre thrust itself into the audience.

This leads to the second affinity between traditional Japanese theatre and Shakespeare. They are fundamentally 'audience-conscious' types of theatre. By this I mean that both accept the existence of the audience as an indispensable element of dramatic experience, while modern realistic theatre is based on a false assumption that the audience belongs to a different world from that of the play, requiring actors to behave as if the audience were simply not there.

Thirdly, language in both Noh and Kabuki and also in Shakespeare shares many characteristics which are not found in modern realistic drama. Both in Noh and Kabuki and in Shakespeare many speeches are delivered as a direct address to the audience. Many characters in Kabuki and almost every character in Noh tell the audience who they are when they make their first entrance, in the way the chorus does in *The Winter's Tale*. But the choric nature of the language is even more prominent in Noh and Kabuki. In a performance of a Noh play, a group of actors sit at the left side of the stage and function as the chorus. They chant speeches which describe not only such visible elements as the setting of the play (which of course are not really visible) but also such invisible elements as the inner feelings of the characters. Sometimes they even chant speeches or parts of speeches which normally would be spoken or chanted by dramatic characters themselves. This is rather like a production of *Hamlet* in which the delivery of soliloquies is shared by the prince and the chorus.

This narrative quality is also noticeable in Kabuki. In a production of many, if not all, Kabuki plays, a small dais is placed on the left side of the fore-stage on which a narrator and a musician take their seats. The narrator gives comment on the action of the play, describes the emotion and inner feeling of the characters, and sometimes even chants the kind of speeches that in realistic drama would be spoken by the actors themselves. What we hear is, if I may use T. S. Eliot's definition which he gave in his essay 'The Three Voices of Poetry', the second voice, the epic voice or the voice of the poet addressing the audience, rather than the third voice, the dramatic voice or the voice of the poet addressing the audience through imaginary characters. If we examine Shakespearean texts carefully, we will find an amazing number of speeches, including of course soliloquies and asides, which have a distinctly choric nature. In Shakespeare the relation between speech and speaker is certainly more complicated than in Ibsen or Chekhov, and in this sense Shakespeare is actually very close to Kabuki and Noh.

Altogether Noh, Kabuki and Shakespeare belong to the kind of theatre where language occupies the central place and where the nature of language is quite different from that in modern realistic theatre. This should be common knowledge, and I shall never understand why in the opening scene of Ninagawa's production of *The Tempest* the speeches were almost totally inaudible because of the 'thundering' sound effect or why English reviewers did not mind this. I know they did not understand Japanese, but the least a professional reviewer can do is to indicate if he or she can hear what actors say.

As many reviewers noticed, Ninagawa's productions of Shakespeare are dominated by a visual framing-device. One of the reviewers, Michael Coveney, felt 'the spectacular shipwreck' was 'worthy of Drury Lane in its Victorian heyday' (*The Financial Times*, 20 August 1988). This critic loved the whole production, but does this mean he would have also loved Victorian productions of Shakespeare with elaborate scenery which was absolutely un-Shakespearean?

Of course not all the reviewers were enthusiastic. Charles Osborne was relatively sober, and I will quote from his review at some length:

Only by reading the director's programme note in advance can one know that one is about to see a production of *The Tempest* set on the island of Sado . . . The remarkably well-equipped amateurs of Sado begin their performance with a spectacular storm at sea, and then settle down to a staging of the play which, while it cannot fail to seem exotic to an English-speaking audience, does not appear to bring any fresh insights to the play . . . Those who like their Shakespeare decked out with attractive stage pictures will enjoy this *Tempest*, as will those who automatically respond positively to Foreign Cultural Experiences . . . But anyone who regards theatre as an art form which communicates primarily by verbal means will derive little pleasure from this production unless he or she can appreciate Yushi Odashima's translation of the play. Caliban . . . is highly acrobatic, Miranda . . . and Ferdinand . . . make a pretty couple, and Goro Daimon's almost naked Stefano seems about as far from Shakespeare as one can get. The Noh-masque of Iris, Ceres, and Juno is exquisite. At no point, however, did I feel that I was watching anything remotely connected with Shakespeare's *The Tempest*. I would have much preferred to be attending an indigenous Noh play. (*The Daily Telegraph*, 20 August 1988)

This kind of response was rather exceptional, and the majority of the reviewers responded very positively indeed. They had their right to do so, but the degree of ignorance about and misunderstanding of Noh and Kabuki they exhibited was really lamentable if forgivable. After all a lot of English-language materials are easily available about these forms, and a little homework would have made them better informed and more cautious. But what is really puzzling is the way they seem to understand Shakespeare. Do they not know what kind of theatre the playwright wrote for? Have they never thought about the nature of this dramatist's language? Do they not notice the difference between Shakespeare and playwrights of modern realism? If they had not done any of these things, they would not be where they are.

So the real mystery is why they responded that way. I hate to say this, but there is little doubt that the exoticism clouded their eyes. If a Greek director, for instance, sets *The Tempest* on a Mediterranean island and fills the production with pseudo-Dionysian rituals so that the play will become more accessible to the Greek audience, will the reviewers be as impressed? What about an Irish director who sets the play in the Synge country and invests it with allusions to Celtic mythology? I very much doubt it.

I could end this essay here, but I had better mention a more recent incident as a kind of postscript. In March 1994 Yukio Ninagawa mounted an English-language production of Ibsen's *Peer Gynt* in London. It was almost unanimously panned by reviewers, many of whom had praised the same director's Shakespearean productions most extravagantly. According to one of them, Paul Taylor, the production was based on a 'questionable concept' and the critic complained about an 'over-arching design' (*The Independent*, 5 March 1994). He described it as follows:

[Ninagawa's] version begins and ends amidst the flashing electronics of a modern games parlour. Standing dreamily apart from the other machine-addicted youths, the boy who becomes Ibsen's hero is imagined as entering the world of virtual reality, sucked into the software that sends him on Peer's journey through life – a vicarious experience of truly epic proportions.

This sounds promising enough, but another of the group, Michael Billington, thought the director's 'strong framing device' did not work (*The Guardian*, 5 March 1994). He said, '. . . while I can see how, in the context of Japan, an audience needs a point-of-entry into an unfamiliar Western classic like *Peer Gynt*, the framing-device seems oddly redundant when grafted on to Frank McGuiness's highly colloquial English version'.

I cannot understand Billington's criticism, because, as the critic realises himself, 'Ninagawa has always been a great one for frames'. I really cannot see any difference between what he did this time and what he did when he directed *Macbeth* and *The Tempest*. If the Western audience does not need 'a point-of-entry' for Ibsen, it certainly would not need one for Shakespeare. Exactly when does the point-of-entry become redundant? One can either accept them both or reject them both.

There were of course some differences this time. For one thing the framing device was not exotic at all. It clashed violently against the expectation on the part of the reviewers of something distinctly Japanese. For another the production was in English, and so the reviewers were able to listen to the speeches and realised for the first time, possibly with some horror, what was really happening. What they do not seem to realise is that their criticism of Ninagawa is actually a reflection on themselves. It is both intriguing and sobering to think how difficult transplanting a work of art to a different cultural context can be. One is never free from the danger of showing oneself as essentially vulnerable even when one responds most positively.

8 Directing *King Lear* in Japanese translation

Tetsuo Anzai

When we produce Shakespeare in Japan, the first problem, as well as the most difficult, and probably the most important, is the question of translation. This I think is obvious enough, but it seems the difficulty and the importance have not necessarily been duly recognised by non-Japanese scholars or critics in discussing Japanese Shakespeare. In a sense this is only natural, for they usually do not have sufficient knowledge of Japanese, but the fact does not therefore lessen its importance. Any translation, especially that of poetry, however skilfully and scrupulously done, cannot but be a pale and feeble imitation of the original, but in the case of the Japanese translation of Shakespeare, in which the distance between the background of the original and that of the translation is linguistically, dramatically, culturally and historically so great, the difficulty is overwhelming. To put it bluntly, it is simply impossible to re-create in Japanese the power and subtlety, depth and wealth of Shakespeare's language. A Japanese director, who is bound to work with a translated text thus enfeebled, is destined to start with a desperate handicap, like a man who is, as it were, thrown into the stormy sea with both his hands tied.

To overcome this disabling handicap, one possible means we can turn to is to make the most of the visual, nonverbal resources available in the theatre: to emphasise, amplify, or even inflate the *theatrical* effects in contrast to the *dramatic* appeal, and thus to try to achieve a piece of powerful theatre in spite of the poor text. Ninagawa's Shakespeare may be regarded as one of the notable examples of such a method. This approach is certainly effective in its own way, for in trying to compensate for the feebleness of the text, it can reveal the powerful potentialities of the non-verbal dimension inherent in Shakespeare, a dimension little explored by English-speaking directors, and thus, paradoxically enough, it can lead to the success Ninagawa has enjoyed in Britain.

However, another way to solve the dilemma is not impossible. We can find, or rather we should find, a way to overcome the difficulty without prematurely losing faith in the translated text. For in the translation of dramatic texts an approach different from that to other, non-dramatic sorts of text is possible, even desirable. The text of a play is no mere verbal artifact complete in itself. Instead, it stands for the dramatic or theatrical experience embodied in it. The experience is the thing. What we have to aim at in translating a dramatic text is therefore not to translate its literal meaning but to re-create this latent theatrical experience. Once this premise is accepted, it can open up a new breakthrough. According to this criterion, it is permissible, legitimate, even imperative in some cases, to sacrifice the literal meaning. The same is true of similes, metaphors, allusions, and other rhetorical figures of speech. The crucial point is to weigh carefully what is essential to the dramatic experience and what is peripheral, and consider the differences between the linguistic, literary, dramatic and cultural background in Elizabethan England and that of modern Japan. Then, based upon these considerations, sometimes drastic adjustment must be made, so that the theatrical experience embodied in Shakespeare's text may be re-created on the modern Japanese stage with as much vividness and immediacy as is possible through translation.

However, this does not mean mere simplification, making the translation so straightforward or streamlined that the modern Japanese audience can follow it with the least resistance, as Professor Odashima's translation seems to be trying to do. What I mean is something quite different, almost opposite. Shakespeare should not be too easy to understand, and that is not simply because Shakespeare's English is archaic and hard to understand even for the English readers or audience. Neither is it merely because the enormous richness of Shakespeare's language would be lost. It is because it contradicts our basic purpose of producing Shakespeare in Japanese at all. It is not to provide the Japanese audience with a popular entertainment, easy to understand, easy to enjoy, and easy to make good box-office. It is to rediscover and experience afresh the most basic, the quintessential elements of theatre, which I believe are more powerfully represented in Shakespeare than in any other playwright. Besides, poetic expression in general is impossible without some sort of strangeness in it, a deviation from the everyday, conventional, stereotyped usage of the language, with which to awaken the reader's sensibility and imagination. Our translation therefore should not be too easy, too plain, too smooth; a certain degree of density or intensity should be retained. Of course, this is quite different from the difficulty on the level of literal meaning. Our translation should be of such a nature that the audience can grasp the literal meaning immediately, while at the same time it is dramatically dense, demanding a certain sort of alertness and receptivity on the part of the audience. And this particular kind of translation will only be possible when we firmly keep in mind the basic premise stated above: our goal is not the communication of the literal meaning of the original text, but the re-creation of the theatrical experience embodied there.

Then, how can we achieve this ideal in terms of the actual process of translation? One of the most serious disadvantages of Japanese as a vehicle for translating Shakespeare is that, while potentially highly power-ful in expressing intense emotion, it is often inadequate to the expression of logical, articulate argument or direct, decisive, forceful statement or assertion. Another weak point is its slowness. It tends to take time in saying something, especially when it comes to expressing strong emotion, with each word stressed deliberately, and with plentiful pauses between phrases. Climactic moments in Kabuki typify this characteristic, though in a somewhat exaggerated manner compared with modern plays. Speeches, words, or even syllables are drawn out almost endlessly to squeeze theatrical excitement out of the passion to the last drop, often with very long pauses full of tears. In Noh plays the prolongation of speeches is still more drastic. Here, even ordinary, straightforward dia-logues are presented in a stately, ritualistic tempo, and the important parts of a play take the form of chanting. This peculiarity of the Japanese theatrical tradition as well as the Japanese language itself can cause great difficulty in translating and producing Shakespeare in Japanese, for if we want to create a genuinely Japanese Shakespeare and not a mere imitation of English Shakespeare, we cannot afford to ignore and leave untapped our own native dramatic tradition and its rich potentialities.

It is not impossible, however, to break through the difficulty, especially in terms of tapping the potentialities inherent in the Japanese theatrical tradition. One of the most effective expedients is reinforcement by various means. For example, if simple statement is felt not to be powerful enough, we can change it to an interrogative form, for it will then be charged with more emotional value, and hence stronger dramatic impact. To take a typical example from the last scene of *King Lear*, when the king re-enters with Cordelia dead in his arms, he laments:

> Howl, howl, howl, howl! O, you are men of stones!
> Had I your tongues and eyes, I'd use them so
> That heaven's vault should crack.   (V.iii. 257–59)

My translation was as follows (I give my version re-translated back into English):

> Howl, howl, howl, howl! Are you stones? Have you no voice, no eyes?
> If you have any voice, why don't you howl so
> That heaven's vault should crack and fall?

If rendered literally, keeping the grammatical form of the original unchanged, the simple, direct, declarative address forms, 'you are men of stones' and 'I'd use them . . .', would not be arresting enough. Because of the disadvantages of Japanese mentioned above, that is, its inadequacy in direct, forceful assertion, the translation would sound neutral, abstract, definitely falling short of the painfully immediate, powerful appeal of the original. To retain its poignant effect, the change into an interrogative form seemed inevitable.

Another possible means of reinforcement is the repetition of words and phrases, one of the favourite techniques in traditional Japanese theatre for intensifying expression. In the lines immediately following the quotation above, Lear continues:

> She's gone for ever.
> I know when one is dead, and when one lives;
> She's dead as earth.   (V.iii. 259–61)

I translated these lines thus:

> She's dead.
> She's dead. Dead and still as earth.

True, my version is a simplification of the original, but to keep the overwhelming effect of the original unimpaired in translation, simplification, as well as judicious deletion or compression, may sometimes be unavoidable. This may sound too drastic, too daring, even sacrilegious, but in some cases, especially in such an intense scene, it is none the less advisable to discern what is truly essential in speeches and to delete, of course discriminatingly, less essential elements, so that the translated text may retain a dramatic impact equivalent to the original. And in this particular instance, the simple repetition of 'dead' three times proved to be highly effective in our own production of the play, at least partly because, I believe, it was reminiscent of one of the favourite techniques in our native theatrical tradition.

Interestingly, this technique is also employed quite conspicuously throughout the last scene of *King Lear*, especially in Lear's speeches. It has already appeared in the repetition of 'howl' in the above quotation, but this is by no means the only instance. It recurs time and again in Lear's later speeches: 'Cordelia, Cordelia! stay a little' (271), 'No, no, no life!' (305), 'Never, never, never, never, never' (308), and lastly in his dying words, 'Look on her. Look, her lips, / Look there, look there!' (310–11). The fact might suggest that the distance between Shakespeare and the traditional Japanese theatre is not so inhibitingly great as is generally supposed, at least in scenes of the highest emotional intensity.

For the sake of reinforcement of translation we can also make effective use of the most widely prevalent verse form in Japanese poetry, whether dramatic or lyrical: the syllabic pattern of 5 and 7 or 7 and 5, which is an almost exact counterpart of iambic pentameter in English poetry. A familiar example will be the syllabic pattern of 5–7–5 in *haiku* and that of 5–7–5–7–7 in *tanka* or *waka*. To draw upon this metrical rhythm and its emotionally evocative potentiality often proves to be effectual. Although my translation is all apparently done in prose (as is the case with virtually all past Japanese translations of Shakespeare), I have intentionally introduced this metrical pattern, especially in such intense scenes as this, though not with too rigid, or obvious a regularity, which would give an impression of artificiality. The syllabic pattern of my version of the passage quoted above ('Howl, howl . . . She's dead as earth') is 6–7–7–7/ 7–7–8/ 5–7–7/ 8–7. This latent metrical pattern, I anticipated, would create an underlying rhythm sustained throughout, thus offering a basis upon which an actor, in delivering the lines, could build up a surge of passion, equivalent to the effect we experience in the most intense scenes of Kabuki or Bunraku.

Still another sort of reinforcement is possible by availing ourselves of yet another aspect of the assets accumulated and handed down in our theatrical tradition: that is, the technique of retrospective narration. The point is, however, rather difficult to explain in abstract terms; it is advisable to describe it by giving a specific example. The instance I choose is one of Gloucester's speeches in Act IV, scene i, where Gloucester, immediately after having had his eyes ruthlessly plucked out by Cornwall, comes onto the stage led by an Old Man, and meets Edgar in the disguise of a mad and naked beggar, without knowing the beggar is in fact his own son:

> I' th' last night's storm I such a fellow saw;
> Which made me think a man a worm. My son
> Came then into my mind; and yet my mind
> Was then scarce friends with him. I have heard more since.
> As flies to wanton boys are we to th' gods –
> They kill us for their sport.   (IV.i. 33–38)

According to the conventional definition, the essence of the dramatic lies in the impassioned conflict between two antagonistic characters or the causes they represent. By this definition Gloucester's speech above is hardly 'dramatic', for there can be no conflict of the kind here. And yet the speech had in fact an overwhelming impact on the stage, at least in our production of the play. The secret is, I believe, in the fact that the speech, though brief, takes the form of narration, and that the form is a technique of central importance in the traditional Japanese theatre, especially in Kabuki and Bunraku. In those dramas the climactic moments often take the form of the protagonist's retrospective narration of his past experiences in which he discovers the true meaning of those experiences. Nothing new happens now in terms of incidents; all the incidents have already taken place. What remains to be done is to explore in retrospect the deep layers of meaning of all the incidents hitherto presented in the play, and thus to reveal to the audience the overall significance of the experiences they have till now witnessed on the stage.

This particular type of narration is not necesarily peculiar to Kabuki or Bunraku; neither is Gloucester's speech an exceptional instance in Shakespeare. In fact it is fairly common in Shakespeare as well as in Kabuki or Bunraku. An obvious example is Othello's final speech, 'I pray you, in your letters, / When you shall these unlucky deeds relate, / Speak of me as I am . . .' (IV.ii. 343ff.), in which he recounts his whole life as 'one that lov'd not wisely, but too well; / One not easily jealous, but, being wrought, / Perplexed in th' extreme'. Similar examples are by no means hard to find: Horatio's request to Fortinbras to let him 'speak to th' yet unknowing world / How these things came about . . . Of carnal, bloody, and unnatural acts; . . . Of deaths put on by cunning and forc'd cause;/ And, in this upshot, purposes mistook / Fall'n on th' inventors' heads' (*Hamlet*, V.ii. 371ff.), or Friar Lawrence's similar account of all the main incidents in the play (*Romeo and Juliet*, V.iii. 228ff.) to show how 'A greater power than we can contradict / Hath thwarted our intents' (153–4). These are no mere redundant summaries of the plot; they in fact form moments of crystallisation of the total meaning of the play, moments of dramatic consummation.

Neither is it peculiar to the final scene of tragedy; a similarly revealing type of retrospective narration often appears in the course of the play. Generally speaking, Shakespeare's plays are constructed by an alternation of two functionally different kinds of scenes: those fast-moving scenes, the main purpose of which is to give information to the audience and drive the plot forward, and those scenes which constitute so to speak still points in the forward movement of the plot, and which explore retrospectively the deeper meaning of the experiences presented up till then. The retrospective, self-searching narration I have been discussing usually appears in this latter type of scene, and often forms its crucial part. The scene now in question, the Act IV scene i of *King Lear*, is a typical example of such a scene, and Gloucester's speech quoted above is a typical instance of such a speech.

While translating this scene, I was not yet fully aware of these points. What I had in mind was simply how to keep the scene intense enough, how to find a style truly appealing, so that every word uttered by the actors, even every breath of theirs, might have the utmost impact upon the audience, as if driving a nail home. For that purpose one of the specific means I only half-consciously turned to was a style of diction reminiscent of the traditional Japanese theatre, Bunraku in particular, upon the basis of the metrical pattern of 5 and 7 discussed above. Not that I directly borrowed words or phrases, or made any specific allusions. What I tried to do was to create a pervading overtone vaguely but hauntingly suggestive of the theatrical experience we have in Bunraku at moments of the highest intensity. Then, while rehearsing the scene and, in close collaboration with the actors, striving hard to discover a genuine, convincing expression, I suddenly realised that the experience we were struggling to create on the stage was essentially the same experience as we have in the climactic, self-searching, revealing narration in Bunraku and Kabuki. This realisation was a decisive turning point in our quest for the authentic Japanese Shakespeare, immediately appealing to our innate theatrical sensibility and imagination. What we were searching for was in fact to achieve the perfect fusion or amalgamation of Shakespeare and our theatrical tradition on the most basic level, and through such fusion to rediscover and create afresh the quintessential, archetypal expressiveness of theatre on our own stage.

Our discussion has already moved onto our second topic, the question of staging and the general style of production. I will keep to *King Lear* as an example and analyse my production of the play in some detail, for in this particular production our fundamental aim, the fusion of Shakespeare and the Japanese theatrical tradition, was, at least to my mind, more successfully achieved than in any of the other Shakespeare productions I have directed. It was presented by Theatre Group En in 1985 at Stage En, a little theatre of our own in the Shinjuku district of Tokyo, with Noboru Nakaya in the title role, Masahiko Arima as Gloucester, Isao Hashizume as the Fool, and Sokyu Fujita as Edgar. The production was revived in 1989 with a slightly different cast, and went on tour from '89 to '90.

The venue, Stage En, was a disused iron-works converted to a little theatre, with a seating capacity of 150, or at most 200. The floor was flat, so that we could arrange the stage and the seats in any position or shape we liked. Taking advantage of this to the full, we set out the theatre in such a way that we could reproduce all the essential features both of an Elizabethan theatre and of the theatres of Noh and Kabuki. In the first place, we constructed a thrust stage, of almost exactly the same dimensions as a Noh stage (about 5 metres square), with the seats surrounding it on three sides. The seats were arranged in five to seven rows, sloping downwards towards the stage, as in an ancient Greek theatre, though ours were not set out in a semi-circular form but in a square, and of course the space was much smaller in size – the distance between the foremost row of seats and the stage was only a few feet. We then made an opening for entrance and exit, with curtains, at the centre of the back wall of the stage.

In addition we prepared two more entrances, a sort of corridor, leading from down-stage corners, both right and left, and running through the seats, which would serve as a functional counterpart of the *hanamichi* in a Kabuki theatre (a bridgeway that runs from the stage through the auditorium to the farthest end of the theatre). We were not able to build an upper stage as in an Elizabethan playhouse, for the ceiling of our tiny theatre was not high enough, but we found, at least in producing *King Lear*, we could dispense with it without any serious disadvantage.

What really matters is, however, not so much the physical shape of the stage as its artistic or conceptual implications. A thrust stage presupposes an idea of drama significantly different from that of the modern stage closed in by a proscenium arch: an idea of drama, not as a mimetic representation of everyday reality, but as the presentation of something mythical, the visitation of something beyond life, the revelation of something that gives meaning and order to life. Another important corollary of this particular form of stage is the more active, immediate involvement of the audience, so that they are by no means passive onlookers of a fictional action but the witnesses of, even participants in, the visitation or revelation.

In the case of Noh all this is fairly obvious, with its origins in Shamanistic rites of calling down spirits and communicating with them. The central action of a Noh play usually consists of the visitation of the ghost of a dead soul, and its crucial moment comes when the spirit emerges onto the stage in the form of the protagonist (*shite*). The *waki*, the secondary character, often in the figure of a Buddhist priest, derives his function as invocator from a Shamanist priest, and plays the role of an intermediary agent between the *shite* and the audience. Furthermore the chorus, led by the *waki*, serves, as in the Greek tragedy, as representative of the audience, inviting them to participate vicariously in the action, and interpreting its meaning to them. In Kabuki or Bunraku, which represent a more secularised form of drama, such ritualistic characteristics may be less apparent, but here we have the *hanamichi* (the bridgeway), which powerfully heightens the active involvement of the audience. The entrance and exit through the *hanamichi* is often effectively employed to introduce or round off a particularly striking sequence of events, while the actors, giving particularly arresting performances on it, elicit excited responses from the audience. The bridgeway runs right through the auditorium, and all this action takes place in the midst of the audience. The whole presentation of a Kabuki play thus takes on the nature of a communal festivity or ritual, still persistently, if not obviously, reminiscent of the ritualistic origins of the theatre.

In the Elizabethan theatre such vestiges may not be so apparent as in

Noh, but perhaps a little more evident than in Kabuki. For example, the Elizabethan theatre represents the stage as the earth, this world, existing between 'heaven' (the ceiling above) and 'hell' (the pit below), the physical structure of the stage as a whole thus standing symbolically for the cosmos, the theatre of the world. And this was not merely a static set of symbols; they were dynamically employed in actual staging – for instance, in the entrance of Jupiter from above descending on an eagle's back in *Cymbeline* (V.iv), or the repeated cries of the Ghost from beneath in *Hamlet* (I.v). A more conspicuous example, this time from Marlowe, is the descent of a golden throne from 'heaven' above and the sulphurous smoke emitted from the mouth of 'hell' in *Doctor Faustus* (scene xiv), visibly symbolising the heavenly bliss Faustus has lost for ever and the agony of hell his soul has to go through from now on.

Another feature of staging in the Elizabethan theatre particularly significant in this connection is the technique of 'discovery', the disclosing of a character or characters hidden in the inner stage by opening the door or drawing the curtains, as when Prospero 'discovers' Ferdinand and Miranda playing at chess in the cave (*The Tempest*, V.i). But here I want to extend the meaning of the term a little further, to include any abrupt, unexpected entrance such as the entrance of the blinded Gloucester led by an Old Man, or Lear's last entrance with the dead Cordelia in his arms. We can readily add further examples out of *King Lear*: the naked Edgar in the disguise of a mad beggar running out from a hovel in the storm (III.iv), and the appearance of the mad Lear, with a wreath of wild flowers on his head, to Gloucester and Edgar in the field near Dover (IV.vi). These scenes do not chiefly serve to drive the plot forward. Instead, their main purpose is, as has already been suggested, to explore the deeper meaning of past developments, and the 'discovery' in each of them marks the moment of this deepened recognition. Indeed these scenes reach their culmination in lines which attest each step in an ever-deepening revelation of the mystery of the world: 'unaccommodated man is no more but such a poor, bare, forked animal' (Lear in the hovel scene, III.iv.109–110), 'As flies to wanton boys, are we to th' gods' (Gloucester, IV.i.37), 'When we are born, we cry that we are come / To this great stage of fools' (Lear in the field near Dover, IV.vi.183–4), and 'Is this the promis'd end? / Or image of that horror?' (Kent and Edgar in the final scene, V.iii.263–4).

We may therefore justly argue that these 'discoveries' betoken moments of revelation, and that in this sense they embody the same basic idea of drama-as-revelation as represented by Noh plays, and to a lesser extent by Kabuki or Bunraku. Besides, we have to remember that all of the speeches quoted, except the last one, belong to that particular type of retrospective, self-searching, revealing narration which, as we have already suggested, often forms climactic moments in Shakespeare as well as in Kabuki and Bunraku. That is to say, what we have observed about this type of narration and what we have noted of 'discoveries' in fact converge; they are the two sides of the same coin, two different manifestations of the same basic idea. It is I hope now reasonably clear that Shakespeare and the traditional Japanese drama share some important common qualities in their fundamental conception and dramaturgy.

To return to the physical structure of a stage and its implications, the stage we prepared for the production of *Lear* could not afford to have its own 'heaven' or 'hell'. However, to recapture the symbolic dimension of the stage as the earth in an Elizabethan playhouse, we painted on the stage, though not very distinctly, the simplified outline of Britain, suggesting first the kingdom Lear divides among his daughters, but more significantly the earth or the world itself, 'this great stage' to which, when we are born, we come crying. And the opening we provided for entrance through the back wall enabled us to make the most of the 'discoveries', to accentuate the revelational effects of this particular kind of entrance. The effects were tangibly heightened by the thrust structure of the stage, for the very position of the opening at the up-stage centre formed the inevitable focus of the audience's intent gaze. In short, with all these physical arrangements of the stage, the entrance ways and the seats, as explained above, we hoped to combine all the essential structures shared in common by the Shakespearean theatre and the traditional Japanese theatre, and explore and realise the symbolic potentialities inherent there. In other words, we tried to achieve the fusion or amalgamation of the two theatrical traditions on the level of stage structure and staging, just as we tried to attain the same sort of fusion in translating the text.

Of course I am not in a position to judge the results, to tell whether, or how far, our attempts proved successful. The only thing I can do here is to report the effects actually produced on me as objectively as possible. One of the results I found most rewarding was the extraordinary effect the 'discovery' entrance brought about on this particular form of stage. At the moment, for instance, at which the curtains of the central door were sharply pulled apart, discovering the standing figure of the blinded Gloucester, who had had his eyes ruthlessly plucked out on the same stage only a few minutes before, the impact was enormous. If we imagine that Gloucester had merely plodded onto the stage from the wings, we can easily see how incomparably great the difference was. In the 'discovery' entrance Gloucester was revealed in a flash, frontally, face to face with the audience, forming a powerful tableau, a living emblem of the absurd atrocity inflicted on humanity. In the next moments, Gloucester, in a loose gown vaguely resembling a traditional Noh costume, with a

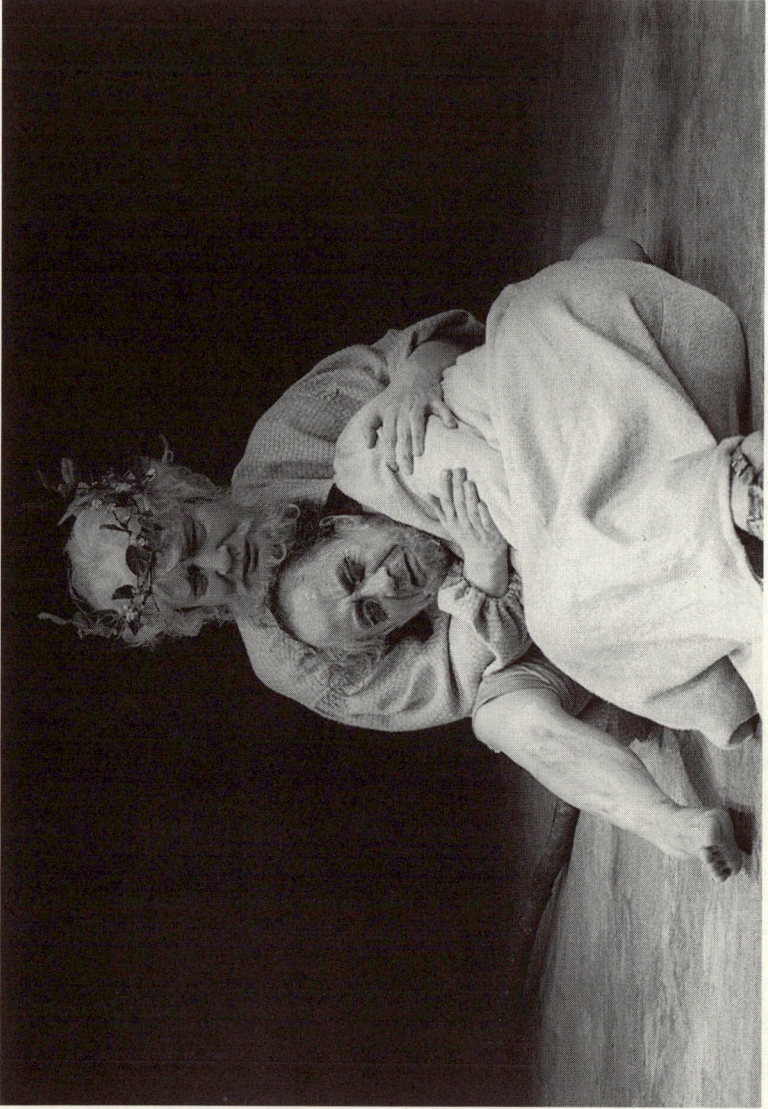

11. *King Lear*, IV.vi. Noboru Nakaya as Lear and Masahiko Arima as Gloucester.

12. *King Lear*, V.iii. Noboru Nakaya as Lear, Jun Karasawa as Cordelia.

long staff formed from the branch of a tree as high as his shoulder, and with his other hand held by the Old Man, slowly, very slowly walked forward a few steps. Edgar, all but naked except for a soiled loin cloth, covered all over with mud and scratches, lay prostrate at the opposite end of the stage, or rather between the foremost row of the seats and the edge of the stage. Seeing the mutilated figure of his father, he groaned, 'My father, O that figure!' He was now, just like the *waki* in a Noh play, representative of the audience breathlessly watching the eyeless figure of Gloucester. Then Gloucester, led by the Old Man, reached the very centre of the stage, walking onto the dim image of the earth painted there, and uttered the key lines of the scene: 'As flies to wanton boys are we to th' gods . . .' I made the lighting of the scene dazzlingly bright, up to the utmost brightness possible within the electrical capacity of the theatre, to make it seem as if this harshly blazing light were the merciless gaze of the gods looking down from above – in other words, I intended this lighting to be a counterpart of the 'heaven' of an Elizabethan stage. Moreover, the light, in this tiny theatre, naturally overflowed profusely over the audience, thus drawing them forcefully into the action on stage. They were now under the same 'heaven', exposed to the same ruthless gaze of the gods. They no longer could remain mere onlookers; they could not but be participants in Gloucester's agony, involved recipients of a revelation of the cruel mystery of the world.

In another 'discovery' scene, where the mad Lear makes his abrupt entrance with a wreath of wild flowers, this sense of participation was even more compelling. After Gloucester's futile attempt to kill himself, and after he is saved by Edgar in what he calls 'a miracle', the transformed figure of the king is 'discovered'. In his following speeches archetypal, almost apocalyptic images of depraved humanity are mercilessly piled up one after another. Then come the crucial lines. Lear, as if suddenly recovering his right mind, says to Gloucester, who is prostrate by his master, crying like a helpless baby:

> If thou wilt weep my fortunes, take my eyes.
> I know thee well enough; thy name is Gloucester.
> Thou must be patient; we came crying hither.
> Thou know'st the first time that we smell the air
> We waul and cry. I will preach to thee. Mark . . .
> When we are born, we cry that we are come
> To this great stage of fools.   (IV.vi. 177–83)

Here again we made the lighting dazzling from 'heaven' above, while on the stage the 'earth' remained painted. This actual stage of ours was then 'this great stage' of the world, between heaven and earth. And it was not only Gloucester who was listening to Lear's words, or Edgar lying flat beside his father, also crying. The audience too was now the congregation listening breathlessly to Lear's preaching. We all shared the same vision revealed in his utterances. At this moment what we were experiencing was *the* theatre. It was no longer an old play, written four centuries before, on the other side of the globe, translated into another language. There was no longer any distinction between Shakespeare and a Japanese play. Simply, it was *the* theatre, the theatre reduced to the ultimate.

I have been discussing the possibility of fusing Shakespeare and the Japanese dramatic tradition. What I have been arguing, however, is not that we can achieve this by arbitrarily adapting the style of Kabuki or Noh to our production of Shakespeare, or by exploiting this or that particular technique or convention already established in Kabuki or Noh. Such an approach will produce only a curious mongrel or hybrid, at best a piece of clever pastiche. Neither do I mean a simplistic 'Japanisation' of Shakespeare, presenting his plays in a Japanese setting and Japanese costume, whether modern or medieval.

I do not believe either that a self-consciously, self-assertively Japanese interpretation will lead to a truly creative result. If we want to create the authentic Japanese Shakespeare, we should go much deeper than that, and search for the fountainhead of particular conventions or styles. We have to dig deep enough to reach the underground stream of our dramatic sensibility and imagination running unseen through established tradition, and tap the great reservoir of its potentiality afresh.

The principal purpose of our producing Shakespeare in Japan is, in the last analysis, to rediscover what is truly essential in drama, what is the ultimate in the theatre. If we want to realise this purpose, we have first to re-examine what is truly essential and ultimate in Shakespeare as well as in our own theatrical tradition. It is only then that the meaningful fusion of the two is at all possible.

Part 2

Shakespeare and the traditional Japanese stage

9 Preface to the Japanese translation of *Renaissance Self-Fashioning*

Stephen Greenblatt

In a remarkable plenary address delivered in August, 1991 at the World Shakespeare Congress in Tokyo, and reprinted in revised form in this book (pp. 145–58 *below*), Professor Takashi Sasayama undertook to compare Monzaemon Chikamatsu with Shakespeare. Acutely aware of the perils that beset such cross-cultural enterprises – the empty enumeration of meaningless parallels, the loss of specificity in a tangle of woolly generalities – Sasayama suggested that beneath the many apparent similarities between the work of the two great dramatists, there lie deep differences. Even if one can identify certain emotions common to the two theatrical traditions – grief, desire, anger, pathos, exaltation, and so forth – and even if these emotions are aroused by strikingly similar plot devices, their significance depends upon their place within divergent aesthetic structures that in turn operate within radically divergent cultural systems. Hence, Sasayama observed, the pity and fear aroused by Chikamatsu are not organised around a powerful, overarching moral judgement, as they would be in Shakespeare, but remain to be savoured by the audience, enjoyed independently of the awareness of sin, punishment, and redemption that shapes the Christian discourse of the late sixteenth century. For the Japanese audience, 'feelings are given a free hand to liberate themselves from moral contexts, so that they may contribute to the emotional rhythms of the scenes which are designed for aesthetic pleasure'. For the Elizabethan audience, by contrast, feelings are tightly woven into a vision of the fate of the individual, a fate inseparable from the psychological and moral depths of his character and the cumulative force of his actions.

It might be possible to question Sasayama's strong insistence on moral judgements in Shakespeare – many of the plays seem to complicate such judgements to the point where they are virtually suspended – but not his sense that feelings in Shakespeare are bound together, organised, and integrated in remarkably intense and insistent structures: what we might call the structures of the fashioned self. Feelings in Shakespeare, and more especially in the tragedies, are not readily detachable from characters; it is difficult for the audience to savour them as discrete entities, to enjoy them as aesthetic experiences independent of powerful individuals whose claim on reality seems, for the duration of the play, as great as our own. We come to know not melancholy, jealousy, and despair, but Hamlet's melancholy, Othello's jealousy, and Macbeth's despair. Shakespeare's use of passion as a principle of individuation and of speech as an expression of deep inwardness serves to bind emotions to particular imagined and embodied selves and gives his drama, and the Western theatre since the Renaissance, its distinctive quality.

Renaissance Self-Fashioning originated in a fascination with such selves – the intense, irreducible individuals who not only are memorably represented in Shakespeare's theatre but also seem to leap out from the historical records of his age. In an earlier book, *Sir Walter Ralegh: The Renaissance Man and his Roles*, I had analysed the life of the celebrated courtier and adventurer from the perspective of role-playing: from the time he had first caught the attention of Queen Elizabeth to the moment he stretched out his neck for the executioner's axe, Ralegh lived his life as if he were improvising a part on stage. I wrote as if this theatrical mode of existence – an identity established in and as performance – were Ralegh's special achievement, and in some sense it was. But I also acknowledged that this achievement depended upon a complex cultural system already in place, and in *Renaissance Self-Fashioning* I set out to try to decode that system. I wanted to know how it was possible for Ralegh, or anyone else in Renaissance England, to experience his identity as something that could be invented, shaped, and deployed, how it was possible to feel that selfhood was not given – determined by parents, profession, religious faith, or simply fate – but invented.

My concerns extended well beyond the boundaries of art: influenced by Clifford Geertz's brilliant meditations on ethnography, *The Interpretation of Cultures*, I saw my inquiry as involving the dense network of constraints and entitlements within which the self was fashioned. But I also saw literature as central, and this for two reasons beyond my own training and pleasure. First, identity of the type I wished to study was principally shaped and displayed in language – it was a rhetorical performance – and, as the career of Ralegh attested, this performance was at its height in poetry. Second, works of art were the crucibles in which imaginary identities were not only fashioned but also tested, challenged, disassembled and reassembled. Literature served as a laboratory in which processes that elsewhere could only be seen through a glass darkly could be seen face to face.

What I observed in this laboratory was not only the triumphant affirmation of life lived as performance. On the contrary, the more I studied Renaissance self-fashioning, in literature and in life, the more it appeared riven by contradictions, conflicts, and intimations of loss. These rifts in the smooth surface of the performance seemed to me to constitute not the negative limits of self-fashioning but the root conditions of its existence. And I felt that I was looking too at the conditions for a mode of identity that had survived the Renaissance and had served as a model in Europe and America to the present day.

For in this book, as in everything I have written, the pressures of the present were registered in my vision of the past. *Renaissance Self-Fashioning* was written in the general context of the American ethos of the self-made man, and it is marked as well by more topical concerns: for example, the story of the armed Englishmen who burn a poor village in Sierra Leone in 1586, which I use to lead into an analysis of Marlowe, conjures up as well images of American soldiers setting fire to Vietnamese huts, images that haunted the United States in the 1970s. This contemporary context does not mean that my book was intended as an allegory; I was and remain committed to a scholarly and truthful account of Renaissance England. But scholarship and passion are not, as is sometimes mistakenly thought, incompatible, and the sources of my passion lay in the twentieth century.

If the self-fashioning of sixteenth-century Englishmen fascinated me in part because of its filiations with the ideology of the self-made man, so too my sense of the costs of this self- fashioning, its tensions, bad faith, and tragic contradictions, was linked to a growing scepticism about self-making in my own culture. In this scepticism I was obviously not alone; like many American intellectuals whose world-view had been deeply shaken by the Vietnam War, I was powerfully influenced by the radical critiques of Western cultural values mounted by such figures as Marcuse, Althusser, Lacan, Foucault, and Barthes.

These critiques often involved an attempt to look elsewhere for alternative models. When Roland Barthes wished to attack the dramatic tradition of the West since the Renaissance, when he sought an alternative to its essential spirit and to the cultural values that underlay that spirit, he turned in *The Empire of Signs* to Japan – at least to the Japan of his imagination – and more particularly to Bunraku. For Barthes, in an interpretation that anticipates certain elements of Sasayama's analysis of Chikamatsu, Bunraku 'abolishes the metaphysical link the West cannot help establishing between body and soul, cause and effect, motor and machine, agent and actor, Destiny and man, God and creature'. It abolishes then the very condition for the Western self which has been constructed, as both Classical and Renaissance moralists understood, around the principle of inward agency, a consciousness hidden deep within the envelope of the flesh, an interior capacity to reflect and to improvise. In the puppet theatre by contrast, Barthes observes, 'the *inside* no longer commands the *outside*'.

Renaissance Self-Fashioning bears traces of this desire to escape from the deep structures of Western selfhood – it begins, after all, with the most famous dream of such an escape, More's *Utopia*, and it ends with Shakespeare's vision of an 'extravagant and wheeling stranger' – but at the same time it never welcomes the abolition that Barthes longs for. The Western theatrical tradition that seemed to Barthes an unredeemable lie seemed to me, at least in the works of Marlowe and Shakespeare, beautiful and enduring. And for all of the deep flaws in the lives I studied, I was, and I still am, far too committed to the Western model of the performing self in the theatre of the world to be able to embrace any of the proferred cultural alternatives, real or imagined.

10   Tragedy and emotion: Shakespeare and Chikamatsu

Takashi Sasayama

Many attempts have been made by scholars and critics of drama in Japan since the Meiji era to compare Monzaemon Chikamatsu (1653–1724) – the greatest figure of the classical popular theatre of Japan – with Shakespeare. The aim of the comparison has often been to gain recognition for Chikamatsu in the world of theatre as a national playwright analogous to Shakespeare in Britain. The result is that Chikamatsu's plays have been ransacked for likenesses to those of Shakespeare in details of plot and characterisation as well as feelings expressed. But very rarely has there been awareness of the differences lying beneath these apparent resemblances, which arise from different cultural contexts.[1]

Among the most notorious of these attempts was the case of a professor of English in Tokyo who in a fit of jingoistic zeal after the first World War, wrote a long literary comparison between Shakespeare and Chikamatsu in Japanese, in which he claimed to have clarified similarities, pseudo-similarities or at least negative similarities between them under no less than twenty-five heads.[2] Like his miserable translation of Chikamatsu's plays published in London in 1926,[3] the essay is too shallow, too meagre in substance to deserve comment here. It only intrigues me to find that the last chapter of this high-spirited treatise is written in a somewhat lugubrious tone. The author here tries to catalogue the heavy handicaps under which the Japanese playwright had to work in an intellectual milieu dominated by rigid conformism with the feudalistic rules of conduct and the established principles of literary rhetoric based on Chinese classics. The essay concludes with words of keen chagrin: 'If only Chikamatsu's genius had been given scope in the cultural climate in which Shakespeare breathed so freely.'[4] Nothing shows more tangibly than this the self-evident truth that naive comparativism necessarily denies its own *raison d'être* once it makes itself open to a historical perspective.

I do not mention this early Japanese attempt at comparative drama as a mere subject of ridicule; nor am I inclined to cry out complacently, 'East is East, and West is West, and never the twain shall meet'. I only want to warn myself against the danger of succumbing to the lure of the romantic idea that two literatures or dramas far removed in time and space, have, unknown to each other, walked on a common path. It is true that analogues of certain elements of a literary creation in one cultural area are often found in the literature of a different area with quite different cultural traditions. One could pick up a couple of popular plays from among 100 attributed to Chikamatsu and say, 'Here are themes and motifs that are common to Euripides and Shakespeare.' This, however, requires close scrutiny, and I should like to look into the matter in concrete terms.

For an illustrative example I will take *Kagekiyo Victorious*,[5] a tragical history in five acts, which Chikamatsu wrote for Bunraku in *c.* 1685. Resemblances between *Kagekiyo Victorious* and Western drama may be discovered on two levels of the action. The main plot revolves around Kagekiyo, the defeated warrior, seeking revenge on the patriarchal ruler of the enemy clan. There is something about the sinister figure of this vindictive hero which reminds us of Hieronimo or Titus Andronicus or even Hamlet. The subplot centres on a complication between the hero and his courtesan-wife, who, after giving him refuge and comfort, is driven by violent jealousy of the noble lady he is going to make his official wife to betray him and reveal his whereabouts to his enemy. Regretting her action immediately afterwards, the courtesan-wife returns to him in prison, craving his forgiveness. Kagekiyo turns her down; he even refuses to recognise her two sons as his own, whereupon she kills the boys before his eyes and then stabs herself. The intensity of passion in this tragic woman who 'loved not wisely but too well' mighty be associated with that of Medea, while the noble stubbornness the hero's legal wife shows when she resolutely refuses to submit under the severest torture has some likenesses to the stoic perseverance of certain heroines of John Ford's tragedies. It is also noteworthy that the hero, Kagekiyo, is an active agent of his fate and that the whole dramatic action depends upon his indomitable will to revenge, so that there is a unity of action in the Aristotelian sense, and all the melodramatic incidents and situations concerning his two mutually antagonistic wives are to be regarded as 'episodes' as they are defined in the *Poetics*.

This, however, does not clinch the argument. The problem starts here. With all those apparent similarities in the component parts of the drama, *Kagekiyo Victorious* creates for us a totally different impression from any European play. This is not, as we tend to think, because of its extravagant finale in which through the *deus ex machina*-like intervention of Kwannon, the Goddess of Mercy, the head of the executed hero is replaced by that of her statue, or because, having been reconciled to his mortal enemy, Kagekiyo plucks out his eyes to become absolved of his obsessive vindictive desire. We know very well that theatre audiences can

Plate 9 Banquo and Macbeth 'on horseback' behind the Butsudan screen which separated an inner stage area from the forestage in Ninagawa's production of *Macbeth*.

Plate 10 Komaki Kurihara as Lady Macbeth in Ninagawa's production of *Macbeth*.

Plate 11 Samisen player and narrator on the Bunraku stage, National Bunraku Theatre, Osaka.

Plate 12 Puppets and manipulators on the Bunraku stage, National Bunraku Theatre, Osaka.

always wink at the inorganic functional outer framework of narrative once they have set their minds on having a meaningful experience of the drama proper *within* the framework.

It seems to me that the difference of impression has more to do with the difference of emotions aroused in scenes with seemingly analogous narrative contents. For instance, if the agony of jealousy in Chikamatsu's courtesan affects us, it is not in the same manner as does the passion of Medea. The proud defiance and abysmal hatred that make Medea's appearance in the open air after the bloody murder of her children such a horrifying and yet moving spectacle in the Greek tragedy are quite out of the reach of a lady of pleasure in medieval Japan. Her atrocity to her own sons as well as to herself seems to be neither a form of protest nor even an act of despair. It is rather a submissive gesture, reconciling herself to responsibility for the sin of betrayal of her husband and lord.

The case is nearly the same with the theme of revenge, which is more closely connected with society's ethical foundations. With God's pronouncement 'Vindicta mihi' ringing in the public's ears, revenge never ceased to be a moral issue having eschatological implications for the Elizabethans. No wonder revenge tragedies in Renaissance England from *The Spanish Tragedy* down to *'Tis Pity She's a Whore* and *The Cardinal* were more or less revenger's tragedies. Chikamatsu's revenge tragedies are also, nearly without exception, revenger's tragedies, but in quite a different sense. To the Japanese in Chikamatsu's age, revenge was nothing less than a sacred duty, the neglect of which had to be subjected to strict censure in the name of society. In most cases revengers were prompted to vindictive actions either by a samurai-like ideal of honour or a citizen-like sense of obligation or moral debt to one's masters or feudal lords. In a number of Chikamatsu's revenge tragedies, the plot so evolves that a husband whose devoted wife succumbs to temptation during his absence, and commits adultery, is forced to go on a long journey for honourable revenge and to kill his repentant wife as well as her seducer, often with the help of her brother or even her own father. These ill-starred 'women killed with *un*kindness' may indeed resemble some of those pathetic female figures who appear in the domestic tragedies and tragicomedies of Thomas Heywood and Thomas Dekker. But the fundamental difference between the two is that no moral consciousness either of sin or punishment is required of the audience of Chikamatsu. In fact, pity and fear are aroused, but they do not function as means for achieving catharsis, but remain submerged in the deeper layers of the audience's mind as emotions to be enjoyed independently of the moral implications of the tragic act.

Such is also the case with the murder of one's own children. Westerners interested in classical Japanese theatre are often perplexed when they see fathers, or even mothers, driven by various senses of duty and obligation, attack their children with daggers. In some cases the cruelty is committed by the parent in order to sacrifice his or her son as a substitute for the young heir of his feudal lord when there is a plot against the prince's life. In other cases like *Kagekiyo Victorious* the parent's slaughter of his or her children is just an act (or even a gesture) of atonement for the guilty and dishonourable deeds perpetrated by him- or herself against the patriarch of his or her family or clan. Chikamatsu wrote some such scenes, and no one can deny that they are moving. But here also feelings are given a free hand to liberate themselves from moral contexts, so that they may contribute to the emotional rhythms of scenes that are designed for aesthetic pleasure.

All these considerations lead us to realise the difficulties that beset our endeavours to draw direct comparison between the two dramatists, each with his own cultural tradition. Being at a loss to find an effective means of dealing with these difficulties, we are driven to doubt even the validity of the endeavours themselves. But are there other ways, we may ask, for us to compare Shakespeare and Chikamatsu so that one may illuminate the other on a level other than the superficial? It seems to me that audience response offers one such possibility.

Instead of looking for coincidences or correspondences between Shakespeare and Chikamatsu to be substantiated in general theoretical terms, I am more inclined to look into myself, or into the audience mind within myself, to see if there is any common factor in my response to each of the two dramatists. However, with a view to treating the subject as objectively as possible, I will start by asking in a general way how one's long-term familiarity with Chikamatsu affects one's reception of Shakespeare. Or it might be more appropriate to ask if it is likely that a theatre-goer whose theatrical experience has been limited to Chikamatsu's work will find anything in Shakespeare that strikes him as familiar. Actually, this is an extremely conceptual question capable of vast expansion, and in answering it in the concrete one is naturally obliged to confine oneself to a few material points. As for myself, I should like to set a framework for my discussion by concentrating on two of Chikamatsu's most popular love tragedies, *The Love Suicides at Sonezaki* and *The Love Suicides at Amijima*, representing respectively the earlier and later phases of his craftsmanship as a Bunraku playwright.

Bunraku, a common appellation for *Ningyo-Joruri*, is a genre of puppet theatre in which mute puppets of about half human size gesticulate behind a platform spanning the entire stage, each puppet being held against his chest by a puppeteer in ceremonious clothes. (Puppets in major roles are handled each by a master manipulator and two assistants in black gowns pulled over their heads.) On a dais on the left wing of the stage are seated several *tayus* or chanters who, while narrating the story of the play, declaim the speeches of the puppet characters, accompanied by the twanging of the *shamisens* played by musicians sitting beside them. Their narration includes descriptions of the scenery of the location, and the facial expressions and bodily movements, or even the psychology, of the puppet characters. Furthermore, scattered over the play, but most frequently at the beginning of a scene, are a number of lyric interludes of intricate poetic tissue. These characteristics of the language in Bunraku can partly be accounted for in terms of literary evolution. Bunraku originated in popular medieval narrative histories and moralities which were recited and chanted before the public by men who made this their profession. Chikamatsu's surpassing merit as an innovator of Bunraku is that he achieved a superb success in integrating the dramatic and the narrative modes to create plays with enormous power. His language is extremely varied, and is flexible enough to switch between racy colloquialism (in speeches) and exalted poetical flourishes (in narrative passages).

In connection with this we must keep in mind that puppets in Bunraku are not mere counterparts of live actors in regular theatre. Indeed, the success of a theatrical performance largely depends on the quality of the puppets' 'acting', which is identical with the skill of their manipulators, but they also have their *raison d'être* on the stage as symbolic images, incarnating the spirit of the words of the text recited by the *tayu*. *Tayus* on their part never aim simply to be vocal impersonators of the puppet characters. Although they have to colour their toning so as to make evident stereotypical characteristics such as the sex, age, social status, and so forth of each of the characters, they rarely alter their natural voice to the extent that they actually simulate a character's personality. The *tayu* is first and last an authorised mediator for the audience between the text and the puppets. The words of the text recited by the *tayu* inspire the audience to animate the puppets so that they can be seen to move freely without cumbersome materiality in a dynamic cosmos of fictive time and space. Paul Claudel, who was attracted by Bunraku while staying in Japan as French ambassador in the 1920s, wrote in a letter to his friend: 'Ce n'est pas un acteur qui parle; c'est une parole qui agit.'[6]

It is nothing less than the mind of the audience that gives shape and meaning to the drama of puppets in order to complete it. Perhaps it is not amiss to recall here what Ernst Gombrich in a work that has become a classic in the psychology of pictorial representation calls 'the beholder's share'. In *Art and Illusion* Gombrich points out as a necessary condition for effective 'projection' from the beholder the existence of a 'screen' or an

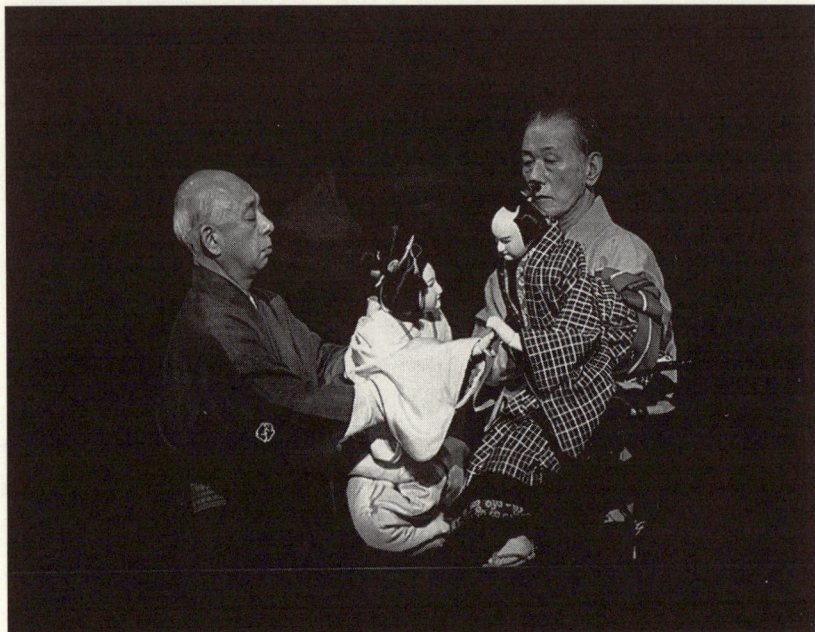

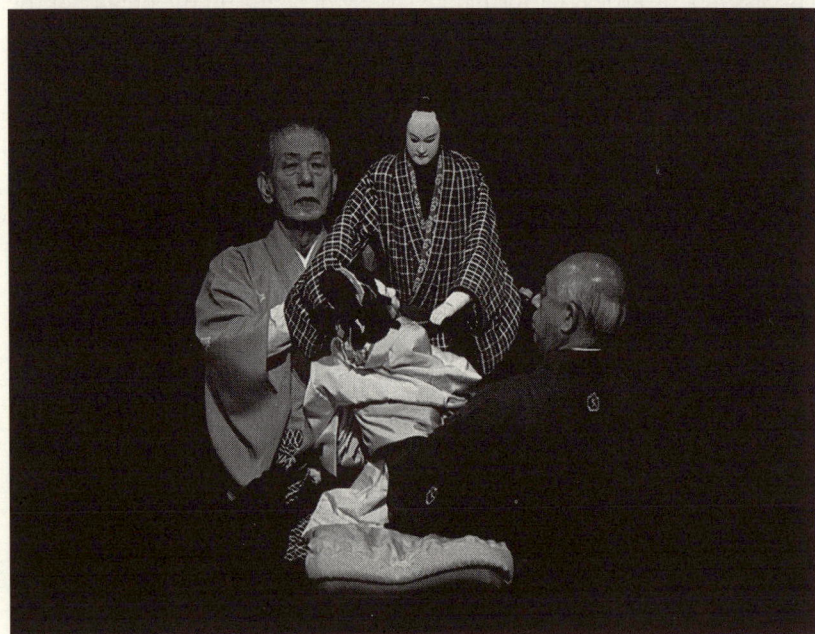

13 and 14. Scenes from Chikamatsu's *The Love Suicides at Sonezaki*.

'empty or ill-defined area' onto which the expected image can be projected.[7] And it need hardly be said that the stage with puppets whose
physical movements are more or less stereotyped and whose speech has to
be supplied by narrators is best qualified as a screen in this sense. The
concept of 'the beholder's share' itself, as Gombrich amply illustrates in
the same book, has long been a tradition of Japanese and Chinese art. A
dry landscape garden is made only of several big stones scattered on
smooth white sand, but it inspires us to imagine in our inner eye a vast
land- or seascape, which can be philosophically cosmic or concretely picturesque according to our preference. In like manner, Chikamatsu audiences, especially of his love-suicide tragedies, are incited during the
performance to picture a virtual world of drama within their imagination,
where crude reality is sublimated and transposed into an upper order to
produce a new dimension of meaning. Herein consists the essence of
Chikamatsvian tragedy.

This special mode of theatrical response is more or less common to all
kinds of classical Japanese drama and is indeed quite unique. But is it
entirely foreign to our experience of Shakespeare? Is it probable that the
Chikamatsu-conditioned theatre-goers first seeing Shakespeare whom
we hypothesised earlier will take in the whole fictional reality of the play as
a world with an autonomous meaning extractable from a structured
sequence of behaviours exhibited by the characters who live that reality?
Will they be content to see each of the speeches as no more than an
expression of the speaker's inner self at that particular moment? The
answer will be negative. I am almost certain that they will hear in some of
the words spoken by Shakespeare's characters something beyond the
voice of the speakers, something that belongs to a different dimension of
existence from the immediate present on the stage. For instance, when
they hear Hamlet speak those memorable ruminations on providence and
human destiny before the fencing match or hear the mad Lear mutter
words of existential sorrow to the blind Gloucester on Dover heath: 'we
came crying hither . . . When we are born, we cry that we are come / To
this great stage of fools'(IV.vi. 178, 182–5), the actors might appear in
their inner vision somehow transformed into puppets that are being
manipulated by ventriloquial narrators, so that it seems as if the voice of
the *play* is reaching their ears through the mouths of the characters. And
since through their theatre-going experience of Chikamatsu they are
habituated to being disengaged from the phenomenal world on the stage
by expository and narrative passages in the text which compel them to
respond to the action with something of an epic detachment, it is possible
that in seeing Shakespeare their mind will be acted on in like manner by
dramatic narrative in the characters' speeches. They will probably make

much of those narrational speeches of petty functional characters, in which beautifully worded accounts of moving scenes are given in *King Lear, The Winter's Tale,* and some other plays. They will be particularly interested in what Francis Berry calls the 'inset' effect of the narrative mode of speech,[8] which they think somehow corresponds to the 'spotlight' effect in Chikamatsu.

That so little critical attention has been accorded to the dramatic use of narration in Shakespeare seems to me rather strange when in some of his plays, including *King Lear,* lines in the narrative mode occupy more than 25 per cent of the whole text. Perhaps it is because narration tends towards actional stasis and is therefore considered to go against the medium of drama. No one could deny, however, that whenever the narrative mode is successfully integrated with the dramatic within an action sequence, the effect is great and multifarious. There is not only a juxtaposition of past and present time, of what is physically before one's eyes and what is imagined; there is also a friction between the epic sense of time and the dramatic time governing the dramatic action. It serves to wean the audience's mind away from its preoccupation with the here and now on the stage and set it groping for a new perspective from which the speaker as well as the object of the narration can be viewed. Othello's long speech preceding his suicide is a notable case of this kind. When Othello starts speaking of the resolute patriotic justice he once inflicted on a Turk, we find ourselves ready to reminisce about the magnificent figure he used to cut in our eyes in the initial acts. Next moment, however, he himself becomes the Turk, the 'circumcised dog', and stabs him, or himself. Thus, the punisher is transformed into the punished, and the heroic act of a Christian executing a pagan offender overlaps with the action of a civilised man annihilating himself in order to execute justice on the barbarian within himself. Narration is fused into speech, stasis into motion, tableau into drama.

Notoriously F. R. Leavis found in Othello at this last moment the posture of a self-dramatiser whose tears are shed for the self-felt pathos of 'the spectacle of himself'.[9] Leavis' view is anticipated by a severe moral criticism of the hero by T. S. Eliot who says that 'Othello succeeds in turning himself into a pathetic figure, by adopting an *aesthetic* rather than a moral attitude, dramatising himself against his environment. He takes in the spectator, but the human motive is primarily to take in himself.'[10] I did not quote Eliot to endorse this curious piece of pseudo character criticism; nor am I inclined to think that the human motive is primarily to take in himself. However, that Othello takes in the spectator is nothing less than true, not of course in the sense in which Eliot says this, but as a statement of theatre psychology working at the ending of a tragedy, for the root of tragic pleasure is evidently in being *taken in* – that is, in being so deluded as to believe in the reality of that which has no existence except as a psychic phenomenon in the audience's mind. As far as audience response at the finale of *Othello* is concerned, it does not matter what kind of personality the hero has ultimately proved himself to be. What is important is that a quiet upsurge of emotions evoked in response to the integrated effect of his narrative speech and his dramatic action works to make the audience free to be *taken in* and accept the beautiful image of a noble Moor into which Othello has fashioned himself at the last moment.

The vigour and intensity of this ending is indeed beyond the scope of Chikamatsu's tragic craftsmanship, but the pattern of audience response operating here seems to have something in common with that which is supposed to work in some climactic scenes of love-suicide tragedies of the Japanese playwright. The Japanese word for narration or narrative, *katari*, can also mean 'deception' or 'delusion'. This is not a mere pun. People in ancient times who believed in the soul of language thought that by narrating something with verve one could exert a miraculous influence on the hearers. And without doubt Chikamatsu was a great practitioner of *katari*, or the art of aesthetic deception in the theatre. Noh is also a theatrical form which is designed to release aesthetic energy for producing a self-deluding inner vision on the part of the audience. In Noh, however, tragedy is not enacted on the stage but is lived through in mime, song, and dance, usually by the ghost of one of its former participants. So the emotions aroused in the audience cannot but be emotions recollected in tranquility. There is indeed pain and regret mixed with them, but it is mitigated and mellowed by memory and nostalgia. On the other hand, in Chikamatsu's love-suicide plays, we are squarely confronted with hard tragic realities which are actually represented on the stage. Both in *The Love Suicides at Sonezaki* and *The Love Suicides at Amijima*, the action centres on a complicated relationship of the protagonist with his beloved prostitute. The adverse circumstances, both social and domestic, in which the lovers find themselves, together with their lively sense of honour and obligation, drive them finally into a tight corner, where they choose to die together.

Writing his plays like Shakespeare for a specific theatre in a big city, Chikamatsu must have thought it advisable in terms of box-office profits to attract those unsophisticated citizens who swarmed to theatres just to see the sensational incidents they had heard or read of enacted on the stage. Accordingly, his dialogues are generally close to everyday language, and his characters' words and conduct are easy to understand from the viewpoint of the behaviour patterns of common people in contemporary society. Yet nothing is more improper than to call Chikamatsu a realist in the normal sense of the word. Chikamatsu never ceased to be conscious of the play as an artifact, in which crude reality was sublimated and woven into fine traceries of emotional figures. Many of his characters are so artfully informed with life, 'in the slender margin between the real and the unreal', as he reportedly put it,[11] that puppets incapable of subtle movement or expression can effectively function as emotive presences for the audience. The male heroes are mostly social misfits or uncontrollable self-wreckers, wanting in purpose and often easily jealous. On the other hand, women, who are usually wives or prostitutes, are possessors of noble and magnanimous hearts, ever ready to sacrifice themselves, even their lives, to the love they bear for their husbands or their lovers. This, however, is not what I meant when I mentioned Chikamatsu's artistic sublimation of crude reality. What I was actually referring to is the peculiarly Chikamatsvian manner in which the theatrical experience of certain catastrophic scenes is made to affect the audience's mental image of the whole play. Let me dwell on this point by taking as illustrative case the scene where the lovers journey through the night shadows towards the suicide spot.

A love-suicide journey is a theatrical set piece permeated by an atmosphere of lyric beauty and pathos which is enhanced by the narration of several *tayus*, now chanting in chorus, now declaiming solo for each puppet-character, accompanied by the continuous, orchestrated twang of *shamisens*. In this final scene there are no new developments of the plot; all that takes place on stage is a slow-paced peregrination in the dead hours of night, followed by the actual suicides at break of day. But the static stage business is amply supplemented by the poetical narration, which gives circumstantial accounts of the locations and scenery along the road, as well as the feelings of the lovers, alternating between agony and ecstasy. It is a critical commonplace to say that the character of the male lover undergoes a spiritual change in the course of this death-bound journey. Indeed, even those weakling protagonists who are so infirm of nature that their decision for a joint suicide with their beloved prostitute seems controlled by the stronger desire of the latter, appear to have grown to spiritual maturity if not heroic stature. But to say that a man's true character is made clear in the face of imminent death is to reduce the artistic problem to a familiar truism about human nature. The approach to this question must be phenomenological.

Let me first make clear that I do not quite agree with the popular notion of Chikamatsu's romanticism in which he allegedly tried to idealise love's consummation in death. In *The Love Suicides at Sonezaki*, there is certainly a sense in which the suicidal journey symbolises the alliance of *eros* and *thanatos*. 'Let us secure our bodies to this twin-trunked tree and die immaculately', says the man, seeing that they have arrived at the pre-arranged spot. But it is also true that the lovers themselves are not entirely infatuated with death. Embracing each other, they continually weep over their hapless lot and the narrators give a rather objective description of the awkward and painful death the woman has to suffer at the hands of her lover as the blade deflects this way and that until it is thrust through her throat. In *The Love Suicides at Amijima* the lovers on their way to death constantly refer to their guilty feelings about those helpless innocents they are going to leave behind. Still conscious of earthly obligations to people around them, they cannot even die together. Cutting their locks to become a nun and a priest, they choose to die physically separated.

Notwithstanding all these points, it is indisputable that there is a metamorphosis of the protagonist's image in the inner eye of the audience during the suicidal journey, which in its turn contributes to the final configuration of its tragic experience. This is, I think, due to a change of the mental perspective on the drama that occurs in the deeper layers of the consciousness of the audience. As in the final act of Thornton Wilder's *Our Town*, in which some of the happenings in the earlier acts are re-envisioned by the audience *sub specie aeternitatis*, so in the last scene of Chikamatsu's love tragedies the entire action of the earlier scenes that has been experienced in terms of this world gradually withdraws into the distance, as if by a long pullback on a zoom lens, and assumes a new aspect in the light of the other world. The result is that the whole body of the unhappy human drama turns itself, as it were, into a long confessional protasis and epitasis for a requiem.

To put it more concretely, those unfortunate events and circumstances that led up to the lovers' double suicides are made to appear, in retrospect, to be episodes in their purgatorial journey through this floating world, of which the present suicide trip is the final phase. Being sinners who have corrupted themselves after the flesh and are experiencing torturing agonies, the lovers dream of being reborn together in the next world, in a lotus calyx. This does not necessarily mean that they are to be saved by Amida Buddha whom they repeatedly invoke before they die. Actually they have not had their earthly desires rarefied yet. Abandoned as they are, they are still not free from feelings that are all too human. However, the audience must be remembering all through this catastrophic scene that significant phrase in the concluding passage of the induction to *The Love Suicides at Sonezaki* in which Kwannon, the Goddess of Mercy, is alluded to as one who, 'taking as many as thirty-three different shapes, appears in the nether world of dust, and guiding and teaching us by means of sensualities and carnal desires, makes love a bridge for us to cross to attain Salvation'.

Behind these homiletic words lies the conception of the prostitute as an incarnation of *das Ewig Weibliche,* an esoteric view which is rather familiar to Oriental religions. And partly because of this the audience is filled with intense anticipation when a group of *shamisen* players, to launch the scene, start twanging in animated concert; now it is about to experience an event which is at once the most horrid discomfiture and the most blessed consummation, at once the most piteous attempt at self-annihilation and the most joyous realisation of freed humanity. The excitement culminates in an ecstasy at the moment of the suicidal murder, when a cruel beauty is born.

Some of Shakespeare's tragedies also have a certain aspect in which the hero's bafflement, defeat or self-destruction can in itself be a realisation, a fruition of his fundamental life. But it is always accompanied by some higher awareness on his part, usually attained in the last phase of his long strife, whether of love, divine providence, or just the futility of all human endeavours. But protagonists in Chikamatsu's love tragedies make no effort to resist their fate, nor are they in any way enlightened on the meaning and values of man's life in this world. They even do not show any sign of conflict within themselves. Once enamoured of a young courtesan, a middle-aged clerk or the owner of a decent shop yields all too easily to temptations of the flesh and degrades himself in a most stupid way. Not knowing how to save himself, not even realising why he has to suffer, like a wild animal who, feeling that its time to die is near, slowly paces towards its death spot, he chooses, in what seems an instinctive manner, to obliterate himself in order to disappear from this transitory world of vanities. This meek submissiveness of the hero to his fate would give the audience an intimation of the existence of another order of nature to which man ultimately belongs. Perhaps it is because of this that the audience curiously feels at ease when the curtain falls on the final death scene of the tragedy.

Pathos is the chief emotional effect for which Chikamatsu seems to have exhausted all his resources as a poetic dramatist, and it is for an abundance of elaborately wrought effects of pathos that his plays, especially his domestic tragedies and some of his history plays, have received the highest praise as well as the severest censure. Pathos of course is not a quality alien to Shakespeare's drama. We do not need Bradley to point out that in a section of the play, immediately before the final movement towards the catastrophe, Shakespeare often appeals to a new emotion which is painful but is accompanied by a sense of beauty and an outflow of affection.[12] The Chikamatsu-conditioned audience may go so far as to find in Ophelia's madness or Desdemona's Willow Song the counterpart of the love-suicide journey in Bunraku. Taking care not to stumble into the fallacy of parallelism, this audience would contend that they are alike not only in their sweetly plaintive mood, but also in the somewhat hidden effect they are assumed to exercise on the structuring of the tragic experience. The deceptive cadence of lyric peacefulness with nostalgic overtones works as potential energy for engendering in the audience's mind a faint expectancy for a transposition of the tragic key.

To the audience who hear Gertrude's picturesque report of Ophelia's drowning, death, so far perceived, in the form of a poisoned or stabbed body, as nothing less than ugly, odious, and infernal, now becomes the alluring sight of a lovely maid's homeward return to her own element. And this can possibly stimulate the audience to fantasise a future in which the tragic *agon* is brought to a harmonious and meaningful conclusion. If the *Hamlet* experience could be likened to a long night's wandering with ever-growing pressures from the impenetrable darkness, this newly nourished wishful vision is like a glimpse of dawn appearing above the horizon to terminate the groping journey. It endears itself to the audience all the more because the audience knows that it is false. It is too well aware that nothing has changed in respect to the problem the hero is confronted with, and that the possibility of a resolution of the tragic conflict remains as poor as ever. But once a mechanism for such psychic response gets started by the energy of this deceptive vision, Hamlet is made to appear to have changed from an agonist rebelling against 'the thousand natural shocks' of life and the horror of the 'undiscovered country' to a mature, enlightened sufferer ready to resign himself to his fate and to death.

A similarly emotional atmosphere of deceptive peace pervades Desdemona's colloquy with Emilia and her singing of the Willow Song. Desdemona appears to have taken on a new aspect here. She is not merely a pathetic figure in wistful stasis. She also has a certain elusive opacity about her, a corporeality that has gradually been rarefied, while at the same time her symbolic spirituality has become so much the more impressive. This transformed image of Desdemona lingers in the depths of the audience's consciousness until the catastrophe, where her death strikes the audience less as a murder than a love-suicide *à la* Chikamatsu. Instead of recoiling from the pain and horror of her strangulation by her husband, which it cannot reconcile with the meaningful purpose of the universe, the audience ecstatically enjoys the pathetic beauty of the excruciatingly cruel scene.

What pathos means to Chikamatsu, however, is not the same as what it means to Shakespeare. Pathos is as old as tragedy, both in Europe and in Japan. Greek tragedy abounds in pathetic scenes; so does English Renaissance drama. But pathos in these Western dramas is not a mere quality of evoking a feeling of pity or compassion. It has something strong and positive in it. To be touched by pathos in Shakespeare or in Euripides is to be implicated in an implicit judgement of the human heart on whatever inhuman force has caused the pitiable situation. We all know that Shakespeare, in a well-known passage in *Macbeth*, likened pity to a 'naked new-born babe, / Striding the blast', who 'Shall blow the horrid deed in every eye, / That tears shall drown the wind' (I.vii.21–5). In all his tragedies a pathetic scene is a scene where the audience is driven half-instinctively to enter a most vigorous protest in the cause of the holiness of human affections against their sacrilegious annihilators. Thus pity can somehow be linked with the spirit of tragedy. Commenting on the pathetic ending of *The Bacchae*, where Agave, whose sanity has gradually been restored, suddenly recognises what she has done – that is, the tearing of her son Pentheus to pieces – William Arrowsmith says, '[in pity] men declare their humanity and a moral dignity which heaven, lacking those limits which make men suffer *into* dignity and compassion, can never understand or equal. This is their moral victory . . . for by accepting their necessities in anguish, they claim the uniquely human skill of *sophia*, the acceptance of necessity and doom which teaches compassion.'[13]

In Chikamatsu, however, emotions aroused do not lend themselves to a humanistic moral judgement on the part of the audience. They are simply there to be enjoyed for their own sake; no order or value, either cosmic or social, is called in question through them. All that is required of us in a situation that strikes a responsive chord in our hearts is to abandon ourselves completely to the worked-up pathos which is so pure and ethereal because it is so free of moral implications. It is easy to call Chikamatsu a second-rate artist for this reason alone. Yet nothing will be harder for us, even for those of us who have been trained in the moral-intellectual literary tradition of the West, than to withstand the bewitching charm of some of his climactic scenes, where pain and pity fuse so sweetly with aesthetic delight.

11 Conflicting authorities: the canonisation of Zeami and Shakespeare

Gerry Yokota-Murakami

The figure of Zeami (1363?-1443?), founder of the art of Noh, has been canonised in Japanese culture as a supreme genius in much the same way as Shakespeare is enshrined in the canon of English literature, and with similar significance to that culture's sense of national identity. That analogy forms a common point of interest for scholars of comparative culture and literature, especially those who share an interest in the issue of canonicity. But is the perception of such an analogy sufficient to justify their comparison? What is the basis of that perception? Is it possible to pursue such a comparative project without perpetuating the dominant colonial mode of comparative criticism, according to which Shakespeare is revered as the superior central figure of world drama and any drama from any other culture treated as inferior and marginal, deserving of recognition only insofar as it exhibits some feature which is comparable to that central, universal standard? I believe it is important to address these questions squarely before commencing with any comparative project.

The analogy between Zeami and Shakespeare as similar cult figures in their respective countries is the point of departure for this essay. But I would not take such a superficial analogy alone as a rationale for comparison of 'similar' works by the two playwrights. The basic rationale for my project is my belief in the value of comparative study of cultural institutions such as Noh and Shakespearean drama, with emphasis on their deployment, both historical and potential, to facilitate oppression; and the historical and potential forms of challenge to such deployment, as a basis for further analysis of the present and future potential of both arts.

For the past century and more, Shakespeare has been central to the educational curriculum throughout a global empire so vast that the sun was said never to set in that realm. The economics of canon establishment in the postcolonial academy worldwide still fundamentally operates according to the same trickle-down principle as ODA economics. As male-dominated academies around the globe seek to incorporate tokens of the Japanese literary tradition into the margins of their curricula, they make their selections from an array offered by the male-dominated academic establishment in Japan as representative of their national heritage as those men perceive it, and so the same discourses are perpetuated. It is with this contemporary context in mind that I argue for the importance of understanding the historical contingencies of the establishment of Noh as an elite fine art representing the zenith of Japanese culture. I would argue that comparative projects that seek to develop alternative strategies of reception, questioning the authority of such traditional aesthetic canons rather than simply accepting them as inherently superior, are justified as long as those canons continue to be promoted in a wide global array as the supreme examples of their respective cultural traditions, and hence to function as powerful cultural institutions affecting the dominant perceptions of women among people all over the world. As long as canonical images of human relationships, images which are no more than stereotypical projections of male fantasies, remain unquestioned, they retain the potential to be deployed effectively to promote an oppressive power-imbalance in the global status quo, as an ever-widening circle of subscribers to those standards proceed to apply them, in the form of unconsciously internalised cultural standards, in the discriminating decisions of everyday life which perpetuate unequal relations.[1]

The following study of the formation of a major canon of traditional Japanese drama is thus an experiment to test the possibility of a method of comparative drama that does not perpetuate the dominant mode of perception, whereby it is tacitly assumed to be natural, rather than historically contingent, that Shakespeare is central, Zeami marginal. The focus of the study is on analysis of the historical process by which one particular Noh play, *Takasago*, came to be canonised as the supreme example of the art through repeated performance, exegesis, and anthologisation. It is hoped that clarification of the specific historical contingencies which affected the conception and reception of this particular play will effectively demonstrate how this art has been manipulated throughout the centuries in order to establish a dominant mythmaking discourse.

In the process of conducting the original research that forms the basis for this analysis, every attempt was made to avoid applying Western categorical constructs in a way that would reproduce the kind of scholarship that reaffirms the centrality of the canonical and the marginality of the other, and so to approach the corpus with a view unmediated by Western critical categories. The present essay is structured on the basis of traditional Western categories of drama studies, which have influenced twentieth-century Japanese spectators and scholars as well as the Western audience, not simply to facilitate communication of the results of this research by couching it in more familiar terms for Western readers, but primarily to demonstrate how the coercive 'universal' application of constructed categories, both Western and indigenous, can often work to obscure rather than illuminate. It is hoped that this approach will ultimately work to motivate the liberation of ways of thinking entrenched in reifying preconceived categories, including ways of thinking about world drama entrenched in analogies with Shakespeare, and perhaps even effect some difference in the balance of power relationships in the global intellectual field.

Historical background

The Noh troupes first gained decisive recognition for their popular form of entertainment during the Ashikaga period (1338–1573), when they attracted the attention of the third Ashikaga shogun, Yoshimitsu (1358–1408), and went on to refine their art into a more ceremonial, sometimes spectacular, performing art under increasingly exclusive shogunal and daimyo patronage. In the Edo period (1603–1867), the actors came to be officially retained by the Tokugawa shogunate, dependent on government stipends of rice and gold, their public performance activities strictly licensed and controlled.

The decision of the Tokugawa shogunate to monopolise Noh as its official court ceremony was clearly motivated by its desire to exploit the potential 'cultural capital' of the art.[2] When Noh was first developed under the patronage of the Ashikaga shogunate, the seat of government was located in Kyoto. The Tokugawa shogunate moved its seat of government to distant Edo in a declaration of independence from the royal court, and the new capital required a culture befitting its grandeur. Noh, while extensively incorporating aristocratic Kyoto court culture, had been developed under shogunal patronage and combined with elements of martial culture to please samurai tastes, and was thus eminently suited to the nationalistic Tokugawa enterprise. In the following analysis, I will show how the play *Takasago* was particularly instrumental in that enterprise, by first introducing the superficial features of the play as it is commonly perceived according to conventional categories of perception and then proceeding to demonstrate the important historical contingencies that are obscured by those categories.

Synopsis

Takasago, by Zeami, is a play belonging to the first of the five traditional categories of Noh, plays featuring a mythological deity. It is structured in two acts. In the first act, a travelling priest on a journey from the provinces to the capital pays a visit to a shrine along the way and encounters an old man and woman there. After a long, quiet discourse on the sentience of plants and trees and on the virtues of marital fidelity and poetry as means of fostering peace and public order, at the end of the first act the two reveal their identities as the spirits of two pine trees growing within the grounds of two different shrines, their conjugal unity transcending the distance that separates them. There is an interlude in which a local villager entertains the visiting priest with a colloquial rendition of the legend of the two spirits. In the second act, the villager and the priest travel together to the other shrine and there witness the revelation of the deity of Sumiyoshi Shrine in masculine form.[3] The masculine manifestation of the deity re-enacts the scene of an immaculate, woman-free divine birth through a ritual of purification performed upon a mythical husband's return from a visit to his deceased wife in the nether world. The intense burst of energy which characterises this solo dance, the highlight of the play, effects a brilliant contrast to the tranquil serenity of the first act.[4]

Authorship

Zeami is now revered as an artistic genius representing the best of Japanese culture. There are numerous book-length studies in Japanese glorifying him and several in English. But this individualistic cult was only developed in the twentieth century with the publication of Zeami's artistic treatises in 1918. These treatises had been jealously guarded as 'secret transmissions' by Zeami's heirs for centuries under the feudal system, still operative today, whereby the five official schools are organised by patrilineage. The publication of the treatises seems to have been strategically timed to enhance the esoteric aura of the art as it came to be commercially marketed after losing the patronage of the state.

For some time after the art of Noh came to be promoted as an intangible cultural asset of the Japanese national heritage, the name of Zeami was promoted as virtually synonymous with Noh, and virtually any play acknowledged as a classic was automatically attributed to him. But those early hasty attributions are not supported by current scholarship. Zeami is now definitively identified as the sole author of thirty-one plays in the canon of some two hundred and fifty plays and tentatively as the sole author of twelve more. This gives a total of forty-three canonical plays. He is also credited with several revisions and the co-authorship of a few other plays.[5]

It is interesting to note that at least eight plays definitively attributed to Zeami have been excluded from the standard repertoire. Zeami's name alone did not carry sufficient authority to guarantee a play a permanent place in the canon. Indeed, Zeami's popularity with the Ashikaga shogunate was limited to one or two generations. Yoshimitsu's successor favoured Zeami's nephew, On'ami (1398–1467) rather than Zeami's son Motomasa (d. 1432), and invoked his prerogative as shogunal patron to appoint the nephew instead of the son to succeed Zeami as the head of the Kanze troupe. Zeami was stripped of his official artistic appointments and eventually exiled. Although there are no official shogunal records extant explicitly stating the reason for his exile, Zeami's own statements in his treatises naming his son-in-law Zenchiku Konparu (1405–1470) as his artistic heir after his son Motomasa's death have fuelled speculation that he was punished for refusing to bequeath the family treatises to On'ami.[6]

It was not that Zeami had not tried to guarantee his own immortality. The first three leaders of the Kanze troupe – Kan'ami (1333–1384), Zeami, and On'ami – took the first characters of their names from the name of the popular bodhisattva (buddha elect) Kanzeon (Avalokitesvara), who is only occasionally depicted visually on the Noh stage but frequently invoked verbally. A parallel might be found in Shakespeare's self-conscious weaving of the word 'will' into many of his texts.

But just as Jonson's publication of his own *Workes* is seen to signal a new conceptualisation of authorship in England, so we must beware of applying an anachronistic view of Zeami's authority as playwright to the history of Noh. For centuries after his death, the playwright Zeami's name was not a major criterion for the selection of plays for canonisation. As we shall see, the play *Takasago* may have, for a host of interesting reasons, come to validate the name of Zeami more than the name Zeami gave authority to the play.

Literary genres

In the traditional hierarchy of the three Aristotelian genres in the West, tragedy is ranked supreme, epic next, and lyric the lowliest. In Japan, *waka* poetry is the supreme art. It was originally the art of the gods and was later co-opted by Buddhism and 'perfected' as a Tao, a Way with a capital W.[7] The narrative *monogatari* eventually won second place in the Japanese literary generic scheme after the success of the eleventh-century *Genji Monogatari*, although there ensued centuries of critical battles over whether Lady Murasaki, the author of that work, should be condemned to hell for her lies or worshipped as a bodhisattva who told parables like the Buddha to guide the masses to enlightenment.

But in stark opposition to the dominance of tragedy in the Western tradition since the time of Aristotle's *Poetics*, the battle in Japan to overcome the bias against play-acting as a form of immoral deception even more threatening to public order than fiction, to gain recognition for drama as a fine art, begins only in the fourteenth century with Noh. Whereas Shakespeare achieved his greatest acclaim for his development of new tragic conventions none the less firmly rooted in the classical tradition, Zeami evoked the divine authority of buddhas and kami such as the deity of Sumiyoshi Shrine to validate his art. (Specific examples of this technique are discussed more fully below in the section on literary sources.) We must also be careful not to make the Eurocentric assumption that the Japanese were destined to develop a triad of literary genres. Noh, Kabuki, and Bunraku are probably more closely associated with the performing arts of music and dance in the Japanese cultural consciousness than they are perceived as literary genres, although printed texts were circulating by the early seventeenth century.

Dramatic genres

The basic initial perception, for both Japanese and non-Japanese, of the art of Noh as a whole is usually guided by the traditional division of the current canon into five genres, largely according to character type: deity, warrior ghost, woman (often a ghost), living man or woman driven by passion, or demon. These five categories are often romantically described as having naturally evolved as a reflection of the supposedly typical Eastern perception of cosmological time as cyclical, as opposed to the Westerner's typically linear perception. Hence, the golden age of the gods is followed by a fall into the chaos of war, which is followed by an age of relative peace when romantic love is the primary pastime, which is in turn followed by another plunge into the chaos of human passion, the cycle ending with apocalypse, the conquest of the demons and the restoration of order.

But this five-category patterning principle is actually a seventeenth-century development for programmes at Edo Castle, three centuries after Zeami first developed the art of Noh under the patronage of the Ashikaga shogunate.[8] It is important to bear in mind that nearly all of the Noh plays in the current canon were written before such a complex classification system was ever applied. The cyclical view of the Noh programme actually obscures the fact that the order of presentation of the five categories or character types is a strictly vertical hierarchical order: from deities (nine out of ten in a masculine manifestation), to elite warriors (all but one male), to women (mostly from the aristocracy), to passionate individuals from lower social classes, to subhuman demons. In fact, when the Tokugawa shogunate chose, in the early seventeenth century, to monopolise the art of Noh as its court ritual, it established a special liaison office to convey the shogunate's wishes to be entertained with a pro-grammed court ritual appropriately representing the Tokugawa world as an order modelled on and sanctioned by divine order.[9] This, rather than any natural cosmological worldview, is the historical basis for the creation of the five-play programme.

Elsewhere I have outlined in detail the historical process of the canon-isation of Noh as a fine art in four stages:

(1) Zeami's systematisation of character types and establishment of the felicitous mode;
(2) revisions of Zeami's standards by On'ami's heir Nobumitsu (1435–1516);
(3) the monopolisation of the Noh drama as the court ritual of the Tokugawa shogunate; and
(4) the organisation of the repertoire for commercial consumption.[10]

In the present study of the process of canonisation of the play *Takasago*, I will provide specific examples of several canonising manoeuvres employed in this process, in connection with related features of that play, in order to demonstrate the historical process through which an orthodox image of an ideal, divine order came to be constructed for programmes at Edo Castle – a system of representations which has strong potential not only to regulate the way we experience the art but also to affect by exten-sion our ways of perceiving individuals, classes, and cultures. These manoeuvres include the elimination and addition of characters, the ranking of plays in a strict hierarchy, changes in masking and costuming so as to effect changes in the perception of power relationships among the characters, and textual revisions.

Let us begin with the manipulation of the category to which *Takasago* belongs, the first group of plays featuring deities – the category which as a whole was manipulated with the greatest deliberation in order to establish a mythmaking discourse. Obviously this group of plays, depicting a divine order suitable for appropriation as the ultimate model for order in human society, promises the highest yield in terms of 'cultural capital'. And just as the Noh repertoire as a whole is divided into five hierarchical cate-gories, so are the deity plays within the first, supremely orthodox cate-gory. These five hierarchical sub-categories are superficially distinguished by the type of dance performed in the play as follows:

Kamimai:	Nine plays, eight of which feature masculine manifestations of deity and one of which fea-tures a deity which may be portrayed in either masculine or feminine form
Hataraki:	Twelve plays, all featuring masculine manifesta-tions of deity

Gaku:	Ten plays, featuring eight masculine manifestations of deity, one feminine, and one pair of animals
Shinnojonomai:	Four plays, featuring three masculine manifestations of deity and one of feminine
Chunomai:	Three plays featuring feminine manifestations of deity.[11]

The ratio of feminine manifestations of deity generally increases in inverse proportion to rank. But this balance is neither a reflection of the typical Japanese image of the world of the *kami*, nor of Zeami's *oeuvre*, nor of the repertoire in his time. The repertoire in Zeami's time primarily featured wild, raging deities in masculine form, often paired with feminine companions of equal or sometimes higher status, deities who appeared in the human world to battle for supremacy, correct injustice, or demand appeasement.[12] The plays often ended with human characters making offerings to them. But after *Takasago*, the repertoire as a whole came to be re-organised to give hierarchical precedence to beneficent deities who appear not to intervene or make any demand but to bestow approbation on the status quo, explicitly praising the ruler for bringing peace and prosperity to the human realm.[13]

Characters

A survey of Zeami's early non-canonical deity plays clearly indicates this secularising shift. It is not, however, apparent from a survey of the current canon because most of Zeami's plays which were excluded from the canon were his deity plays – especially those featuring feminine manifestations of deity. Zeami's choreography for these plays featuring feminine manifestations of deity, the *tennyomai*, was artistically appreciated, but the powerful feminine manifestations of deity were not. And so Zeami decided to incorporate the popular *tennyomai* dance into his plays featuring masculine manifestations of deity, such as *Takasago*, instead. After *Takasago* achieved such great success, it became necessary to establish a clear distinction between the two styles. The plays featuring feminine manifestations of deity were either re-choreographed with a different dance, the dance used to characterise the human women of the third-category plays (with obvious implications in terms of a far lower hierarchical status), or simply dropped from the repertoire.[14]

The success of *Takasago* led to another major trend in the editorial revision of older plays. It will be recalled that both man and woman are central to the narrative in Act I of *Takasago*, but only the masculine form of the deity appears in Act II. After *Takasago* became established as the orthodox standard for its sub-genre, other plays originally written to feature masculine and feminine manifestations of deity together came to be edited so as to exclude the feminine, resulting in the heavy predominance of masculine manifestations of deity throughout the first category of the standard canon.[15]

The demand for ceremonial formality that dictated such specialisation also fundamentally changed the role of the deuteragonist or *waki*. The *waki* (in *Takasago*, the traveling Shinto priest) was once the leader of the chorus; he was thus far more active on the stage, and the chorus must also have appeared much more part of the action.[16] Today, the *waki*'s lines and movements are extremely limited, his chief role that of witness. But in the first-category plays especially, he is not simply a passive witness by chance but often rather an official envoy, appointed by and validated by an invisible authority, usually either divine or royal authority. Whereas the main character (*shite*), a masked role, may be masculine or feminine, the *waki* is male and played without a mask in every known Noh play. Relieved of his role as leader of the chorus, the *waki*'s silent, fixed gaze becomes doubly oppressive. The masked main characters are far too unearthly for a spectator to identify with. The *waki*'s unmasked face and his position on the stage effectively control the audience's point of view. In the presence of a masculine manifestation of deity in a first-category play, the gaze of the celebrant is one of awe and reverence. But in the presence of a condemned human woman in a third-category play, the gaze of the Buddhist priest, whose mission is to save such corrupt creatures and whose attitude functions to control the spectator's point of view, is intensely demeaning.[17]

The history of stage productions of first-category plays – especially addition and deletion of personae and the costumes and masks utilised in their depiction – is fraught with such strategic manoeuvres to enhance the aura of male authority, both divine and human. Just as the dance for portraying feminine manifestations of deity was changed from the divine *tennyomai* to the human *chunomai*, so were the mask and costume: the mask from the divine *Zo* or *Naki-zo* to the human *Ko-omote*, the costume from the wide split skirt allowing freedom of movement to a tight skirt much like the common kimono worn by modern traditionalists today.[18] The depiction of masculine manifestations of deity was also changed. To create an illusion of continuity between the divine order and the male-dominated human realm, masculine manifestations of deity come to be depicted with more human features, most often as benevolent white-haired patriarchs instead of the originally wild, ferocious figures with bright red or black manes and glittering, bulging eyes.[19] Decorative characters such as angels and dragons (representing slaves and barbarians, trophies of conquest) were added to magnify the glory of the ruler and his reign.[20] In perhaps the most extreme case of revision, even the supreme Sun Goddess Amaterasu is depicted in some stage productions in masculine rather than feminine form. [21]

Literary sources

Many Noh plays, like many plays by Shakespeare, may be characterised as neoclassical adaptations of tales from antiquity. The five categories of Noh plays are primarily organised on the basis of character types, but one may also find considerable correspondence with the genres of their chief sources: myth for the deity plays, 'epic' for the warrior plays, court 'romance' for the woman plays, contemporary events frequently dramatised in the fourth category featuring passionate individuals, and folk tales for the demon plays.

But just as Shakespeare almost certainly read the Greeks only in translation and also probably became acquainted with the Latin classics primarily through grammars and handbooks more than by direct recourse to the Latin originals, so the Noh playwrights frequently drew on medieval commentaries and handbooks for their knowledge of ancient and classical court poetry and narrative.[22] Zeami's knowledge of the mythical characters he depicts in many of his deity plays can be clearly traced not directly to the cryptic eighth-century mytho-historical chronicles, *Kojiki* (712) and *Nihongi* (720) but rather to an intermediate source: the book of Shinto poems in *Shinkokinshu* (1201), the eighth royal anthology of *waka*.

Another major source for Zeami's deity plays, including *Takasago*, is the early tenth-century *Ise Monogatari*, which was recognised by Zeami's contemporaries, the medieval *renga* (linked-verse) poets, as one of the *monogatari* classics central to their art. The *renga* connection suggests that Zeami is likely to have become acquainted with that work initially through handbooks and lectures, although he may also have referred directly to the original. *Ise Monogatari* is most commonly characterised in Western terms as a verse romance of courtly love, its episodes often erotically charged, its composite 'hero' viewed as a model for Genji and many later literary characters who are frequently (and problematically) compared to Don Juan. A rigid conception of generic distinctions might prompt one to find it curious that such a collection of tales should be a source for plays depicting the world of the gods – or, even worse, prevent one from even bothering to investigate such works as potential sources. But deity plays in Noh often depict not a separate divine world but rather revelations of the divine in the human world. The *waka* selected by Zeami for *Takasago* include one quoted in *Ise Monogatari* as having been composed by a *tenno* on the occasion of a pilgrimage to the shrine of the deity who manifests himself in Act II – and the deity's response, also in *waka* form, giving the *tenno* his blessing. But some medieval *Ise* commentators assumed that the court poet Narihira Ariwara (825–880), one of the personalities forming the composite 'hero' of the tales, was the author of the first poem rather than the *tenno*.[23] Zeami was undoubtedly influenced by this layered interpretation, which would constitute neither sacrilege nor *lèse majesté* in the Japanese context.

The extensive editing performed in the process of canonisation of Noh did not include outright bowdlerisation, but the ritualistic effect achieved by such techniques as the ceremonial programming and the slowing of the tempo seems to have functioned sufficiently to modify the conventions of reception so that erotic elements came to be sublimated in a process of spectatorial self-censorship.[24] Erotic elements subliminally present in *Takasago* include the fertility ritual of raising the phallic mast in the womb-like boat and the deity's act of rubbing his loins against the root of the pine.[25]

Theme

Comparatists looking at Noh have for too long been preoccupied with the urge to seek romantic 'universals' such as the belief in a god, eternal love, or the transcendental power of art, without considering the possibility that those 'universals' may be no more than projections of individual or nationalist values. The tendency to view *Takasago* as a paean to conjugal fidelity is a prime example of such a presumption, similar to the reading of a play such as *Othello* as an affirmation of innate male jealousy rather than as the depiction of a male product of a society where wives are considered their husbands' possessions. A re-reading of *Takasago* in its historical context likewise suggests a different dominant effect: a glorification of repressive institutions such as marriage, poetry, and religion to promote their utilisation in the interests of stable government.

The performance history of first-category Noh plays is particularly influenced by the attitudes of the artists' ruling-class patrons, the shoguns, toward the two major established religions, Shinto and Buddhism. Zeami's fourteenth-century patrons, the Ashikaga shoguns, were heavily involved in diplomatic relations with the Asian continent and with the importation of Zen Buddhism, and by far the dominant trend in the early plays is to portray the supplanting of the indigenous Shinto *kami* by their Buddhist counterparts. The not-so-peaceful co-existence of Shinto and Buddhism in Japan is expressed by the dual concept of *honji-suijaku*, 'original ground, manifest trace,' which holds that the indigenous

Shinto deities were inferior local manifestations of the central, supreme Buddha.[26] But the Tokugawa shoguns who monopolised Noh as their court ritual in the seventeenth century promoted a nationalistic nativist culture, and many Buddhist elements in Noh plays, especially those of the first category, were eliminated.[27]

This is the major trend that led to the elimination of many of Zeami's plays from the standard canon. But if we look back at the older, larger corpus, we find many plays like Zeami's *Hakozaki*, in which the Shinto religion is represented by a deity in feminine form passively waiting (in the shade of another pine tree) to be saved by masculine, continental Buddhism. The gender difference in such plays is emphasised by the language, which alternates between fluid, polysyllabic native Japanese and solid, monosyllabic Chinese compounds from the sutras. Tokugawa editors sometimes attempted to rehabilitate such plays by changing the Buddhist priest to a Shinto priest or royal courtier, but most were eventually dropped from the repertoire.[28]

But it would seem that a major reason that *Takasago*'s place was so firmly secured on programmes at Edo Castle was the utility of the image of the pine. Just as the laurel, the premier symbol of fidelity in the Petrarchan sonnet, is doubly significant, being not only evergreen but also homonymous with the name of the object of the poet's affection, so is *matsu*, the Japanese word for pine, not only evergreen but also homonymous with the Japanese word for waiting. The tree is "naturally" suited to symbolise both the eternal fidelity of husband and wife and the loyalty of subjects passively waiting upon their ruler because its constant colour implies that it is undisturbed by chaotic passions.[29] Too often, it seems, the solution to such disturbances is the exclusion of women; this is true of the priesthood in many sects of Buddhism as it is in Catholicism. In *Takasago*, the monolithic form of the tree would appear to have facilitated the acceptance of the appearance of the masculine deity alone in Act II as 'natural.'

Language

The sense of eternity associated with the evergreen pine in *Takasago* is reinforced by the characteristic grammatical ambiguity of subject, gender, number, or person in the language of Noh. Noh artists' treatises provide ample evidence that this ambiguity was often exploited politically: lines of praise for the ruler depicted in the play were often redirected with subtle glances, for example, to pay complimentary tribute to the ruling-class patron in the current audience.[30]

These grammatical ambiguities make it extremely difficult to translate

Noh plays into English. But awareness of the potential irony in these ambiguities can suggest techniques of translation and stage production that preserve such multivalence. For example, in the Penguin Classics translation, the 'God' of Sumiyoshi cries 'soothe His heart, ye of the shrine!' (290) where in fact there is no possessive pronoun, whether neutral or gender-specific, first or third person, singular or plural. Awareness of the potential irony in that ambiguity might prompt another translator to seek a rendering that retains that ambiguity, such as 'appease this spirit'. The same awareness might prompt the editor to note not simply that the triple marine deities (all male) born from their father's solo ritual of purification are subsumed under the name 'Sumiyoshi deity' but also that the fourth party of that quadripartite deity is female – the Regent Jingu, conqueror of the kingdom of Korea.[31]

Structure

It was noted in the synopsis that *Takasago* has a very long first act and a very short second act. In the long first act, the aged couple embody and extol the peace and harmony of the realm, as literary and visual techniques create multiple layers to their identity. They are identified first with that of a pair of ancient evergreens like the one in whose shade they appear, the colours and patterns of their costumes visually reinforcing the poetic language which describes the falling pine needles as forming their cloaks. Next, they are identified with the deities of the two Shinto shrines where the famous paired pines are located. They are further identified with the two premier examples of the art of Japanese poetry, the *Man'yoshu* (759) and the *Kokinshu* (905). In the short second act, a masculine manifestation of a quadripartite deity encompassing both masculine and feminine aspects appears alone. Let us consider what other structural techniques are employed, and to what combined dominant effect.

In terms of musical structure, the technique of reciting a long monologue in the first act to the rhythm of a musical sequence called the *kurisashi-kuse* was invented by Zeami's father Kan'ami and further developed by Zeami especially for orthodox deity plays such as *Takasago*. The spectacular theophany enhances the sense of approbation for the peace and harmony brought to the realm by the ruler's just government, especially as it is followed by a choral epilogue in the *rongi* mode, a musical mode developed from monastical chanting. By contrast, most two-act plays depicting human conflict (neatly contained in the second to fourth categories of the five-play programme) have short first acts and long second acts, focusing on emotional suffering.

The textual layering of the characters' multiple identity forms a more complex structure. One may be tempted to approach it synchronically, but functionally it works diachronically, in combination with temporal and spatial movement. Act I is set at Takasago, a marginal location, the home of the feminine spirit; to witness the revelation in Act II, the priest travels to Sumiyoshi, cultural and political centre of Japan and home of the masculine spirit. The feminine spirit is identified with the archaic *Man'yoshu* poetry, the wild; the masculine spirit is identified with the *Kokinshu*, the civilised court style.[32]

In a typical metaphysical move, the unity of two as one is proclaimed in *Takasago* when in fact only one of the pair, the masculine and not the feminine, is privileged to appear in the glorious finale.[33] There is no evidence that *Takasago* was originally composed to feature both aspects in the second act and that the feminine aspect was later eliminated, as was the case in many early deity plays. The logic of *Takasago* dictates from the start that the feminine must disappear.

In *The Tempest*, presumably, all the characters suddenly found their garments fresh as new after the spell was broken, but in *Takasago*, only the male deity sheds his cloak of dead brown pine needles to be admired by the Chorus with the praise, 'a thousand years' fresh green brims from your hands'.[34] This is not to say that Miranda was allowed much more of a voice than the female deity of *Takasago*; it is to say that the silences of the women in both plays inevitably produce irony in any conceivable historical context. In *The Tempest*, Prospero constantly feels compelled to ask whether Miranda is really listening to his patriarchal wisdom (I.ii *passim*). Similarly, the long, lulling narrative in Act I of *Takasago* is modelled on Kan'ami's most famous deity play, *Shirahige*, which first established the success of the Kanze troupe. In *Shirahige*, Kan'ami had parodically recontextualised a long tale which was employed as a method of filibustering. The tale of this clever strategy to silence one's opponent originally appeared in the contemporary and controversial *Taiheiki*, a chronicle of bloody civil war ironically entitled *Record of Great Peace*. Likewise, the 'reunion' of Pericles with his wife and daughter may appear from a different perspective as the man's recovery of his female possessions, just as the revival of Hermione in *The Winter's Tale* may be viewed as essentially serving to aid in the restoration of the friendship of the two men, Leontes and Polixenes, although that male friendship, like the conjugal fidelity of the old man and woman in *Takasago*, had of course always had the potential to transcend the miles that separated Sicily and Bohemia – the two men had always 'seemed to be together, though absent' (I.i.30).

The attraction of such logic guaranteed *Takasago*'s enthusiastic reception by the shogun and secured its premier place in the canon. The play went on to become the play with the most extensive performance record throughout the centuries. And through the years, it accumulated more and more authorisation in the form of esoteric performance codes and their exegesis – from the number symbolism of the drumbeats, to the cosmological significance of the directions in which the dancer faces, to any number of taboos.[35]

Challenges

As this brief survey has demonstrated, conservative revisions of the Noh repertoire to bring insubordinate plays in line with more orthodox standards set by *Takasago* were accomplished primarily by manipulating features of visual representation, including the elimination of female characters, changes in mask and costume that elevate the status of masculine manifestations of deity and compromise that of feminine manifestations of deity, changes in dance patterns, and the addition of decorative subordinate characters to enhance the aura of authority of masculine deities. The ruling-class patrons of Noh appear to have recognised the subliminal power of spectacular visual images and to have worked just as actively to support their employment to enhance the mythmaking project (for example, by commissioning gorgeous costumes) as did the patrons of the Elizabethan masque, as documented by Stephen Orgel in *The Illusion of Power* (1975).

But in their zeal to exploit that power, the makers of Tradition seem to have severely underestimated the subversive power of the text. As Catherine Belsey notes in her Afterword to *The Matter of Difference*, 'The heterogeneous text is one which is not readily co-opted on behalf of either subversion or containment'.[36] This is a view frequently expressed specifically about Shakespearean texts: as Stephen Greenblatt says in *Renaissance Self-Fashioning*, 'Shakespeare's plays offer no single timeless affirmation or denial of legitimate authority'.[37] Having documented the above trends in strategies of attempted containment, let us next examine ways in which all these conservative revisions and erasures are yet challenged.

Despite attempts to obscure historical fact in order to capitalise on the appeal of esoteric mystique, Noh is clearly a sophisticated, self-consciously ironic product of an age of constant civil war characterised in Japanese as the era of *gekokujo*, literally, when 'the low overturned the high'. Gender reversal is one major source of irony. There are a number of plays in which indigenous deities traditionally conceived as male are portrayed as revealing themselves in feminine form to heighten the sense of the anguish of their oppression under the tyranny of Buddhism, as well as many plays in other categories featuring human characters.

The ironic potential of silences and absences is also increasingly coming to be recognised and exploited. The most famous example is *Dojoji*, a prime example of a woman scapegoated as whore to absolve a Buddhist priest of the sin of sexual desire. In *Kanemaki*, the earlier form of this two-act play, the woman continues to speak even after her metamorphosis into a serpent. In the later canonical version, she is silent after the metamorphosis, but her silenced voice is all the more striking to the spectator attuned to such silence. The same technique is used in non-canonical deity plays such as *Hitokotonushi*, literally, 'Master of the One Word', the spirit of the mountain echo driven out of its territory by the invading Buddhist priest. Contemporary awareness of this issue is indicated by the fact that more and more plays featuring feminine manifestations of deity, plays once totally excluded from the canon, are being revived on the stage. Just as recent stage productions of *A Midsummer Night's Dream* place greater emphasis on the sinister, nightmarish aspects of the forest,[38] so the staging and reception even of the most orthodox Noh plays may also some day change so that they no longer automatically perpetuate unwarranted assumptions based on impressions internalised from artificially constructed categories: *Takasago* may come to be recognised not as the supreme articulation of a vision of an ideal world but as a nightmare for women.

One example from Shakespeare which I find emblematic of this problem is the following exchange between Hermione and Leontes in *The Winter's Tale*.

HERMIONE: My life stands in the level of your dreams
                      Which I'll lay down.
LEONTES: Your actions are my dreams. (III.ii.79–80)

In the end, the statue mocks Leontes's attempt to dominate Hermione, just as all imitation ultimately mocks our desire to control others – even when men such as Pygmalion and Genji attempt not only to create women in their desired images but to render them silent and invisible.

Increasingly widespread recognition of the prominence of such ironic features in non-canonical Noh plays is already being seen to affect the dominant mode of both stage production and reception of the art. It has led to a renewed awareness of the ironic potential of the play-within-a-play and other methods of re-contextualisation in plays in the traditional canon as well. Such dramatic techniques have been put to brilliant use in plays from both Noh and Elizabethan traditions to create subtly ironic depictions of conflicting authorities. Should that genius be attributed to Zeami and Shakespeare alone? Or might it be viewed as testimony to a wider and deeper understanding, collectively and accumulatively achieved by a far more inclusive community of artists and spectators of both cultures, of the pathos inherent in the futile desire of any author to own or control the ways in which any text may be re-read or re-staged once it has been released?

12 Shakespearean drama and the Noh: *theatrum mundi* and nothingness

Izumi Momose

In spite of the fact that Shakespearean drama and the Noh are strikingly different in their appearance on stage, there are unexpected points of contact between them. To begin with, scholars have noticed the similarity between the structures of the original theatres designed for both.[1] Then, the authors of both kinds of drama typically began their careers as actors, and in addition to acting took over the writing of play texts for their own theatrical companies, which were in turn deeply rooted in the dramatic tradition of the populace. They achieved such success that their companies came to be granted the patronage of the highest authorities, that of the Stuart monarchs on the one hand, and that of the Ashikaga Shogunate on the other. In both kinds of drama actors took the initiative, a characteristic reflected in the structure of the two kinds, particularly in such devices as the use of the 'play-within-the -play' and the topos of *Theatrum Mundi*, 'the theatre of the world'.[2] In this essay, I should like to concentrate on several of these similarities, especially the role of actors as intermediaries between the action and the audience, and the place of 'nothingness' in both kinds of drama.

I

Among the six lovers in the wood of Athens in *A Midsummer Night's Dream* the most pathetic in the beginning is Helena. Oberon, the Fairy King, pities her, and Puck puts into practice his master's order to change her beloved Demetrius's mind, through pouring the magic juice of Cupid's herb in his eyes. But Puck's repeated mistakes play havoc with the loving game of the young men and maids, and turn it into a nightmarish chaos of complex love affairs. The immediate cause is a fantastic trick in an enchanted fairy tale, but the events are a reflection or projection on to the stage of an actual 'madness' inherent in fertility rituals which were still being practised in woods and hills around the villages of contemporary England. We know from Philip Stubbes, for example, of similar young men and maids who 'against Maie, Whitsonday, or some other tyme' assemble 'to goe some to the Woodes and Groues, some to the Hilles and Mountains . . . where they spend all the night in pleasant pastymes'.[3]

A connection with actual rituals can also be observed in Noh drama. The performance of Noh, as Shimpei Matsuoka has made clear in his recent study,[4] harks back to the rituals for the appeasement of deceased souls. These included not only *sutra* recitation, prayers and the preaching of sermons by *hijiri* (holy ones) in front of a statue of Amitabha Buddha, but also various inverted ceremonials in the form of dramatic performances, such as carnivalesque dances and the composition of *renga*-poems. Ultimately, there would have been a sacred stage presentation in which devils and good demons struggled with each other to the eventual expulsion of the former.

Victor Turner calls the chronospace of festive rituals *liminality* and its inner experience *communitas,* and says that the spontaneity and immediacy of this *communitas* can seldom be sustained for long, although 'when even two people believe that they experience unity all people are felt by these two, even if only for a flash, to be one'. We thus face 'the paradox that the *experience* of communitas becomes the *memory* of communitas'.[5] In *A Midsummer Night's Dream*, as I have suggested, the rituals are transformed into a drama of complicated love relationships.[6] The connection of ritual and drama is as strong, or even stronger, in the case of Noh, which seems originally to have been a paradoxical enterprise, comprising a half-ritual, half-theatrical chronospace, whose purpose was to let the *memory* world revert to and recompose the original *communitas* experience. The plays thus bring into focus the inherent core of festive rituals and give it expression through the interaction of ordinary human beings.

Izutsu (The Well Cradle), is often regarded as the 'masterpiece among masterpieces' of Zeami's *mugen*-Noh, the Noh of Dream Vision.[7] Izutsu, the *shite*-character, is first introduced by the *waki*-priest as a humble village woman, who comes to the ancient Ariwara Temple at Isonokami in Nara province to pray to the Amitabha Buddha. The temple was founded in the distant past by a courtier, Ariwara no Narihira, who was an outstanding poet as well as an enterprising lover. In the course of her verse monologue and prose dialogues with the *waki*, complemented from time to time by comments and narration from the chorus, it becomes clear that the woman's prayers are for the soul of Narihira, who has been buried in the grave-mound in one corner of the Temple garden. In addition, it is revealed at the end of the first part that she herself is the incarnation of the soul of Narihira's old sweetheart and spouse, Ki no Aritsune's daughter, whose love of Narihira caused her much pain in her lifetime.

The latter half of the play is staged within the *waki*-priest's dream vision, in which Izutsu's ghost appears wearing the hat and robe left her by Narihira. She approaches the mouth of an old well in the garden, and peers into it, amazed at how vividly her figure mirrored in the water is reminiscent of her former lover and husband:

> I've grown old, yes!
> Just as he looked, the Man of Old,
> his robe and headdress
> conceal the woman, show me a man,
> Narihira:
> there before me, and so dear!
> I see myself, yet I still love him![8]

It seems that only through a performance recalling the past can the moment of supreme ecstasy be transparently embodied and acknowledged as a real experience. But, as is symbolised by the fact that Izutsu usually wears a *wakaonna* (young woman) mask, her performance at the same time faces the future and eternalises her inner strength, through confirming her pitiable and ultimately innocent love. The pair's mutual love grew up as a childhood affection when the two children came to the same well-cradle to talk and look at each other in the mirror of the water, and developed into a mature love during adolescence. But once their married life began, the man's love divided, as he had a mistress in Kawachi province whom he used to visit each night. The young wife's sufferings caused by her husband's neglect were painful to an unbearable degree, and (according to one interpretation) led her to commit a solitary indiscretion. Unfortunately, her husband found out and, in her ensuing pursuit of him, she collapsed exhausted at a clear spring. She died after writing a last poem in blood on a rock.

During a beautiful, quiet and dignified *jo-no-mai* dance by the ghost of Izutsu just before the end of the play, accompanied by flute and drums and the chanting of the chorus, each experience of the love affair with Narihira is vividly recalled in terms of present emotion, as she transmutes desperate, grievous and vengeful feelings into rare moments of erotic ecstasy, and then into a blissful conviction of conjugal happiness, confirmed by her ultimate reliance on her own innocence. She is observed, and supported with prayer, by the *waki*-priest. In such exquisite dramatic circumstances alone could *yugen*, Zeami's ideal of supreme beauty, be given full expression.[9]

The lady Izutsu is the supreme creation among similar *shite*-characters of the *mugen*-Noh – mainly female but sometimes male – who have had similar innocent, pathetic and indeed tragic experiences of love. The latter part of the play, in which her supreme moments of *yugen* are presented in the *waki*-priest's dream vision, is a kind of play-within-the-play staged by the *waki*-priest's mediating role. The play's action is wholly

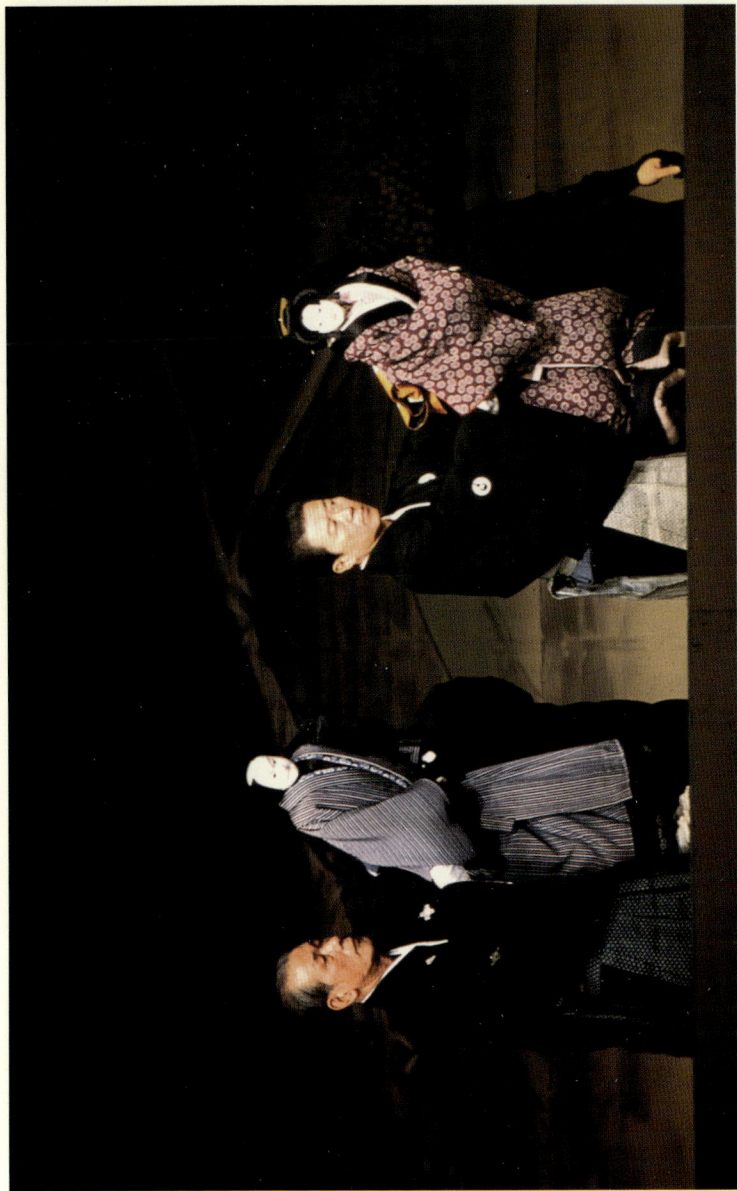

Plate 13 Publicity photograph of puppets and manipulators for the Bunraku stage, National Bunraku Theatre, Osaka.

Plate 14 A scene from Chikamatsu's *The Love Suicides at Sonezaki*, National Bunraku Theatre, Osaka.

Plate 15 Tamao Yoshida manipulating the puppet of Prospero and
Minosuke Yoshida that of Miranda in the 1992 Bunraku adaptation of
The Tempest.

Plate 16 Mansaku Nomura as Falstaff in the Tokyo Globe-Mansaku Company production of Yasunari Takahashi's *The Braggart Samurai*, a Kyogen adaptation of *The Merry Wives of Windsor* (Tokyo and on tour, 1991).

subsumed into it, and the audience is led into its dream world as though it were a potently real experience. But, when dawn comes, the *waki*-priest awakes and his dream vision is utterly dissolved. The audience is left with a desolate sense of vacancy, evoking the ruinous Ariwara Temple, or the mundane yet turbulent historical reality of Japan's middle ages outside the theatre.

II

To return to *A Midsummer Night's Dream*, the tortuous course of love affairs in that play is merged with an atmosphere heavy with festive rituals, the mythical logic of which is embodied in Oberon's plot, mediated especially by Puck. At the same time, however, there takes place a drama of human passion, and this merging of the two aspects seems to be responsible for the ultimate success of the play as one of the masterpieces of Shakespearean comedy. For the essential love-action to evolve and be completed, without being diverted or absorbed into festive ritual, there must necessarily be an intermediary being between the audience and the stage who will function in a stage-manager-like role as well as being a character in the play. Such a pliant, delicate role is very much the counterpart of the Noh drama's *waki*-character, and can be said to be taken jointly by Puck and Bottom, together with the amateur-drama group of mechanicals.

Puck and Bottom act in more immediate conjunction with the audience than with the other characters. Their genealogy is complicated. At a primordial stage in Greek Old Comedy two types of comic characters have been identified in conflict with each other, the Alazon (ἀλαζών), the boaster or imposter, and the Eiron (εἴρων), the ironical man.[10] In medieval and Renaissance English festival, entertainment and drama, there existed in a continuous series a similar pair of comic types, apparently inherited from Greek Old Comedy. For example, Philip Stubbes reports that 'all the wild-heds of the Parish, conuenting togither, chuse them a Ground-Captain (of all mischeefe) whome they innoble with the title of "my Lord of Mis-rule"'. This Lord, whom 'they crowne with great solemnitie and adopt for their king', came to be accompanied by a recognised specialist Fool. Eventually these two types merged into one in such great comedians and comic characters as Richard Tarlton, William Kemp and Sir John Falstaff.[11] Puck the fool and Bottom the clown seem to represent the last stage of this evolution, just before, or in parallel with, the merging of the two characters into one.

Through the mediation of these comic characters the nightmarish tragedy of love in the wood of Athens is transformed into a comedy of love which extends its revitalising influence to all the community. In particular, Bottom's response to his experience in the wood witnesses the dramatic necessity of his and Puck's mediation. Whereas other characters reflect upon it as 'dotage' (IV.i.44), 'the fierce vexation of a dream' (l. 66) and 'sickness' (l. 170),[12] Bottom gives a positive account of his experience:

Methought I was – there is no man can tell what. Methought I was – and methought I had – but man is but a patched fool if he will offer to say what methought I had. The eye of man hath not heard, the ear of man hath not seen, man's hand is not able to taste, his tongue to conceive, nor his heart to report what my dream was! (IV.i.202–7)

Critics have pointed out that these sentences, in which Bottom ponders the 'most rare vision' (IV.i.200) of his amorous encounter with Titania, are a parody of St Paul's words on God's spiritual wisdom, 'secret and hidden', in 1 Corinthians ii.9.[13] Frank Kermode tells us that the blindness of love is a means to grace as well as to irrational animalism.[14] But this is a partial truth only, and seems to be saying too much, or too little, because Bottom's parody remains on the level of an exercise in rhetoric – so much so that the substantial meaning of the Biblical passage is if wholly maintained also wholly submerged.

In terms of psychological analysis, there seems to be figured in Bottom the process through which, according to a Jungian interpretation, a suffering person necessarily goes in the course of his journey towards the Individualisation of Personality. The journey is one from personal unconsciousness to collective unconsciousness, going through the hardships of experiencing and internalising various archetypes. According to Jung, the confrontation with Anima (in the case of the male), or Animus (in the case of the female), which is nothing other than a frontal encountering of one's own erotic impulses, is the most critical moment.[15] The clues to the right solution to a dichotomised personality are most often given through dreaming a meaningful dream, and interpreting it in the deepest way. Bottom overcomes the critical dilemma, as Annabel Patterson suggests,[16] so far as to embody in terms of his adventurous yet ridiculously humble corporeal being a precarious unity between mind and body, in whose deteriorated bi-polar sphere all the other lovers, including even Theseus and Hippolyta, are for the moment wandering.

A further dimension of Bottom's 'most rare vision' is illuminated by considering it in relation to another tradition of Western spiritual thought originating in Plotinus. Particularly in the writings of Pseudo Dionysius, Plotinian Godhead as fundamental Oneness is deepened and transformed into a joyous experience of union with God, who is hidden and ineffable beyond knowledge. Pseudo Dionysius boldly tries to unify the

Greek idea of Eros with the Christian idea of Agape, and says, explaining the phrase 'the foolishness of God' (1 Corinthians i.25), that Paul celebrates this identification 'by calling it that which appears contrary to reason and absurd in itself but which leads us to the ineffable truth before all logos'.[17] This seems to be in close agreement with Bottom's speech above. Moreover, the author says that such a hidden, ineffable God alone could create the cosmos with its overflowing fecundity and that the unity and peace necessarily pervading all created beings are never in contradiction with the individuality and distinctness of each one of them. On the contrary, they are the indispensable basis on which each created being grows, develops and is kept alive to the most perfect degree, in particular through the loving-kindness of Christ 'Who worketh all things in all', uniting all things and binding extremes together. It may be argued that the connotations of this thought of Pseudo Dionysius are also present in Bottom's speech.[18]

In calling to mind these associations, Bottom and his troupe turn a tragedy of love into a revitalising comedy. 'A tedious brief scene of young Pyramus and his love Thisbe' becomes 'very tragical mirth'. (V.i.56–7) This is taken further in Duke Theseus's discussion of the function of audience response towards a performance on stage:

HIPPOLYTA: This is the silliest stuff that ever I heard.
THESEUS: The best in this kind are but shadows; and the worst are no worse, if imagination amend them.
HIPPOLYTA: It must be your imagination then, and not theirs.
THESEUS: If we imagine no worse of them than they of themselves, they may pass for excellent men. (V.i.204–10)

His compassionate attitude, putting himself in the place of others, can be said to be a union of Eros and Agape. The speech also provides a keen insight into the significance of audience identification with the action on stage.

A Midsummer Night's Dream presents three kinds of unified vision: the marriage of three couples, the union of Eros and Agape, and that of mind and body. All of these are attained through the workings of dream vision as the supreme form of reminiscence that can 'apprehend / More than cool reason ever comprehends' (V.i.5–6). Just after the 'tragical mirth', Bottom and the others throw themselves into the performance of a jig, a carnivalesque dance called a 'Bergamask', the excitement of which seems to meet with enthusiastic applause.[19] Thus at the very point at which the story reaches its culmination, the audience is no longer presented only with text, but with a much more participatory format. The 'Bergamask' probably lasted for some time, and may be compared to the *mai*-dance of the Noh. The invitation to audience participation is even more marked when another stage-manager-like figure, Puck, replaces Bottom and speaks the epilogue directly to the audience. He talks of the shadow-like nature of both fairies and actors, then calls the audience's attention to the screeching of an owl, which

> Puts the wretch that lies in woe
> In remembrance of a shroud.   (V.i.355–6)

We cannot but be reminded of the existence of a chaotic nothingness behind the historical realities which surround the audience and the theatre.

III

At the time of composing *Izutsu* and other *mugen*-Noh plays in his sixties, Zeami wrote a treatise of dramatic theory and actor training which sympathetically vibrates with Theseus's speech on audience response. Zeami attached great importance to the audience and said repeatedly that the aim of a Noh performance is to gain the love and respect of people of diverse tastes, places and classes. In *Kakyo*, or a Mirror Held to a Flower, one of his sixteen major treatises, he insists, as a vital necessity, that the actor and the audience should share the same image. To realise this, an actor must come to see himself as the audience does, which means he must make efforts to transform the outer image of himself, which the audience sees, into his own internalised outer image, a step possible only through assiduous training.

If the actor cannot somehow come to a sense of how he looks from behind, he will not be able to become conscious of any possible vulgarities in his performance. Therefore, an actor must look at himself using his internalised outer image, come to share the same view as the audience, examine his appearance with his spiritual eyes and so maintain a graceful appearance with his entire body. Such an action truly represents 'the eyes of the spirit looking behind'.[20]

In a Shakespearean play such as *A Midsummer Night's Dream*, the sharing of the same image between actor and audience, or, to put it another way, the attainment of the play's ultimate meaning (which is dependent on audience response) is pursued and promoted by mediating stage-manager-like characters. Basically the same principle applies also to Noh performance, in which the *waki*-character first presents the narrative as a large-scale play-within-a-play, as well as observes and protects with prayers the ghost-changed *shite*-character in the latter half of the play, just as we have seen in *Izutsu*.

In the case of the Noh, however, the religious function of a mediator is consolidated at a deeper level in terms of the stylisation of the actor's performance, as Zeami noted. In other passages, Zeami substitutes different expressions for this corporeal power of spiritual insight, such as 'inner concentration' or 'inner state of control', which enables the audience to experience as enjoyable and informative even those moments when the actor does nothing, the moments of pause when even the chanting, the dance and the action have ceased. At the same time, this power must never be such as to allow an audience to observe the actor's inner tension as deliberate. Otherwise such concentration will merely become another ordinary skill or action.

This spiritual state, or transcendent inner concentration, cannot but derive its genesis and nurture from religious practice, in particular from Zen Buddhism, as the words of Zeami himself strongly suggest: 'Morning and night alike, and in all the activities of daily life, an actor must never abandon his concentration, and he must retain his resolve'.[21] Zen religious contemplation is a fundamental spiritual state in which an ultimate cosmic truth becomes known like an epiphany, through a delicately balanced union of body and mind. By this embodied spiritual state alone man can penetrate through the perpetual flow of life and death to eternity. The awkward movements and strange appearance of Noh actors, which derive from Zen practice, are like those of a puppet in a puppet show, as Zeami says, quoting a poem by a Zen priest, Gettan Soko.[22] Just as puppet figures, he writes, are manipulated by strings, only to fall and crumple when the strings are cut, so the illusions of the Noh performance are supported and given life by the actor's continuing inner concentration. Yet this concentration must never be made evident, not only to the audience, but even to the actor himself.

The metaphors of puppet and death vividly evoke the stylisation of Noh performance, which includes masks (*men*), costumes (*isho*), chanting (*utai*), musical instruments (*hayashi*), posture (*kamae*), movement (*hakobi*) and other elements that generally seem peculiar and grotesque to present-day sensibilities. W. B. Yeats, however, realised that there is a true artistic meaning behind this 'separating strangeness', on first seeing fragments of a Noh performance in a London drawing-room. With remarkable insight, he perceived in the actor's way of moving, exactly as Zeami indicated, 'those movements of the body copied from the marionette shows of the fourteenth century':

There are few swaying movements of arms or body such as make the beauty of our dancing. They move from the hip, keeping constantly the upper part of their body still, and seem to associate with every gesture or pose some definite thought. They cross the stage with a sliding movement, and one gets the impression not of undulation but of continuous straight lines.[23]

This strangeness, for him, turns in an instant into 'an august formality' and a 'style according to the subject', for it alone can evoke 'a deep of the mind'. Such expressiveness is entirely beyond the ability of any modern realistic art. The actor's mask, according to Yeats, becomes a work of art because 'being is only possessed completely by the dead'.

Yeats's perceptions can be read as the best exposition of Zeami's idea of supreme beauty, *yugen*, which is realised and embodied at the climactic moment of a Noh performance. This is the moment at which body and mind are exquisitely unified in a most delicate balance. Zeami calls it, in another treatise written at the same period, the highest degree of performance, a 'performance at ease in the style of Nothing',[24] since it lies beyond every possibility of verbal expression and logical analysis. And it is well known that Zeami likens the beauty of *yugen* to a flower. But the point of the metaphor is not merely the fascinating grace of a perfect creation of nature. On the contrary, what Zeami stresses is the 'epiphanical' character of the flower's blooming, which is full of surprise, mystery and yet absolute integrity with the life-nexus of the cosmos and nature. This was most profoundly expressed by a Zen priest, Dogen, a great spiritual leader of the time who was also Zeami's mentor, when he wrote in 'Plum Blossom in Bloom': 'A flower blooms in spring, and the whole universe rises in full bloom. The flower is the spring; it is the spring of all things.'[25]

IV

King Lear is a tragedy which contains, as a kind of residue, an inherent form of festive ritual drama, as is shown by the fact that there appear several Eiron- and Alazon-like characters. These are all outcast people, including the Fool, Edmund, Edgar, Kent and even Cordelia. They are like representatives or extensions of the audience, leading the hero and his surrounding people on a way of 'pilgrimage' (V.iii.196) to the final climactic moment. In the course of this process the play is, so to speak, divided into three layers of plays-within-the-play, one telescoped into another. The first, comprising Acts I and II, resembles a tragedy concerning an Aeschylean Prometheus, the second, Acts III and IV, recalls a mystery or miracle play concerning a Prodigal Father, and the third, Act V, constitutes an appalling tragical History.

In common with the Noh, *King Lear* is a drama of 'epiphany'. But this epiphany is revealed stage by stage, following the sequential logic of the plot. At the end of the first play-within-the-play, the storm takes place like a divine act; then at the end of the second occurs the Prodigal Father's miraculous redemption; and lastly the father and daughter's ineffably miserable but strangely cathartic deaths bring about a conclusive and comprehensive revelation. All three stages are sustained by an awareness of a fundamental apocalyptic eschatology, in turn produced through the mediation of Eiron- and Alazon-like characters culminating in a Christ-like Cordelia. Thus the mythical logic of festive rituals, most abundantly reflected in the second play-within-the-play, is transformed, and in close parallel with it, Chaos or Nothingness is faced, tackled and, if only just, overcome. In contrast, the epiphanical outcome of Noh drama is like a flower (as we noted above), which takes place in an instant, and is not sequentially presented. But the sense of joyousness emanating from the overcoming of Chaos or Nothingness is just as powerful.

Thus Shakespearean drama and the Noh both pursue and develop the theatre of the world to the limit of its dramatic possibility, a process guided and sustained by the topos of Chaos and Nothing which can be said, in turn, to derive ultimately from the mythology of festive rituals. And it is none other than this topos that makes them turn again and face the historical realities, breaking open the text as an ultimate consequence of their performance. It also makes them inherently different from other contemporary or related dramas, which evolve similar theatres of the world, but more or less exhibit a finished, inclusive completeness of form. We might think of such Renaissance dramas as those of Marlowe, Jonson and Calderón, on the one hand, and the Bunraku-puppet theatre and Kabuki on the other.

Shakespearean drama and the Noh each creates its own world. Everything is achieved with some radical religious philosophy as ultimate, intercommunicative, basis and source. Both dramatic worlds are presented in a way that realises the religious philosophers' insights as real and true, through their respective and peculiar dramaturgy: the apocalyptic eschatology tinged with Plotinian restlessness in Shakespeare, and the epiphanically directed and formalised performance in the case of the Noh, connected as it is with Zen meditation. In the end, both kinds of drama eventually face and overcome Chaos and Nothingness, without ignoring historical realities.

13   Tradition and the Bunraku adaptation of *The Tempest*

Minoru Fujita

Tradition is restrictive, hampering and often stifling, but I have never ceased to be impressed by the activating force of the tradition that has allowed Japanese drama to remain over the centuries an effective means of representing life. The vitality of the Japanese theatre tradition may partly be due to an unswerving commitment to the highest artistic skills of performance and, as a necessary complement to this, to the practice of bequeathing the secrets of the trade to actors or performers belonging only to certain privileged families or restricted groups. This latter circumstance has doubtless been a serious drawback in the growth and development of Japanese theatre, and the National Theatre in Tokyo and the National Bunraku Theatre in Osaka are currently training additional performers in order to mitigate this disadvantage to some degree. Another reason for the continuing vitality of Japanese drama is its success in preserving the individual forms of Noh, Bunraku and Kabuki and in preserving their performance spaces essentially in their original shapes.

When I was asked to plan a production of a Shakespeare play in Bunraku form, I immediately turned my mind to circumstances relating to the living tradition of Japanese drama. Up to now I have always imagined Shakespeare's drama as it was performed in the original conditions of the Elizabethan or Jacobean public theatre, on the open stage. Shakespeare was referring to the wide stage of the newly opened Globe playhouse when the Duke in *As You Like It* spoke of 'this wide and universal theatre'. And he had in mind the nature of the cosmic theatre of the Renaissance when he wrote the storm scene of *King Lear* in which the hero 'Strives in his little world of man to out-scorn / The to-and-fro conflicting wind and rain'. To revive the Renaissance idea of the *theatrum mundi* and combine the nature of its stage-space with the messages inscribed in Shakespeare's own texts, has afforded the modern interpreter the most convincing way to re-evaluate the original power and energy of the plays of Shakespeare. Since Renaissance theatres in England were totally lost in the 1640s, together with the theatre tradition from which Shakespeare's plays must have derived their expressive power, my dream now was to expose a Shakespeare play to some traditional principles that remain in the sphere of world theatre. Bunraku seemed to me to provide the conditions for the realisation of this dream. At about the same time, I was engaged in preparing an annotated edition of *The Tempest*, and the elements of tragedy, comedy and fantasy in the romance seemed at least to have something in common with this genre of Japanese drama.

1992 saw the Bunraku version of *The Tempest* produced under the auspices of a committee of which I was chairman and in cooperation with the National Bunraku Theatre. It was first presented in the Kintestsu Art Museum in Osaka and then brought to the Tokyo Globe Theatre. The adaptation started with the making of the libretto, which was undertaken by Mr. Shoichi Yamada, who had long been involved with productions of Bunraku plays. Due to shortage of time and other circumstances, he chose to base the composition of his Bunraku version upon the translation of the play by Shoyo Tsubouchi. Tsubouchi began his work as a Shakespeare translator as early as the 1890s, when Japanese theatre was still strongly under the influence of Kabuki and Bunraku. His earliest translation of Shakespeare, that of *Macbeth* (1892), was admirable since it attempted to translate Shakespeare's rhetorical style into a rich Kabuki idiom. The choice of Tsubouchi's translation as the basis for his adaptation of *The Tempest* was a factor in enabling Mr Yamada to achieve his aim of transmuting Shakespeare's language into the passionate 'resonance' of traditional *joruri* (chanting accompanied by *shamisen* music) in the Bunraku. This Banraku version was given a title based upon the traditional way of naming a Bunraku play: *Tenpesuto Arashi Nochi Hare* (literally meaning '*The Tempest*: the storm followed by fine weather').

What did the adaptation of Shakespeare into the idiom of Bunraku entail? In the case of Noh, Kyogen and Kabuki, as soon as the adaptation is completed copies of the play-book can readily be distributed to the cast, and rehearsals can be started almost immediately. In the case of Bunraku, however, when it is completed the text is passed to the *shamisen* composer to be set to music. Seiji Tsurusawa was chosen as the composer, and he succeeded in finding a creative means of affording the text a certain rhythm and melody of pathos. Oritaiu Takemoto, one of the greatest Bunraku chanters today, gave a vocal rendering of the narrative, aided effectively by the music to which the words of the text had been set. The chanter in Bunraku intones the words according to his own understanding of the internal logic of the drama, down to the smallest detail of the narrative, and the puppet manipulators then devise steps and figures for their puppets in accordance with the thoughts and emotions of the characters now vocalised by the chanter. I believe this extended process well illustrates the kinds of barriers Shakespeare's drama has to overcome in order to achieve successful adaptation to a form of theatrical artifice such as Bunraku.

From the start of planning the Bunraku *Tempest*, a primary consideration was to limit the number of characters, since one Bunraku puppet has to be operated by a set of three manipulators. (These are the head puppeteer, usually dressed formally in kimono and unhooded, exposing his face to the audience, the left-arm manipulator and the leg manipulator, the latter two always hooded and clad in black.) The puppeteer who operates the head and right arm should be a skilled and experienced veteran. The result of the limitation in the number of characters was to retain Prospero, Miranda, Ariel, Caliban, Alonso, Ferdinand, Antonio, and Stephano as characters operated by three manipulators each, with minor characters such as the spirits being controlled by single operators. Celebrated puppeteers such as Tamao Yoshida (for Prospero), Minosuke Yoshida (for Miranda), Bunjaku Yoshida (for Alonso) and Iccho Kiritake (for Ferdinand) were among those selected.[1]

As to the theme of the adapted version of *The Tempest*, the adapter placed his main emphasis on the hero's revenge on his enemy, a theme by no means prominent in the original Shakespearean romance of harmony and reconciliation. According to Mr. Yamada, however, Prospero's revenge comes when his daughter Miranda marries his enemy's son Ferdinand, allowing Prospero to mix his blood with his enemy's through matrimony.[2] From a Japanese perspective, as Mr Yamada points out, the reconciliation achieved through marriage with the enemy's house essentially means a victory over it. In Shakespeare's script, the Neo-Platonic theme of harmony is combined with the harmony of music and the cosmos, and this finds remarkable expression in the poetry of *The Tempest*. This quality is diluted in the traditional rhetorical idiom of Tsubouchi's Japanese translation, in which the metaphysical theme is given less emphasis. The adapted *Tempest* gave the drama of feudal conflict, and the resulting tragedy of banishment, a more central emphasis. Bunraku is essentially not a drama of ideas but of conflict and passion, and it is here that the virtue of the adaptation of *The Tempest* asserted itself. The chanter's vocal narrative and singing evoked intensely the hero's long endured agony of a life of banishment, and his mental struggle to live through the extreme ordeal.

Material circumstances associated with Bunraku also affected the adaptation of *The Tempest*. The Bunraku puppet has a hand-carved wooden head permanently attached to a handgrip, which is inserted into the framework of the puppet's body and held by the right hand of the main manipulator. The heads for the puppet characters are usually chosen from among those kept in reserve in the Bunraku Theatre. For

Miranda and for Ferdinand the typical heads for young lovers were of course chosen. The same head is often shared by several puppet characters, but, from character to character the way the puppets are manipulated varies, and hence the delicate, skilful characterisation proper to Bunraku arises.[3] As to the puppet head for Prospero, it was at first planned that this should be specially sculpted for this production. It was then found however that Prospero could be represented by the head of Shunkan.

The role of Shunkan is one of the most intensely studied among puppeteers and Kabuki players alike. Before Chikamatsu adapted the story in 1719, the Noh drama *Shunkan*, based upon a tragic episode from the great classic *Tale of the Heike (Heike Monogatari)*, had already fully expressed Shunkan's great sorrow in his fatal banishment. In Chikamatsu's version, *The Heike Island of Exile (Heike Nyogo no Shima)*, Shunkan plots against tyranny and is banished to an islet with his comrades. After years of life in exile, they are eventually pardoned and permitted to leave the lonely island for the mainland. But, seeing that a friend of his, who married a girl of the island during his banishment, will have to leave her behind because of the limited number of people listed on the pardon, Shunkan decides to remain and to let her go on board in his stead. (He has already heard the tragic news of his own wife having been killed in the capital Kyoto, because she had refused the tyrant's advances.) In his extreme sadness, Shunkan climbs to the top of a huge rock on the shore and, almost petrified there, gazes after the vanishing boat. The self-discipline of Shunkan, his superb intellect, his upright, honest personality, his indomitable spirit of endurance, his tough and magnanimous mind, all of which have not been affected by adversity, find expression in the carving of the puppet head, with the characteristically thick eyebrows, moustache and beard adorning its gaunt face. The puppet head of Shunkan is generally accepted as expressing, in artistic form, all the accumulated aspects of the dramatic character Shunkan.[4] The magus-like character of Prospero in the Bunraku version of *The Tempest* is a perfect counterpart to this, and the choice of Shunkan's head is therefore highly appropriate. The head is traditionally matched with a worn-out, patched kimono which eloquently speaks of long years of hard and austere life in banishment.

The Bunraku puppet head of Shunkan has also been used for the role of Kan Shojo, the best known tragic hero in Bunraku and Kabuki, during the scene of his banished life in Act IV of the renowned drama *Sugawara and the Secrets of Calligraphy (Sugawara Denjyu Tenarai Kagami)*, written by Takeda Izumo and first performed in 1746. This is a play about a noble sage and court statesman, who is falsely accused of a crime and banished to a distant land. In the scene in Act IV known as 'Mt Tempai' the hero puppet wears a new head with 'the eyes larger and more deeply set . . . [and a] striking brownish red accent about the eyes and nostrils. The general countenance is a mixture of grief and anger'.[5] Shojo's anger against his enemy's evil is certainly great, and the dignity of the character as he endures inward sorrow and rage during his banishment gives a superb sculptural expression to the puppet head. In a great fury he says that his 'ghost will become chief of the one hundred and sixty eight thousand rumbling thunders that reverberate through the heavens',[6] and at the close of the scene he, still alive, is seen to soar up and change into a Jupiter-like thunder god.

In 1930, *The Heike Island of Exile* (*Heike Nyogo no Shima*), a Bunraku play originally written by Monzaemon Chikamatsu, was revived after a long hiatus in its performance history. Since the Bunraku theatre had been destroyed by fire and its store of puppet heads lost in 1926, no proper head was then available for the banished Shunkan. The puppeteer therefore used the old head of Kan Shojo. The result was very satisfactory. Since then, the use of the puppet head of Kan Shojo to represent Shunkan in the scene of his banished life in the very remote Island of Kikaigashima has been accepted practice. No other head can express so effectively the full realisation of Shunkan's passion as it reaches its climax. Thus the Shojo–Shunkan type of puppet head traditionally carries, for Japanese audiences, associations of tragic banishment and rage. By using the same head-type for Prospero, the banishment theme, as elaborated in Bunraku and Kabuki over hundreds of years, carried its powerful associations into the new adaptation of *The Tempest*.

I first proposed the adaptation of *The Tempest* in the form of Bunraku because a Shakespearean romance seemed to me to be compatible with the classical genre of Bunraku in weaving together 'a vast array of historical and legendary characters into a marvellous day-long drama with comic, tragic, realistic, and fairy-tale-like elements'.[7] I realised that my proposal was even more justifiable when I saw that the Shunkan-Shojo head, and the banishment theme represented by it, corresponded closely to the Shakespearean drama with its banished noble prince as hero. Of course the stories of Prospero, Shunkan and Kan Shojo are different from one another in detail. Nonetheless, for a Japanese audience that has cultivated its sense of the nature of tragedy via the drama of Shunkan and Kan Shojo, the banishment theme in *The Tempest* offered an opportunity for developing the sense of the tragic in a new way.

All aspects of the adapted drama had to conform to this new structure of feeling. The adapter was expected to make his language as pathetic and moving as Shunkan's. The narrator and the musician had to make the rendition as deeply emotional as that in the recital of Shunkan's story. The sculptural solemnity of the Shojo-Shunkan head implicitly required that the entire quality of the adapted drama should be appropriate to the force derived from the matrix of the banishment theme in Bunraku. The adaptation necessarily differed in several ways from the original Shakespeare script: the wonder of the island, so delicately wrought through the magical workings of the airy spirits, had to be largely eliminated; the strong sense of the opposition between civilisation and wilderness, between culture and nature, mainly inspired by Caliban, proved beyond the scope of the adaptation. However, the Bunraku version of *The Tempest* acquired a new consistency from its impassioned re-creation in the mould of the classical Japanese drama of rage and renunciation.

In comparison with the advantages the figure of Prospero obtained from Bunraku and Kabuki, Ariel's character posed serious problems, since Japanese classical drama offers nothing that would even remotely correspond to the dramatic representation of a Western supernatural spirit. In the Japanese adaptation of *The Tempest*, however, the combined work of the musician and the chanter created a 'song' that might tolerably be compared with Shakespeare's own 'Full fathom five . . .' With its aria-like melody, it inspired the puppeteers to manoeuvre the puppet of the kimono-clad Ariel to look lingering and air-supported within the stage space. This freedom from gravitation in Ariel was indeed a theatrical innovation, which will, when more ingeniously choreographed, develop into an asset to Bunraku performance.

The representation of Caliban proved to be a challenging case to deal with on the Bunraku stage. Japanese theatre has created no imaginary creatures truly comparable to this wild monster immune from any kind of nurture or culture but remotely reminiscent of a noble savage. It was amusing to see the monkey-like creature of the Bunraku Caliban behaving like a rebellious young rascal, cursing and abusive in an Osaka accent. He remained, however, no more than a resentful country hoodlum, and never provided a genuine antithesis to the civilisation, reason and benevolence represented by Prospero and Miranda in Shakespeare's original.

In the adaptation, emphasis was laid on the portrayal of conflict arising out of the bitter feud over political power which, in Shakespeare's version, is spoken of by Prospero in his narrative recapitulation in the second scene of Act I. In the Bunraku version with its seven scenes, this retrospective sequence of the hero's story is brought forward in scene v, which thus becomes the crucial centre of the drama. In the previous scene, Miranda narrowly escapes being violated by Caliban, but is rescued by Ferdinand. This young man has been controlled by Ariel's magical music, and induced to sleep until the moment he hears Miranda's shriek. 'At the

first sight they have changed eyes', though in this case through no stratagem of Prospero's, as in the original.

In scene v of the Bunraku version, Prospero meets the young man and
Ferdinand tells him who he is. Hearing that he is no other than his arch-
enemy's son, the old man shows extreme anger and tries to drive him out,
to the great sorrow of Miranda. Prospero then tells his daughter everything that has happened to them twelve years earlier. His daughter's
astonishment is enormous. Ferdinand's surprise is similarly great on
hearing the old lord's story. He offers to be killed by Prospero when he
learns that his family has so long been the object of the old man's hatred,
and that Prospero will not allow his daughter to marry their enemy. In the
Bunraku theatre, a chanter, chanting the narrative of a given story, can
create a moment in the course of the drama when, like a singer in an opera
or oratorio, he voices a melody so deeply expressive as to create 'sounds
that convey the essence of the femininity of a woman in love or the distilla-
tion of the rage of a vengeful man'.[8] What is no more than a past event
remembered by Shakespeare's Prospero becomes, in the hero's utterance
in Bunraku, an occurrence in the dramatic present which requires an
intense and elaborate vocal rendition of nobility and wisdom in thought,
and of fury and sorrow in passion. The art of the traditional *joruri* recitation enables the old lord, the young girl and the young samurai to give the
most delicate and intense expression to their respective mental agony and
suffering. Thus, in this Bunraku adaptation, *The Tempest* achieved a rarefied artistic presentation quite different from that ever experienced in a
Western performance.

This production of *The Tempest* also provided a really outstanding
shamisen score for the tempestuous storm in the opening scene. The
entire scene, set in almost complete darkness, proceeded for a duration of
three to five minutes (according to the play-text), solely with a dynamic
shamisen performance making the formidable sea storm audible. It totally
omitted any human voice such as those incorporated in Shakespeare's
text. On top of the fortissimo strokes of the *shamisen* a barely perceptible
flute melody hovered as a clever counterpoint to the tempestuous music.
The delicate flute music created the impression that the raging of the elements, unmistakably a natural phenomenon, was somehow moderated by
a mysterious influence, which became visible when, in the following
scene, the Bunraku Ariel hovered over the stage space, accompanied by
this increasingly audible air on the flute, to meet the magus Prospero at
his magical practice.

One aspect of the production I found less than satisfactory related to
the use of the puppets. The head puppeteers were all dressed in black and
hooded exactly like the hooded assistant manipulators throughout the

seven scenes of the performance, in order to obliterate or at least mini-mise the obtrusive sense of their presence. Paradoxically, however, I was struck by the fact that normally it is not only the lifelike behaviour of the puppets that the spectators enjoy seeing. The unhooded head pup-peteers' serene facial expressions (always exposed to the eyes of the spec-tators) signal the ultimate empathic dimension, as they convey into their puppets thoughts and emotions shared, as if they were their own. Their faces mirror the delicate art, the exquisite poses and movements of the puppets. This is what unmistakably takes place between the Bunraku audience and the *omozukai* (chief puppeteers) when, with their character-istic decency and solemnity of deportment, they perform, unhooded, on the Bunraku stage. If the audience could have watched the elderly manip-ulator Tamao Yoshida, in his regular kimono costume and unhooded, operating the puppet Prospero, the nobleness of character and the agony of mind that imbues the puppet would have far more forcefully and effectively moved the souls of the spectators.

The Bunraku version of *The Tempest* was followed by a pseudo-Kabuki production by a newly formed troupe of non-traditional actors. The play with the same Japanese title (*Tenpesuto Arashi Nochi Hare*) was based upon the identical Japanese version that the Bunraku group had used. However, it was more freely adapted in parts and more comically ampli-fied, with Trinculo and even Sycorax joining the list of characters. The same *shamisen* music was employed, but female instead of male *joruri* chanters sang in this mock-Kabuki production. To discuss in detail this production, which often parodied while seriously trying to re-evaluate the tradition of Kabuki, might be the topic for another essay. Nevertheless, we can say that the repeated enactment of the same play in two different but closely related modes of Japanese classical drama served to promote the intercultural re-creation of Shakespeare in Japan. In the Kabuki or Bunraku performances a sophisticated and efficient co-operation was found between the actor or puppet-manipulator, the chanter and the *shamisen* musician. These three parts, with their respective skilled tech-niques, assimilated the thoughts and emotions of Shakespeare's drama and developed a new and original artistic way of unfolding a Shakespearean play. This tripartite work seems to me to signify something resembling what Peter Brook calls 'collective creation', and is indeed a far cry from a drama dictated by an individual director's conception.

Directors of Shakespeare's plays in the West today seem to be trying to give their own personal or individualised reading to Shakespearean texts, and to stage the plays according to their own particular interpretation. What distinguishes classical Japanese drama more than anything else is its almost self-perpetuating theatrical tradition. In both Kabuki and

15. A publicity photograph of the Miranda puppet and its manipulator (Minosuke Yoshida) in the 1992 Bunraku adaptation of *The Tempest*.

Bunraku, Chikamatsu's texts have been spoken in a traditional, orthodox way, hardly varying for hundreds of years. The working concept behind these 'play books' in the theatre is that they are no more than the visible counterpart of what is actually kept in the chanter's memory. He must make the manipulation of the puppets (or actors' performance), the execution of the musicians, and his own narration work in harmony, so as to orchestrate the total unfolding of the drama. In the Bunraku theatre a reading desk of splendid appearance is set in front of the chanter. A play-book bound in an old style is placed on the desk. The chanter is seen to lift it up, offer a prayer and open it on the desk. Needless to say, all the language in the text is preserved in his memory, and this ceremony only signifies the determining role of the 'text' in Bunraku. The chanter's dignified desk called 'kendai' is the symbol of the supreme authority that the chanter, who leads the unfolding of the Bunraku drama, confers on its 'texts', or its 'metatext'.

The true text of a Bunraku play does not consist only of the words written by the author. It also includes the cues and choreography for the

16. The scene from *Sugawara Denjyu* showing the head of the puppet Kan Shojo, hero of the play, which was also used for the Prospero puppet in the Bunraku adaptation of *The Tempest*.

puppets' movements, the notations of pitch and length for the accompanying *shamisen* music, and the vocal elaboration by the chanters to express the delicacy of human sentiments and the strength of human passion. The visible, readable text is the 'outer' one. The text which is kept in the performers' minds and bodies, combined with their art and skill, and synthesising the whole setting and staging of a play, is the 'inner' one. The text of a Shakespearean play as we have it is essentially the former, open to everyone's interpretation. The text of a Chikamatsu play, consecrated by the chanter is merely the visible counterpart of the 'meta-text (or unwritten text of the *mise-en-scène*)'[9] developed by the chanter and shared by the rest of the performers.

To the eyes of a Western audience the Bunraku version of *The Tempest* may seem merely another new and ephemeral interpretation of a Shakespearean play, exotic in every possible way. Yet, this production meant something remarkable for the Japanese audience, being intended to create a new type of Bunraku drama to be included in the permanent repertory.

14   The performance of gendered identity in Shakespeare and Kabuki

Yoko Takakuwa

At the turn of the sixteenth century a new kind of theatre came into existence in Japan. A little earlier in Britain, the Shakespearean theatre created a new paradigm with several similar features. In both Shakespeare and Kabuki, drama and popular culture meet centre stage and produce a dynamic form of theatricality.

While generic classifications are different in the Shakespearean and Kabuki theatres, both forms of drama tend to include mixed comic and tragic modes. In each case, history plays based on the chronicles are anachronistic, ignoring or fictionalising historical 'facts' and exploiting historical frameworks to represent issues in contemporary culture as modern drama. During the Edo era (1603–1867) the Tokugawa shogunate did not allow the theatre to make topical allusions, and so Kabuki had to distance modern problems in the guise of remote (hi)story (*histoire*) as 'fiction', irrelevant to current reality. Most significantly, however, the powerful theatricality of both Kabuki and Shakespeare is produced precisely on the ambiguous boundary between social 'fact' and literary 'invention' or, in the words of one of the greatest Japanese playwrights, Monzaemon Chikamatsu (1653–1724), on 'the membranous confines between fiction and reality'.

Both the Shakespearean and Kabuki theatres are also all-male theatres where female roles are performed by men. The clear distinction between masculine and feminine genders does not hold there. In impersonating 'woman' on stage, both theatrical practices defy the law of genre/gender, which we so easily take for granted as defining our own meaning-and-identity. The law of genre/gender commands us: 'one must respect a norm, one must not cross a line of demarcation, one must not risk impurity, anomaly or monstrosity . . . genres [genders] should not intermix'.[1] An excess of meaning produced as theatrical surplus, however, overflows the restriction of the law of genre/gender and brings to light contradictions in the ideological meanings, constitutive of our identity in the nexus of class, race and gender. As a result, both early modern Puritans and the Tokugawa shogunate came to regard the theatre's transgression of the law of genre/gender and its subversive power of 'fiction' as a menace to the cultural order and, by locating the theatres on the margins of the city, did their best to regulate a dynamic of theatricality.

Paradoxically, the history of Kabuki's prosperity was also the history of being driven out of the city centre of Edo, the present Tokyo.[2] In 1603 Ieyasu Tokugawa (1542–1616), the founder of the Tokugawa shogunate, chose provincial Edo as the new capital. In the course of the urbanisation of Edo, the shogunate first appropriated Kabuki to attract people and populate Edo,[3] and then confined the Kabuki theatres to licensed quarters and repeatedly moved them, in accordance with its city planning, and later owing to its oppression policy.[4]

The shogunate ordered the first theatre-town in Nakahashi to move to Negi-cho around 1635, for the reason that it was too near Edo Castle. In 1651, the shogunate again moved two Kabuki theatres to two adjacent towns, Sakai-cho and Fukiya-cho, near the brothel-town, Yoshiwara. In 1663, it limited the theatre-towns to Sakai-cho, Fukiya-cho and Kobiki-cho.[5] Also the head of the company needed the sanction of the shogunate to perform Kabuki. In the keen competition for performance rights, four companies survived as the licensed 'grand theatres' in Edo: the Nakamura-za, the Ichimura-za, the Morita-za and the Yamamura-za. In 1714, however, the Yamamura-za lost its license because it caused a scandal about a love affair between an actor and a high-ranking lady-in-waiting to the shogun's mother.

The shogunate then restricted the number of Kabuki theatres to three in Edo and came to control the relations between the Kabuki players and the 'citizens' more severely. The class system was strict, recognising only samurai, farmers, artisans and merchants. As 'classless' people, neither the Kabuki players nor the prostitutes had citizenship. The players were separated and confined as were the prostitutes in licensed quarters called the *aku-sho* (bad places). The shogunate used Confucian ethics as its ideological basis to regulate class and gender, and tried to establish a system of hierarchical identities advantageous to the ruling samurai. The players were excluded from this ideological system.

None the less, the shogunate could not completely repress the creative yet subversive power of Kabuki, which unsettled the seemingly stable meanings-and-identities of samurai or citizen, or of man or woman, and suspended social and sexual 'reality'.[6] Consequently, the more prosperous Kabuki became, the less the shogunate could ignore its social influence. With the Tempo Reforms (1841–1843), the shogunate accused the theatres of demoralising social order and the players of forgetting their 'proper' position in society, and it again ordered the three Kabuki theatres to move to Saruwaka-cho, further away from the city centre of Edo. Near

Saruwaka-cho, there was Shin-Yoshiwara, the brothel-town, which was moved after the Great Fire of Edo in 1657. In assigning these two *aku-sho* (the Kabuki theatres and the brothels) to the margins of the city, the shogunate attempted to bring their dangerous power under control.

Pointing to a similar marginality for Elizabethan drama, Steven Mullaney has argued that 'a social and cultural distance' established by confining the Renaissance theatres to the outskirts of the city gave the stage 'a critical distance' – 'a freedom' to portray the contradictions of their own culture from 'decentred perspectives'.[7]

What is more, however, Shakespeare and Kabuki integrated their own cultures. They were both popular and licensed by high authority. Both theatrical practices break with the conventions and, in the process, reveal that they are conventional. The ways in which they offer the alternatives at the heart of culture *and* outside, however, are generally subversive *and yet* culturally acceptable for the audience. That Shakespeare and Kabuki occupy very ambiguous places in culture thus makes them dangerous.

Shakespeare and Kabuki have much in common. In this essay I propose to isolate their treatment of women and to reconsider the problem of gender as performance by comparing two parallel theatrical representations of femininity, in the light of current poststructuralist theory. I shall first outline a history of Kabuki as an all-male theatre and then discuss the theatricality and fictionality of gendered identity, by deciphering the textual inscriptions of the fatal woman performed by male actors, focusing on the *keisei* (high ranking courtesan) in Kabuki and Shakespeare's Cleopatra.

II

Japanese cultural history locates the 'origin' of Kabuki in the initially religious *Furyu* (unusually elaborated decorativeness) dancing, which became popular after the Ohnin-Bummei disturbances (1467–1477). Through the following century, when the whole country was at war, a widespread craze for *Furyu* dancing involved many people from different classes, who zealously designed decorative costumes and properties, and tried to forget their anxiety about their precarious existence in uneasy times, by pursuing such secular, transient pleasures. The prolonged turbulence finally seemed to draw to an end, when Ieyasu Tokugawa founded the new shogunate in 1603 in Edo, gradually centralising power.

In the same year, 1603, a female entertainer called Okuni (?1572–?1620) started Kabuki dancing with her travelling company in Kyoto, the former capital. The noun Kabuki comes from the verb *kabuku* (to incline),which meant, according to *The Japanese Portuguese Dictionary* published in 1603, 'to conduct out of rule, or act more freely than one is allowed to'.[8] The word *kabuki* signified an 'unusual' deviation from orthodox standards or rules. People whose clothing, speech and conduct were unconventional or eccentric were called *kabuki-mono*. Okuni put on 'unusual', sumptuous men's clothes, stylish properties and swords, performed as a *kabuki-mono*, dancing and singing love songs, and staging an amorous flirtation with a male comedian disguised as the mistress of a house of pleasure. Okuni Kabuki was simple and yet modern, representing the latest fashion in popular culture and an atmosphere of the fickle world. Not only gender roles but also the idea of (heterosexual) love are here parodied and fictionalised as Kabuki.

As soon as Okuni's Kabuki dancing enjoyed widespread popularity, many imitators appeared. The managers of large brothels promoted Yujo Kabuki, in which many courtesans in male disguise danced to the music, singing and playing flutes, drums and the imported, exotic *shamisen* (the main stringed instrument of Kabuki). Yujo Kabuki's luxurious, sexy stages attracted large audiences. The shogunate was so anxious to establish a new social order and discipline that it gathered all the brothels of Edo in Yoshiwara, the licensed pleasure quarters, in 1617. The shogunate then banned Women's Kabuki, Women's *Joruri* and Women's Dancing in 1629, forbidding women to perform with men, in accordance with Confucian ethics. Women's Kabuki was brought to a close only twenty-six years after Okuni started Kabuki.[9]

Young Men's Kabuki, in which boy actors played female roles, became very popular. The third shogun, Iemitsu Tokugawa (1604–1651) enjoyed Young Men's Kabuki, inviting the performers to Edo Castle. After Iemitsu's death, however, the government criticised boy actors for causing social disorder (homosexuality and prostitution) and condemned female entertainers for still performing among the boy actors in female disguise, and so in 1652 it put a ban on Kabuki as a whole.

The Kabuki players' petitions and the audience's strong demand to see Kabuki again made the shogunate lift the ban the following year, on the condition that only adult men who shaved their forelocks should appear on stage. In the next three decades, Men's Kabuki developed the art of female impersonation by the actor called *onnagata*, who plays the *onna-kata* (woman's part). The introduction of the drawing curtain in 1664 enabled Kabuki to stage more complicated plays, consisting of more than two acts. The performing styles and plots of Kabuki were differently developed in Edo, Kyoto and Osaka: for example, the *aragoto* plays on the hero who conquers evil with his supernatural power were popular in Edo, while the *wagoto* plays on the noble hero's love affair with the *keisei* were favoured in Kyoto. Primarily the basic modes of drama and performing styles of Kabuki were almost established in the Genroku period (1688–1703), when with the rapid growth of the urban economy prosperous merchants appeared and popular culture thrived. Through the Edo era, Kabuki was more and more elaborated and developed into one of the most popular entertainments. Although the Kabuki theatres were located on the margins of the city, Kabuki became the centre of Edo culture, exercising, especially since the mid eighteenth century, a great influence on people's lives. Thus *Seji Kenbunroku* ('an observation on current events') written in 1816 says: 'Today's plays do not imitate (re-present) the world. Conversely the play is the base and the world imitates the plays'.[10]

The 264-year Edo era finally came to an end with the collapse of the Tokugawa shogunate. The Meiji Restoration in 1868 inaugurated the Westernisation and capitalisation of Japan as a 'modern' nation. The movement to 'improve' traditional theatres produced *Shin* (New) Kabuki. Through trials and experiments, Kabuki survived great social and cultural changes in almost 400 years of evolution since Okuni's Kabuki dancing.

Kabuki is both classical and unorthodox. While the performing styles are conventional, the richness and vitality of Kabuki is sustained by its enterprising spirit (against the conventions). Kabuki has not only energetically produced original plays, but also adapted plays from other theatres (Bunraku and Noh), and later from Western theatres and from novels. For example, many *Joruri* plays, first written for Bunraku by Chikamatsu, became important in the Kabuki repertoire, such as *Sonezaki Shinju* (1703), *Kokusenya Kassen* (1715), and *Shinju Ten no Amijima* (1720). Kabuki first encountered Shakespeare when the Kabuki version of *The Merchant of Venice* was performed in 1885 under the title of *Sakuradoki Zeni no Yononaka*. Today Kabuki still attracts both old and young audiences; it is alive with the dynamic power of theatricality.

Even the new theatrical movement, however, could not bring actresses back to the Kabuki theatre. Kabuki had already completed the art of *onnagata*, whose female impersonation is fundamentally different from that of any other theatre. (For example, the Noh player uses masks to symbolise 'woman'.) Okuni's performance as a *kabuki-mono* and her transgression of the law of gender precisely anticipates the *onnagata*'s art as one of the most characteristic features of Kabuki. The *onnagata* highlights the contemporary question of gendered identity – deep in the heart of Kabuki (to *kabuku*).

III

What does it mean to be woman? The answer seems obvious – until we examine the theatrical (fictional) traditions of sixteenth- and seventeenth-century England and of Japan since the seventeenth century. At this chronological moment in two quite different cultures, male actors played the parts of women and put on display the possibility that femininity is a question of impersonation and representation.

In the Japanese Kabuki theatre, woman has been impersonated by the actor called *onnagata* for more than 300 years. Beyond the footlights – beyond the *onnagata*'s male body – the audience find a beautiful illusory woman who is often said to be more feminine than real women. The *onnagata* does not try to imitate or re-present a 'real' woman, but he *becomes* the *onnagata* through the stylisation of femininity, by representing the meaning of femininity shared with the audience in the specific historical, political and cultural contexts of Japan – as the signifier 'woman'. The *onnagata*'s art enables him to keep the balance between becoming the *onnagata* as a 'fictitious' woman and revealing his 'real' identity as a man. Through his theatrical performance of femininity, the *onnagata* 'fictions' the symbolic identity of 'woman' on stage.

An interesting parallel in Shakespeare is the representation of Cleopatra. Cleopatra is primarily regarded as the transcendental 'woman' – as the embodiment of the meaning of femininity. How is Cleopatra represented or 'boyed' as fiction in *Antony and Cleopatra*? Enobarbus relates Cleopatra's 'infinite variety' and her irresistible power of seduction. Antony calls Cleopatra both 'enchanting' and 'cunning', oscillating between the undecidable meanings of 'woman'. Cleopatra's sexual power over Antony is, ironically enough, acknowledged by Caesar's dialogue with Agrippa and Maecenas. The image of Cleopatra as a fatal woman is usually re-presented in and by a third person's words, paradoxically often when she is *not* on stage. Possibly it is the power of representation that helped the Elizabethan audience to reconstitute the image of the eternal feminine – beyond the male body of a boy Cleopatra. I shall return to this question of representation of Cleopatra and its contradictory implications.

In *Antony and Cleopatra*, Cleopatra embodies Egypt-Orient-as-feminine. Caesar wants to appropriate Cleopatra as his differentiating other in order to substantiate both his cultural and sexual identity and his patriarchal and imperial power by way of the theatrical demonstration of the supremacy of 'man'-Occident over 'woman'-Orient. Imagining herself led to Rome by Caesar in triumph, Cleopatra vividly visualises a parody scene staged by the 'quick comedians' (V.ii. 215) for the Roman audience: 'I shall see / Some squeaking Cleopatra boy my greatness / I' th' posture of a whore' (218–20).[11] This self-mocking speech discloses the ironic 'reality', perhaps as the moment of dramatic disillusionment for the Elizabethan audience, that it is not a 'real' woman but a boy actor who is performing Cleopatra and *boying* the fatal woman as 'fiction' on stage.[12] His/her speech reveals self-referentially the split between the actor's 'fictitious' identity as the fatal woman and his 'real' identity as a boy. Cleopatra, as a transcendental signifier 'woman', is re-presented by *a boy*. The moment paradoxically brings to light the non-sense of Caesar's patriarchal project of parading male supremacy by putting on display an other who is also the same, and calls into question the logic of identity based on the dialectics of binary oppositions between the sexes.

At the same time, in this speech of Cleopatra, s/he posits the transcendental 'Cleopatra' whose *essence* of femininity no actors could 'boy' (represent and appropriate) by 'squeaking'. The audience are invited to attend to the irony that this speech of Cleopatra is spoken by the very boy actor whose travesty of the eternal feminine s/he denounces.

Womanliness masqueraded on both the English Renaissance and the Kabuki stage. Mentioning the 'all-male theatrical traditions, such as Kabuki and Noh', Stephen Orgel says that 'womanliness is simply a matter of acting'.[13] Is what we call female identity fulfilled even by the 'opposite' sex by means of putting on a theatrical mask of womanliness, to the extent that, as Joan Riviere puts it, there is no difference between genuine, innate womanliness and the masquerade or the (theatrical, fictional) mask of womanliness?[14] There is, this implies, no essence of femininity. Femininity is impersonation, whether radical or superficial.

Along with Riviere's significant writing on the feminine masquerade, both Marjorie Garber and Judith Butler help to clarify the performative, constructed status of gendered identity in terms of masquerade. Quoting Riviere, Garber writes: 'The woman constructed by culture is already an impersonation. Womanliness *is* mimicry, *is* masquerade'.[15] Garber has argued that gender is a question of code, and that cross-dressing as transgression brings about a crisis in the set of social codes or categories (class, gender, sexuality, race, ethnicity). Specifying gender identity parodied by drag and cross-dressing, Butler has similarly argued that gender parody as performance destabilises 'the naturalised categories of identity and desire'.[16] I agree with Garber and Butler that transvestism parodies the idea of 'natural' or 'original' man or woman and denaturalises identity, whether male or female. Despite their useful work, however, it seems to me that Garber and Butler tend to over-celebrate the idea of gender performance.[17] Perhaps I might be more sceptical, insofar as I think that the idea of gender performance gives us the possibility of inhabiting the symbolic as 'man', 'woman' or 'wo-man' in various ways, but that it also might cause us speaking animals other problems which present themselves as the drawbacks of transgression, for desire is inconsistent and never satisfied. Impersonation performed by the subject is always already inhabited by desire, inasmuch as the subject can never be complete or become the Other.

In discussing the question of gendered identity, I should like to reconsider the problem, neither simply as 'a category' (which seems to be in danger of reducing the undecidable play of meaning) nor only in terms of cross-dressing, but in more general contexts, as regards the meaning and representation that constitutes and in-forms gendered identity as an after-effect of image – as 'fiction' in the symbolic (theatre). A sense of being male or female is not self-present but comes into being only in the process of citing and re-citing the meaning of masculinity or femininity inscribed in and by language. As meaning is conventional, an effect of citation and re-citation (repetition) in the textual system we inhabit, gendered identity is *citational*.

IV

The *onnagata* has to learn to impersonate 'woman'. Ayame Yoshizawa (1673–1729), the *onnagata* representative of the late seventeenth-century Genroku Kabuki, counts the training for the *keisei* role as the most important among female roles. *Keisei* literally means a castle toppler who, in Chinese legend, brought to ruin the lord of a castle and his kingdom. The *keisei* was a high-ranking courtesan during the Edo era, who was not only graceful but cultivated, and her refined beauty was sometimes likened to that of a heavenly woman. At the same time, like Cleopatra, the cause of Antony's death, the *keisei* personified the fatal woman who infatuated man and sometimes lured him to his social and financial ruin. In his talk on the *onnagata*'s art, Yoshizawa delineates 'how best to prepare oneself for the profession':

if an *onnagata* made a success of a *keisei* role, all others were easy to perform. The reason for this is that, since he is basically a man, he possesses, by his nature, a faculty of strong action, and he must carefully bear in mind the softness of the *keisei* and her feminine charm. Thus, the greatest attention should be paid to the training for *keisei* roles.[18]

Yoshizawa regards the *keisei* as the embodiment of femininity, because she personifies 'feminine charm' or 'female softness', which he believes is opposite to 'male strength' and the *essence* of femininity. However, the *keisei*'s feminine charm is not given but moulded as the object of the gaze and desire in the brothel. It is interesting that the *onnagata* finds the idea(l) of 'woman', whom he wants to represent by his theatrical (citational) performance, in the *keisei*'s artificially elaborated femininity. The 'fictional' femininity of the *keisei* is more perfect and more desirable than 'innate' femininity. The *onnagata* and the *keisei* are both 'fictitious' women self-fashioned to represent the supposed essence of femininity through their (theatrical, citational) performances of 'woman'.[19]

During the Edo era, a shogunal policy of separation and confinement of Kabuki and prostitution produced the seemingly unmitigated space of desire called the *aku-sho* (bad places). Located outside the citizen's daily life, the *aku-sho* provided both the *onnagata* and the *keisei* with the space of fiction to personify the idea(l) of 'pure' femininity, at a distance, disowning the everyday nearness of the ordinary women for procreation. Their (theatrical) performances of the eternal feminine were parts of their 'real' life. In order to impersonate the highly fantasised woman, for example, the *keisei* would drink but not eat in front of her customers. Yoshizawa also says that the *onnagata* must bear in mind that he is the *onnagata* even backstage and should not spoil his image of the ideal feminine, for example, by eating greedily. Moreover, the traditional *onnagata* smiled but did not laugh on stage, in order on the one hand to feature the idea(l) of reticent, modest woman as required in the feudal system, and on the other, by laughing with his mouth wide open, not to disintegrate a theatrical mask of womanliness and reveal the 'real' face of man.[20] The *onnagata*'s smile in the *keisei* role, which they say shows feminine charm, is the smiling mask of the courtesan as sexual commodity. The *keisei* and the *onnagata* both objectify their bodies as the objects of the gaze and desire and so theatricalise the idea(l) of feminine beauty.

Can we then tell genuine womanliness from a theatrical mask of womanliness? Tamotsu Watanabe discusses the *onnagata* in terms of the logic of mask. He takes as an example the last representative *onnagata* of Edo Kabuki, Iwai Hanshiro VIII (1829–1882). Watanabe describes his sense of strangeness when he sees the photograph of Hanshiro in male clothes, for even without makeup Hanshiro's facial expressions (his beautiful, amorous eyes and gentle smile) and postures are exactly a woman's. (To be more precise, I should like to add that these meanings (beautiful, amorous or gentle) are what Watanabe attributes to the signifier 'woman'.) Except when he appeared on stage, Hanshiro lived as if he were a woman, in seclusion within the enclosed space of the theatre town in the *aku-sho*. Watanabe mentions the fictionality of Hanshiro's 'feminine' secluded room as an extension of the stage. According to the logic of mask, Hanshiro denied his own male body and private life to serve the sacred space of the stage, which is more real than his 'real' life. In

Hanshiro's gender-ambiguous face like a smiling mask, Watanabe finds the fictionalised body of the *onnagata* who has impersonated women in the long tradition of Kabuki.[21] It is almost impossible, we realise, to distinguish Hanshiro's 'real' face as a man from his theatrical, 'fictitious', mask of womanliness. It is the space of fiction that enabled Hanshiro to relativise sexual 'reality' in the world outside and transform his 'natural' but culturally defined body into a 'fictitious' body.

In traditional Japanese dancing, the male beginner starts his practice by learning female parts and the female beginner first practises male parts, in order to get free from his or her everyday body and produce the 'fictitious' body capable of being transformed into various roles. The *onnagata*'s art is based on dancing – on this interchangeability of gender roles. Among many Japanese dance repertoires, *Kyoganoko Musume Dojoji* is said to contain all the basic movements and gestures of woman, for example, ways of treating the long kimono sleeves.[22] The *onnagata* represents what it means to be woman in and by body language, by learning how to cast a sidelong glance or incline his head. The *onnagata*'s art is based on the cultural convention of reading the female body as the text.

In the course of the Westernisation and 'modernisation' of Japanese culture after the Edo era, the *onnagata* came to perform differently, for example in the role of the *keisei* Yatsuhashi, the fatal woman, in *Kagotsurube Sato no Yoizame* (1888), written by Shinsichi Kawatake III (1842–1901). This drama is based on a murder committed in Yoshiwara, the brothel-town, in the early seventeenth century and describes the manners and customs of Yoshiwara of those days in detail. A rustic, pock-marked wealthy merchant, Jirozaemon comes to showy Yoshiwara and is dazzled by a splendid procession of the exquisite *keisei* Yatsuhashi, who is accompanied by other beautiful courtesans, male attendants and little servant girls. In passing before him, Yatsuhashi unexpectedly gives Jirozaemon a seductive smile, which deeply fascinates him to the point where he forgets himself, just as Antony is immediately enchanted by Cleopatra in the barge. Jirozaemon becomes desperate to possess her as his own, spending a great deal of money. Yatsuhashi's jealous lover forces her to refuse Jirozaemon, and she gives him the cold shoulder before other people, in order to prove herself faithful to her lover. Jirozaemon is shocked and humiliated, but keeps his composure and leaves Edo. After a long absence he re-visits the Tachibana-ya brothel to see Yatsuhashi again – and then suddenly murders her, her lover and others with his fine sword called Kagotsurube. 'Kagotsurube cuts well', he even grins, but he is finally arrested. The *keisei* Yatsuhashi is precisely the *fatal* woman for Jirozae'mon, obsessed by the desire to possess her at all costs.

Though today the *keisei* Yatsuhashi's smile is very important and well-known in the play, there were originally no stage directions about it. While other *onnagata* did not smile in this role before World War II, Utaemon Nakamura V (1865–1940) was the first to smile alluringly as Yatsuhashi.[23] As Japan's democratisation proceeded as a result of the American occupation, moreover, a new type of *onnagata* is found in Utaemon Nakamura VI (1917–   ), who first 'almost laughed' (showing his teeth but without making any sounds) when he performed Yatsuhashi.[24] From smile to laughter – representations of the fatal woman based on the existing meaning of femininity have changed with the shift in the cultural paradigm. The changing *onnagata*'s art demonstrates that the meaning of femininity is not stable but variable.

V

How is Cleopatra represented in *Antony and Cleopatra*? Enobarbus 'fictions' Cleopatra: 'I will tell you' (II.ii. 200), he says. He starts spinning a *story* about his 'experience' of the other – Cleopatra in Egypt. Earlier, he banters with Antony and defines Cleopatra as 'a wonderful piece of work' (I.ii.160–61), the product of art, a 'fiction'. In the barge speech, Enobarbus paraphrases Plutarch's historical account and tries to cite and summon Cleopatra in the immediacy of the truth of 'woman' as (hi)story (*histoire*). In order to set the sensuous stage for the beautiful heroine and make her entrance more seductive, he invokes the literary conventions of desire and love figured as conflagration and flow: burning water, love-sick winds and resplendent colour imagery. Antony (and the audience) here might fall in love not so much with Cleopatra herself but with this staging and the very idea of desire and love. Enobarbus continues,

> For her own person,
> It beggared all description: she did lie
> In her pavilion, cloth-of-gold of tissue,
> O'erpicturing that Venus where we see
> The fancy outwork nature. (II.ii. 207–11)

All this description, however, evokes the *idea* of Cleopatra's unparalleled but absent beauty. Cleopatra is neither present on the actual stage nor in Enobarbus' speech, but conjured up as the absent object of desire on the empty stage – in the fantasy-scene. Enobarbus does not give a full account of Cleopatra's beauty, by particularising her complexion, eyes, lips or hair, but solely emphasises the impossibility of re-presenting the beauty of the eternal feminine in and by language. And yet the audience already know what 'beauty' is or, more precisely, think that they know what 'it' constitutes. In addition, a description of Cleopatra 'O'erpicturing *that*

Venus' as squired by the two 'pretty dimpled boys, like smiling cupids' (II.ii.212) is a citation of Renaissance paintings of Venus (the mythical signifier of 'beauty' and 'love') accompanied by Cupid, in which Cupid makes Venus more seductive on the postulate that the female body should be more sexy than a little *naked* boy. Referring to this combination of two seductive figures, Catherine Belsey points out that the gender of the object of desire may be indeterminate and undermines the possibility of a fixed distinction between homosexual and heterosexual desire.[25] Above all, it is the process of citing other images of beauty that induces the very effect of Cleopatra's singularity as the eternal feminine.

Introducing Cleopatra as the object of the gaze and desire, Enobarbus says that not only have her people all gone to see her, even the air 'but for vacancy, / Had gone to gaze on Cleopatra, too, / And made a gap in nature' (II.ii. 226–8). The more unseeable and unimaginable a figure Enobarbus portrays, the more it excites the audience's imagination. Unimaginable pleasure alone, as Jacques Derrida explains the paradox of the imagination, 'arouses or irritates desire but also it alone, and for the same reason, in the same movement, extends beyond or divides presence'.[26] The audience takes pleasure from the unimaginable. The impossibility of re-presenting the idea(l) of the eternal feminine differs and defers the 'pure presence' of Cleopatra as an effect of *differance*,[27] and endlessly proliferates her 'infinite variety' in fantasy – as an absent and thus more desirable object, appealing to the audience's imagination. Here 'we see / The fancy outwork nature'.

VI

The seemingly transcendental woman, Cleopatra is not entirely feminine, and neither is the *keisei*.[28] The fatal woman disrupts sexual difference and identity. In the cross-dressing scene, Cleopatra dresses the drunken Antony in her 'tires and mantles' and wears 'his sword Philippan' (II.v. 21–3). The phallic image of this 'stolen' sword stages male fear of the demonic, fatal woman. Antony and Cleopatra confer and confirm each other's identity as 'man' or 'woman', while an excess of their desire destabilises the identities *proper* to themselves. Caesar criticises Antony for being

> not more manlike
> Than Cleopatra, nor the Queen of Ptolemy
> More womanly than he.   (I.iv.5–7)

Even Cleopatra, the signifier 'woman', may well be masculine in comparison with the effeminate Antony. Caesar, a representative of patriarchal ideology, regards Antony's effeminisation and Cleopatra's manliness as dangerous to the cultural order based on the founding separation of the sexes.

The instability of a demarcating line between the sexes discloses the vulnerability of the symbolic identity of 'man'. Thomas Laqueur and Stephen Orgel have drawn attention to the Renaissance man's fear of effeminisation. Until the end of the seventeenth century, according to the anatomists, man and woman were believed to possess essentially homologous genital organs, either inside or outside their bodies.[29] This idea of 'the interchangeability of the sexes' caused male anxiety that lust or love for woman effeminised man. Therefore, the puritan anti-theatrical tracts, which censured the boy actor's female clothes and roles as a blasphemous violation of God's law prohibiting cross-dressing, were deeply concerned with 'the fear of a universal effeminisation'.[30] The fear of effeminisation inscribed in the anti-theatricalist claim, according to Laura Levine, is that there is no 'essence' of masculinity or masculine gender. In her reading of *Antony and Cleopatra*, Levine notes Caesar's longing for the theatricality which he attacks and the link between 'hypermasculinity' and anti-theatricality as a defence.[31] In contrast with Antony's failure to be masculine enough as 'man', Caesar carries through his (performance of) masculinity as male display.

Does Caesar's 'puritan', anti-theatrical objection to Cleopatra's theatrical performances of femininity *and* masculinity impart his covert anxiety that the symbolic identity of 'man' or 'woman' is not given but is thoroughly citational and performative, arbitrarily defined by the context? Possibly Caesar, a spokesman of anti-theatricality, realises the dangerous power of theatricality, which mimes but also parodies the ideological meaning of 'man' or 'woman' and dis-places the single normative subject-position assumed in the system.

The identity of 'man' may also be established in contradistinction to 'boy', while the precarious line of demarcation between 'man' and 'boy' cannot but cause another male anxiety. Antony often calls Caesar 'boy' to insult him and reinstate his own endangered male identity. Cleopatra says to Dolabella, 'You laugh when boys or women tell their dreams' (V.ii.73). Both women and boys are second-rate members of the community as the counter-image of 'man'.

The masculine and the feminine ideals are both exaggerated and dramatised in Kabuki. In order to correspond to the *onnagata*'s stylised performance of femininity, the *tachiyaku* (male lead) equally puts on male display, by citing and overstating the meaning of masculinity shared with the audience. As this Kabuki practice shows, gender identity is a meaning, and therefore an effect of difference. The meaning of masculinity or femininity is induced only in the differential or relational structure of cultural signification. Concerning the notion of the transvestite mask as 'travesty,' Jacques Lacan says that it is 'through the mediation of masks that the masculine and the feminine meet in the most acute, most intense way'.[32] The relationship with the other sex conditions and constructs the masculine or the feminine sexual attitude as components of gendered identity.

At the same time, as Lacan elsewhere mentions, 'the curious consequence of making virile display in the human being itself seem feminine',[33] the paradox of the sexual attitude, either feminine masquerade or masculine display (or *parade* in French), brings to light the undecidability of the ideological meaning of femininity or masculinity.

VII

Frequent references to 'show' and 'play' in *Antony and Cleopatra* highlight the theatricality and fictionality of Cleopatra's performance of the fatal woman. Her self-dramatisation presupposes (the desire of) audiences. Not only Antony but also other men in Rome try to pin down Cleopatra in terms of the available ideological female stereotypes. The whore, the temptress, the witch, the queen of Egypt, the mother of procreation or death: what is the 'real' face of Cleopatra?

Cleopatra, who is both seductive and dangerous, is difficult to define, because she plays the game of the meanings of 'woman'. She seems to endorse and yet elusively bypasses the taxonomies of ideological female stereotypes and suspends the decisive, decidable meaning of 'woman'. Man cannot easily place woman on his map of knowledge. Cleopatra's female identity is always *fading*, substituted and displaced by one signifier 'woman' after another within a chain of signifiers. Lacan points out 'an affinity between the enigmas of sexuality and the play of the signifier'.[34] It is the effect of a distance between the signifier and the signified 'woman' that brings about the enigma of 'woman', which fascinates and yet agonises the subject of the desire to know. The absolute truth of 'woman' is forever lost, being differentiated from itself. Cleopatra seduces man at a distance as the eternal enigma, tantalisingly suspending the truth of 'woman'. Nevertheless, desire is sustained precisely by this absent truth of 'woman' – by that which Lacan calls 'the lost object' defined by male fantasy – for desire is 'the metonymy of all signification' or 'interpretation itself'.[35]

In *Kagotsurube Sato no Yoizame*, likewise, for a male desiring subject Jirozaemon, the *keisei* Yatsuhashi has two Janus-like faces: as a heavenly woman, who entrances him with the hope of the fulfilment of desire, even in the fleeting dream-moment of *jouissance*, and as a demonic woman, who spurns his illusion and humiliates him in front of his colleagues. Jirozaemon reproaches Yatsuhashi for callousness and asks her why she did not refuse him from the start. It is not Yatsuhashi herself, however, but the very image of the *keisei* Yatsuhashi, beautifully (fictionally) represented in Yoshiwara, whom Jirozaemon desires as *his* 'dream woman'. The *aku-sho* stages the 'love' scene with the ideal feminine performed by the *keisei*, on the confines of 'fiction' and 'reality'. Confusing her (professional, theatrical) performance of the ideal feminine with her 'truth', Jirozaemon is too naive to play the love game with the *keisei* Yatsuhashi in the *aku-sho*.

The image of the eternal feminine is reproduced and re-presented as 'fiction' in the non-everyday space of the *aku-sho* (the theatres and the brothels). Both the theatres and the brothels visualise and put on display the fantasy, by means of which '*we learn "how to desire"*'.[36] The *keisei* as the highly fantasised woman thus endlessly seduces man, re-presenting the eternal feminine, *jouissance*, desire or the death drive – as the *fatal* woman.

Both Cleopatra and the *keisei* are products of male fantasy. The male subject is situated and constituted in language and thus bound up with the desire to know – the desire of/for the Other (language) which forms him. It is this subject of desire (for impossible knowledge) who produces the eternal enigma of 'woman' as her infinite variety in the locus of language and/or the unconscious. In his psychical reality, man 'fictions' the *fatal* woman.

VIII

As women's country, Egypt stands for an excess of desire – lust, eating and drinking. Enobarbus calls Cleopatra Antony's 'Egyptian dish' (II.vi.128). Pompey likens Cleopatra to an Epicurean cook and wishes her to keep captivating Antony in Egypt, 'a field of feasts', with her 'witchcraft' combined with beauty and lechery (II.i.20–24). Cleopatra is also the 'serpent of Old Nile' (I.v.26), who feeds desiring subjects with 'most delicious poison' (28). Like the *pharmakon* which, as Derrida explains, gives play to the undecidability of opposite meanings between cure and poison, Cleopatra, the 'Egyptian dish' is both delicious (remedy) *and* lethal (poison), superabundant *and* insubstantial; and so 'she makes hungry / Where most she satisfies' (II.ii.247–8).

It is the undecidable play of the meanings of 'woman' that makes Cleopatra's seduction irresistible. Antony glorifies the infinite variety of Cleopatra,

Whom every thing becomes – to chide, to laugh,
To weep; whose every passion fully strives
To make itself, in thee, fair and admired!   (I.i.50–52)

While Antony suspects the theatricality of Cleopatra's feminine masquerade, he is deeply fascinated by the idea of the *true* 'woman' who incarnates 'every passion'. The fact that '*Woman* [La *femme*] doesn't exist' makes her the object of desire. Lacan accounts for the absence of the truth of 'woman' for man:

Man [*L'homme*], in fooling himself, encounters *a* woman, with whom everything happens: namely that usual misfiring, of which the successful sexual act consists. Its protagonists are capable of the most lofty deeds, as the theatre teaches us.

The noble, the tragic, the comic, the farcical . . . the full range of what is produced in the scene through which it is staged – the scene that severs love relations from every social bond – the full range, then, is realised – producing the fantasies through which speaking beings subsist in what they call . . . 'life'.[37]

It is Antony himself who dramatises and fictions 'Cleopatra' and stages all signification of 'life' in the kingdom of 'woman' – in fantasy.

Like the theatre town and pleasure quarters in the *aku-sho*, Egypt symbolises the terrain of desire as the space of 'fiction', where not only Antony, and men in Rome, but also the audience can indulge their fantasies of 'woman'. None the less, as I have suggested in the contradictory implications of Cleopatra and the *keisei*, fantasy exceeds the circumscription of what it means to be woman, in contradistinction to man, a circumscription by which propriety wants to define male or female subject-positions and secure the cultural and social order. Certainly it is the authorities themselves who realise the subversive power of theatricality, which seems to endorse and reproduce the ideological meaning of 'man' or 'woman', but also parodies and unsettles it. That is why Caesar, the Puritans or the shogunate strongly objected to the theatres – the space of 'fiction'. Theatrical surplus discloses the very fictionality of social, sexual 'reality', on which the organisation of the system is dependent.

Perhaps it is more than a sheer coincidence that in both the English Renaissance and the Kabuki theatres actors impersonated women, taking different gender roles and transgressing the law of gender. To impersonate 'woman' – that is to say, to masquerade womanliness, either in the 'fictitious' space of theatre or in the 'reality' of everyday life – is to represent what it means to be woman in and by (body) language. Both the *onnagata* and the boy actor bring into relief the fictionality of gendered identity, which can be reproduced *citationally* even by the 'opposite' sex, and thus, open up radical possibilities of *fictioning* our own identity of 'man' or 'woman', by challenging the ideological meaning of masculinity or femininity.

At the same time, our performance of the differentiating 'I' is never completed in this world theatre, since the effect of gendered identity is induced, re-presented as 'fiction', and dispersed in and by the very undecidable play of the meaning of 'man' or 'woman' – as an incomplete (hi)story of the 'I'. We find the conditions of our possibility in this incompleteness of our being as ever-deferred in the open space of textual practices.

15 Kyogenising Shakespeare / Shakespeareanising Kyogen: some notes on *The Braggart Samurai*

Yasunari Takahashi

Critique and homage

Why Shakespeare in a Kyogen manner? And/or, why Kyogen based on Shakespeare? The bilateral structure of the question may be precisely matched by the two-way fashion in which I would like to answer. In making a Kyogen adaptation of *The Merry Wives of Windsor*, my concern was, on the one hand, to re-create the original in a completely different, almost opposite style, or, to put it more graphically, to transform the fertility of a Shakespearean forest into the simplicity of a Japanese garden. Verdi's opera *Falstaff* was a great example and source of inspiration for my foolhardy attempt. Obviously, Kyogen being a far more stylised theatre form than opera, a correspondingly more radical re-structuring in the direction of simplification would be needed. This in itself would have a double implication: the act of selecting what seemed to me certain important, potential emphases from the original text would be a form of interpretation and *critique* just as much as writing a critical essay. But the same act might also be a converse form of paying *homage* to Shakespeare's comic vision and energy which, even in this generally undervalued 'farce', should survive any tolerable adaptation.

On the other hand, I wanted to challenge the tradition of Kyogen. It was only too clear that, no matter how simplified, a Shakespeare comedy would prove too gigantic to be adapted to the Procrustean bed of traditional Kyogen dramaturgy. Would Kyogen ever be ready to step out of its too firmly established form and open up its horizon to accommodate Shakespeare's complexity and scale? The kinds of attempt that have been made to take a very thin slice of the story-line from a Shakespearean play and adapt it into a familiar tiny-sized Kyogen piece[1] seem to me too subservient to the tradition and unaware of the potential *self-criticism* involved in the very act of grappling with this giant of a foreign dramatist. If, however, the adaptation should succeed in giving a new shape to a Shakespearean play in ways that could only be possible to the rich heritage of Kyogen dramaturgy and technique, then it would be a form of *tribute* to the art of Kyogen.

Our project, then, must work two ways – both on the basis of, and at the same time against the grain of, the tradition(s). It must not kowtow to the Western tradition of bardolatry, which has been shared by Japanese theatre as part of Japan's imitative adoration of Western civilisation since the Meiji Restoration. Encouragement may come from the alternative tradition which includes such bold alterations of the original plays as Onsui Emi's *Othello*, Yukio Ninagawa's *Macbeth* (though this was faithful as far as the text was concerned), and Tadashi Suzuki's *King Lear*, not to mention Kurosawa's film adaptations of *Macbeth* and *King Lear*. On the other hand, we must not succumb to the jingoistic self-satisfaction or arrogance, which wallows in the half masochistic pleasure of being regarded by foreigners as 'special' and 'impenetrable'. Of course, throwing away the baby with the bath water would be the worst of all; our goal should be to give birth to a baby which hopefully would have the best of both parents, unconstrained by inherited glories. The fact is you cannot Kyogenise Shakespeare without at the same time Shakespeareanising Kyogen. And one has a feeling that a really worthwhile adaptation is bound to look like a forest in comparison with traditional Kyogen plays.

Plebeian aesthetics

The characteristics of Kyogen may be best brought out by comparison with Noh. Noh deals mostly with people of noble birth, emperors and empresses, princes and princesses, high-ranking courtiers and samurais, poets of legendary renown and their sweethearts. Especially in plays belonging to the representative type called *mugen noh* (dream Noh), heroes and heroines are either ghosts of these personages (more often than not they have been dead for a couple of centuries), or spirits of trees and flowers, or even deities incarnate. In accordance with the high seriousness of the subject matter, the language of Noh is profoundly and (some might say) relentlessly poetic. And the way actors chant with masks multiplies ambiguity, defying easy comprehension. The acting style, with its slow tempo (the American avant-gardist Robert Wilson learnt much from this) and its high tension (one is sometimes reminded of Samuel Beckett), can be fiercely demanding or intensely soporific to ill-attuned spectators. Smiling, let alone laughter, either on the stage or in the audience, is out of the question. Noh is 'holy theatre' *par excellence*, powerfully retaining the memory of its origin in the religious rite of calming dead souls and invisible spirits. Nothing, except undying passion, seems real in a drama which looks at life from the point of view of the dead.

Kyogen is the opposite of all this: its world is one of everyday reality. Things preposterous and absurd do occur from time to time (there is for instance an Ionesco-like piece which presents numerous mushrooms propagating themselves on stage and finally expelling humans), and we do come across a few ghosts (there are some comic spirits like that of a crab), but most of the characters who populate the Kyogen stage are common people such as towns-folk and rustics, masters (but none more dignified than country landlords) and servants, thieves and gulls, blind men and priests, and so on. Kyogen pokes fun at all kinds of follies and rogueries perpetrated by these human beings. It captures the wonderfully vivacious ethos of popular culture in an age of bustling social change which saw the emergence of an incipient form of 'citizenry' (*machishu*). The point of view hardly ever shifts from that of people who are living here and now. Story and plot could not be more straightforward. Dialogue is conducted in a colloquial style whose intelligibility to the twentieth-century ear is surprising. Characterisation, performed with a physical and vocal clarity which verges on overacting, is hilariously clear-cut. Acting is realistic compared with Noh, though more stylised than certain Kabuki plays. And laughter which clinches a Kyogen play has a festive ring to it, making us realise that it is *joie de vivre* that Kyogen celebrates with its wonderful repertory, currently comprising some 250 plays, surely one of the most remarkable archives of comic art in the history of world drama.

Kyogen, thus, could be considered a kind of antidote to, or an act of exorcism of, the spirituality of Noh. There is great wisdom in the long-established custom of sandwiching Kyogen pieces between a few Noh plays for an evening's programme (somewhat comparable to dramatic practices in ancient Greece and early modern England). And it should be clear by now that it is this 'plebeian' character of Kyogen that justifies in the first place an attempt to adapt *The Merry Wives of Windsor* into Kyogen. For the play is unique in the Shakespeare canon in being pure 'citizen comedy'. For once in his writing career, Shakespeare devotes a whole play to depicting the everyday life of ordinary people in a contemporary English town, totally forgetting about histories or foreign countries, about noble lords or supernatural beings. Even the spirits making their eerie appearance by Herne's oak are nothing but mock-spirits. The result is a play abounding in follies and rogueries, which are exposed to genial and wry criticism (including self-criticism) from the point of view of middle-class values. It praises their sense of reality and virtue, while it manages to end in the mood of a 'festive comedy'.

Having said this, however, it must be stressed that the gap separating Kyogen and *The Merry Wives* is no less great. To say nothing of the differences in the nature of 'citizenry' in their respective historical and social backgrounds, they are poles apart in their aesthetics. The clarity of story and plot, so imperative in Kyogen, necessarily entails brevity; all plays are in one act, and performance does not last on the average longer than twenty minutes. How can this art cope with Shakespeare's polyphonic dramaturgy which has produced in the comedy in question (requiring three hours for performance) a densely woven picture of a whole town life with its complex network of desires and intrigues – unless by focusing on a rigorously selective number of characters and motifs?

Aesthetics is inescapably determined by material conditions. The Kyogen company Mansaku no kai, for which I wrote the play, comprises only six actors, a normal size for a Kyogen troupe. This would necessitate the dismissal of many a character: Master Page, Mistress Quickly, Shallow, Slender, Caius, Evans, and others would have to go. Servants are indispensable but must be reduced in number. Even Anne Page and Fenton, so important in the original play (and in Verdi), must be sacrificed. Kyogen in its turn must try, for instance, to accommodate a complicated plot requiring more than a few scenes (which might mean the use of something out of the question in traditional performance: lighting) and lasting more than an hour. There would be many more taboos to be broken.

The hero and his name

My title *Horazamurai* (The Braggart Samurai) indicates that I have shifted the focus onto Falstaff, making him the titular hero. This is of course following in the footsteps of Verdi. But, as the English version of the title also suggests, the play is, more fundamentally, meant as a nod to Plautus's *Miles Gloriosus* (The Braggart Soldier). It is true that Shakespeare is less indebted to the Roman playwright in *The Merry Wives* than he is in *The Comedy of Errors* (an obvious borrowing from *Menaechmi*), but no one will deny that Falstaff is (if not so grandly in *The Merry Wives* as in the *Henry IV* plays) the greatest example of variations on the classic type of comic character made popular by Plautus.

On the other hand, my hero and title are something of an innovation in the context of Kyogen tradition, since a 'samurai' seldom makes his appearance in the genre. The only piece that has a samurai for titular hero (*Asahina*) does not portray him in a comic way at all. Kyogen fights shy of samurais, who, besides belonging to a more elevated social class than citizens, are considered to be highly serious people, unfit for laughter. But, in my view, low-ranking samurais such as *ronins* (masterless samurais, e.g. Kurosawa's 'seven samurais') could be just as low as Sir John Falstaff, who in *The Merry Wives* is apparently masterless, too. And I see no reason why one of the *ronins* should not qualify as a Kyogen character, i.e. as an object of ridicule, thus joining the global brotherhood of 'braggart soldiers'. Surely Falstaff would not mind being metamorphosed into a drunkard, a familiar hero in Kyogen?

But Falstaff is more than a simple drunkard. His name alone should be enough to stagger us with its rich ambiguity. It is true that, compared with his overwhelming stature in the history plays, where he could hold his own against the powers that be – where the fool's bauble, though a 'false staff', had a symbolic contrapuntal relation with the king's sceptre – the knight has his size and dignity much diminished in a civilian farce played out in a local town. But in this new situation his name acquires an additional ironical overtone: thrown into the milieu of middle-class values, he is inevitably looked upon as an odd man out, a suspicious outsider, a kind of 'false stuff'. Even his much-flaunted virility comes under suspicion: the big belly may be deceptive, hiding in fact a 'false staff' dangling between his legs. Nevertheless, this gigantic hero has not completely lost mythical ambiguity; he can still thrive on paradoxes, escaping binary distinctions of false/true or vice/virtue.

As much of all this ambiguity as possible must be assimilated. My hero is named Horata Suke-emon. The surname 'Horata', with its faint phonetic echo (Falstaff/Horata), aims to approximate the semantic richness of the original name. 'Hora' in Japanese means 'brag', 'false pretension'. But the same sound, though in different notation (*kanji*), can also mean 'cave', suggesting an image of hollowness. A hollow cave is not necessarily a negative symbol; a great concave is the other side of a great convex, and hollowness and emptiness could paradoxically signify plenitude just as 'nothing' in the language of mysticism overlaps with 'all'. You never can tell whether a big belly contains authentic or deceptive virility. And '-ta' in the surname is 'field', one of the commonest components of Japanese surnames. As for the given name, 'suke' usually suggests 'help', ironically pointing to the hero's actual cowardice and egoism, as evinced by his frightened cry 'Help me!' at the approach of the jealous husband, or by his recoiling from a woman's appeal for 'help' in the wood; but 'suke' can also hint at something altogether different but not too irrelevant to our hero, i.e. 'sukebei' (lecher or philanderer). In brief, our hero's name might be roughly anglicised as 'Lech Bragfield'.

Self-introduction

The play opens with the hero introducing himself: 'I am a samurai, and I am a resident of this neighbourhood', which, while it sounds in keeping with the typical Kyogen style of opening, may strike connoisseurs as somewhat anomalous. The sense of anomaly aroused by the sheer fact of his being a samurai will be augmented when he immediately corrects himself: 'Or, perhaps I should rather say, a temporary resident', for most Kyogen characters are either 'permanent residents' (citizens, landlords, and servants) or 'non-residents' (thieves and conmen). The status of 'temporary resident', coupled with that of samurai, cannot but prompt a 'metatheatrical' question: what can a samurai', sojourning 'temporarily' in the neighbourhood, be doing in a 'citizen drama'? (Locality does not matter very much except that Kyogen is usually assumed to be set in Kyoto, the then capital of Japan, or its suburbs and that here the nearness to Kyoto is supposed distantly to echo Windsor's relation to London.)

Horata is already tipsy. (The translatability of 'sack' into 'sake' is sheer luck.) Although there is no dearth of drunken heroes in Kyogen, Horata must go far beyond these stereotyped rowdy, often lovable, but always simpleminded braggarts to match his Shakespearean model, however remotely. He must be endowed with a degree of complicated social awareness as well as a hint of philosophical and cosmic depth. So he goes on to affirm the pleasure principle embodied by his belly against the 'work ethic' of citizenry (just as Falstaff fretted over the prim frugality of Protestants). His revelation about his former friendship with the new Shogun and his subsequent banishment (interpolated, of course, from the *Henry IV* plays), as well as another intertextual borrowing from Feste's song ('The rain, it raineth every day'), is aimed at expanding the dramatic implication of his self-portrait as a malcontent. (It should perhaps be mentioned in passing that Shakespeare's popularity in Japan today is such that there is reason to expect that these allusions and quotations will not be entirely lost on the audience.) All this culminates in Horata's passionate denial of the famous Kyogen cliché that 'we live in a happy and peaceful reign', casting a wry commentary on the ideological assumptions underlying Kyogen, which is often summarised as 'the spirit of peace and fraternity'. The tension implied in the opening self-introduction between insider and outsider will be seen to develop throughout the play.

Master and servant

In his pecuniary plight, Falstaff sacks Bardolph and orders Nym and Pistol to deliver identical love-letters to Mistresses Ford and Page in an attempt to 'cony-catch' them (I.iii.31–2).[2] But Nym and Pistol not only refuse to play Pandarus but also decide to betray the secret to the Wives. Similar shaky and tense relationships between master and servant can be observed in many theatrical traditions the world over, but the Western theatre seems particularly rich in this archetypal pair: Plautus'

Pyrgopolynices/Artotrogus, Pantalone/Arlecchino, Lear/Fool, Prospero/ Ariel, Don Giovanni/Leporello, Beckett's Pozzo/Lucky and Hamm/Clov, etc. (not to mention the great parallel in the novel, Don Quixote/Sancho Panza).

It happens that Kyogen, too, finds one of its most popular characters in the trickster-servant named Taro Kaja, whose half-recalcitrant dutiful-ness towards his master, peppered with nimble actions and sharp witti-cisms, much enlivens the show. And since he is often found in the company of a younger colleague Jiro Kaja, it should not be too difficult to compress the triad of Bardolph/Pistol/Nym into the familiar Kyogen couple. A more exciting challenge would be to find an equivalent of the charming idiosyncrasies of Shakespearean servants. For instance, can one transpose Nym's obsessive predilection for the word 'humour'? My Taro Kaja has an unstoppable penchant for quoting (or mis-quoting) old sayings. In scene i, in covert response to Horata's violence, Taro Kaja says aside, 'My mother used to tell me there were three things in the world you would never win against: a weeping child, a wilful landlord, and a drunken lecherous Master', of which the last item is an improvised addi-tion to the otherwise familiar Japanese proverb. His verbal wit will mani-fest itself at its sharpest and wildest when he comments on Horata reading Omatsu's letter in scene v.[3]

I have in fact put much greater emphasis on master-servant scenes than Shakespeare does, not only because I believe in the thematic importance of the master–servant relation for the play but also because I know that they can be depended upon for excellent theatrical effects in Kyogen per-formance. This is, I hope, proved in scene i when they are maltreated by Horata, who, grabbing them both by the neck in an exaggerated stylised way, gives them the famous 'honour' speech smuggled from *I Henry IV* (in which I am again anticipated by Verdi). It is also hoped that the compres-sion of the followers, page, servants and even Quickly (as messenger) into the two servants has served us well, e.g. in adding an extra irony to scene iii where Horata is carried off in the laundry basket. The job is done by Taro Kaja and Jiro Kaja who have now deserted Horata to serve Omatsu, whereas in Shakespeare John and Robert, otherwise insignificant servants to the Fords, are assigned the task. (Shakespeare was probably obliged to spread the roles over minor actors of the Lord Chamberlain's Men, as I was obliged to reduce the roles for my company.)

Man and woman

The Merry Wives is one of Shakespeare's most explicit plays about the question of gender. It is obviously the Wives, the titular heroines, who emerge as triumphant victors. The male chauvinist version of the 'plea-sure principle' as embodied by the fat knight proves to be perfectly resistible by the 'reality principle' of these women who know that 'wives may be merry and yet honest too' (IV.ii.91). Master Ford, a husband drowned sado-masochistically in jealous fantasies, is another chauvinist who gets soundly punished by the fun-loving and admirably sensible women.

It is one of the happiest coincidences in the history of world theatre that these Shakespearean strong women (or 'tattling' women, III.iii.80) find their distant cousins in the female characters in Kyogen. Mostly wives, and invariably portrayed as more powerful and garrulous than men, these heroines of so-called 'female pieces' in the repertory have won themselves the nick-name of *wawashii onna* (noisy loquacious women) – a healthy counterblow to the myth (if there still is one) of 'quiet submissive Japanese ladies'. One of them pursues her lazy husband with a sickle tied to a stick;[4] another proposes divorce to her idle husband and outwits his attempt to dodge the situation;[5] another recruits an army of her neigh-bouring wives against her vainglorious, wife-beating husband and tri-umphantly shaves off his proud beard.[6]

The play *Hanago*, one of the 'weightiest' pieces in the whole repertory, deserves a detailed synopsis. The husband, residing in a suburb of Kyoto, is anxious to have a tryst with a woman (named Hanago) with whom he had an affair some time ago while on a journey, and who has now informed him that she is staying at an inn in Kyoto. He pretends to his wife that he is going to spend the night at a temple practising Zen Meditation, and having put Taro Kaja in his place (with strict instructions never to divest himself of the special hood and mantle during the Meditation), he hastens to the *rendez-vous*. The wife visits the temple to inquire after her husband; getting suspicious, she strips Taro Kaja of the hood. Driving the servant away, she then puts herself in his place in the same disguise, and waits for her husband, who returns to the temple at dawn and starts telling her (believing her of course to be Taro Kaja) how thrilling it was and how sad the parting. Proceeding to slander his wife, he takes away the hood from what proves to be her face, which is now mad with jealousy and anger. The play ends as the flabbergasted husband flees apologising, pursued by the screaming wife.

It would be easy to see how some elements – strong wife, tension between a married couple, extramarital love and jealousy, anger and pun-ishment, disguise and mistaken identity, etc. – are shared by *Hanago* and *The Merry Wives*. But it should be equally obvious that similarities do not go much further. Wives in Kyogen are often even more shrewish than Shakespeare's Kate; they are certainly more savage than the Wives of

Windsor in their revolt against masculine power. The other side of the same coin is that Kyogen's delineation of women is so radical and caricatural as to deprive them of audience sympathy, which in fact is what is implied by the malicious nick-name, *wawashii onna*, obviously a male invention. (And does one need to be reminded that performance of Kyogen has been monopolised by men throughout its history?)

That my heroines Omatsu and Otake have lost the ferociousness of their Kyogen ancestors might be regretted by certain Shakespearean critics who complain that female power in *The Merry Wives* misses 'an opportunity radically to undermine the men's proprietorial assumptions',[7] and who might have expected to see this corrected in my new Kyogen. But insofar as my heroines know how to be 'Merry and yet honest' rather than 'noisy and loquacious', thus acquiring an endearing likeableness and depth of character, thanks are due to their models, Mistresses Ford and Page, who have a richer sense of humour and a more complex sense of human relationships than wives in Kyogen. When, for instance, Omatsu and Otake make fun of Horata's letters (scene ii), or execute their plan for his punishment and then improvise on the actual arrival of the husband (scene iv), they demonstrate one of the desiderata in the theatre of Kyogen by radiating the charm of women who are possessed of a good sense of humour and even of a gift for playacting. Or, for that matter, it looks as though, in the two *rendez-vous* scenes (scenes iv and vi), they are mischievously enjoying infuriating the purists who would frown upon the slightest intimation of eroticism on the Kyogen stage such as, for example, a man's hand about to fondle a woman's breast.

It hardly needs stressing that no one has ever heard of a samurai courting a citizen's wife in Kyogen, much less of her counterattack against him. More significantly, it is under the aegis of Shakespeare that one has been able to reverse the normal Kyogen pattern of the husband/wife relationship, where it is almost always wives who are jealous, just as the adulterous party is always male, never female.[8] To see a wife triumphing over a madly jealous and miserably scolded husband (scene iv) is something new in Kyogen. The comic thrust of Mistress Ford's line, 'I know not which pleases me better – that my husband is deceived, or Sir John' (III.iii.166–7), will lose none of its exquisite point here; rather, it will sound even more hilarious in the mouth of a Japanese wife in Kyogen. It is with an added pleasure that one remembers that wives are impersonated by male actors in both Shakespeare and Kyogen, with this difference that the latter acquires a greater alienation effect through the fact that Kyogen actors do not conceal their adult voices at all.

Scapegoat and denouement

As has been seen earlier, my version underlines from the outset Horata's awareness of his own social position more strongly than is the case with Falstaff. As if being a 'temporary' resident and a masterless samurai, and accumulating a pile of unpaid bills were not enough to mark him as a suspicious outsider, he starts seducing citizens' wives and coaxing them out of money. This transgresses the two fundamental tenets of proto-bourgeois society, the marital and monetary order, which are of course held together by a belief in the sanctity of property, a wife being no less a husband's property than money. Falstaff/Horata, therefore, commits a double theft against property. This crime and its punishment are foregrounded as the main motivating force of my adaptation, whereas the Ann/Fenton plot has to be cut for two reasons: because the Shakespearean principle of complexity must yield here to the Kyogen principle of simplicity and concentration, and also because the subject of romantic love lies outside the territory of Kyogen, belonging as it does by definition to Noh.

The second punishment of Falstaff (the 'Witch of Brainford' episode) is abandoned in obedience to both the Kyogen aesthetic and Verdi's wisdom, whereas, in the final scene vi, the ritual resonance of Horata's punishment may be felt to be more pronounced than Falstaff's. Herne's oak is replaced by an abstract or stylised pine tree, a design which 'quotes' the constant image painted on the back panel of the Noh stage where Kyogen has been performed along with Noh for centuries. The pine tree (*matsu*) has a special significance in Japanese folklore as the symbolic site of a god's epiphany, with a religious pun on the verb *matsu* (to wait for, to keep vigil). That is why the tree always looms so visibly at the back of the stage where epiphanic moments are enacted by Noh actors. The symbolic implication of the pine tree suffers a slight slippage in *The Braggart Samurai*: the pine tree (*matsu*) is where Omatsu (i.e. Mistress Pine) and Horata wait for (*matsu*) each other. Arata Isozaki's design, meanwhile, visually suggests a gigantic antler as well as a pine tree. The image, meant to suggest the buck's horn on Falstaff's head, may be an ambiguous symbol both of virile potency and cuckoldry (though logically the horn should grow on the cuckold's forehead, and even though the association of cuckoldry with horn is not familiar to the Japanese mind). The old knight disguised with a buck's horn becomes a samurai with a mask of *tengu*, a popular folkloric demon with a red face and an extraordinarily long, patently phallic nose.

Falstaff is tortured by the 'fairies' as the 'Fairy Queen' sings, 'Pinch him, fairies, mutually, / Pinch him for his villainy' (V.v.97–8). As far as this element of *charivari* is concerned, I do not diverge from the original too much: Horata, having 'counterfeited dying' in the manner of Falstaff on the battlefield (*1 Henry IV*, V.iv.119), is mocked with a ritualistic catalogue of preposterous curses and then tickled to near-death by the masked figures to the refrain, 'Kutsu, kutsu' (the traditional onomatopoeia for tickling, just like Verdi's unforgettable 'Pizzica, pizzica'). The greatest difference is perhaps in the festive spirit in the ending. A great master of ambiguously merging realism with ritualism, Shakespeare does not overdo mythologising. The ending of *The Merry Wives* can even look bathetic. Forgiven and yet a little disgruntled, Falstaff makes only a feeble last rebuttal against the insiders: 'I am glad, though you have ta'en a special stand to strike at me, that your arrow hath glanc'd [referring to the failed plots over Anne Page's betrothal] . . . When night-dogs run, all sorts of deer are chas'd' (V.v.221–5). This realistic and ironical touch deprives Falstaff of the extraordinary stature which the author conferred upon him in the *Henry IV* plays.

I have chosen to tip the Shakespearean balance and reinstate the fat hero in the centre of the play, treading of course in Verdi's footsteps, but going beyond him. Omatsu says, as no one in Shakespeare or Verdi does, 'Thus we join tonight to quell a fat sake-reeking demon and offer him up to our patron god', thus adding to Horata's mythical stature. Curses flung at him, escalating from 'a barrel' to 'a pig' to 'a meteorite', are expected to have a paradoxically glorifying effect. And then, intimidated by a string of interrogations which culminate in 'Do you swear to become a virtuous man?' he does seem to succumb. But his answer, 'I do, I do. I swear to become whatever you wish', has a stubborn ring to it which gives the lie to his ostensible meekness. In fact, he turns the tables (as he, at this point, literally turns around to face the audience) at the last moment. 'No, no . . . I refuse to apologise', he says, and goes on to deliver a braggadoccio's credo – a final brag, if you like – in a mishmash of borrowed phrases from Jaques (*As You Like It*), Verdi, and Beckett (*Waiting for Godot*): 'All the world is but a joke, and all men and women merely jesters . . . The quantity of laughter in this world is constant. For every one who stops laughing, someone starts laughing somewhere. I for one will go on laughing until the end . . .' And he laughs a Gargantuan laugh, which is indeed a far cry from Falstaff's discomfited grumbling.

Not only does this denouement go against the grain of Shakespearean wry humour but it also defies the normal Kyogen pattern. One of the familiar endings of Kyogen plays is called *oikomi* (chasing out) whereby the villain (a husband, a crafty servant, a conman, etc.) exits with a cry, 'Pardon me, pardon me', fleeing from the angry victim (a wife, a master, a gull, etc.) who chases him with a cry, 'I'll get you, I'll get you'. Another is *warai-dome* (laughing end) or *ukare-dome* (euphoric end) which, with a typical illogicality, brings all the characters together in a joyous circle of laughter and dance. It will be clear that my ending resists the easy-going exorcism of the former, and that it inclines towards the latter. But it just does not seem possible for Horata's huge belly to be conveniently incorporated into a complacent compromise of 'peace and harmony' as celebrated by many of the traditional Kyogen plays. Horata as a scapegoat must be aggrandised into a great embodiment of the spirit of carnival, going beyond both the life-sized realism of Shakespeare and the customary euphoria of Kyogen.

It seems fitting to me that the play should end with a quaint grand finale of dance and songs. The choreography is of course anything but Shakespearean; it may look pure Kyogen, but not quite. Never has Kyogen seen an ending with such reverberating festivity.[9] *The Braggart Samurai*, born out of the marriage of Shakespeare and Kyogen, and yet refusing to be confined to either of its parents, is hopefully a *tertium quid*.

In this essay I have focused on the dramatic text and structure of *The Braggart Samurai*, but it goes without saying how entirely the play relies on the performance of Kyogen actors for its impact upon the audience. In writing the text, I always had of course the actors' physical actions and voices in my mind's eye and ear, but it was amazing and exhilarating to watch how they expanded and enriched my words into a living theatre with their boundless energy and resourceful improvisation. What may look like a rule-bound stylisation is in fact a tense control of physical power through a complex network of time-honoured techniques; nothing is arbitrary, and yet nothing is constrained. In a way, I thought my job was to provide these wonderful actors with new technical challenges, so that I felt very glad when they told me that in no single Kyogen play had they ever been able to make such a full use of their traditional skills. The sense of their sheer delight in acting was manifest everywhere, and not solely in the most talked-about scene in past productions, the one where Horata was carried away by Taro Kaja and Jiro Kaja in a laundry basket, all done in mime, with the fat samurai tumbling along between the servants who are carrying nothing but a stick. I thought the entire performance was exhilarating, but I would prefer to leave the task of analysis and evaluation to others, who can take a detached view of the realisation on stage of my work.[10]

16   The Braggart Samurai

Yasunari Takahashi

An English version of *Hora-zamurai*, a Kyogen adaptation of Shakespeare's *The Merry Wives of Windsor*, translated from the Japanese by the author.

Characters:

Horata Suke-emon   *Mid-sixties, ronin (masterless samurai), grossly fat drunkard, glutton, braggart, lecher, fraud, welsher, coward.*
Taro kaja   *Servant of Horata.*
Jiro kaja   *Servant of Horata.*
Yakibei   *Jealous merchant (disguises himself as* Mochibei).
Omatsu   *Wife of Yakibei (played by a male actor).*
Otaké   *Wife of merchant Heibei (played by a male actor).*

Music (live): A flute and a stick-drum.
Scenery: Empty except for a semi-abstract sculpted pine-tree upstage centre. A bridgeway connects main stage with exit extreme right. No change from scene to scene, except for some lighting effects.
Costume: Traditional Kyogen costume (Horata wears a big beard).
Time: Vaguely late medieval.
Place: Somewhere near Kyoto.

Notes on names:

HORATA (surname) – 'hora' means tall tale as well as hollow cave; 'ta', meaning field, is often a component of family names. Suke-Emon (given name) suggests help, also lecher.

TARO KAJA and JIRO KAJA – prototypical servants' names in Kyogen.

YAKIBEI and MOCHIBEI – combine to form 'yaki-mochi', literally 'baked rice-cake', but a colloquialism meaning jealousy.

OMATSU – common female name based on 'matsu' (pine tree), which is also identical in pronunciation with the verb 'matsu' (to wait, to pine for).

OTAKÉ – common female name based on 'take' (bamboo).

Scene 1

(Horata's room at the inn.) Enter Horata, tipsy, followed by Taro Kaja and Jiro Kaja, who sit upstage until they are called.

HORATA: (*Stopping downstage centre.*) My name is Horata Suke-emon. I am a samurai, and I am a resident of this neighbourhood – or perhaps I should rather say, a temporary resident. Hic! Oh, I'm a bit drunk. There's nothing under the sun as pleasant as getting oneself drunk, and yet most of the world's idiots stay sober and work. Inside this belly of mine are stuffed all the sensual pleasures known to mankind. No wonder it has such an admirable rotundity. Hic! (*Sitting down on a stool which a stage assistant, coming forth from behind the tree, has carried in.*) I can't but observe these days how rotten the world has gone. Once I was the closest of friends with the young heir of the Shogun. We drank a lot together, we played at highway robbers, we played countless practical jokes. Those were golden days when we enjoyed ourselves to our hearts' content. But on the day that young man succeeded his father and became Shogun, he banished his old bosom friend, me, Horata Suke-emon. Indeed he went so far as to call me a corruptor of public order and morals. Rightly is it said that the milk of human kindness is thinner than water or paper. The whole world now is nothing but a pack of uptight puppets, from the Shogun at the top to soldiers, merchants, and farmers at the bottom. I'm horrified to hear people say that we live in a happy and peaceful reign. On the contrary, I would say that the end of the world is nigh. These are really hard times for a lofty-minded samurai of my stamp. As they say, the rain it raineth every day. So, off I must go to sake! Where else, indeed! Bring me sake! Hey, Taro Kaja! Are you there?

TARO KAJA: (*Coming forward.*) Here, sir, at your service.

HORATA: Now, listen. The despicable state of the world is all the more reason why we must live triumphantly for pleasure – here and now. To indulge in memories of good old days is a sign of old age. I may be without a master, but I'm not without youth. So, drink ye sake while ye may, that's what I say. Sake! Bring me sake!

TARO KAJA: Yes, sir. (*Stage assistant hands to Taro Kaja a vessel of sake and a large cup.*) Here I have brought you sake.

HORATA: Well done! You are so quick. (*Receiving the cup.*) Pour for me. Be quick.

TARO KAJA: With all my heart, sir. (*Pouring. Onomatopoeic.*) Dobu, dobu, dobu.

HORATA: (*Drinking.*) You drink, too.

TARO KAJA: I am most grateful. (*He takes out of his belt a fan which, opened, functions as a cup. He pours for himself and drinks.*)

HORATA: Jiro Kaja, are you there?

JIRO KAJA: (*Coming forward.*) Here, sir.

HORATA: You must drink, too.

JIRO KAJA: Much obliged, sir. (*Fills fan as above.*)

TARO KAJA: (*Pouring for Jiro Kaja.*) Go ahead.

HORATA: Pour me more! (*Taro Kaja does so. Horata drinks up and forestalls Taro Kaja just as he is about to pour for himself.*) Pour me more! More! (*Taro Kaja, having done so and then turning round to pour for himself, is again interrupted.)* More!

TARO KAJA: (*He does so. As he pours for himself, he finds the bottle almost empty. Trying to get the last few drops. Onomatopoeic.*) Pisho, pisho, pisho!

HORATA: Hey, Taro Kaja, why do you look so glum?

TARO KAJA: Well, there's no more sake.

HORATA: What? You idiot! Why didn't you prepare more? Go get more! Be quick!

JIRO KAJA: Well, there's no more money.

HORATA: Money? What are you jabbering about? Who needs money? Tell the host to put it on my bill.

TARO KAJA: He says he can't do that any more.

JIRO KAJA: He says you must pay for your room first.

TARO KAJA: Your bills for room and sake are piled up mountain-high, and he keeps clamouring for payment. It's so very humiliating that I'm ashamed even to walk in the street.

HORATA: You coward! (*Beating Taro Kaja.*) How can you serve under the great Horata Suke-emon with such a paltry spirit?

TARO KAJA: Ouch! Ouch!

HORATA: Hey, Jiro Kaja, you go.

JIRO KAJA: Well, I too dare not face the host without at least a part of your room charge in my hand.

HORATA: You rascal! (*He beats Jiro Kaja.*)

JIRO KAJA: Ouch! Ouch!

HORATA: Nothing but talk of money, money, money. As if that were a new note that all the bees of May had started buzzing! It's enough to make my sake go sour. (*He takes a deep breath.*) Now, I've got a bright idea. In this town live two merchants named Yakibei and Heibei, and their wives, named Omatsu and Otaké, are both crazily in love with me. I have proof of that. Oh yes I have. But even if I had none, I should be resigned to the situation. I mean, it's my fate to have all women fall for me. So I will now write a love-letter to each of these two women . . . (*Stage assistant hands him sheets of paper.*)

TARO KAJA: (*To Jiro Kaja.*) Look, the worm of his other passion has started wriggling inside him.

JIRO KAJA: (*To Taro Kaja.*) Shame on him! Sake is not his only passion.

HORATA: (*Giving a sheet of paper to each servant.*) You hold this so that I can write. (*He takes out his fan, which serves as a pen, and begins to write.*) I will set times for meeting with these women. Making women happy and coaxing money out of them – doesn't this go far beyond the usual game of killing two birds with one stone? (*Signing the letters with a flourish.*) There, complete with signatures. Now, go and deliver these to the ladies by your hands. (*They tentatively receive the letters.*) Be quick.

TARO KAJA: I'm afraid, sir, even an order from my dread master can't possibly force me to obey such a . . . such a . . . I will not simply go running about for anybody's illicit affairs. (*Offering to return the letter to Horata.*) Even I have a sense of honour, sir.

HORATA: What! You speak of honour, you moron! (*He angrily kicks Taro Kaja, who rolls about on the ground in pain. To Jiro Kaja.*) What about you? Do you have some sense of this thing called honour, too?

JIRO KAJA: (*Offering to return the letter.*) Er . . . yes . . . just a little . . .

HORATA: (*Grabbing Jiro Kaja by the neck.*) What nonsense you are talking, fools! What is honour? Tell me. It's a word. It's a breath of empty air. Suppose a samurai goes out to battle for the sake of honour, can honour set to a leg? No. Or an arm? No, dunces, never. (*Grabbing Taro Kaja by the neck who was trying to sneak away.*) Or can it take away the grief of a wound? No, imbeciles, never. There's only one way for a wise man to survive in this vile world. I'll tell you what it is. (*Dragging both servants along by the neck.*) Listen with your both ears wide open. 'Be the first in the banquet hall, be the last on the battle-field.' So stop talking rubbish about honour and such stupid ideas. Go on your errand, quick! Otherwise, you're banished out of my sight forever, is that clear?

TARO KAJA and JIRO KAJA: Ouch, all right, we will go.

HORATA: (*Letting them go.*) Be on your way quickly.

TARO KAJA: (*Sarcastically.*) My mother always told me that there were three things in the world which you'd never win against: a weeping child, a wilful landlord, and a drunken lecherous master.

HORATA: What did you say?

TARO KAJA: Nothing. I was just recalling an old saying. (*He and Jiro Kaja turn to exit with the letters.*)

HORATA: (*Yawning.*) Oh, how sleepy I feel. Hey, you slow-wits, what are you doing here? Off to the women, and come back with good news! Quick! I must take a nap. (*He lies down downstage centre, and falls asleep, snoring audibly. The servants are now on the bridgeway.*)

TARO KAJA: Don't you remember our master in the old days? He used to be a man of some importance, and it was a joy to serve him then.

JIRO KAJA: It was, indeed.

TARO KAJA: But then, he became masterless, which made him penniless, which made him witless. And here he is, stranded in a country town, long over-staying his welcome at this tiny inn, which has made him particularly domineering and gruff. When he gets violent as he did just now, it's really more than I can bear.

JIRO KAJA: I cannot take it any longer either.

TARO KAJA: Oh yes, I have an idea. When I give this letter to Mistress Omatsu, I'll tell her all about his trick. And we'll plot together to outwit him. That'll be a good revenge. What do you say to this?

JIRO KAJA: Excellent! I'll tell all to Mistress Otaké.

TARO KAJA: I'll leak this to Master Yakibei as well. (*Exeunt both.*)

Scene 2

(*Omatsu's room. However, Horata is left lying asleep as before, in the shade.*) *Enter Omatsu and Otaké, reading their letters to each other, and comparing the contents.*

OMATSU: (*Reading her letter aloud.*) 'Shall I compare thee to . . .' what? . . . 'Nay, I do not know what to compare you to. Nor do I know how to describe my burning desire for you.'

OMATSU and OTAKÉ: 'I have heard of a famous Western drama in which . . .' (*The flute starts playing the well-known tune from Zeffirelli's film 'Romeo and Juliet'. The women read the following sentence with overt theatricality, mimicking a gesture of love.*)

OMATSU: 'A youth named Romeo . . .'

OTAKÉ: '. . . falls in love with a maiden named Juliet.' (*Both laugh raucously.*)

OMATSU: 'I am aware that I am a little too aged to call myself a youth.'

OTAKÉ: 'A little?'

OMATSU: 'Nor is it entirely appropriate to refer to you as a maiden.' Well, certainly not. (*They giggle.*)

OTAKÉ: 'But it is surely not for nothing that both you and I have grown somewhat older. This great belly of mine . . .'

OMATSU: '. . . symbolises powers of middle age unpossessed by men of lesser years . . .'

OTAKÉ: What impudence!

OMATSU: '. . . just as the wrinkles at the corners of your eyes serve only to enhance your middle-aged charms.'

OTAKÉ: I see, he puts himself in the same category with us.

OMATSU: 'We, in the middle of our lives, are destined to embrace each other and tear our pleasures through the iron gates of life. The amorous fire burning in my mountainous belly waits yearning for your favourable answer. With profound respect and appetite.'

OMATSU and OTAKÉ: (*Chanting in unison in a special Kyogen tone.*) 'From your furiously devoted slave of love, the samurai, Horata Suke-emon, to the most beauteous . . .'

OMATSU: 'Milady Omatsu.'

OTAKÉ: 'Milady Otaké.' (*Both laugh heartily.*)

OMATSU: This is just as Taro Kaja reported. Completely identical, word for word, except for our names.

OTAKÉ: This is exactly as Jiro Kaja told me. Such a brazen joke, and from such an old rogue!

OMATSU: How apt his name is! Horata the braggart, and Suke-emon the lecher. I humbly desire more acquaintance of your lordship, my dear Sir Lech Bragfield. (*Good laugh.*) According to Taro Kaja, this braggart samurai boasts that it is his lot to be adored by all women.

OTAKÉ: What a conceit!

OMATSU: How dare he treat respectable wives of citizens in such a manner? Should we let him get away with it? This self-styled gallant samurai deserves a sound drubbing like a hot moxa treatment, don't you agree?

OTAKÉ: With all that plentiful extra flesh on his bones, I'm sure he'll make a good bonfire.

OMATSU: If only my husband could see this letter. It would give eternal food to his jealousy.

OTAKÉ: Don't say such a horrible thing.

OMATSU: (*Laughing.*) It's only a joke. Come on, let's devise some smart plan against this greasy samurai. (*Exeunt both.*)

Scene 3

(Horata's room, with Horata still lying as before in the shade.) Enter Yakibei, disguised as Mochibei, a crooked old man, with a walking stick.

YAKIBEI: *(Soliloquises on the bridgeway.)* My name is Yakibei. I am a merchant residing in this town. Truly, I believe that nothing on earth is more like pure hell than jealousy. If you wish to avoid being roasted by this cruel flame, you should never take a wife. I say this because – well, I have a wife – her name is Omatsu – and I am warned by Taro Kaja that there is a samurai who is trying to woo her. His name is Horata Suke-emon. My suspicion has grown so excruciating that I can't stand it any longer. I have come to the conclusion that the only way to get rid of the torture is to confirm the suspicion. So, disguising myself in these garments and assuming a false name, I pay a visit to this samurai. *(Calling out towards the main stage.)* Hello in there! Sir Horata Suke-emon, are you there?

HORATA: *(The stage is lit up. Awakened by Yakibei's voice, Horata gets to his feet.)* Who is there? Do come in.

YAKIBEI: *(Coming onto the stage.)* My name is Mochibei. I am a merchant residing in this town. I have come to ask for a very special favour of you.

HORATA: And what might that be, Master, er, Master Mochibei?

YAKIBEI: Well, to make a most embarrassing confession, I'm deeply enamoured of the wife of a merchant of this town named Yakibei. But this woman, Omatsu by name, is as hard as adamant, refusing to take the slightest notice of me. A veritable mirror of wifely virtue, or so she seems. However, it is my belief that all this is only a mask concealing a wanton nature.

HORATA: And what is it you desire of me?

YAKIBEI: Well, what I would implore you to do, Sir Suke-emon, is to seduce her, to embrace her, to bed her. For that purpose, you shall want no money. *(Swinging a money-bag.)* I will provide you amply.

HORATA: It is strange, I must say, asking another man to enjoy the woman you are in love with yourself. I don't know what to make of this.

YAKIBEI: You may well wonder, but I'll tell you why. If this woman were once bedded by a man other than her husband, then this infidelity could be used by me as a weapon to assail her seemingly impenetrable citadel of honour and virtue. Surely she would have to open her treasure to me as well.

HORATA: What a superb plan! I'm totally convinced. *(Snatching the bag.)* I'll make bold with your battle fund without further ado. In actual fact, I'm going to have a tryst with this same Omatsu – by her own appointment, for it happened that only a while ago a letter arrived from her informing me of the hour during which her husband would be out. So I'm just on my way to visit her. Do come back tomorrow, Master Mochibei, I'll tell you all about how I've made a horned monster of her husband Yakibei. Rest assured that you'll hear every detail of his cuckolding straight from her paramour's mouth, that is, from this mouth of mine.

YAKIBEI: That will be more than I wished, indeed. I humbly beg you to remember that my happiness depends on your success.

HORATA: Wait till tomorrow and look forward to a great revelation. I must hurry

on my way to be treated to the sweetest of delicacies. Oh, what a pleasure it is
to imagine the great pleasure that is in store. (*Exit Horata.*)

YAKIBEI: Oh, this is worse than hell! To request to be made a cuckold is painful
enough. But to have this request carried out in such a way – it is a torture
beyond words. Oh, frailty, thy name is wife! Oh, lecherous, treacherous
villain! I'll catch you both in the act of love-making, and make four pieces of
your two bodies as you lie on top of each other. Oh, anger, consume my heart
with your flame! (*He tears off his false beard and throws away his walking stick.
Crying as he exits.*) Anger! Anger! Anger! . . . (*Stage assistant comes forth and
takes away the stick.*)

Scene 4

(*Omatsu's room.*) *Enter Taro Kaja and Jiro Kaja, to the slow beat of a drum,
carrying a huge laundry basket and putting it down downstage left. (Actually,
they carry nothing, all being done in mime.) They are followed by Omatsu and
Otaké.*

OMATSU: Now, Otaké, don't forget to give us a timely knock on the door, as we
discussed earlier.

OTAKÉ: You can depend on me, Omatsu. Till I do so, enjoy your sweet tryst as
much as you like.

OMATSU: Certainly I will. (*Exit Otaké. To Taro Kaja and Jiro Kaja.*) And are you
two prepared to do as I ordered?

TARO KAJA: Yes, madam. When you call, we will come out in all haste, and carry
this laundry basket out of the room no matter what happens, and empty it in
the river. We will do the job trimly and to perfection. We warrant you that . . .

TARO KAJA and JIRO KAJA: (*In unison.*) . . . nothing shall go amiss.

OMATSU: All right. Wait inside.

TARO KAJA and JIRO KAJA: We shall.

OMATSU: Now all I have to do is just to wait for the arrival of that blister-bellied
water-melon goblin of an old philanderer. Oh, speak of the devil, here he
comes.

Enter Horata.

HORATA: Oh, my loveliest one! When I heard that you, Milady Omatsu, were
pining for my arrival, my heart started to pine for your gracious sight.

OMATSU: Oh, my dearest Sir Suke-emon, I'm overwhelmed by your great presence.

HORATA: Oh, the joy of gathering my long-adored you at last in these arms! My
impossible dream come true! How I was haunted by your fragrant visage! (*He
tries to embrace her.*)

OMATSU: (*Slipping out of his arms.*) You speak so nicely, but is it not Mistress
Otaké, the wife of Master Heibei, who has truly enthralled your heart?

HORATA: What nonsense you are talking! I'm just as much enamoured of her as I
am of a fat sow or a rotten persimmon.

OMATSU: (*Coquettishly.*) Can I really believe what you say? I'd be mortally wounded if you meant to hold a rose in each hand. You will soon find out just how much I yearn for you.

HORATA: (*Taking off his cape, and trying to manoeuvre around his fat belly to embrace her.*) I assure you that you'll not regret having repaid my love. A look at this belly should abundantly show you just how perfectly I'm the man for you.

OMATSU: It certainly does.

Enter Otaké in a pretended flurry. Horata hides himself behind Omatsu.

OTAKÉ: Omatsu, Omatsu, it's awful! You are undone!

OMATSU: How now? What is the matter?

OTAKÉ: Is it possible, Otaké, that you have a paramour?

OMATSU: What a foolish thing to say!

OTAKÉ: That is precisely what I told Master Yakibei, and I did my best to stop him.

OMATSU: What? What's that about my husband?

OTAKÉ: He is madly shouting in the street that you are at this moment in the arms of your paramour and that he's going to punish the guilty couple. He's approaching, with such a ferocious look on his face and a sword in his hand.

OMATSU: Oh, I'm undone, as you say, for there is in fact a man here.

OTAKÉ: What? There's a man in this room?

OMATSU: Yes, it's a fact.

OTAKÉ: Oh, I'm appalled! If he finds him here, he'll most certainly cut you both to pieces.

OMATSU: Oh, I'm frightened! You know how extraordinarily jealous my husband is. Oh, help! What shall we do with Sir Suke-emon?

OTAKÉ: What? Did you say Sir Suke-emon? (*Horata tries to sneak away hiding his face behind his cape, which Otaké snatches off.*) Indeed! Sir Suke-emon, what on earth does this mean, if I may ask, after that letter of yours to me?

HORATA: I love you and none but you, but more of that later. Help me away now. I hate pain of any sort whatsoever, but I would hate being cut to pieces more than anything else. Help, oh, help!

OMATSU: How disgusting! How disappointing! Go squat down in that corner and hide your head.

OTAKÉ: Yes, that looks like the only safe place. (*Horata goes upstage left and crouches on the floor hiding his head. Quick drumbeats.*)

OMATSU and OTAKÉ: What is that noise?

Enter Taro-Kaja and Jiro-Kaja, also wondering at the noise. Taro Kaja runs to the bridgeway to look into the distance.

TARO-KAJA: Look! It's really him!

OMATSU and OTAKÉ: Oh, no, it cannot be!

ALL FOUR: What shall we do? (*They mime an instant conference. Exeunt Taro Kaja and Jiro Kaja.*)

[Note: Yakibei's arrival is unexpected to the wives and the servants: it was meant to be a pretence to scare Horata. With Yakibei actually rushing in, they must from this moment on partly improvise.]

Enter Yakibei, to the quick beat of the drum, slashing at the air with his sword, exactly as described by Omatsu earlier.

YAKIBEI: Hey, where are the adulterous couple? It's not enough to run them through with this and chop them to pieces. Come out and show yourselves!

OMATSU: Come, come! What are you so worked up about? Do calm yourself a little, I beseech you.

YAKIBEI: You be silent! Where have you hidden him? Bring out your paramour! I have proof he's here.

The wives ostentatiously hide the (invisible) basket. Yakibei rushes to it, and begins throwing the (invisible) dirty clothes all over the room. Finding no one inside, he begins desperately searching all corners. While he is searching behind the tree, the dismayed Horata comes out of hiding, thus making it easier for the women to act according to their scenario.

OMATSU: (*To Horata.*) You are in danger there. Oh, what shall we do? Look, what's that I see over there? Is it not a laundry basket?

OTAKÉ: Indeed it is! How lucky! You can climb into it.

OMATSU and OTAKÉ: Come, come. Hurry up!

HORATA: What! You want me to get into this tiny smelly thing?

OMATSU: Would you rather be butchered by my husband?

HORATA: I'll get in, I'll get in. (*The women shove him into the basket and pile dirty clothes on him.*) Oh, it stinks! I'm choking!

OMATSU: Shhh! My husband is coming.

OTAKÉ: How terrifying ! Look how he slashes about with his sword!

At Omatsu's signal, Taro Kaja and Jiro Kaja come in with a (visible) long pole, with which they carry out the (invisible) basket with Horata inside. He mimes being carried off by rolling along between the servants. They are intercepted by Yakibei on the way.

YAKIBEI: (*Suspiciously.*) Wait a minute.

JIRO KAJA: This is a laundry basket.

YAKIBEI: I know that. I looked in it before. (*Throwing out a few pieces of laundry.*) Just to make sure.

TARO KAJA: Do you want to smell the same stench once more? Crazy taste, I must say. Maybe it will smell of rotten baked rice-cake, which I remember my mother comparing to the smell of jealousy.

YAKIBEI: All right! Go! Go away!

Taro Kaja and Jiro Kaja, with Horata between them, start on their journey around the stage, circling behind the tree, and singing the song, 'Fair is foul, white is black . . .' (see below). The following conversation between Omatsu, Otaké, and Yakibei takes place on the bridgeway while the procession is circling around the tree.

OMATSU: (*To Yakibei.*) I wonder how you can treat your own wife with such an ignoble suspicion. What will you do if word gets about in the world?

OTAKÉ: Truly, jealousy is a miserable disease.

YAKIBEI: I'm ashamed, I'm sorry, I acted foolishly. (*Aside.*) But I don't understand. Why is this? Was that rascally samurai simply bragging to me? (*To Omatsu.*) Oh, I'm ashamed, I'm sorry, I apologise. Do pardon me, pardon me. (*Exit Yakibei dejectedly.*)

Meanwhile, Taro Kaja and Jiro Kaja, having come back downstage centre, dump Horata onto the floor (now taken to be a river) with a big shout. Horata tumbles out shrieking, and is immediately carried down into the trap. (Where the trap is unavailable, he should perhaps be flung off into the left wing.) Exeunt Taro Kaja and Jiro Kaja after a hearty laugh, which is echoed by the wives on the bridgeway.

OMATSU: (*Laughing.*) Oh, what fun it was! But how on earth did my husband know about it?

OTAKÉ: It was not in our scenario. I was scared out of my wits.

OMATSU: But it was all the more fun.

OTAKÉ: We have killed two birds with one stone.

OMATSU: I don't know which pleases me better, to have deceived the samurai or my husband.

Enter Taro Kaja and Jiro Kaja to join the women.

OMATSU: (*To Taro Kaja and Jiro Kaja.*) Did all go well?

TARO KAJA: Very well indeed. He squawked so inside the basket, but we silenced him by telling him that Master Yakibei was close upon our heels. But oh, the weight of the basket!

JIRO KAJA: Emptying it into the river was also a bit of trouble.But with all our might and main combined together, we did it, and down he went with a resounding echo – (*onomatopoeic splash of water*) BOTCHAAN!

TARO KAJA: (*Onomatopoeic sinking into water.*) BUKU, BUKU, BUKU!

(*All four laugh raucously.*)

OTAKÉ: That old braggart seems to me really too good to let go with a single drubbing, don't you think?

OMATSU: Quite so. My husband may be pardoned, but that samurai deserves at least another lesson to remember us by.

OTAKÉ: Indeed he does. Together with your husband, let us discuss what to do next.

TARO KAJA: This is getting more and more amusing.

ALL FOUR: (*Singing and dancing to flute and drum accompaniment.*)

> Fair is foul,
> White is black,
> Fat is slim.
>   Hey nonny-no!

> Big is small,
> Red is blue,
> High is low.
>   Hey nonny-no!

They continue singing and dancing as they exit. Then, Horata, emerging out of the trap, comes to his senses. (If he has been in the wings he crawls onto the stage.)

HORATA: Oh, I'm soaking wet! Damn it! Atchoo! (*Exit.*)

An interval of about five minutes, during which the audience is entertained by performance of flute and drum.

Scene 5

(Horata's room.) Enter Horata, sneezing horribly, followed by Taro Kaja.

HORATA: Atchoo! And what do you want?

TARO KAJA: (*Offering a letter to Horata.*) A letter for you, sir.

HORATA: Fie upon letters! Who is it from?

TARO KAJA: From Mistress Omatsu, sir.

HORATA: What? From Omatsu?

TARO KAJA: Yes. I don' t know why, but she looked, when she told me to deliver this to you, as though she had something greatly tormenting her heart, so I made haste to bring it.

HORATA: (*Reading the letter aloud.*) Let me see. 'I am most deeply chagrined that we were interrupted at the very moment of consummating our love yesterday. It is my damned husband who is to blame.' It is, indeed. Just as I was about to touch those white pearly breasts with this hand of mine, that stupid green-eyed monster of a husband . . .

TARO KAJA: (*Aside.*) A half-witted paramour is laughing at a foolish husband. This is just like a belch laughing at a fart, as the old saying goes.

HORATA: 'We were fortunate, however, that nobody was hurt, no blood shed.' True enough, for I hold no love, however sweet, or no gold, however glittering, to be worth a drop of blood.

TARO KAJA: (*Aside.*) As some philosophical coward said, 'To be or not to be, that is the question.'

HORATA: 'Please forgive me for allowing that awful thing to happen. My sole concern ever since has been whether you returned home safe and sound.' Bitch! What does she mean safe and sound? Choked by stinking laundry, dumped without ceremony into the freezing river, and seized by a deathly cold. Atchoo!

TARO KAJA: (*Aside.*): The old saying never goes wrong: 'Blood is thicker than water just as ice is colder than water.'

HORATA: What else does she say? 'Oh please do not let that discourage you, for I am longing for a second chance, another sweet joy of tryst.' Well, I'm not above scratching your back if you are willing to scratch mine.

TARO KAJA: (*Aside.*) One is obliged to amend the proverb a little: Once bitten, twice hot.

HORATA: 'Which brings me to a proposal. Tonight, in the grove on the outskirts of the town, there is an annual festival dedicated to the patron god of our town, and people will gather in fanciful costume to celebrate. I will be there wearing the mask of a maiden. It would be thrilling if you could come wearing the mask of a long-nosed demon. I look forward with passionate yearning to the pleasure of seeing you by the ancient pine in the depths of the grove. To my dearest Sir Horata Suke-emon. From your love-tormented Omatsu.' The pleasure of seeing me? It is all mine, all mine. The mask of a long-nosed demon? I will wear anything. This is going to be a most unforgettable rendezvous. Go get ready, Suke-emon, you the luckiest of men, go get ready! Oh, my beloved Omatsu, wait for me, I will come to you. (*Exit.*)

TARO KAJA: As the old saying goes . . . alas, I've run out of old sayings. (*Exit.*)

Scene 6

(The dark grove on the outskirts of the town.) Enter Omatsu upstage right.

OMATSU: (*Stopping on the bridgeway, she calls towards the wings on the right.*) Let me confirm what I hope is clear to everyone. When I shout, 'Look there! Those weird shadows!' that is the signal for you all to come forth. And then it is all up to you whether to pinch him, or scratch him, or beat him. Do whatever you feel like – to your hearts' content. Thus we join tonight to quell a fat sake-reeking demon and offer him up to our patron god. (*Groping her way upstage centre towards the pine.*) Now I have already arrived at the appointed spot. I will wait here, by this pine-tree. (*She dons the comic mask of a maiden.*) Already I seem to smell a whiff of sake in the air.

Enter Horata upstage left, wearing the mask of a 'tengu', long-nosed demon.

HORATA: (*Groping his way towards the pine.*) How bothersome! I can't see well, for I'm not accustomed to wearing a mask. On top of that, it's pitch-dark night. She said, 'By the ancient pine', but I can't make out where the bloody tree is. Was she punning on her name, which means pine? I guess this is it. Here I will pine for Lady Pine who must be pining for me by the pine. (*Laughing at himself.*) How foolish of me! This is no time to indulge in pineal puns. (*They both go about the stage in dumb groping gestures, till they bump into each other. He falls over backward in fright.*) Haaaagh! Who is it!

OMATSU: Oh, how frightful!

HORATA: Oh, is it Omatsu?

OMATSU: Oh, Sir Suke-emon?

HORATA: What do you mean springing upon me like this? You nearly scared me out of my wits.

OMATSU: Why, what a coward! You are a samurai, aren't you?

HORATA: A samurai is human just like any other man. We too are subject to surprises and consternations. Especially on a night like this.

OMATSU: And yet people say, 'Tender is the night', and they are right, are they not? For a tryst with your dear sweetheart, no place is fitter than a dark spot.

HORATA: I couldn't agree with you more on that. The thicker the dark, the more vigorous the power of pleasure that swells inside my belly. (*He tries to embrace her.*)

OMATSU: How ravishingly manly you sound! But wait. I've been feeling that there's some strange presence around us. Could it be some spirits lurking about, or some humans spying on us?

HORATA: Stop talking nonsense, and surrender your sweet body into my desiring arms.

OMATSU: (*Loudly.*) Look there! Those weird shadows!

Enter Otaké, Taro Kaja, Jiro Kaja, and Yakibei, all wearing different weird masks, accompanied by scary music on the flute.

HORATA: Haaaagh, what are these?

OMATSU: Oh! how fearsome! They must be evil demons inhabiting this grove. I'm scared! Oh, Sir Suke-emon, please help me, help me!

HORATA: No, no! I'm just as frightened as you are. Helping others is out of the question. This is no child's play. Yes, I know what I will do, I will lie down on the ground and pretend I'm dead. Look, everybody, I am dead.

Horata lies down on his back. All the others start circling around him to the menacing sound of the flute till they finally come to a stop, surrounding him.

OTAKÉ: What can this be? A sake barrel with all its hoops loose? (*She pinches Horata.*)

TARO KAJA: Not a sake barrel, but a pig that has eaten itself into immobility. (*He stamps on Horata.*)

JIRO KAJA: Not a pig, but a drowned body. (*He twists Horata's arm.*)

YAKIBEI: No, no, this is a meteorite fallen from the sky. (*He kicks Horata.*)

OMATSU: Or rather that meteorite grown fat and rotten. (*She tickles Horata. The others join her in tickling Horata, whispering 'Kutsu, kutsu'. [Japanese onomatopoeia when tickling a person, similar to Verdi's Italian onomatopoeia for pinching, 'Pizzica, pizzica'.]*)

HORATA: (*Unable to take it any more, he begins to shriek.*) Forgive me, you evil demons – I mean good Masters Demons. (*Sitting up, he kowtows shamelessly.*) I will do anything you say if only you spare my life.

OTAKÉ: Then do you apologise for using women disgracefully?

HORATA: I do, I do.

TARO KAJA: Do you admit you have told braggart lies?

HORATA: I do, I do.

JIRO KAJA: Do you repent having drunk far too much sake?

HORATA: I do, I do.

YAKIBEI: Do you make public confession that you ignored the solemn vows of marriage . . .

OMATSU: . . . and ask pardon for violating the laws of society?

HORATA: I do, I do.

OMATSU: Do you swear that you will henceforth become . . .

ALL: (*in unison.*) . . . A VIRTUOUS MAN?

HORATA: I do, I do, I swear to become whatever you wish.

OMATSU: (*Taking off her mask and then pulling off Horata's mask.*) Sir Suke-emon, you look more handsome without the mask than with it.

HORATA: (*Looking around.*) Well, I say, what is all this?

OTAKÉ: (*Taking off her mask.*) My esteemed Sir, you seem to look a little pale. Did you, perhaps, have a bad dream?

HORATA: Oh, it is you, Mistress Otaké.

TARO KAJA: (*Taking off his mask.*) I just remembered one more old saying . . .

HORATA: And you are Taro Kaja.

JIRO KAJA: (*Taking off his mask.*) How heavy that basket was!

HORATA: Jiro Kaja, you rascal!

YAKIBEI: (*Taking off his mask.*) I am the familiar jealous cuckold.

HORATA: Why, Master Mochi . . . no, Master Yakibei.

YAKIBEI: (*Dragging Horata by the hand to face the others who now stand in a line.*) Come on now, bow down with your head to the ground, and apologise in earnest once more.

HORATA: (*Shaking himself free of Yakibei's grasp.*) No, no, what's the use of it? I refuse to apologise. (*Turning around to face the audience.*) All the world is but a joke, and all the men and women merely jesters. Life is made up of laughing at just as much as of being laughed at. The quantity of laughter in this world, just like that of tears, is constant. For every one who stops laughing, someone starts laughing somewhere. I for one will go on laughing until the very end. I shall be the one to laugh last and best. (*Sitting down triumphantly.*) And I swear by this gigantic belly that my philosophy shall never change. (*He laughs a typical Kyogen laugh, a thundering, Gargantuan-scale laugh.*)

YAKIBEI: There's no cure for him. Well, I admit defeat.

TARO KAJA: No old saying could ever cope with that primeval belly.

OMATSU: We have meted out sufficient chastisement. Our revels are now ended, so let us forgive our dear old braggart samurai.

YAKIBEI: And let us every one celebrate the festival of our patron god. We will dance the night joyfully away, Sir Suke-emon and all.

ALL: Let us do so.

Horata leads the others in a cheerful song [which incorporates a very popular folk dance-song, The Fool Dance of Awa] and a Kyogen dance to the music of flute and drum. A sort of grand finale.

ALL: All the world is a Kyogen farce.
         All the men and women are jesters.
                 Hey, hey, nonny-nonny, hey, nonny-no!

         If it be so, I would rather be

A dancing Jester than a watching one.
Hey, hey, nonny nonny, hey, nonny-no!

A fortissimo note of flute at the climax, and black out.

THE END

Part 3

Afterword

17   A playgoer's journey: from Shakespeare to Japanese classical theatre and back

Robert Hapgood

Imagine an uncut performance of *Hamlet*, lasting over four hours, that includes everything Shakespeare wrote except the fencing match in which the prince takes his long-awaited revenge. Imagine *Romeo and Juliet* performed in its entirety except for the final love-death. To my knowledge no such performances have ever been given. Whatever else may have been cut, those climactic moments come so close to being what the tragedies are 'about' as to make their omission unthinkable. Yet when analogous Japanese classics are performed their finales are truncated in just these ways, and not as an experimental innovation but as common practice. It is one measure of the distance between Japanese and Western traditional theatre.

It was early in my two years of intensive Japanese theatre-going that I realised the extent of the distance a Western playgoer, accustomed to Shakespeare and modern drama, would need to traverse.[1] I had the opportunity on successive weekends to see the quintessential Japanese revenge tragedy *Kanadehon Chushingura* done in Kabuki and Bunraku (puppet) versions, both lasting all day. Everything in the play points toward the climactic act of revenge, yet to my astonishment and frustration both productions simply skipped that scene (although it is written in the original text) and went on to the next, which concluded the play. A short while later I saw my first Chikamatsu love-suicide play. In it too the scene he wrote depicting the death of the lovers was left out in performance. When I asked a Japanese friend why these climaxes had been omitted, he said, 'Well, it is customary; and anyway everyone knows how it turns out so there is no need to show it.' At the time I found this hard to accept. But as my exposure to Japanese theatre continued, I came to see that these omissions led deeper and deeper into a distinctive way of understanding the performing arts: to what constitutes a satisfying theatre-event and beyond that to so fundamental a matter as where the essential drama occurs – on the stage, in the eyes of the beholders, in the hearts of the performers, or in the mind of the playwright. Not that I feel I have travelled the whole distance between Western and Eastern theatre, or ever will. Indeed, as will be discussed, I remain unpersuaded as to the wisdom of cutting the tragic catastrophes. After all, their performance was clearly part of the playwrights' original conception. Yet their omission no longer seems so baffling as to be unthinkable. And this improved understanding of the aesthetic principles that lie behind this practice has not only extended to Japanese classics generally but has also influenced fundamentally my subsequent view of Shakespeare and Shakespearean production.

Bafflement was by no means the chief part of my initial reaction to Japanese classical theatre. For the most part I was simply and delightedly astounded by its bold and expert theatricality, excitements that made Western theatre seem pallid and unadventurous by comparison. On a daily basis the Japanese actors went to extremes that only an Olivier or a Peter Brook dared to risk. What I found especially surprising and thought-provoking was that the features that struck me as most daringly theatrical turned out to be traditional. Their excitement derived from the past whereas in the West the whole emphasis has been to supplant the past lest it lead to 'museum theatre', the goal being always to discover a break-through into the future, to 'make it new'. It is not that Western actors disregard or lack respect for their forerunners. Olivier's Richard III was very much in Anthony Sher's mind when he conceived his own, as Sher's Richard was in Simon Russell Beale's when he conceived his. Each actor confessed as much in presentations at the Shakespeare Institute. Yet in each case although the younger actor may have been inspired to carry on the heroic scale of his immediate predecessor, his chief concern was to differ from what had become definitive: if in the words of Queen Elizabeth's curse (*Richard III*, IV.iv.80) Sher as Richard resembled a 'bottled spider', then Beale would resemble a 'foul and bunch-backed toad'.

Western directors have similarly sought a fresh approach to classic plays, often looking for inspiration to modern playwrights. In particular, my own tastes as a Shakespeare-goer had been formed on the Royal Shakespeare Company productions of the Peter Hall era. Following their approach I fully subscribed to the line of thought that contemporary playwrights have the surest sense of what is most dramatic today and that therefore their plays are our best guides to what is dramatically most alive in Shakespeare. I could see the reductiveness of claiming a direct equivalence between *King Lear* and *Endgame* as Jan Kott provocatively did in *Shakespeare Our Contemporary* (1965). Yet it did seem beneficial for the same directors and actors to be doing Shakespeare at Stratford-upon-Avon and Pinter at the Aldwych in London; the two 'rubbed off' on one another, Shakespeare gaining immediacy from the juxtaposition and

Pinter scope. So wholeheartedly did I accept this view that in my own teaching I had deliberately sought the same kind of conjunction.

In Japan this whole set of assumptions was called into question. Instead of the play's dramatic potential being energised by an infusion of contemporary perspectives, it was the extreme stylisation from the past that provided this stimulus. For a newcomer, it is true, this excitement was at first partly in its novelty. There was, for example, an element of exoticism in the appeal of the bizarre Kabuki make-up and the strutting, declamatory *aragoto* style of the play *Wait a Moment (Shibaraku)*. Yet a year later, when the traditions had become familiar, they still retained their power. The electrifying single click of the wooden clappers, the striking of a statuesque pose that crystallised a moment or a relationship, the raising of a puppet to its full commanding height, the lifting of the curtain at a Noh play to reveal the *shite* (leading actor) as his spirit self – all asserted with absolute confidence: 'This is a dramatic moment'. And it was!

These realisations have since made me wonder if beneath the apparent contradiction between tradition and contemporaneity there were not a common performance value. Did both Eastern and Western kinds of energy derive from a special conviction on the part of the actors? In Japan the authority came from the great actors of the past; in the west from affinity with contemporary playwrights and scholars (for Hall from Jan Kott and E. M. W. Tillyard) and from the searching and uncompromising re-investigation of the text that the RSC itself had become famous for. However that may be, the Japanese productions made me see that updating a classic was only one way of enhancing the excitement of its performance.

My sense of the whole theatrical occasion was stretched in Japan. In sheer length a programme of Japanese classical theatre lasts about twice as long as is now customary in the West. Instead of the ordinary 'two (or three) hours traffic' of Shakespeare's stage Noh programmes typically start in mid-morning and end four or five hours later, including three Noh plays plus a Kyogen (farce); Bunraku and Kabuki programmes are of comparable length.

In genre all three forms stretch beyond the Western 'theatre of words,' combining the performing and visual arts into their distinctive brands of total theatre. It is in Noh that the integration of music and dance with one another and with the drama is most complete. Even the glacially slow yet gliding walk of the *shite* seems a form of dance that leads up to his sometimes frenzied dancing at the climax of the drama. His singing, the chanting of the chorus, and the strange yelps of the drummers go together with the playing of the drums and flute to make a whole with the rest of the work. Visually, the elegant robes and ancient masks are no less integral to the drama – in fact, the actors enter into their roles through meditating on their masks. The result is a composite art of great complexity, as if drama, opera and ballet were amalgamated into one. Noh can at first seem tediously static, with nothing much happening and at a very slow pace! Yet the more I came to understand its components the harder I found it to keep up with everything that was going on. Noh stretches its viewer's powers of witness to the limit.

In the other forms of classic Japanese theatre the blending of the performing arts is not so extensive or thoroughgoing. In Bunraku, the *samisen* music is integral to the chanter's narration and rendering of the dialogue, but dance is not important. In Kabuki, moments of high intensity may be rendered in song and/or dance. Yet in general the two are more separable from the drama than in Noh. Still, in all three forms non-verbal performing arts are much more important than in modern drama, where apart from musicals dance almost never occurs and music is at most atmospheric. As in so many ways Shakespeare stands between the two extremes by occasionally including music and dance, especially in his comedies, but subordinating them to the verbal drama.

If the Japanese sense of a theatre event is larger than that in the West, it is held together by a looser sense of unity. The Japanese have a taste for dramatic fragments. It is one aspect, I believe, of their general avoidance of the obvious and their preference for leaving unspoken what can be communicated by suggestion and intuition. The novelist Junichiro Tanizaki mounted a whole aesthetic on this well-known national trait, *In Praise of Shadows* (1933). In it he makes the case for the beauty and magic of oriental obscurity as opposed to Western clarity. 'In the mansion called literature', he concludes, 'I would have the eaves deep and the walls dark. I would push back into the shadows the things that come forward too clearly.' In the theatre this reticence often takes the form of substituting the part for the whole. In contrast to the currently prevailing Western demand that a performance consist of a single complete play (a demand so strong that even an evening of complete one-act plays is rare) most Bunraku and Kabuki programmes are anthologies of excerpts. There is something to be said for such anthologies. They can serve to salvage living portions from plays that as a whole are no longer playable, a practice that might be emulated in the West. And they allow aficionados to see favourite actors in favourite scenes. But when most programmes are made up of such excerpts, the spectator is deprived of the satisfactions of an Aristotelian complete action. A Noh programme composed of a set of complete plays is much more satisfying; in this respect it is rather like a symphony concert. Even Noh programmers, however, frequently indulge in *shimai* (excerpted dances) done without mask or costume, each by a different dancer.

The fragmentation of forms becomes abusive, in my judgement, when it is applied to dramas that are still playable as wholes. And the abuse is especially objectionable when, as already mentioned, it leads to the truncation of tragic finales. I grant that Japanese spectators are more inclined than their Western counterparts to supply in their imaginations what is missing from the stage performance. Yet even Noh does not expect its viewer to supply everything. It provides a visual trigger to release the audience's imagination – perhaps no more than a folded kimono to evoke an absent lover. Less can be more. All the same there must be some prompting of the imagination, or else why have a performance at all? To the reply that the scenes preceding the tragic finale serve this purpose, I can only say that in the truncated love-suicide tragedies I have seen the intensity of passion displayed earlier was not so compelling as to necessitate a fatal outcome. For me, when a scene is completely deleted and the audience is expected to supply everything, nothing comes of nothing.

A positive aspect of the Japanese kind of loose unity is that in Bunraku and Noh it allows the script a certain autonomy. In these forms the playwright's words are coordinated with the rest of the work yet remain more distinct than in the West, where every effort is expended to make the language seem solely what the characters say. In Bunraku there is no pretence that the words are being spoken by the puppets rather than the chanter, who is visible throughout on a small stage to the right of the main stage. Words are given primacy. The puppeteers time their movements to fit the chanter's rendering of the dialogue, but he never looks at the stage. At the beginning of the play and between episodes he and his narration have the audience's total attention. In turn he begins his performance by saluting the playwright's text, lifting it high above his head. Out of regard for a Chikamatsu classic, even star puppeteers may remain hooded throughout. All the same, Bunraku chanters have felt free to modernise Chikamatsu's language and take other liberties with the original text. In Kabuki, playwrights have always been seen as mere purveyors of vehicles for star actors.

Only in Noh is a classic text given the respect that Shakespeare has received in twentieth-century performance. Indeed, in Noh the dramatist's words are accorded a remarkable autonomy, almost as though a dramatic poem were being acted out. So far from the literal can the dialogue become that at certain points the Chorus may chant the *shite*'s thoughts. Many in the audience have their own copies of the text, which since the houselights are always up they can follow as the play proceeds. (Whenever possible I too would have to hand my copy of an English translation, of which there are many.)

Although primacy is given to the text, the Noh playwright is not a dictator. The players and playgoers are free to interpret because, especially with the Noh master Zeami, the text itself is allusive and ambiguous, even more so than Shakespeare's. For a knowledgeable Noh spectator, to attend a play is to meditate upon its text in the presence of a performance. And for a Noh performer there is a spontaneous aspect to what might seem a ritualistically fixed occasion, because Noh productions these days are one-time-only events.[2] The participants already know their parts. Often only a single rehearsal will be thought necessary, devoted to special points of interpretation the *shite* may wish to emphasise. The essential coming together of *shite*, musicians, and chorus thus occurs at the time of performance. When the parts jell satisfyingly, its spontaneity adds an extra excitement. But this does not always happen. For instance, neither of the two Noh productions I have seen of *Dojoji* gave a satisfying rendering of the episode in which the heroine climbs an imaginary flight of stairs to meet her fate, to which more than twenty minutes of performance time was devoted: in one, the climax built too fast, came too soon, and thus left the performers with nowhere to go; in the other, it did not build steadily enough, causing the audience to lose interest in the middle. At such times one wishes for the kind of coordination that rehearsals and a director could have provided.

The same may be said of Kabuki, only more so. A good deal of what I saw of it struck me as tired. The grand effects require the burning of a commensurate amount of energy; and I did not find in many of the older actors the kind of dynamism so evident in the *ukiyo-e* prints, films of earlier leading actors, and the best of the current young actors. Even in the most rip-snorting *aragoto*-style pieces, this was true. For instance, in *Wait a Moment* the villain orders two of the sympathetic characters to be executed. As the executioner prepares to carry out the order, the Kabuki Handbook explains: 'A voice is heard shouting, "*Shibaraku*, wait a moment" from the back of the audience. Takehira [the villain] pays no attention and urges his men to hurry. Goro [the executioner] says the voice sends cold shivers down his spine. The retainers ask each other who the newcomer can be and confusion reigns.'[3] When I saw this done in Tokyo, confusion did not reign, or even come close to doing so. Instead, there was no visible on-stage reaction beyond that of the retainers, with their enormously padded bellies, standing in line and in turn spouting their assigned speeches. The 'big moment' simply did not happen. As here I often felt the lack in Japan of that directorial concern for an overall coordination of text, design, and performance now taken for granted in a Western Shakespeare production.

Perhaps the Japanese spectator is expected to bring all the parts together. Certainly the loose unity and autonomy of parts in Japanese classical theatre give the spectator a larger role in the dramatic event than is customary in modern Western drama. It is the spectator who must connect the chanter's voice with the puppets and in Kabuki transform an *onnagata* (male performer of female roles) into a beautiful maiden. The latter transformation, I confess, has yet to happen for me. Tamasaburo Bando is the exception that can help to clarify my general difficulty. One of the world's best actors, he has never in my experience failed in his depiction of women, whether performing Kabuki in Tokyo, traditional dances in New York, or modern roles in Kyoto. In a Kabuki-style *Othello* in Nagoya, I saw this Japanese man successfully impersonate an Italian lady of the Renaissance. Unlike a 'female impersonator' Tamasaburo does not exaggerate conventionally female characteristics. His portrayal of a woman is not basically different from that done by an actress except that through a process of selection from what men find most attractive about women, he distills an essence of beauty that is more purely and concentratedly feminine than that of a real woman. His artistry has been readily available for a Western beginner like me precisely because so much of it is accomplished on the stage that there is little need for the viewer to accomplish it, through theatrical convention, in the imagination. By contrast, despite the gracefulness of their movements, other *onnagata* remain for me no more than cackling men in white-face.

In general, I have not as yet been able to lose myself in the world of Kabuki, perhaps because of the three forms it most resembles Western theatre. Previous conditionings get in my way, particularly because the demonstrativeness of Kabuki style in many respects recalls 'ham' Shakespearean acting. On the other hand, I had had no previous experience with serious puppet theatre and have found it readily accessible. After all, if Bunraku is to have any dramatic effect at all, a viewer's imagination has to be active. For me it was. I have often been so caught up in an episode that, without my being aware of it, the puppets have in my mind grown to life-size; I usually don't realise that this has happened until the episode is over, and I am startled to see that the characters who then come on are mere puppets.

The necessity of relying on the viewer's imagination is even more pronounced in Noh, and – perhaps for that reason – it was there that I found it easiest to enter the imaginary world of the play. The test comes when, as is often the case, the *shite* abandons his initial corporeal identity and returns to the stage revealed in his true, ghostly self. For this moment to succeed the spectator must have been brought to accept that the spirit world is more real than the material one – that a boatman is in fact a fallen warrior, a village woman a poetess, an old couple the embodiment of two gods. At the time it happens, this acceptance seems quite natural and, again, only becomes remarkable in retrospect. Just how it comes about is complex. Partly it is prompted by what happens on stage. Even the uninitiated can see that the *shite* is transformed: he wears a different mask and costume; his whole bearing and way of moving have changed. Partly it is prompted by the script, which by recalling the past cues the audience to regard the *shite*'s final return to it as a revelation of the truth. But for full conviction to be achieved the drama must be lived in the heart of the *shite* and somehow communicated to the imagination of the audience.

In this process the Noh mask is crucial. Now in certain respects a mask can be directly expressive: its single expression realises an archetype, whether that of a demon or warrior or demented woman; and by artful tipping this expression can be subtly varied. Yet primarily the mask constitutes an extreme limitation on the vast range of facial expressions that a Shakespearean actor, say, might employ. The limitation is of the essence. I once observed a promising young Noh actor vigorously rehearsing a climactic dance and generating a direct charge of energy that was to me far more exciting than that of the numerous mature professionals I had been watching in performance. At first I attributed the difference to the fact that he was not wearing a costume or mask. But further thought made me realise that the young actor was not wearing an 'inner mask' either, whereas the artistry of a consummate professional like Hisao Kanze lay in a certain reserve, a sense that no matter how energetic his acting he always had further resources on call – 'pushed back in the shadows'. It is precisely because the outer and inner masking require indirect expression that the *shite*'s identification with his character must be heartfelt and total and that the audience must be attuned to its slightest indication, responsively supplying what his reticence leaves to the imagination. That is why in Noh as compared with Western theatre so much more of the drama takes place inside the minds and hearts of the actors and audience than is visible on-stage.

And that is why in this highly charged imaginative atmosphere the lyrical autonomy of the words in Noh can at times seem to put one directly in touch with the mind of the author. For me one such moment came at the end of *Hagoromo,* performed at the outdoor theatre of Miyajima, where the tide flows between the stage and the auditorium. As the moon-maiden made her twirling exit, I felt that I shared the poet's vision of her flight (as rendered by Arthur Waley):

> Sky-cloak of feathers fluttering, fluttering,
> Over the pine-woods of Mio,
> Past the Floating Islands, through the feet of the clouds she flies
> Over the mountain of Ashitaka, the high peak of Fuji,

Very faint her form
Mingled with the mists of heaven;
Now lost to sight.
    The No Plays of Japan (London: George Allen, 1921), p. 226

II

When I returned home my playgoing in Japan left me with no desire to see Western productions of Shakespeare Japanised in any literal way. Japanese attempts to do so have in my experience tended toward pastiche and interesting experiment more than genuine artistic accomplishment. They may serve to assimilate Shakespeare into the Japanese repertoire (as with the recent Bunraku *Tempest* in Osaka) but without adding much that is distinctively Japanese to the general understanding of Shakespeare. Another recent version of *The Tempest*, Ninagawa's at the Barbican, provides a case in point. Within a realistic set, it eclectically mixed the performance styles of various Japanese genres. Although Noh dominated, Caliban was brilliantly portrayed as a Kabuki character of the most flamboyant kind. In other respects, however, the eclecticism was too freewheeling for me. In a sense I was the worst possible spectator for this production. A Westerner unfamiliar with Japanese traditions could take the Japonisms for their direct theatrical values, uncomplicated by generic conventions; a Japanese aficionado, for whom these conventions were second nature, might find their recombination intriguing and easy to take in stride. But for someone like myself, whose rudimentary understanding of these forms was a studied acquisition, the mixture of idioms was too much for ready acceptance. A Ceres who was costumed to look like a Noh goddess but spoke with a Kabuki intonation was, to my taste, too hybrid to ring true. Ninagawa's earlier *Macbeth* at the National Theatre was more successful. Here again the least effective parts were the most direct translations of Shakespeare into Japanese conventions: there was nothing sinister about the three *onnagata* who played the Weird Sisters, they were merely peculiar; and the Kabuki-style posturing in the scene between Malcolm and Macduff made that episode seem even more interminable than usual. The greatest strength of this production had nothing to do with cross-cultural matters. It came simply from the fact that Masane Tsukayama as Macbeth and Komaki Kurihara as Lady Macbeth were so intensely and convincingly living their tragedies from within.

The new perspectives on Shakespeare that I brought home have not involved direct transplants from Japanese traditions. They have been of a more general sort, involving analogous approaches to Western traditions. As I have said the extremes of extravagance and subtlety in Japanese performance have made me realise how narrow a band most Western classic performers have limited themselves to. And that realisation has made me more receptive than I might otherwise have been to such bold strokes as Kenneth Branagh's Henry V delivering 'Once more unto the breach' from a siege-ladder attached to the front curtain, or Anthony Sher's declamation of one of Tamburlaine's monologues while hanging upside-down from a rope, or Judi Dench's prolonged wail as sleepwalking Lady Macbeth in the RSC video. In such instances I felt a Japanese-like release from the literal that freed the imagination. I have found that marathon sequences of Shakespeare's history plays, performed in single weekends by the Royal Shakespeare and English Shakespeare companies, have challenged my attention-span and stretched my imagination just as had the long programmes of Noh, Kabuki, and Bunraku.

The deepest and most pervasive Japanese influence on my understanding of Shakespeare has had to do with matters of relative realism and stylisation. Previously I had approached Shakespeare from modern Western drama, a form less stylised and more realistic than his. My exposure to Japanese classical theatre gave me first-hand experience of a kind of drama that was more stylised and less realistic. Comparison of Shakespeare with the two has thus allowed me to plot more precisely where he stands on a scale between Arthur Miller at one pole and Zeami at the other. Shakespeare's characters, for example, are much more individualised than those in Japanese classical drama (it is hard to imagine them wearing stock masks); yet the blank verse they speak could not be reduced to modern dramatic prose without great loss.

On this scale Shakespearean drama now seems more formalised than it did before. Here one must not exaggerate. Noh is undoubtedly closer to religious ceremonial than is Shakespeare; at the *omatsuri* celebration in Nara, a Noh play seemed very much at home as part of the worship at the god's temporary shrine. Yet the resemblance of the Noh chorus to Buddhist chanting has made me wonder if the varied verbal texture of Shakespeare's dialogue (from prose to blank verse to rhyming verse to song) may not be comparable to that of a Church of England service, where the levels of discourse range from the reading of scriptures to the formal rhetoric of sermons and prayers to the melodic chanting of psalms to the singing of hymns and anthems. Certainly, with few lighting effects, little scenery, and no actresses, Shakespeare was like the Japanese obliged to locate more of his drama in the imagination of his audience than do modern playwrights. While recognising that affinity, one also sees that the working of his imaginative appeal is much less rigidly conventionalised than in Japanese classical theatre. The farcical Kyogens, for example, are regularly included in a Noh programme but as separate playlets that are not integrated into the flow of serious action, as is comedy in Shakespeare's tragedies and histories.

What stands out most from such comparisons is the variety of balances that Shakespeare strikes between realism and stylisation and the suppleness with which he moves from one to another. The balances differ from play to play, scene to scene, character to character. They are most clearly registered in the dialogue. Consider, for example, the range of styles that Helena must negotiate in the opening scenes of *All's Well That Ends Well*. When she first appears she must deliver convincingly sincere blank verse soliloquies on either side of light-minded prose repartee about virginity with Parolles. In the next scene she must begin with submissive half-line responses to the Countess's long speeches and then herself give long speeches confessing her love in response to the Countess's half-line questions. At her next appearance (I.ii) she must first make a humble offer of her medical services to the King and humble acceptance of his rejection of them (the word 'humble' is prominent in both of her speeches); yet she then must proceed to make a confident and persuasive invocation of miraculous, religious powers, and finally rise to a rhyming incantation that promises a complete cure 'Ere twice the horses of the sun shall bring / Their fiery torcher his diurnal ring.' At her next appearance she must one by one dismiss other prospective husbands in incisive couplets but then declare her choice of Bertram in the most submissive way imaginable and finally accept his rejection by telling the king in the simplest of terms: 'That you are well restored, my lord, I'm glad. / Let the rest go.'

My Japanese experience has enhanced my respect for such differences in verbal form. Modern Helenas tend to level the differences to a single kind of speech that she might realistically employ; but if Shakespeare's whole idea of a theatre is seen as more stylised than that, the differences can be given full play. These various forms of expression might then allow her state of mind to be conveyed to the audience in the most rhetorically vivid ways – never mind whether or not she would use them in ordinary life.

In general I came home with a greater resistance to Western productions that seek to curtail the spectatorly freedoms I had exercised in Japan. Directors who try to impose a single line of interpretation and designers who insist on tendentious period costumes and scenery fall into this category. Conversely, I have found that I appreciated more than most reviewers the less heavily interpreted, more open, Shakespeare productions that Peter Hall directed at the National Theatre.

In particular my Japanese experience has made me less tolerant than before of cuts in Shakespeare's complete texts. When the words are regarded as simply 'what the characters say,' they seem much more expendable than if they are seen as part of a semi-independent literary construct that makes its own contribution to the whole. This autonomy is not so pronounced in Shakespeare as in Noh, yet his plays are poems as well as dramas, with unifying patterns of words, images, and modes of speech. Although consideration of such features has gone out of vogue in literary analysis, they deserve renewed attention as part of an audience's experience of the play in performance, whether or not the poetic lines are realistically motivated or fit a particular interpretation and whether or not the audience is aware of their contribution. Subliminally the poetry makes its effect, and it cannot be cut without loss because its imaginative appeals are integral to the dramatic event.

The example of classical Japanese theatre has thus led me to value a kind of Shakespearean performance that is less confined to the literal than is usual in the west and that gives fuller sway to what is poetic about the dialogue. Minimising the preformulations of a director or designer, productions of this sort assign their audiences a larger role than usual in imagining the play and permit the author's presence to be more directly felt, especially through recurring poetic features in the dialogue. As in Noh, playgoers are thus freed for an imaginative encounter with the playwright and his play, prompted in the most compelling fashion by its representation on stage but not confined to it. It is by suggesting ways, through performance, of enhancing this encounter with Shakespeare in the realm of his own imagination that the Japanese example seems to me most helpful.

Part 4

A chronological table of Shakespeare productions in Japan 1866–1994

18   Chronological table of Shakespeare productions in Japan 1866–1994

Ryuta Minami

This chronological table traces the stage history of Shakespeare in Japan from 1866, the year in which the first public reading of some speeches from Shakespeare was given by a foreign resident in Yokohama, up until 1994.

Until 1945, the listing is intended to be comprehensive. After that date, due to a shortage of information, the list of productions is limited primarily to those given in the greater Tokyo area, unless otherwise stated. As the table shows, the proliferation of productions after 1970 makes it almost impossible to list every Shakespeare production in Japan. Amateur productions, including productions by university students, are not given in the tables, aside from some particularly notable ones. When a company toured a production around Japan, only performances in the Tokyo area are listed.

The chronology is briefly annotated when explanation seems necessary or useful. An English translation of the title of an adaptation is given in parentheses on its first appearance. The names of translators, adapters and directors are given, whenever possible, followed by the name of the theatre company in square brackets. Where the production was the responsibility of a commercial production company such as the Tôhô or Shôchiku Co. Ltd., this is indicated in the form [Tôhô Production] or [Shôchiku Production]. The following abbreviations, or their plurals, are used:

(tr.) translator   (adpt.) adapter   (dir.) director.

A macron (ˆ) over a vowel means that the pronunciation is lengthened. Designations of vowels in this way avoids the possibility of confusion with other Japanese words spelled in a similar fashion. Familiar names such as Tokyo, Osaka and Kyoto are however left without macrons. Please note that in these tables Japanese names are given *in the Japanese order*, that is family name followed by given name.

Date	Title	Translator/director [Theatre company]
1866		
February	Mr Seare's Lecture Entertainment: 'Hamlet's Instructions to the Players' and selection from *A Midsummer Night's Dream* (Mr Seare was one of the foreign residents in Yokohama. This entertainment was performed at the Silk Salon exclusively for foreign residents in Yokohama.)	
1869		
November	*Romeo and Juliet* (Act II Scene 1: Balcony Scene) (This extract was performed as part of an entertainment for foreign residents at a theatre in the foreign settlement in Yokohama.)	[Miss Fanny Raynor and Mr Benee Company]

257

Date	Title	Translator/director [Theatre company]
1875 January	*King Henry the Fourth, Part One* (Performance of only a few extracts from the play at the Gaiety Theatre in Yokohama. This production was mounted in English primarily for foreign residents in Yokohama.)	[an amateur production by foreign residents in Yokohama]
1879 November	Scenes from *The Taming of the Shrew* and other Shakespeare plays (This performance was given in English at the Gaiety Theatre in Yokohama, primarily for foreign residents.)	[Mr B. Fairclough and Miss Elcia May with amateur players
1885 May June	*Sakura-doki Zenino Yononaka* ('It's a World Where Money Counts for Everything': a Kabuki adaptation of *The Merchant of Venice*, based on Udagawa Bunkai's novel adaptation of the story taken from Charles and Mary Lamb's *Tales from Shakespeare*. This is the first Shakespearean production mounted by Japanese theatre professionals. This play which was performed from 16 May to June was a sell-out.)	Katsu Genzô (adpt.) [Nakamura Sôjûrô Ichiza] (at Ebisu-za in Osaka) ('*Ichiza*' means 'theatre company')
May June	*Sakura-doki Zenino Yononaka* (The success of *Sakura-doki* at the Ebisu-za led to another Kabuki company presenting the same play. The play was performed from 31 May to 21 June.)	Katsu Genzô (adpt.) [a Kabuki company including Jitsukawa (Kurotani) Ichizô] (at Asahi-za in Osaka)
1886 February	*Sakura-doki Zenino Yononaka*	Katsu Genzô (adpt.) [a Kabuki company] (at Benten-za in Osaka)
1888 May	*Hamlet* (Performance of extracts from *Hamlet* and Richard Sheridan's *School for Scandal*: This production at the Public Hall in Yokohama was presented in English exclusively for foreign residents in Yokohama.)	[Louise Crawford Company]
1889 May	Extracts from *Hamlet* and other plays (a production at the Public Hall in Yokohama for foreign residents)	[Wanderers Company]

Date	Title	Translator/director [Theatre company]

1891

May   *Hamlet*   [Miln Company]
The Merchant of Venice
Macbeth
Othello
Romeo and Juliet
Julius Caesar
Richard the Second
[These were the first complete productions of Shakespeare's plays performed in Japan, though in English. Tsubouchi Shôyô saw this company's *Hamlet* and *The Merchant of Venice*. Other Japanese to see the Miln Company's productions were Kitamura Tôkoku and a number of Japanese students. The performances at the Public Hall in Yokohama were primarily for foreign residents in Yokohama]

November *Momiji-doki Zenino Yononaka*   Katsu Genzô (adpt.)
(Another Kabuki company's production   [a Kabuki company in
of Katsu's script based on Udagawa's   Osaka]
novel version of *The Merchant of Venice*, with a slight alteration in the
title. 'Sakura-doki' which means 'the
time of cherry blossoms' was changed to
'the time of coloured maple leaves'.)

1893

January *Nanjakaja Zenino Yononaka*   Katsu Genzô(adpt.)
('Anyway, It's a World Where Money   [a Kabuki company]
Counts for Everything'. Another
production of Katsu's script based
on Udagawa's novel adaptation
of *The Merchant of Venice*, with a
slight alteration in the title.)

November *Nanjakaja Zenino Yononaka*   Katsu Genzô (adpt.)
                                            [a Kabuki company in
                                          Osaka]

           Sakura-doki Zenino Yononaka   Katsu Genzô (adpt.)
                                            [a Kabuki company]

1894

August *Zenino Yononaka* ('It's a World Where   Katsu Genzô (adpt.)
Money Counts for Everything': a Kabuki   [a Kabuki company in
adaptation of *The Merchant of Venice*.   Osaka]
The script is similar to that of *Sakura-doki
Zenino Yononaka*, first performed in
1885.)

1895

March *Nin'niku Saiban*   [a Kabuki company]
('The Judgement with Regard to Human   (at Tokiwa-za in Tokyo)
Flesh': another Kabuki adaptation
probably based on Katsu's adaptation.)

Date	Title	Translator/director [Theatre company]
1899 June	Scenes from Shakespeare plays (Famous scenes with Juliet, Beatrice, Rosalind and other heroines: this production was staged in English at the Public Hall primarily for foreign residents in Yokohama.)	[Janet Waldorf Company]
1901 July	*Shîzaru Kitan* ('A Strange Story of Caesar': a *shimpa* company's production of two scenes from *Julius Caesar*. They staged the scenes of the Murder at the Capitol and of the Speeches at the Forum. Although it was adapted, the script retained the original names and settings.)	Tsubouchi Shôyô (tr.) Hatakeyama Kohei (adpt.) [Ii Yôhô Ichiza] (at Meiji-za in Tokyo)
September	*Shîzaru Kitan*	Tsubouchi Shôyô (tr.) Hatakeyama Kohei (adpt.) [Fukui Mohei Ichiza] (at Kado-za in Osaka)
1902 September October	*Yami to Hikari* ('Darkness and Light': an adaptation of *King Lear*)	Takayasu Gekkô (adpt.) [Fukui Mohei Ichiza (a *shimpa* company) in association with Kyoto Engeki Kairyô Kai (Kyoto Theatre Reformation Society)]
October	*Momiji Goten* ('The Maple Palace': This is the first adaptation of *Hamlet* staged in Japan.)	[Shin Engeki Ichiza (New Theatre Company): Seibi-dan (a *shimpa* company)]
1903 January	*Yami to Hikari*	Takayasu Gekkô (adpt.) [Fukui Mohei Ichiza with Kyoto Engeki Kairyô Kai; first performance in Osaka]
February March	*Othello*	Tozawa Koya (tr.) Emi Suiin (adpt.) [Kawakami Otojirô Ichiza]
June	*The Merchant of Venice* (a production of the trial scene in a faithful translation)	Doi Shunsho (tr.) [Kawakami Otojirô Ichiza]
July	*Jin'niku Shichiire Saiban* ('Judgement with Regard to the Pledging of Human Flesh': an adaptation of the trial scene of *The Merchant of Venice*. This is probably a stage adaptation of Inoue's translation of Lamb's *Tales from Shakespeare*)	Inoue Tsutomu (tr.) (adapter unknown) [Shin Engeki Yamaguchi Sadao Ippa (New Theatre Group Led by Yamaguchi Sadao)]

Date	Title	Translator/director [Theatre company]
	The Merchant of Venice (a production of the trial scene only)	Doi Shunsho (tr.) [Kawakami Otojirô Ichiza]
August October	*Yami to Hikari*	Takayasu Gekkô (adpt.) [Fukui Mohei Ichiza]
October November	*Hamlet*	Yamagishi Kayô and Doi Shunsho (adpts.) [Kawakami Otojirô Ichiza)
1904 January	*Twelfth Night*	[Itô Fumio Shin Engeki Ichiza (Itô Fumio New Theatre Company)]
February	*The Merchant of Venice* (a production of the trial scene only)	Doi Shunsho (tr.) [Kawakami Otojirô Ichiza]
May	*Zenino Yononaka*	Katsu Genzô (adpt.) [a Kabuki company]
	Othello	Tozawa Koya (tr.) Emi Suiin (adpt.) [Murata Masao Ichiza]
June	Public reading of *Julius Caesar* Public reading of *Much Ado About Nothing* (at the Public Hall in Yokohama for foreign residents)	Mr Hannibal Williams Mrs Hannibal Williams
August	*Othello*	Tozawa Koya (tr.) Emi Suiin (adpt.) [Murata Masao Ichiza]
October November	*Hamlet*	Doi Shunsho and Yamagishi Kayô (adpts.) [Kawakami Otojirô Ichiza] (In Kyoto, Kobe and Tokyo)
November	*Romeo and Juliet*	Osanai Kaoru (adpt. and dir.) [Ii Yôhô Ichiza]
	Hamlet	Doi Shunsho and Yamagishi Kayô (adpts.) [Kawakami Otojirô Ichiza]
1905 February	*Macbeth* [The play is set in Korea.]	Hatakeyama Kohei and Shima Kasui (adpts.) [Fukui Kitamura Ichiza]
April	*Romeo and Juliet*	Osanai Kaoru (adpt.) [Shizuma Kojirô Ippa]
June	*Jin'niku Shichiire*	[a Kabuki company in Osaka]
July	*Hamlet*	Yamagishi Kayô and Doi Shunsho (adpts.) [Kawakami Seigekiha (Kawakami Genuine Drama Company)]

Date	Title	Translator/director [Theatre company]
October	*Othello*	Tozawa Koya (tr.) Emi Suiin (adpt.) [a *shimpa* company]
	Nanjakaja Zenino Yononaka	Katsu Genzô (adpt.) [a Kabuki company]
1906		
June	*Hamlet*	Yamagishi Kayô and Doi Shunsho (adpts.) [Itô Shiraishi Ichiza]
July	*Henrî Ô* (an adaptation of *King Henry the Fourth*)	Iwasaki Shunka and Kojima Koshû (adpts.) [a *shimpa* company including Fukui Mohei]
August	*Hamlet*	Yamagishi Kayô and Doi Shunsho (adpts.) [Sudô Sadanori Ichiza]
September	*The Merchant of Venice*	Doi Shunsho (adpt.) [Shizuma Kojirô Ippa]
	Othello	Tozawa Koya (tr.) Emi Suiin (adpt.) [Itô Fumio Ichiza]
	Shin Othello ('New *Othello*': a comedy)	Masuda Tarôkaja(adpt.) [Kawakami Otojirô and Kawai Takeo Ichiza]
November	*The Merchant of Venice* (Bungei Kyôkai's first production of the trial scene in Tsubouchi's translation only with male actors.)	Tsubouchi Shôyô (tr.) [Bungei Kyôkai (Literary Society)]
1907		
January	*Shin Hamlet* ('New *Hamlet*')	Satô Kôroku (adpt.) [Takada Kitamura Ichiza]
April	*Hamlet*	Yamagishi Kayô and Doi Shunsho (adpts.) [Joyû Ichiza: 'Joyû' means 'an actress']
May	*Shîzâ: Julius Caesar* (a production of several scenes in English by Japanese amateur players: Dr Arakawa Shigehide who studied in America played Brutus, and a young Kabuki actor Sawamura Sônosuke played Caesar, with all the other parts played by English teachers at junior high schools.)	[Yôgeki Kai (Society of Western Drama)]
June	*As You Like It* (a production in English at Tokyo Women's School by British and American residents in Japan)	

Date	Title	Translator/director [Theatre company]
August	*Shin Hamlet*	Yamagishi Kayô and Doi Shunsho (adpts.) [Yamazaki Chônosuke Ichiza]
October	*Hamuretto* (a Kabuki adaptation of *Hamlet*)	Yamagishi Kayô (adpt.) [Ichikawa Kodanji Ichiza]
November	*Hamlet*	Tsubouchi Shôyô (tr. and dir.) [Bungei Kyôkai]
1908 January	*The Merchant of Venice* (A production of the trial scene: in this production, 'actresses' who were not trained as *On'na Yakusha* appeared on the stage for the first time. Until this production, female players seen on the stage were either *On'na Yakusha*, women with Kabuki actor training, or ex-*geishas*.)	Tsubouchi Shôyô (tr.) [Ichikawa Kodanji Ichiza]
February	*Hamlet*	Doi Shunsho and Yamagishi Kayô (adpts.) [Kawakami-ha Seigeki Kampani (Kawakami's Genuine Drama Company)]
	Othello	Tozawa Koya (tr.) Emi Suiin (adpt.) [Sudô-ha, Kumagai Engeki]
	The Merchant of Venice (a production of the trial scene)	Tsubouchi Shôyô (tr.) [Ichikawa Kodanji Ichiza]
March	*Hamuretto* (a Kabuki adaptation of *Hamlet*)	Yamagishi Kayô (adpt.) [Nakamura Ganjirô and other Kabuki actors in Osaka]
	Shin Othello	[Shirakawa Kôichi Ichiza]
May June	*The Merchant of Venice* (a production of the trial scene)	Tsubouchi Shôyô (tr.) [Ichikawa Sadanji Ichiza]
November	*Nanjakaja Zenino Yononaka*	Katsu Genzô (adpt.) [a Kabuki company]
1909 January	*The Merchant of Venice*	Yamagishi Kayô (adpt.) [Joyû Ichiza]
April	*Hibiki* ('Echoes': an adaptation of *Timon of Athens*)	Kojima Koshû (adpt.) [Jitsukawa Enjirô Ichiza]
May	*Hibiki*	Kojima Koshû (adpt.) [Joyû Ichiza]
July	*Hibiki*	Kojima Koshû (adpt.) [a *shimpa* company]

Date	Title	Translator/director [Theatre company]
August	*Hibiki*	Kojima Koshû (adpt.) [Nagasaki Chônosuke Ichiza]
November	*Yami to Hikari*	Takayasu Gekkô (adpt.) [a *shimpa* company]
1910 January	*Othello*	Tozawa Koya (tr.) Emi Suiin (adpt.) [Kawakami Otojirô Ichiza]
March	*Hamlet* (a production of Act Three)	Tsubouchi Shôyô (tr.) Doi Shunsho (dir.) [Bungei Kyôkai]
	The Merchant of Venice (a production of the trial scene)	Tsubouchi Shôyô (tr.) Tôgi Tetteki (dir.) [Bungei Kyôkai]
	Kôryô (an adaptation of *Hamlet*, based on Yamagishi and Doi's adaptation)	Yamagishi Kayô and Doi Shunsho (adpts.) [Mishima Ichiza]
April	*Hibiki*	Kojima Koshû (adpt.) [Mishima Ichiza]
May	*The Merchant of Venice*	Tsubouchi Shôyô (tr.)? [Kumagai Takeo Ichiza]
	Public reading of scenes from *The Merchant of Venice*, *Julius Caesar*, *Twelfth Night*, and *The Comedy of Errors* (at the Gaiety Theatre in Yokohama for foreign residents)	Marshall Darrach
June	*Goando* ('Relief': an adaptation of *Much Ado about Nothing*)	Yanagawa Shun'yô (adpt.) [Ii Fujisawa Ichiza]
July	*Hibiki*	Kojima Koshû (adpt.) [a *shimpa* company]
1911 January	*Hibiki*	Kojima Koshû (adpt.) [Jitsukawa Enjirô Ichiza]
March	*Kampu Narashi* (an adaptation of *The Taming of the Shrew*)	Kako Zam'mu (adpt.) [Rakuten kai]
	Romeo and Juliet	Osanai Kaoru (tr. and adpt.) [Kawakami Fukui Ichiza]
April	*Saiai no Tsuma* ('My Dearest Wife': an adaptation of *The Taming of the Shrew*)	Matsui Shôyô (adpt.) [a *shimpa* company with Ii, Takada and Fujisawa]
	Othello	Tozawa Koya (tr.) Emi Suiin (adpt.) [a *shimpa* Company]
May	*Hamlet*	Yamagishi Kayô and Doi Shunsho (adpts.) [Mishima Ichiza]

Date	Title	Translator/director [Theatre company]
	Saiai no Tsuma	Matsui Shôyô (adpt.) [Kitazawa Ikoma Ippa]
May June	*Hamlet* (This is the first complete production of *Hamlet* in translation.)	Tsubouchi Shôyô (tr.) [Bungei Kyôkai]
June	*Saiai no Tsuma*	Matsui Shôyô (adpt.) [Kitazawa Ikoma Ippa]
	King Lear	[Kakumei Geki Kyôdai Ippa (Revolutionary Drama Brothers Group)]
July	*Hamlet*	Tsubouchi Shôyô (tr. & dir.) [Bungei Kyôkai]
	Yami to Hikari	Takayasu Gekkô (adpt.) [Jiyû Ippa]
	Hibiki	Kojima Koshû (adpt.) [Matsuo Jirô Ichiza]
August	*Yami to Hikari*	Takayasu Gekkô (adpt.) [a *shimpa* company]
October	*Hibiki*	Kojima Koshû (adpt.) [a *shimpa* company]
	Hamlet	[Nihon Kindaigeki Ichiza (Japan Modern Drama Company)]
November	*Saiai no Tsuma*	Matsui Shôyô (adpt.)
	Hibiki	Kojima Koshû (adpt.) [Hanabusa Tarô Ichiza]
	The Merchant of Venice (a production of the trial scene)	Tsubouchi Shôyô (tr.) [Bungei Kyôkai]
	Hibiki	Kojima Koshû (adpt.) [Nakamura Kasen Ichiza]
1912 February	*Yôkina Nyôbô* ('Merry Wives': an adaptation of *The Merry Wives of Windsor*)	Matsui Shôyô (adpt.)
March	*The Merchant of Venice* (a production of the trial scene)	Tsubouchi Shôyô (tr.) [Bungei Kyôkai]
April	*Hibiki*	Kojima Koshû (adpt.) [Matsuo Ichiza]
May	*A Midsummer Night's Dream* (an amateur production in English by foreign residents in Japan)	
August	*Hibiki*	Kojima Koshû (adpt.) [Chûkyô Seibi-dan, Nishi Manbei Ichiza]

Date	Title	Translator/director [Theatre company]
September	*Hibiki*	Kojima Koshû (adpt.) [Itô Ayanosuke Ichiza]
October	*Twelfth Night*	[Matsuo Ichiza]
October November	*The Merchant of Venice* *Romeo and Juliet* *Hamlet* *Othello* *The Taming of the Shrew* (in English)	[Allan Wilkie Company] (The company presented the plays not only at the Gaiety Theatre in Yokohama but also at the Imperial Theatre in Tokyo and at the Naka-za Theatre in Osaka. This means that the company staged Shakespeare plays in English for the Japanese audience in Tokyo and Osaka.)
1913 January	*The Merchant of Venice* (an amateur production in English by foreign residents in Japan)	
January February	*Shin Hamlet* ('New *Hamlet*')	Satô Kôroku (adpt.) [a *shimpa* company]
February	*The Merchant of Venice* (a production of the trial scene)	Tsubouchi Shôyô (tr.) [Ichikawa Sadanji Ichiza]
	Hibiki	Kojima Koshû (adpt.) [a *shimpa* company]
May	*Hibiki*	Kojima Koshû (adpt.) [a *shimpa* Company]
June	*Julius Caesar*	Tsubouchi Shôyô (tr.) [Bungei Kyôkai]
September	*Macbeth*	Mori Ôgai (tr.) Kamiyama Sôjin (dir.) [Kindaigeki Kyôkai (Modern Drama Society)]
October	*Hibiki*	Kojima Koshû (adpt.) [a *shimpa* company]
November	*The Merchant of Venice* (a production of the trial scene)	Tsubouchi Shôyô (tr.) [Kindaigeki Kyôkai]
1914 January	*Othello*	Ikeda Daigo (tr. and dir.) [Mumei Kai]
September	*Hibiki*	Kojima Koshû (adpt.) [Nakamura Kasen Ichiza]
	Romeo and Juliet	Tsubouchi Shôyô (tr.) [Geijutsu Club]
	Hibiki	Kojima Koshû (adpt.) [a *shimpa* company]

Date	Title	Translator/director [Theatre company]
November	*Kureopatora* (Cleopatra) (an adaptation of *Antony and Cleopatra*)	Shimamura Hôgetsu (tr., adpt. and dir.) [Geijutsu-za]
	Hibiki	Kojima Koshû (adpt.) [Matsuo Ichiza]
1915 January	*Hibiki*	Kojima Koshû (adpt.) [Atami Koshû Ichiza]
May	*The Merchant of Venice* (a production of the trial scene in English by Japanese actors and actresses)	[Teikoku Gekijô Production]
	The Merchant of Venice (a production of the trial scene in Japanese) [In these two productions at the Teikoku Gekijô (the Imperial Theatre), Portia was played by the same actress, Mori Ritsuko.]	Tsubouchi Shôyô (tr.) [Butai Kyôkai (Stage Society)]
1916 February	*The Tempest*	Ikeda Daigo (tr., adpt. and dir.) [Tenkatsu Ichiza]
May	*The Winter's Tale* (in English)	[Zairyû Gaijin Shirôto Geki Kurabu (Amateur Drama Club of Foreign Residents in Japan)]
June July	*Macbeth* (This was the production to mark the occasion of the tercentenary of Shakespeare's death.)	Tsubouchi Shôyô (tr.) Tsubouchi Shikô (dir.) [Mumei Kai]
August	*Macbeth*	Tsubouchi Shôyô (tr.) Shimamura Hôgetsu (adpt. and dir.) [Geijutsu-za]
October	*Shamuro-bune* (a Kabuki adaptation of *Hamlet*: 'Shamuro-bune' is the name of a big merchant ship built in Thailand. Shamuro-bune visited Japan from the 17th to the 19th century when Japan had an isolation policy.)	Ômori Chisetsu (adpt.) [Shôchiku Production in Osaka]
1917 March	*Othello* (In this production, a Kabuki actor Matsumoto Kôshirô played the title role with *shingeki* actors.)	Tsubouchi Shôyô (tr.) [Tôgi Tetteki and Matsumoto Kôshirô Ichiza]

Date	Title	Translator/director [Theatre company]
1918		
February	*Hamlet*	Tsubouchi Shikô (tr. and dir.) [Teigeki Joyû-geki]
	Yami to Hikari	Takayasu Gekkô (adpt.) [Fukui Mohei Ichiza]
April	*Gekichûgeki Hamlet* ('A Play within a Play *Hamlet*')	[Seibi-dan, a *shimpa* company]
June	*The Merchant of Venice*	Ikuta Chôkô (tr.) Kamiyama Sôjin (dir.) [Kindaigeki Kyôkai]
	King Lear	Tsubouchi Shôyô (tr.) Kamiyama Sôjin (dir.) [Kindaigeki Kyôkai]
September	*The Merchant of Venice*	[Tokyo Sôsakugeki Kyôkai]
	King Lear	Takayasu Gekkô (adpt.) [a *shimpa* company]
	Shin Hamlet	Satô Kôroku (adpt.) [a *shimpa* company]
November	*Romeo and Juliet*	Tsubouchi Shôyô (tr.) Hayashi Nagomu (adapt. and dir.) [Bungei-za]
1919		
February	*King Lear*	Tsubouchi Shôyô (tr.) Kamiyama Sôjin (dir.) [Kindaigeki Kyôkai]
July	*Dochiraga Yumeda* ('Which is a Dream?': an adaptation of *The Taming of the Shrew*)	Ikeda Daigo (tr. and adpt.) [a *shimpa* company with Ii, Kawai and Tôgi Tetteki]
November	*Hamlet*	Tsubouchi Shôyô (tr.) Hayashi Nagomu (adpt. and dir.) [Bungei-za]
1920		
January	*Saiai no Tsuma* (an adaptation of *The Taming of the Shrew*)	Ochiai Shimiroku and Matsui Shôyô (adpts.) [a *shimpa* company]
July	*Macbeth*	[Kasei-za] (Kasei-za was a leading company in the *shingeki* Movement in Osaka.)
August	*Romeo and Juliet*	[Tokyo Opera-za]
December	*The Merchant of Venice* (a production of the trial scene as part of a year-end entertainment called Bônen Sukatan-kai)	[Horie Yûkaku Geiko Ren (*Geishas* in the red-light district of Horie)]

Date	Title	Translator/director [Theatre company]
1921 February	*The Merchant of Venice* (a production of the trial scene)	Tsubouchi Shôyô (tr.) [Gekijutsu Kai (Dramatic Art Society)]
April	*Hamlet*	Nobuchi Akira (dir.) [Elan Vital] (Elan Vital was a *shingeki* company that played a leading part in the *shingeki* Movement in Kyoto.)
June	*Hamlet*	Tsubouchi Shôyô (tr.) [Gekijutsu Kai]
	Hamlet (Act One)	Tsubouchi Shikô (tr. and dir.) [Gikyoku Kenkyû Kai (Society for the Study of Drama)] (This society was formed in Osaka by Tsubouchi Shikô.)
October	*Hamlet*	Tsubouchi Shikô (tr. and dir.) [Gikyoku Kenkyû Kai]
November	*The Merchant of Venice* *Romeo and Juliet* *Hamlet* *Othello* (in English)	[Allan Wilkie Company]
	Hamlet	Tsubouchi Shôyô (tr.) [Gekijutsu Kai]
	King Lear	Tsubouchi Shôyô (tr.) [Gekijutsu Kai]
	The Merchant of Venice	Tsubouchi Shikô (tr. and dir.) [Gikyoku Kenkyû Kai]
December	*Hamlet*	Tsubouchi Shikô (tr. and dir.) [Gikyoku Kenkyû Kai]
1922 May	*The Merchant of Venice*	Tsubouchi Shôyô (tr.) [Gekijutsu Kai]
November	*Macbeth*	Tsubouchi Shôyô (tr.) [Gekijutsu Kai]
1923 January	*The Merchant of Venice*	Tsubouchi Shôyô (tr.) Tsubouchi Shikô (dir.) [Gikyoku Kenkyû Kai]
April	*The Merchant of Venice*	Tsubouchi Shôyô (tr.) [Gekijutsu Kai]
June	*Hamlet*	Tsubouchi Shôyô (tr.) [Gekijutsu Kai]

Date	Title	Translator/director [Theatre company]
July	The Merchant of Venice (a production of the trial scene)	Tsubouchi Shôyô (tr.) [Gekijutsu Kai]
	Julius Caesar	Tsubouchi Shôyô (tr.) [Butai Kyôkai]
August	Macbeth	Tsubouchi Shôyô (tr.) [Gekijutsu Kai]
	A Midsummer Night's Dream	Tsubouchi Shôyô (tr.) Tsubouchi Shikô (dir.) [Geijutsu Kyôkai]
1924 February	The Merchant of Venice (a production of the trial scene)	Tsubouchi Shôyô (tr.) [Aoi Tori Gekidan]
May June	Hamlet	Tsubouchi Shôyô (tr.) [Gekijutsu Kai]
October	The Merchant of Venice	Tsubouchi Shôyô (tr.) [Geijutsu Kyôkai]
1925 January	Julius Caesar	Tsubouchi Shôyô (tr.) Hijikata Yoshi (dir.) [Tsukiji Shôgekijô (Tsukiji Little Theatre)]
March	Julius Caesar	Osanai Kaoru(tr. and dir.) [Ichikawa Sadanji Ichiza]
September	Othello	Osanai Kaoru (tr. and dir.) [Ichikawa Sadanji Ichiza]
1926 January	The Merchant of Venice	Osanai Kaoru (tr.) Hijikata Yoshi (dir.) [Tsukiji Shôgekijô]
March	Hamlet–Amakusa-jidai no Nihon-fuku wo Kita ('Hamlet in Japanese Kimono of the Amakusa Period')	Literary Department of the Aoi-tori (adpt.) [Aoi-tori Gekidan]
July	The Merry Wives of Windsor	Tsubouchi Shôyô (tr.) Tsubouchi Shikô (dir.) [Takarazuka Kokumin-za]
August	Coriolanus	Tsubouchi Shôyô (tr.) Matsui Shôyô (adpt. and dir.) [Shinkoku Geki]
1927 February	Macbeth	Mori Ôgai (tr.) Osanai Kaoru and Aoyama Sugisaku (dirs.) [Tsukiji Shôgekijô]
May	The Merchant of Venice (probably a performance of only the trial scene: part of a variety show presented with ballet, a farce, conjuring tricks etc.)	[Shôkyokusai Tenka Sôgô Geijutsu-za]

Date	Title	Translator/director [Theatre company]
July	*Hamlet*	Tsubouchi Shôyô (tr.) Tsubouchi Shikô (adpt. and dir.) [Takarazuka Kokumin-za]
1928 June	*Twelfth Night*	Tsubouchi Shôyô (tr.) Katô Nagaharu (dir.) [Chikyû-za (or the Globe Theatre)]
July	*A Midsummer Night's Dream*	Tsubouchi Shôyô (tr.) Osanai Kaoru, Hijikata Yoshi and Aoyama Sugisaku (dirs.) [Tsukiji Shôgekijô]
1929 February	*Hamlet*	Tsubouchi Shôyô (tr.) Tsubouchi Shikô (dir.) [Takarazuka Kokumin-za]
March	*The Taming of the Shrew*	Tsubouchi Shôyô (tr.) Katô Nagaharu (dir.) [Chikyû-za]
April	*Othello*	Tsubouchi Shôyô (tr.) Tsubouchi Shikô (dir.) [Takarazuka Kokumin-za]
May	*Hamlet*	Tsubouchi Shôyô (tr.) Tsubouchi Shikô (dir.) [Takarazuka Kokumin-za]
June	*Gendaifuku no Benisuno Shônin* ('*The Merchant of Venice* in Modern Clothes')	Yokoyama Yûsaku (tr.) Katô Nagaharu (dir.) [Chikyû-za]
November	*Much Ado About Nothing*	Tsubouchi Shôyô (tr.) Katô Nagaharu (dir.) [Chikyû-za]
1930 March	*Twelfth Night*	Tsubouchi Shôyô (tr.) Katô Nagaharu (dir.) [Chikyû-za]
April	*The Taming of the Shrew*	[Tokyo Gaijin Shirôto Gekidan (Tokyo Amateur Theatre Company of Foreign Residents)]
June	*The Taming of the Shrew*	Tsubouchi Shôyô (tr.) Tsubouchi Shikô (dir.) [Takarazuka Kokumin-za]
1931 January	Scenes from *King Henry the Fourth, Part One*	Tsubouchi Shôyô (tr.) Katô Nagaharu (dir.) [Chikyû-za]

Date	Title	Translator/director [Theatre company]
April	Scenes from *Othello, The Tempest,* and *The Taming of the Shrew*	Tsubouchi Shôyô (tr.) Katô Nagaharu (dir.) [Chikyû-za]
December	Scenes from *King Henry the Fourth, Part Two*	Tsubouchi Shôyô (tr.) Katô Nagaharu (dir.) [Chikyû-za]
1932 April	*Macbeth*	Tsubouchi Shôyô (tr.) Katô Nagaharu (dir.) [Chikyû-za]
October	*The Merchant of Venice*	Tsubouchi Shôyô (tr.) Katô Nagaharu (dir.) [Chikyû-za]
1933 May June	*A Midsummer Night's Dream* (a revue adaptation)	Aoyama Sugisaku (adpt. and dir.) [Shôchiku Shôjo Kagekibu (Shôchiku Girls' Revue Company)]
September	*Romeo and Juliet* (a revue adaptation)	Aoyama Sugisaku (adpt. and dir.) [Shôchiku Shôjo Kagekibu]
	Scenes from *Julius Caesar* and *Hamlet*	Tsubouchi Shôyô (tr.) [Shinshun-za]
October	*The Merchant of Venice* (a production of the trial scene)	Tsubouchi Shôyô (tr.)
	Hamlet	Tsubouchi Shôyô (tr.) Kume Masao (dir.) [Gekidan Tsukiji Shôgekijô]
December	*Hamlet* (Hamlet was played by a *shimpa* actress Mizutani Yaeko.)	Tsubouchi Shôyô and Tsubouchi Shikô (trs.) Katô Nagaharu (dir.) [Shôchiku Production]
1934 January	*The Taming of the Shrew*	Tsubouchi Shôyô (tr.) Katô Nagaharu (dir.) [Nihon Haiyû Gakkô Gekidan (Japan Actors School Company)]
	The Merchant of Venice (a production of the trial scene)	Tsubouchi Shôyô (tr.) Katô Nagaharu (dir.) [Nihon Haiyû Gakkô Gekidan]
April	*Othello*	Tsubouchi Shôyô (tr.) Katô Nagaharu (dir.) [Nihon Haiyû Gakkô Gekidan]

Date	Title	Translator/director [Theatre company]
	Othello	Tsubouchi Shôyô (tr.) Kume Masao (dir.) [Shin Tsukiji Gekidan]
	The Merchant of Venice	Tsubouchi Shôyô (tr.) Toyo'oka Saichirô (dir.) [Shinjin Gekijô] (in Osaka)
June	Hamlet	Tsubouchi Shôyô (tr.) Kume Masao (dir.) [Shin Tsukiji Gekidan]
August	A Midsummer Night's Dream	Tsubouchi Shôyô (tr.) Katô Nagaharu (dir.) [Nihon Haiyû Gakkô Gekidan]
September	A Midsummer Night's Dream (a production with actors different from those in the previous production in August)	Tsubouchi Shôyô (tr.) Katô Nagaharu (dir.) [Nihon Haiyu Gakkô Gekidan]
November	Romeo and Juliet	Tsubouchi Shôyô (tr.) Tsubouchi Shikô (tr. and dir.) [Tôhô Senzoku Gekidan]
1935 March	Hamlet (with Mizutani Yaeko, an actress, as Hamlet)	Tsubouchi Shôyô and Tsubouchi Shikô (trs.) Katô Nagaharu (dir.) [Tôhô Production]
April	King Lear	Tsubouchi Shôyô (tr.) Katô Nagaharu (dir.) [Nihon Haiyû Gakkô Gekidan]
1936 September	Fukurono Nezumi (an adaptation of The Merry Wives of Windsor)	Ikkai Tsuribito (adpt.) [Soganoya Gorô Ichiza]
1937 January	The Merry Wives of Windsor	Mikami Isao and Nishikawa Masami (trs.) Senda Koreya (dir.) [Shin Tsukiji Gekidan]
1938 May June and December	Hamlet	Mikami Isao and Okahashi Hiroshi (trs.) Yamakawa Yukiyo (dir.) [Shin Tsukiji Gekidan]

Date	Title	Translator/director [Theatre company]

1940
May
June
A Midsummer Night's Dream: A Revue — Katô Tadamatsu (adpt. and dir.) [Takarazuka Kageki-dan (Takarazuka Revue Company)]

[The Second World War]

1946
June
July
A Midsummer Night's Dream — Tsubouchi Shôyô (tr.) Hijikata Yoshi (dir.) [Tokyo Geijutsu Gekijô]

1947
November   The Merchant of Venice (Zenshin-za company started touring around Japan in September, and mounted the play in Tokyo in November.) — Tsubouchi Shôyô (tr.) Miyagawa Masao (dir.) [Zenshin-za]

December   Hamlet — Mori Hôsuke (tr.) Miyata Teruaki (dir.) [Tokyo Seinen Gekijô]

1948
January   The Taming of the Shrew — [Teatoro Soreiyu (Théâtre Soleil)]

The Merchant of Venice — Tsubouchi Shôyô (tr.) Miyagawa Masao (dir.) [Zenshin-za]

March   Much Ado About Nothing — Tsubouchi Shôyô (tr.) Miyagawa Masao (dir.) [Zenshin-za]

July   The Merchant of Venice — Tsubouchi Shôyô (tr.)

October   The Merchant of Venice (This performance was given to celebrate the 20th anniversary of Waseda Theatre Museum as well as to commemorate the company's successful one-year tour around Japan. Zenshin-za presented this play more than 600 times and gathered over a million people as their audience.) — Tsubouchi Shôyô (tr.) Miyagawa Masao (dir.) [Zenshin-za]

1949
March   A Midsummer Night's Dream — Tsubouchi Shôyô (tr.) Miyagawa Masao and Hijikata Yoshi (dirs.) [Zenshin-za]

Date	Title	Translator/director [Theatre company]
1950		
May	*Romeo and Juliet*	Mikami Isao (tr.) Hijikata Yoshi (dir.) [Zenshin-za]
	Twelfth Night	Tsubouchi Shôyô (tr.) Katô Nagaharu (dir.) [Kindai Gekijô]
October	*The Tempest*	Tsubouchi Shôyô (tr.) Katô Nagaharu (dir.) [Kindai Gekijô]
	The Tempest	Toyoda Minoru (tr.) Tsubouchi Shikô et al. (dirs.) [Bungei Gekijô]
1951		
January	*The Comedy of Errors*	Tsubouchi Shôyô (tr.) Katô Nagaharu (dir.) [Kindai Gekijô]
February	*Ôji to Tôzoku* ('The Prince and Robbers', an adaptation of Act II Scene iv of *King Henry the Fourth, Part One*)	Wada Shôichi (adpt. and dir.) [Gekidan Minshû-za]
June	*The Taming of the Shrew*	Tsubouchi Shôyô (tr.) Katô Nagaharu (dir.) [Kindai Gekijô]
November	*Othello*	Kinoshita Junji (tr.) Aoyama Sugisaku (dir.) [Haiyû-za Seinen Gekijô]
	A Midsummer Night's Dream	Tsubouchi Shôyô (tr.) Katô Nagaharu (dir.) [Kindai Gekijô]
1952		
January	*The Merry Wives of Windsor*	Mikami Isao and Nishikawa Masami (trs.) Aoyama Sugisaku (dir.) [Haiyû-za]
May	*The Merchant of Venice*	Tsubouchi Shôyô (tr.) Katô Nagaharu (dir.) [Kindai Gekijô]
November	*Much Ado About Nothing*	Tsubouchi Shôyô (tr.) Katô Nagaharu (dir.) [Kindai Gekijô]
1953		
May	*Macbeth*	Tsubouchi Shôyô (tr.) Katô Nagaharu (dir.) [Kindai Gekijô]
October	*The Taming of the Shrew*	Tsubouchi Shôyô (tr.) Katô Nagaharu (dir.) [Kindai Gekijô]

Date	Title	Translator/director [Theatre company]
1954		
April	*Twelfth Night*	Tsubouchi Shôyô (tr.) Katô Nagaharu (dir.) [Kindai Gekijô]
July	*A Midsummer Night's Dream*	Tsubouchi Shôyô (tr.) Katô Nagaharu (dir.) [Kindai Gekijô]
November	*The Comedy of Errors*	Tsubouchi Shôyô (tr.) Katô Nagaharu (dir.) [Kindai Gekijô]
December	*The Taming of the Shrew*	Tsubouchi Shôyô (tr.) Katô Nagaharu (dir.) [Kindai Gekijô]
1955		
January	*The Tempest*	Tsubouchi Shôyô (tr.) Katô Nagaharu (dir.) [Kindai Gekijô]
May	*Hamlet*	Fukuda Tsuneari (tr. and dir.) [Bungaku-za]
	The Winter's Tale	Tsubouchi Shôyô (tr.) Katô Nagaharu (dir.) [Kindai Gekijô]
August	*Much Ado About Nothing*	Tsubouchi Shôyô (tr.) Katô Nagaharu (dir.) [Kindai Gekijô]
October	*King Lear*	Tsubouchi Shôyô (tr.) Katô Nagaharu (tr.) [Kindai Gekijô]
1956		
January	*Hamlet*	Fukuda Tsuneari (tr. and dir.) [Bungaku-za]
May	*Othello*	Tsubouchi Shôyô (tr.) [Bungei-za]
July	*Twelfth Night*	Tsubouchi Shôyô (tr.) Hijikata Yoshi (dir.) [Bungei-za]
	*Hamlet (*a Bunraku adaptation*)*	Ônishi Toshio (adpt.) Nozawa Matsunosuke (composer) [Chinami Kai] (Chinami Kai was one of the leading Bunraku companies in Osaka.)
1957		
February	*The Merchant of Venice*	Tsubouchi Shôyô (tr.) Katô Nagaharu (dir.) [Kindai Gekijô]

Date	Title	Translator/director [Theatre company]
May	*The Merchant of Venice*	Tsubouchi Shôyô (tr.) Katô Nagaharu (dir.) [Kindai Gekijô]
July	*Othello*	Tsubouchi Shôyô (tr.) Tanaka Tokihide (dir.) [Bungei-za]
September	*The Merchant of Venice* (a production of the trial scene)	Tsubouchi Shôyô (tr.) Katô Nagaharu (dir.) [Kikugorô Gekidan]
October	*The Merry Wives of Windsor*	Mikami Isao and Nishikawa Masami (trs.) Aoyama Sugisaku (dir.) [Haiyû-za]
November	*The Taming of the Shrew*	Tsubouchi Shôyô (tr.) Katô Nagaharu (dir.) [Kindai Gekijô]
1958 October	*Macbeth*	Fukuda Tsuneari (tr. and dir.) [Bungaku-za]
	The Winter's Tale	Tsubouchi Shôyô (tr.) Katô Nagaharu (dir.) [Kindai Gekijô]
1959 May	*Twelfth Night*	Ozu Jirô (tr.) Nakamura Shun'ichi (dir.) [Gekidan Nakama]
	Julius Caesar	Tsubouchi Shôyô (tr.) In'nami Takashi and Katô Nagaharu (dirs.)
October	*Twelfth Night*	Mikami Isao (tr.) Ozawa Eitarô (dir.) [Haiyû-za]
1960 January	*Twelfth Night*	Mikami Isao (tr.) Ozawa Eitarô (dir.) [Haiyû-za]
May	*Hamlet*	Jean-Louis Barrault [Théâtre de France]
June	*Othello* (A production with *shingeki* actors, Kabuki actors and film actors: Matsumoto Kôshirô played the title role.)	Fukuda Tsuneari (tr. and dir.) [Yoshida Fumiko and Sankei Hall Production]
July	*Romeo and Juliet*	Mikami Isao (tr.) Yamakawa Yukiyo and Uriu Masami (dirs.) [Bungei-za]

Date	Title	Translator/director [Theatre company]
1961 May	*Macbeth*	Kurahashi Takeshi (tr.) Shimizu Kôji (dir.) [Ningyô Gekidan Hitomi-za (Puppet Company Hitomi)]
	The Merchant of Venice	[Yûki Magosaburô, Hitoito Ichiza, Ningyô-za(Puppet Theatre) and Kindai Gekijô]
June	*King Lear*	Tsubouchi Shôyô (tr.) Katô Nagaharu (dir.) [Kindai Gekijô]
	A Midsummer Night's Dream (a musical adaptation)	Kinotôru (tr. and adpt.) Tobe Shin'ichi (dir.) [Théâtre Écho]
October	*A Midsummer Night's Dream*	Tsubouchi Shôyô (tr.) Katô Nagaharu (dir.) [Kindai Gekijô]
	Julius Caesar	Fukuda Tsuneari (tr. and dir.) [Bungaku-za]
1962 March	*King Richard the Third*	Fukuda Tsuneari (tr.) Kitamura Eizô (dir.) [Kyoto Kurumi-za] (in Osaka)
March April	*A Midsummer Night's Dream*	Fukuda Tsuneari (tr. and dir.) [Gekidan Kumo]
June	*Macbeth*	Kurahashi Takeshi (tr.) Natsume Shunji (dir.) [Dôke-za] (in Kobe)
1963 June	*Macbeth*	Kurahashi Takeshi (tr.) Natsume Shunji (dir.) [Dôke-za] (in Kobe)
October	*King Lear* (a production for the quadricentennial of the birth of Shakespeare)	Tsubouchi Shôyô (tr.) In'nami Takashi (dir.)
1964 March	*King Richard the Third* (A Kabuki actor Nakamura Kanzaburô played the title role.)	Fukuda Tsuneari (tr. and dir.) [Gekidan Kumo, Gekidan Shiki et al.]
June	*Hamlet*	Mikami Isao (tr.) Senda Koreya (dir.) [Haiyû-za]
October	*The Merry Wives of Windsor*	Kurigoma Masakazu (tr.) Inoue Takeshi (dir.) [Yagino-kai]

Date	Title	Translator/director [Theatre company]
	Shakespeare no Gensô ('A Vision of Shakespeare')	Kawajiri Taiji (adpt. and dir.) [Puppet Theatre Puk]
1965 February	Hamlet	Mikami Isao (tr.) Senda Koreya (dir.) [Haiyû-za]
April	Romeo and Juliet	Fukuda Tsuneari (tr.) Michael Benthall (dir.) [Gekidan Kumo]
July	A Midsummer Night's Dream	Fukuda Tsuneari (tr. and dir.) [Gekidan Kumo]
	The Taming of the Shrew	Tsubouchi Shôyô (tr.) Katô Nagaharu (dir.) [Kindai Gekijô]
	Romeo and Juliet	Mikami Isao (tr.) Kazama Sô (dir.) [Shingeki-kai]
September	Much Ado About Nothing	Fukuda Tsuneari (tr.) Kitamura Eizô (dir.) [Kyoto Kurumi-za] (in Osaka)
1966 February	The Taming of the Shrew	Fukuda Tsuneari (tr. and dir.) [Gekidan Kumo]
October	Twelfth Night	Tsubouchi Shôyô (tr.) Katô Nagaharu (dir.) [Kindai-za]
1967 July	Julius Caesar	Fukuda Tsuneari (tr. and dir.) [Gekidan Kumo]
August	Henry The Fourth, Part One	Fukuda Tsuneari (tr. and dir.) [Gekidan Shiki]
December	King Lear	Fukuda Tsuneari (tr. and dir.) [Gekidan Kumo]
1968 January April	The Merchant of Venice	Fukuda Tsuneari (tr.) Asari Keita (dir.) [Gekidan Mingei]
June	The Merchant of Venice	Suga Yasuo (tr.) Hayashi Omou (dir.) [Kyoto Drama Gekijô]
July	A Midsummer Night's Dream	Tsubouchi Shôyô (tr.) Nemoto Yoshinari (dir.) [Kindai-za]

Date	Title	Translator/director [Theatre company]
October	*Min'nano Shakespeare/ Waga Itoshino Kimiyo* ('Everyman's Shakespeare/ My dear Love': a production of famous scenes taken from several Shakespeare plays)	Peter Potter (adpt. and dir.) [London Shakespeare Group]
	Hamlet: Mono-drama	Chûjô Masao (adpt. and dir.)
November	*Hamlet*	Fukuda Tsuneari (tr.) Asari Keita (dir.) [Gekidan Shiki]
December	*Antony and Cleopatra*	Fukuda Tsuneari (tr.) Arakawa Tetsuo (dir.) [Gekidan Kumo]
	Romeo and Juliet	Odashima Yûshi (tr.) Nishi Kôichi (dir.) [Teatoro Q] (in Osaka)
1969 April	*Hamlet*	Kamokawa Seisaku (adpt. and dir.) [Takarazuka Kageki-dan (Takarazuka Revue Company)]
	Othello (The title role was played by a Kabuki actor Onoe Shôroku)	Fukuda Tsuneari (tr.) Asari Keita (dir.) [Gekidan Shiki with a Kabuki actor as Othello]
	Omuretto (an adaptation of *Hamlet*)	Kataoka Teru (adpt.) Takahashi Toshiaki (dir.) [Gekidan Baron]
June	*Hamlet*	Fukuda Tsuneari (tr.) Asari Keita (dir.) [Gekidan Shiki]
July	*The Comedy of Errors*	Tsubouchi Shôyô (tr.) Nemoto Yoshinari (dir.) [Kindai-za]
September	*Much Ado About Nothing*	Fukuda Tsuneari (tr. and dir.) [Gekidan Keyaki]
November	*Titus Andronicus*	Kimura Masaru (tr. and dir.) [Engeki Shûdan Hana]
December	*The Winter's Tale*	Tsubouchi Shôyô (tr.) Nemoto Yoshinari (dir.) [Kindai-za]
1970 January	*The Merry Wives of Windsor*	Terry Hands (dir.) [Royal Shakespeare Company]

Date	Title	Translator/director [Theatre company]
	The Winter's Tale	Trevor Nunn (dir.) [Royal Shakespeare Company]
March	The Rape of Lucrece	Kitamura Eizô (adpt. and dir.) [Môri Kikue Engeki Kenkyûjo] (in Kyoto)
	Hamlet Kyôsô ('Hamlet in a Frenzy')	Kanehachi Yoshikane (adpt. and dir.) [Shin-Butai]
April	Hamlet '70	Abe Ryô (adpt.) Abe Ryô and Sasaki Ken'ichi (dirs.) [Actors' Studio]
	Hamlet Geki: Wakamono Tachini Yoru ('Hamlet by Young People')	Fukuda Tsuneari (tr.) Chikyû-za(adpt.) [Chikyû-za]
June	Hamlet Kyôsô	Kanehachi Yoshikane (adpt. and dir.) [Shin-Butai]
July	Hamlet Yakusha, Hamlet ('A Hamlet Actor, Hamlet')	Satsuki Shunsuke (adpt.) Yoshioka Hiroshi (dir.) [Engeki Kenkyû Centre, Hiroba]
September	Romeo and Juliet	Fukuda Tsuneari (tr.) Arakawa Tetsuo (dir.) [Gekidan Kumo]
	Macbeth	Tsubouchi Shôyô (tr.) Nemoto Yoshinari and Arai Yoshio (dirs.) [Kindai-za]
	Hamlet	Fukuda Tsuneari (tr.) Asari Keita (dir.) [Gekidan Shiki]
November	Scenes from The Winter's Tale, Twelfth Night, Othello and Hamlet	Peter Potter (dir.) [London Shakespeare Group]
	King Lear	Odashima Yûshi (tr.) Nishi Kôichi (dir.) [Teatoro Q] (in Osaka)
1971 February	Othello	Mikami Isao (tr.) Senda Koreya (dir.) [Haiyû-za]
April	The Two Gentlemen of Verona	Katô Kyôhei (tr.) Arai Yoshio (dir.) [Kindai-za]

Date	Title	Translator/director [Theatre company]
	Hamlet	Mikami Isao (tr.) Masumi Toshikiyo (dir.) [Haiyû-za]
May	*Twelfth Night*	Ozu Jirô (tr.) Deguchi Norio (dir.) [Bungaku-za]
June	*Shin Hamlet* ('New *Hamlet*': Dazai Osamu's closet-play adapted for the stage.)	Kinotôru(adpt.) Naya Gorô and Kumakura Kazuo (dirs.) [Théâtre Écho]
	Macbeth	Odashima Yûshi (tr.) Nishi Kôichi (dir.) [Teatoro Q] (in Osaka)
September	*Coriolanus*	Fukuda Tsuneari (tr.) Fukuda Tsuneari and Arakawa Tetsuo (dirs.) [Gekidan Kumo]
	The Taming of the Shrew	Tsubouchi Shôyô (tr.) Kikuchi Akira (dir.) [Kindai-za]
	Romeo and Juliet	Mikami Isao (tr.) Uriu Masami (dir.) [Seinen Gekijô]
	As You Like It	Fukuda Tsuneari (tr.) Ôhashi Narito (dir.) [Gekidan Kumo]
November	*Bara Sensô matawa Chi* ('The Wars of the Roses or Blood': an adaptation of *King Henry the Sixth* and *King Richard the Third*)	Abe Ryô (adpt and dir.) [Dômei and Shinjuku Bunka Joint Production]
1972 January	*Hamlet*	Mikami Isao (tr.) Masumi Toshikiyo (dir.) [Haiyû-za]
February	*Othello* *Twelfth Night* *Henry the Fifth*	John Barton (dir.) [Royal Shakespeare Company]
March	*Hamlet*	Etsu Aruto (adpt. and dir.) [Engekisha Ken]
April	*Nobutora* (an adaptation of *King Lear*)	Katô Kyôhei (adpt. and dir.) [Kindai-za]
	Macbeth	Kushida Kazuyoshi (adpt. and dir.) [On-Theatre Jiyû Gekijô]

Date	Title	Translator/director [Theatre company]
	Troilus and Cressida	Odashima Yûshi (tr.) Jeffrey Leavis and Deguchi Norio (dirs.) [Bungaku-za]
May	*Hamlet*	Odashima Yûshi (tr.) Deguchi Norio (dir.) [Bungaku-za]
	Romeo and Juliet	Odashima Yûshi (tr.) Kimura Kôichi (dir.) [Bungaku-za]

The theatre company, Bungaku-za, held a 'Shakespeare Festival' and produced three plays of Shakespeare at the Bungaku-za Atelier from April to June.

Date	Title	Translator/director [Theatre company]
June	*Hamlet by Women*	Etsu Aruto (adpt. and dir.) [Engekisha Ken]
July	*Hamlet Now*	Charles Marowitz (adpt.) Mikami Isao (tr.) Masumi Toshikiyo (dir.) [Roppongi Shôgekijô]
	Hamlet	Tsubouchi Shôyô (tr.) In'nami Takashi (dir.) [Kindai-za]
August	*Hamlet* (The title role was played by a Kabuki actor Ichikawa Somegorô, who later became Matsumoto Kôshirô)	Fukuda Tsuneari (tr.) John David (dir.) [Tôhô Production]
	A Midsummer Night's Dream	Mikami Isao (tr.) Hirowatari Tsunetoshi (dir.) [Tokyo Engeki Ensemble]
	Romeo and Juliet	Odashima Yûshi (tr.) Kimura Kôichi (dir.) [Bungaku-za]
	Don Hamlet	Suzuki Tadashi (adpt. and dir.) [Waseda Shôgekijô]
	Macbeth	Mikami Isao (tr.) Okamura Yoshitaka (dir.) [Joint Production of *shingeki* companies in Osaka]
October	*Hamlet*	Fukuda Tsuneari (tr.) Asari Keita (dir.) [Gekidan Shiki]
	Macbeth	Fukuda Tsuneari (tr.) Arakawa Tetsuo (dir.) [Gekidan Kumo]

Date	Title	Translator/director [Theatre company]
November	*King Lear*	Mikami Isao (tr.) Senda Koreya (dir.) [Haiyû-za]

1973
January	*Much Ado About Nothing*	Odashima Yûshi (tr.) Deguchi Norio (dir.) [Gekidan Shiki]
February	*Aisuru-toki mo Shisuru-toki mo* ('When in Love and When I Die, Too': an adaptation of *Hamlet*)	Fujita Toshio and Tanaka Motoi (adpts.) Matsuura Takeo (dir.) [Matsuura Kikaku]
March	*A Midsummer Night's Dream*	Fukuda Tsuneari (tr.) Kitamura Eizô and Kamisawa Kazuo (dirs.) [Môri Kikue Engeki Kenkyûjo] (in Kyoto)
	Othello	Fukuda Tsuneari (tr.) John David (dir.) [Tôhô Production]
May	*A Midsummer Night's Dream*	Peter Brook (dir.) [Royal Shakespeare Company]
June	*The Tempest*	Fukuda Tsuneari (tr. and dir.) [Gekidan Kumo]
	The Merchant of Venice	Fukuda Tsuneari (tr. and dir.) [Gekidan Keyaki]
July	*Makubesu Fujin no Genso to Genjitsuno Majiwari: Sonetto* ('Lady Macbeth's Vision and Reality: Sonnets')	Kikuchi Akira (adpt. and dir.) [Isoda Aki Recital]
November	*Macbeth*	Peter Potter and Nicholas Kent (dirs.) [London Shakespeare Group]
	The Merchant of Venice	Ôoka Kinji (dir.) [Gekidan Chôryû] (in Osaka)

1974
January	*Tempô Jûninen no Shakespeare* ('Shakespeare in the 12th Year of the Tempô Era': a parodic play which combines various plots taken from Shakespeare's plays, with allusions or references to all Shakespeare's plays. The 12th year of the Tempô Era (1841) is the year when the name of Shakespeare was first mentioned in Japanese.)	Inoue Hisashi (playwright) Deguchi Norio (dir.) [Abe Yoshihiro Jimusho]
	King Richard the Third	Mikami Isao (tr.) Masumi Toshikiyo (dir.) [Haiyû-za]

Date	Title	Translator/director [Theatre company]
	As You Like It	Mikami Isao (tr.) Uchigaki Keiichi (adpt. and dir.) [Rekishi-za]
	Twelfth Night	Mikami Isao (tr.) Uchigaki Keiichi (adpt. and dir.) [Rekishi-za]
March	Tsuyazakura no Homare On'nano Oshie ('The Honour of Cherry Blossoms and Instructions for Women': an adaptation of The Taming of the Shrew)	Mizuhara Akito (adpt.) Nemoto Yoshinari and Kawashima Seiichirô (dirs.)
May	Romeo and Juliet (A Kabuki actor Ichikawa Somegorô played the role of Romeo)	Odashima Yûshi (tr.) Ninagawa Yukio (dir.) [Tôhô Production]
	Danjo Kigi: Hamlet ('Men and Women's Comic Play: Hamlet)	Endô Takurô (adpt.) Takeuchi Toshiharu (dir.) [Takeuchi Drama School]
July	Twelfth Night	Odashima Yûshi (tr.) Nemoto Yoshinari (dir.) [Kindai-za]
August	Twelfth Night	Fukuda Tsuneari (tr.) Terence Knapp (dir.) [Gendai Engeki Kyôkai and Gekidan Kumo]
September	As You Like It	Fukuda Tsuneari (tr.) Miyajima Haruhiko (adpt. and dir.) [Gekidan Shiki]
November	Ofêria to Makubesu Fujin ('Ophelia and Lady Macbeth')	Tsubouchi Shôyô (tr.) Kikuchi Akira (adpt. and dir.) [Isoda Aki Recital]
December	The Merchant of Venice	Takahashi Saemon (dir.) [Tokyo Geijutsu-za]
1975 January	Shin Hamlet	Dazai Osamu (author) Akutagawa Hiroshi (adpt.) Murata Ganshi (dir.) [Gekidan Kumo]
March	Scenes from Hamlet	Fukuda Tsuneari (tr.) [Môri Kikue Engeki Kenkyûjo] (in Kyoto)
	A Midsummer Night's Dream	Uriu Masami (adpt. and dir.) [Seinen Gekijô]
May	Berôna no Koibitotachi ('Lovers of Verona': an adaptation of The Two Gentlemen of Verona as a musical play, first performed in America in 1971 under the title of The Two Gentlemen of Verona.)	Mel Shapiro and John Guare (adpts.) Aoi Yôji (tr.) Asari Keita (dir.) [Gekidan Shiki]

Date	Title	Translator/director [Theatre company]
	Twelfth Night	Odashima Yûshi (tr.) Deguchi Norio (dir.) [Shakespeare Theatre]
June	*Much Ado About Nothing*	Odashima Yûshi (tr.) Deguchi Norio (dir.) [Shakespeare Theatre]
July	*King Lear* (The title role was played by a Kabuki actor Ichikawa Somegorô.)	Odashima Yûshi (tr.) Ninagawa Yukio (dir.) [Tôhô Production]
	Romeo and Juliet	Odashima Yûshi (tr.) Deguchi Norio (dir.) [Shakespeare Theatre]
August	*A Midsummer Night's Dream*	Odashima Yûshi (tr.) John David (dir.) [Tôhô Production]
	Botomu no Yume ('Bottom's Dream': an adaptation of *A Midsummer Night's Dream*)	Tsubouchi Shôyô (tr.) Hayashi Kyôhei (dir.) [Gekidan Tochinomi]
	The Comedy of Errors	Odashima Yûshi (tr.) Deguchi Norio (dir.) [Shakespeare Theatre]
	Hamlet	Iwaki Kîko (dir.) [Gekidan Shimai]
September	*Itariano Koimonogatari* ('An Italian Love Story': an adaptation of *Romeo and Juliet*)	Karisaka Akira (adpt.) Masumi Toshikiyo (dir.) [ASA]
	Hamlet	Odashima Yûshi (tr.) Deguchi Norio (dir.) [Shakespeare Theatre]
	A Midsummer Night's Dream	Hirowatari Tsunetoshi (dir.) [Tokyo Engeki Ensemble]
October	*Twelfth Night*	Tsutsui Yôsuke (dir.) [Gekidan Academy] (in Osaka)
	Toki to Tokei ('Time and a Clock': an adaptation of *Macbeth*)	Tsubouchi Shôyô (tr.) Suzuki Tadashi (adpt. and dir.) [Waseda Shôgekijô]
November	*Measure for Measure*	Odashima Yûshi (tr.) Deguchi Norio (dir.) [Shakespeare Theatre]
	Hamlet	Odashima Yûshi (tr.) Kodama Hisao (dir.) [Isoda Aki Recital]
December	*Twelfth Night*	Odashima Yûshi (tr.) Deguchi Norio (dir.) [Shakespeare Theatre]

Date	Title	Translator/director [Theatre company]
	Much Ado About Nothing	Odashima Yûshi (tr.) Deguchi Norio (dir.) [Shakespeare Theatre]
	The Comedy of Errors	Odashima Yûshi (tr.) Deguchi Norio (dir.) [Shakespeare Theatre]
1976 January	*Twelfth Night*	Odashima Yûshi (tr.) Deguchi Norio (dir.) [Shakespeare Theatre]
February	*King Richard the Third*	Yadaka Masaru (tr., adpt. and dir.) [On-Theatre Jiyû Gekijô]
	Macbeth	Odashima Yûshi (tr.) Masumi Toshikiyo (dir.) [Shôchiku Production]
	Hamlet	Odashima Yûshi (tr.) Deguchi Norio (dir.) [Shakespeare Theatre]
March	*Much Ado About Nothing*	Odashima Yûshi (tr.) Deguchi Norio (dir.) [Shakespeare Theatre]
April	*Julius Caesar*	Odashima Yûshi (tr.) Deguchi Norio (dir.) [Shakespeare Theatre]
	The Taming of the Shrew (a Kyogen adaptation)	Miake Tôkurô (adpt.) [Izumi Sôke]
May	*As You Like It*	Odashima Yûshi (tr.) Deguchi Norio (dir.) [Shakespeare Theatre]
June	*The Taming of the Shrew*	Odashima Yûshi (tr.) Deguchi Norio (dir.) [Shakespeare Theatre]
July	*Twelfth Night*	Odashima Yûshi (tr.) Deguchi Norio (dir.) [Shakespeare Theatre]
	Much Ado About Nothing	Odashima Yûshi (tr.) Deguchi Norio (dir.) [Shakespeare Theatre]
	As You Like It	Odashima Yûshi (tr.) Deguchi Norio (dir.) [Shakespeare Theatre]
	The Taming of the Shrew	Odashima Yûshi (tr.) Deguchi Norio (dir.) [Shakespeare Theatre]
	The Comedy of Errors	Odashima Yûshi (tr.) Deguchi Norio (dir.) [Shakespeare Theatre]

Date	Title	Translator/director [Theatre company]
	Romeo and Juliet	Mukôjima Sanshirô (adpt. and dir.) [Gekidan Shibaraku]
July August	*A Midsummer Night's Dream*	Odashima Yûshi (tr.) Deguchi Norio (dir.) [Shakespeare Theatre]
September	*Hamlet*	Odashima Yûshi (tr.) Kimura Kôichi (dir.) [Bungaku-za]
	Measure for Measure	Odashima Yûshi (tr.) Deguchi Norio (dir.) [Shakespeare Theatre]
October	*The Comedy of Errors*	Odashima Yûshi (tr.) Deguchi Norio (dir.) [Shakespeare Theatre]
	Pericles	Anzai Tetsuo (tr. and dir.) [Engeki Shûdan En]
	King Lear	Tsubouchi Shôyô (tr.) In'nami Takashi (dir.) [Kindai-za]
November	*King Richard the Third*	Odashima Yûshi (tr.) Deguchi Norio (dir.) [Shakespeare Theatre]
	Titus Andronicus	Fukuda Tsuneari (tr.) Murata Ganshi (dir.) [Gekidan Subaru]
December	*Ofêria/Makubesu Fujin* ('Ophelia/ Lady Macbeth': an adaptation of *Hamlet* and *Macbeth*)	Tsubouchi Shôyô (tr.) Terasaki Yoshihiro (dir.) [Isoda Aki's One Woman Play]
	The Merchant of Venice	Odashima Yûshi (tr.) Deguchi Norio (dir.) [Shakespeare Theatre]
	Macbeth	Odashima Yûshi (tr.) Akagi Saburô (adpt.) Seki Kiyoshi (dir.) [Ikebukuro Shôgekijô]
1977 January	*Julius Caesar*	Odashima Yûshi (tr.) Masumi Toshikiyo (dir.) [Haiyû-za]
	Hamlet	Odashima Yûshi (tr.) Deguchi Norio (dir.) [Shakespeare Theatre]
February	*As You Like It*	Odashima Yûshi (tr.) Deguchi Norio (dir.) [Shakespeare Theatre]

Date	Title	Translator/director [Theatre company]
	The Merchant of Venice	Tsubouchi Shôyô (tr.) Isoda Aki (dir.) [Gekidan Tochinomi]
March	Macbeth	Odashima Yûshi (tr.) Akagi Saburô (adpt.) Seki Kiyoshi (dir.) [Ikebukuro Shôgekijô]
	Twelfth Night	Odashima Yûshi (tr.) Deguchi Norio (dir.) [Shakespeare Theatre]
April	Measure for Measure	Anzai Tetsuo (tr.) Terence Knapp (dir.) [Engeki Shûdan En]
	Othello	Odashima Yûshi (tr.) Masumi Toshikiyo (dir.) [Shôchiku Production]
	King Lear	Odashima Yûshi (tr.) Deguchi Norio (dir.) [Shakespeare Theatre]
	A Midsummer Night's Dream	Takeuchi Issei (dir.) [Group Zatto]
	Twelfth Night	Mikami Isao (tr.) Nishiki Kazuo (dir.) [Haiyû-za]
May	Coriolanus	Odashima Yûshi (tr.) Deguchi Norio (dir.) [Shakespeare Theatre]
	King Lear	Fukuda Tsuneari (tr.) Yadaka Masaru (dir.) [On-Theatre Jiyû Gekijô]
June	The Merchant of Venice	Fukuda Tsuneari (tr.) Asari Keita (dir.) [Gekidan Shiki]
	The Taming of the Shrew	Fukuda Tsuneari (tr.) Arakawa Tetsuo (dir.) [Gendai Engeki Kyôkai Subaru]
July	King Richard the Third	Odashima Yûshi (tr.) Deguchi Norio (dir.) [Shakespeare Theatre]
	Hamlet	Odashima Yûshi (tr.) Deguchi Norio (dir.) [Shakespeare Theatre]
	King Lear	Odashima Yûshi (tr.) Deguchi Norio (dir.) [Shakespeare Theatre]

Date	Title	Translator/director [Theatre company]
	Coriolanus	Odashima Yûshi (tr.) Deguchi Norio (dir.) [Shakespeare Theatre]
	King Richard the Third	Odashima Yûshi (tr.) Deguchi Norio (dir.) [Shakespeare Theatre]
	A Midsummer Night's Dream	Hidaka Hitoshi (dir.) [Gekidan Fuji]
August	*A Midsummer Night's Dream*: *Ningyô niyoru Mugen-geki* ('A Dream Play Performed by Puppets')	Odashima Yûshi (tr.) Shimizu Kôji (dir.) [Ningyô no Ie and Seibu Gekijô]
	A Midsummer Night's Dream	Odashima Yûshi (tr.) Deguchi Norio (dir.) [Shakespeare Theatre]
	Othello	Odashima Yûshi (tr.) Masumi Toshikiyo (dir.) [Shôchiku Production]
September	*Twelfth Night*	Mikami Isao (tr.) Nishiki Kazuo (dir.) [Haiyû-za]
	The Winter's Tale	Odashima Yûshi (tr.) Deguchi Norio (dir.) [Shakespeare Theatre]
1978 January	*As You Like It*	Odashima Yûshi (tr.) Deguchi Norio (dir.) [Haiyû-za]
	Twelfth Night	Odashima Yûshi (tr.) Deguchi Norio (dir.) [Shakespeare Theatre]
February	*King Lear*	Odashima Yûshi (tr.) Deguchi Norio (dir.) [Shakespeare Theatre]
	Hamlet	Fukuda Tsuneari (tr.) Yadaka Masaru (dir.) [On-Theatre Jiyû Gekijô]
March	*Othello*	Odashima Yûshi (tr.) Deguchi Norio (dir.) [Shakespeare Theatre]
April	*Hamlet*	Odashima Yûshi (tr.) Deguchi Norio (dir.) [Shakespeare Theatre]
May	*Titus Andronicus*	Odashima Yûshi (tr.) Deguchi Norio (dir.) [Shakespeare Theatre]

Date	Title	Translator/director [Theatre company]
June	*Romeo and Juliet* (an adaptation as a rock 'n' roll musical)	Mori Daigo (adpt., dir. and lyricist) Kondô Hiroaki (composer) [Izumi Taku Follies]
	A Midsummer Night's Dream (an adaptation as a musical)	Uriu Masami (adpt.) Yamakawa Keisuke (lyricist) Horiuchi Kan (dir. and choreographer) [Izumi Taku Follies]
	Twelfth Night	Kawano Takehiko (dir.) [Gekidan Mainâ Theatre]
July	*Troilus and Cressida*	Odashima Yûshi (tr.) Deguchi Norio (dir.) [Shakespeare Theatre]
August	*Hamlet*	Odashima Yûshi (tr.) Ninagawa Yukio (dir.) [Tôhô Production]
	A Midsummer Night's Dream	Odashima Yûshi (tr.) Deguchi Norio (dir.) [Shakespeare Theatre]
	The Merchant of Venice	Odashima Yûshi (tr.) Deguchi Norio (dir.) [Shakespeare Theatre]
	Twelfth Night	Odashima Yûshi (tr.) Deguchi Norio (dir.) [Shakespeare Theatre]
	Utageno Yoru, 3 ('The Night of a Banquet, 3': an adaptation of *Macbeth)*	Mikami Isao (tr.) Suzuki Tadashi (adpt. and dir.) [Waseda Shôgekijô]
September	*Love's Labour's Lost*	Odashima Yûshi (tr.) Deguchi Norio (dir.) [Shakespeare Theatre]
October	*Hamlet*	Fukuda Tsuneari (tr.) Okamura Yoshitaka (dir.) [Gekidan Puromete] (in Osaka)
	The Merry Wives of Windsor	Odashima Yûshi (tr.) Deguchi Norio (dir.) [Shakespeare Theatre]
	Berôna Monogatari ('Verona Story': an adaptation of *Romeo and Juliet)*	Yokoyama Yoshikazu (adpt.) Saitô Toyoharu (dir.) [Ongaku-za]
November	*A Midsummer Night's Dream*	Odashima Yûshi (tr.) Seki Kiyoshi (dir.) [Ikebukuro Shôgekijô]
	Macbeth	Odashima Yûshi (tr.) Deguchi Norio (dir.) [Shakespeare Theatre]

Date	Title	Translator/director [Theatre company]
December	*Othello*	Kawano Takehiko (dir.) [Gekidan Mainâ Theatre]
	Pericles	Odashima Yûshi (tr.) Deguchi Norio (dir.) [Shakespeare Theatre]
1979 January	*Macbeth*	Odashima Yûshi (tr.) Masumi Toshikiyo (dir.) [Haiyû-za]
	Romeo and Juliet	Odashima Yûshi (tr.) Shibata Yukihiro (adpt. and dir.) [Takarazuka Kageki-dan]
	The Winter's Tale	Odashima Yûshi (tr.) Deguchi Norio (dir.) [Shakespeare Theatre]
	Titus Andronicus	Odashima Yûshi (tr.) Deguchi Norio (dir.) [Shakespeare Theatre]
March	*The Taming of the Shrew*	Odashima Yûshi (tr.) Deguchi Norio (dir.) [Shakespeare Theatre]
	Hamlet	Fukuda Tsuneari (tr.) Okamura Yoshitaka (dir.) [Gekidan Puromete] (in Osaka)
	Macbeth	Fukuda Tsuneari (tr.) Yamaguchi Takehiko (dir.) [Môri Kikue Engeki Kenkyûjo] (in Kyoto)
April	*Henry the Fourth, Part One*	Odashima Yûshi (tr.) Deguchi Norio (dir.) [Shakespeare Theatre]
	A Midsummer Night's Dream	Odashima Yûshi (tr.) Moriizumi Hiroyuki (dir.) [Engeki Shûdan En]
	Romeo and Juliet	Odashima Yûshi (tr.) Shibata Yukihiro (adpt. and dir.) [Takarazuka Kageki-dan]
	Ayashii Kazeyo Rarabai ('Lullaby of a Mysterious Breeze': an adaptation of *A Midsummer Night's Dream*	Odashima Yûshi (tr.) Kushida Kazuyoshi (dir.) [On-Theatre Jiyû Gekijô]
May	*Henry the Fourth, Part Two*	Odashima Yûshi (tr.) Deguchi Norio (dir.) [Shakespeare Theatre]

Date	Title	Translator/director [Theatre company]
	Antony and Cleopatra	Mikami Isao (tr.) Senda Koreya (dir.) [Haiyû-za]
June	Much Ado About Nothing	Odashima Yûshi (tr.) Deguchi Norio (dir.) [Shakespeare Theatre]
	Much Ado About Nothing	Anzai Tetsuo (tr. and adpt.) Terence Knapp (dir.) [Engeki Shûdan En]
	Much Ado About Nothing	Odashima Yûshi (tr.) Natsume Shunji (dir.) [Gekidan Kobe] (in Kobe)
July	Romeo and Juliet	Odashima Yûshi (tr.) Deguchi Norio (dir.) [Shakespeare Theatre]
	Hamlet (a rock musical)	Odashima Yûshi (tr. and supervisor) Nakajima Azusa (adpt.) Satô Hiroshi (dir.) [Nakano Sun Plaza Production]
	My Richard the Third (a musical adaptation)	Fujiwara Tomonori (adpt. and dir.) [Mister Goodman]
August	Romeo and Juliet	Odashima Yûshi (tr.) Ninagawa Yukio (dir.) [Tôhô Production]
	Macbeth	Odashima Yûshi (tr.) Deguchi Norio (dir.) [Shakespeare Theatre]
September	Henry the Fifth	Odashima Yûshi (tr.) Deguchi Norio (dir.) [Shakespeare Theatre]
	Yôseitachi no Mori ('A Forest of Fairies': an adaptation of A Midsummer Night's Dream)	Hirata Minoru (adpt. and dir.) [Gekidan Tôhai]
October	As You Like It	Odashima Yûshi (tr.) Masumi Toshikiyo (dir.) [Haiyû-za]
	Pericles	Odashima Yûshi (tr.) Deguchi Norio (dir.) [Shakespeare Theatre]
	Hamlet	Toby Robertson (dir.) [Old Vic Company]
	Macbeth	Odashima Yûshi (tr.) Kushida Kazuyoshi (dir.) [On-Theatre Jiyû Gekijô]

Date	Title	Translator/director *[Theatre company]*
	Ofêria/ Makubesu Fujin	Odashima Yûshi (tr.) Isoda Aki (adpt. and dir.)
November	*The Tempest*	Odashima Yûshi (tr.) Deguchi Norio (dir.) [Shakespeare Theatre]
December	*King Richard the Second*	Odashima Yûshi (tr.) Deguchi Norio (dir.) [Shakespeare Theatre]
1980 January	*Hamlet*	Odashima Yûshi (tr.) Masumi Toshikiyo (dir.) [Haiyû-za]
February	*Macbeth*	Odashima Yûshi (tr.) Ninagawa Yukio (dir.) [Tôhô Production]
	The Comedy of Errors	Anzai Tetsuo (tr. and dir.) [Engeki Shûdan En]
April	*Hamlet*	Odashima Yûshi (tr.) Masumi Toshikiyo (dir.) [Haiyû-za]
	King Lear	Odashima Yûshi (tr.) Deguchi Norio (dir.) [Shakespeare Theatre]
May	*Cymbeline*	Odashima Yûshi (tr.) Deguchi Norio (dir.) [Shakespeare Theatre]
	Berôna no Koibitotachi	Mel Shapiro and John Guare (adpts.) Aoi Yôji (tr.) Asari Keita (dir.) [Gekidan Shiki]
June	*The Comedy of Errors*	Anzai Tetsuo (tr. and dir.) [Engeki Shûdan En]
	King John	Odashima Yûshi (tr.) Deguchi Norio (dir.) [Shakespeare Theatre]
July	*Romeo and Juliet*	Odashima Yûshi (tr.) Deguchi Norio (dir.) [Shakespeare Theatre]
	The Merchant of Venice	Odashima Yûshi (tr.) Takimoto Shin'ichirô (dir.) [Gekidan Mainâ Theatre]
	Hamlet (a rock musical adaptation)	Odashima Yûshi (tr.) Nakajima Azusa and Satô Hirofumi (adpts.) Fujii Tomonori (dir.) [Nakano Sun Plaza Production]

Date	Title	Translator/director [Theatre company]
	Phantom Lady (a rock musical adaptation of Romeo and Juliet)	Fujii Tomonori (adpt. and dir.)
	A Midsummer Night's Dream	Natsume Shunji (tr. and dir.) [Gekidan Kobe] (in Kobe)
August	Much Ado About Nothing	Odashima Yûshi (tr.) Deguchi Norio (dir.) [Shakespeare Theatre]
	Macbeth Rhapsody	Satô Yasuaki (adpt.) Ôtani Akira (dir.) [From East and Fujioka Kikaku Joint Production]
September	The Two Gentlemen of Verona	Odashima Yûshi (tr.) Deguchi Norio (dir.) [Shakespeare Theatre]
	King Richard the Third (The title role was played by a Kabuki actor, Onoe Tatsunosuke.)	Tsubouchi Shôyô (tr.) Wada Yutaka (dir.) [Shôchiku Production]
October	Twelfth Night	Odashima Yûshi (tr.) Deguchi Norio (dir.) [Shakespeare Theatre]
	A Midsummer Night's Dream	Odashima Yûshi (tr.) Deguchi Norio (dir.) [Shakespeare Theatre]
	Macbeth 12	Kushida Kazuyoshi (adpt. and dir.) [On-Theatre Jiyû Gekijô]
November	Twelfth Night	Ôta Kazuo (dir.) [Theatre 2+1]
	King Richard the Third (The title role was played by a Kabuki actor, Onoe Tatsunosuke.	Tsubouchi Shôyô (tr.) Wada Yutaka (dir.) [Shôchiku Production]
	The Merchant of Venice	John Fraser (dir.) [London Shakespeare Group]
	All's Well That Ends Well	Odashima Yûshi (tr.) Deguchi Norio (dir.) [Shakespeare Theatre]
	Timon of Athens	Odashima Yûshi (tr.) Deguchi Norio (dir.) [Shakespeare Theatre]
1981 January	Romeo and Juliet	Odashima Yûshi (tr.) Masumi Toshikiyo (dir.) [Haiyû-za]
	Romeo and Juliet	Odashima Yûshi (tr.) Deguchi Norio (dir.) [Shakespeare Theatre]

Date	Title	Translator/director [Theatre company]
January February	*Hamlet*	Odashima Yûshi (tr.) Emori Tôru (dir.) [Bungaku-za]
March	*Hamlet*	Odashima Yûshi (tr.) Takatsu Sumio (dir.) [Kikansha]
	Yume no Hamlet ('*Hamlet* in the Dream')	Yasuda Masao (adpt. and dir.) [Gekidan Fruit Jam]
	The Comedy of Errors	Anzai Tetsuo (tr. and dir.) [Engeki Shûdan En]
	King Henry the Eighth	Odashima Yûshi (tr.) Deguchi Norio (dir.) [Shakespeare Theatre]
	King Richard the Third	Takeuchi Kazuhide (dir.) [Group Zatto]
	Macbeth	Ôta Kazuo (dir.) [Theatre 2+1]
April	*King Henry the Sixth, Part One*	Odashima Yûshi (tr.) Deguchi Norio (dir.) [Shakespeare Theatre]
	King Henry the Sixth, Part Two	Odashima Yûshi (tr.) Deguchi Norio (dir.) [Shakespeare Theatre]
	King Henry the Sixth, Part Three	Odashima Yûshi (tr.) Deguchi Norio (dir.) [Shakespeare Theatre]
	Berôna Monogatari ('Verona Story: an adaptation of *Romeo and Juliet*)	Yokoyama Yoshikazu (adpt.) Igarashi Susumu (dir.) [Ongaku-za]
May	*Antony and Cleopatra*	Odashima Yûshi (tr.) Deguchi Norio (dir.) [Shakespeare Theatre]
June	*Twelfth Night*	Odashima Yûshi (tr.) Deguchi Norio (dir.) [Shakespeare Theatre]
	Much Ado About Nothing	Odashima Yûshi (tr.) Deguchi Norio (dir.) [Shakespeare Theatre]
	A Midsummer Night's Dream	Odashima Yûshi (tr.) Deguchi Norio (dir.) [Shakespeare Theatre]
July	*King Lear*	Odashima Yûshi (tr.) Deguchi Norio (dir.) [Shakespeare Theatre]

Date	Title	Translator/director [Theatre company]
	A Midsummer Night's Dream	Odashima Yûshi (tr.) Masumi Toshikiyo and Watanabe Kyôko (adpts.) Masumi Toshikiyo (dir.) [Haiyû-za and Shôchiku Joint Production]
September	*Love's Labour's Lost*	Odashima Yûshi (tr.) Deguchi Norio (dir.) [Shakespeare Theatre]
October	*Twelfth Night*	Iwata Hiroshi (tr.) Uesugi Kiyofumi (adpt.) Uriu Ryôsuke (dir.) [Hakkenno Kai]
	Julius Caesar	Fukuda Tsuneari (tr.) Fukuda Hayaru (dir.) [Gendai Engeki Kyôkai Subaru]
	Julius Caesar	Odashima Yûshi (tr.) Deguchi Norio (dir.) [Shakespeare Theatre]
	Macbeth	Odashima Yûshi (tr.) Deguchi Norio (dir.) [Shakespeare Theatre]
1981 January	*Romeo and Juliet*	Odashima Yûshi (tr.) Masumi Toshikiyo (dir.) [Haiyû-za]
	Romeo and Juliet	Odashima Yûshi (tr.) Deguchi Norio (dir.) [Shakespeare Theatre]
February	*Hamlet*	Odashima Yûshi (tr.) Emori Tôru (dir.) [Bungaku-za]
March	*Hamlet*	Odashima Yûshi (tr.) Takatsu Sumio (dir.) [Kikansha]
	Yumeno Hamlet ('*Hamlet* in the Dream')	Yasuda Masao (adpt. and dir.) [Gekidan Fruit Jam]
	The Comedy of Errors	Anzai Tetsuo (tr. and dir.) [Engeki Shûdan En]
	King Henry the Eighth	Odashima Yûshi (tr.) Deguchi Norio (dir.) [Shakespeare Theatre]
	King Richard the Third	Takeuchi Kazuhide (dir.) [Group Zatto]
	Macbeth	Ôta Kazuo (dir.) [Theatre 2+1]

Date	Title	Translator/director [Theatre company]
April	*King Henry the Sixth, Part One*	Odashima Yûshi (tr.) Deguchi Norio (dir.) [Shakespeare Theatre]
	King Henry the Sixth, Part Two	Odashima Yûshi (tr.) Deguchi Norio (dir.) [Shakespeare Theatre]
	King Henry the Sixth, Part Three	Odashima Yûshi (tr.) Deguchi Norio (dir.) [Shakespeare Theatre]
	Berôna Monogatari ('Verona Story': an adaptation of *Romeo and Juliet*)	Yokoyama Yoshikazu (adpt.) Igarashi Susumu (dir.) [Ongaku-za]
May	*Antony and Cleopatra*	Odashima Yûshi (tr.) Deguchi Norio (dir.) [Shakespeare Theatre]
June	*Twelfth Night*	Odashima Yûshi (tr.) Deguchi Norio (dir.) [Shakespeare Theatre]
	Much Ado About Nothing	Odashima Yûshi (tr.) Deguchi Norio (dir.) [Shakespeare Theatre]
	A Midsummer Night's Dream	Odashima Yûshi (tr.) Deguchi Norio (dir.) [Shakespeare Theatre]
July	*King Lear*	Odashima Yûshi (tr.) Deguchi Norio (dir.) [Shakespeare Theatre]
	A Midsummer Night's Dream	Odashima Yûshi (tr.) Masumi Toshikiyo and Watanabe Kyôko (adpts.) Masumi Toshikiyo (dir.) [Haiyû-za and Shôchiku Joint Production]
September	*Love's Labour's Lost*	Odashima Yûshi (tr.) Deguchi Norio (dir.) [Shakespeare Theatre]
October	*Twelfth Night*	Iwata Hiroshi (tr.) Uesugi Kiyofumi (adpt.) Uriu Ryôsuke (dir.) [Hakken no Kai]
	Julius Caesar	Fukuda Tsuneari (tr.) Fukuda Hayaru (dir.) [Gendai Engeki Kyôkai Subaru]
	Julius Caesar	Odashima Yûshi (tr.) Deguchi Norio (dir.) [Shakespeare Theatre]

Date	Title	Translator/director [Theatre company]
	Romeo and Juliet	Odashima Yûshi (tr.) Kimura Kôichi (dir.) [Mitsukoshi Royal Theatre]
	Macbeth	Odashima Yûshi (tr.) Deguchi Norio (dir.) [Shakespeare Theatre]
1982 January	*The Merchant of Venice*	Odashima Yûshi (tr.) Masumi Toshikiyo (dir.) [Haiyû-za]
February	*Cymbeline*	Odashima Yûshi (tr.) Hirabayashi Tsuneshige (dir.) [On-Theatre Jiyû Gekijô]
	Love's Labour's Lost	Odashima Yûshi (tr.) Deguchi Norio (dir.) [Shakespeare Theatre]
March	*Noh Hamlet* (a Noh adaptation of *Hamlet* in English)	Munakata Kuniyoshi (adpt. and dir.) [Noh Shakespeare Group]
April	*Ito-ayatsuri Ningyô-shibai Macbeth* ('A Puppet Play *Macbeth*)	Odashima Yûshi (tr.) Satô Makoto (dir.) [Yûki-za]
May	*Ofêria/ Makubesu Fujin*	Odashima Yûshi (tr.) Isoda Aki (adpt.) [Gekidan Tochinomi]
	King Henry the Sixth (Parts One, Two and Three)	Odashima Yûshi (tr.) Deguchi Norio (dir.) [Shakespeare Theatre]
June	*King Henry the Fourth*	Fukuda Tsuneari (tr. and dir.) [Gendai Engeki Kyôkai Subaru]
	The Taming of the Shrew	Odashima Yûshi (tr.) Deguchi Norio (dir.) [Shakespeare Theatre]
	Romio to Furîjia no Aru Shokutaku ('A Dining Table with Romeo and a Freesia on It': a play based on *Romeo and Juliet*)	Kisaragi Koharu (playwright) Deguchi Norio (dir.) [Shakespeare Theatre]
	Twelfth Night	Odashima Yûshi (tr.) Deguchi Norio (dir.) [Shakespeare Theatre]
	A Midsummer Night's Dream	Odashima Yûshi (tr.) Deguchi Norio (dir.) [Shakespeare Theatre]
July	*The Merchant of Venice*	Odashima Yûshi (tr.) Isoda Aki (dir.) [Gekidan Tochinomi]

Date	Title	Translator/director [Theatre company]
	A Midsummer Night's Dream	Odashima Yûshi (tr.) Deguchi Norio (dir.) [Shakespeare Theatre]
	The Merry Wives of Windsor	Odashima Yûshi (tr.) Takasaki Kunihiro (dir.) [Gekidan Kobe] (in Kobe)
August	*Berôna Monogatari*	Yokoyama Yoshikazu (adpt. and dir.) [Ongaku-za]
October	*Hamlet*	Fukuda Tsuneari (tr.) Asari Keita (dir.) [Gekidan Shiki]
November	*Macbeth*	Odashima Yûshi (tr.) Ryû Tomoe (dir.) [Nakadai Project and PARCO Joint Production]
	Twelfth Night	John Fraser (dir.) [London Shakespeare Group]
December	*Hamlet*	Arima Norizumi (tr.) Uriu Ryôsuke (dir.) [Hakken no Kai]
	Julius Caesar	Fukuda Tsuneari (tr.) Fukuda Hayaru (dir.) [Gendai Engeki Kyôkai Subaru]
1983 January	*The Merry Wives of Windsor*	Odashima Yûshi (tr.) Masumi Toshikiyo (dir.) [Haiyû-za]
February	*Noh Hamlet*	Munakata Kuniyoshi (adpt. and dir.) [Noh Shakespeare Kenkyû-kai]
March	*The Merry Wives of Windsor*	Odashima Yûshi (tr.) Masumi Toshikiyo (dir.) [Haiyû-za]
April	*Pericles*	Odashima Yûshi (tr.) Deguchi Norio (dir.) [Shakespeare Theatre]
	A Midsummer Night's Dream	Fujita Asaya (adpt. and dir.) [Gogatsu-sha]
	King Lear	Odashima Yûshi (tr.) Deguchi Norio (dir.) [Shakespeare Theatre]
May	*Ria Ô no Aoi Shiro* ('King Lear's Blue Castle')	Kisaragi Koharu (playwright) Deguchi Norio (dir.) [Shakespeare Theatre]

Date	Title	Translator/director [Theatre company]
	Hamlet Q1	Anzai Tetsuo (tr. and dir.) [Engeki Shûdan En]
June	*Romeo and Juliet '83*	Odashima Yûshi (tr.) Michael Bogdanov (dir.) [Tôhô Production]
	The Merchant of Venice	Fukuda Tsuneari (tr.) Sueki Toshifumi (dir.) [Gendai Engeki Kyôkai Subaru]
July	*A Midsummer Night's Dream*	Takarada Akira (dir.) [TAC]
August	*King Henry the Sixth*	Odashima Yûshi (tr.) Deguchi Norio (dir.) [Shakespeare Theatre]
September	*King Henry the Fourth*	Odashima Yûshi (tr.) Deguchi Norio (dir.) [Shakespeare Theatre]
October	*Macbeth*	Odashima Yûshi (tr.) Kushida Kazuyoshi (dir.) [On-Theatre Jiyû Gekijô]
November	*Julius Caesar*	Odashima Yûshi (tr.) Deguchi Norio (dir.) [Shakespeare Theatre]
	Twelfth Night	Odashima Yushi (tr.) Deguchi Norio (dir.) [Shakespeare Theatre]
	Othello	Odashima Yushi (tr.) Emori Tôru (dir.) [Bungaku-za]
	Hamlet	Odashima Yûshi (tr.) Ryû Tomoe (dir.) [Mumei-juku]
	King John	Abe Ryô (adpt. and dir.) [Zen Shakespeare (Complete Shakespeare)]
1984 January	*The Tempest*	Odashima Yûshi (tr.) Masumi Toshikiyo (dir.) [Haiyû-za]
February	*Hamlet* (The title role was played by a Kabuki actor, Kataoka Takao.)	Fukuda Tsuneari (tr.) Kimura Kôichi (dir.) [Nissei Gekijô Production]
April	*The Merchant of Venice*	Isoda Aki (adpt. and dir.) [Gekidan Tochinomi]
June	*Butano Sekai: King Henry the Fourth* ('Swines' World: *King Henry the Fourth*')	Abe Ryô (dir.) [Zen Shakespeare]

Date	Title	Translator/director [Theatre company]
	A Midsummer Night's Dream	Odashima Yûshi (tr.) Deguchi Norio (dir.) [Shakespeare Theatre]
	A Midsummer Night's Dream	Shibata Toshiyuki (dir.) Yamaguchi Keiko (producer)
October	*Romeo and Juliet*	Odashima Yûshi (dir.) Endô Eizô (dir.) [Itabashi Engeki Centre]
November	*Hamlet*	Fukuda Tsuneari (tr. and dir.) [Gendai Engeki Kyôkai Subaru]
	Much Ado About Nothing	Odashima Yûshi (tr.) Deguchi Norio (dir.) [Shakespeare Theatre]
	Macbeth	John Fraser (dir.) [London Shakespeare Group]
	Noh Hamlet	Munakata Kuniyoshi (adpt. and dir.) [Noh Shakespeare Kenkyû-kai]
	Macbeth	Ôwada Isamu (dir.) [Theatre 2+1]
1985 January	*Ôtachi* ('Kings'): *King Richard the Second, King Henry the Fourth, King Henry the Fifth*	Abe Ryô (adpt. and dir.) [Zen Shakespeare]
February	*A Midsummer Night's Dream*	Odashima Yûshi (tr.) Haichi Jun (dir.) [Tokyo Actors in Tanaka Production]
March	*Twelfth Night*	Odashima Yûshi (tr.) Wada Toshihichi (dir.) [Theatre 2+1]
	Twelfth Night	Odashima Yûshi (tr.) Nishizawa Akira (dir.) [Rhyming]
	Noh Hamlet	Munakata Kuniyoshi (adpt. and dir.) [Noh Shakespeare Kenkyû-kai]
April	*Ningyô-shibai Macbeth* ('A Puppet Play *Macbeth*')	Odashima Yûshi (tr.) Satô Makoto (dir.) [Yûki-za]
	King Lear	Anzai Tetsuo (tr. and dir.) [Engeki Shûdan En]
May	*Twelfth Night*	Takagi Tôru (dir.) [Honda Studio]

Date	Title	Translator/director [Theatre company]
	A Midsummer Night's Dream	Odashima Yûshi (tr.) Endô Eizô (dir.) [Itabashi Engeki Centre]
	The Taming of the Shrew	Odashima Yûshi (tr.) Deguchi Norio (dir.) [Shakespeare Theatre]
July	*I Am Portia.* (an adaptation of *The Merchant of Venice*: one woman play)	Odashima Yûshi (tr.) Isoda Aki (adpt. and dir.) [Gekidan Tochinomi]
	Twelfth Night	Wada Toshihichi (adpt. and dir.) [Theatre 2+1]
September	*King Richard the Third*	Odashima Yûshi (tr.) Ôsugi Hiroshi (dir.) [Katô Ken'ichi Jimusho]
	Eiyû: Coriolanus ('A Hero, Coriolanus')	Abe Ryô (adpt. and dir.) [Zen Shakespeare]
November	*King Lear*	Odashima Yûshi (tr.) Tanaka Tetsurô (dir.) [Rhyming]
	A Midsummer Night's Dream	Odashima Yûshi (tr.) Deguchi Norio (dir.) [Shakespeare Theatre]
	The Taming of the Shrew	Odashima Yûshi (tr.) Deguchi Norio (dir.) [Shakespeare Theatre]
	Twelfth Night	Odashima Yûshi (tr.) Deguchi Norio (dir.) [Shakespeare Theatre]
	A Midsummer Night's Dream	Fukuda Tsuneari (tr. and dir.) Higuchi Masahiro (dir.) [Gendai Engeki Kyôkai Subaru]
1986 January	*Aru Ningyô-ichiza niyoru Hamlet* ('*Hamlet* Staged by a Puppet Company')	Fukuda Yoshiyuki (adpt. and dir.) [Yûki-za]
	Caesar	Abe Ryô (adpt. and dir.) [Zen Shakespeare]
April	Shakespeare Recital: *Noh Hamlet*	Arai Yoshio (supervisor) Munakata Kuniyoshi (adpt. and dir.)
	Ofêria/Makubesu Fujin	Isoda Aki (adpt. and dir.)
May	*Love's Labour's Lost*	Odashima Yûshi (tr.) Deguchi Norio (dir.) [Shakespeare Theatre]

Date	Title	Translator/director [Theatre company]
June	*Shylock matawa Ijime* ('Shylock or Maltreatment': an adaptation of *The Merchant of Venice*)	Abe Ryô (adpt. and dir.) [Zen Shakespeare]
July	*Noda Hideki no Twelfth Night* ('Noda Hideki's *Twelfth Night*')	Odashima Yûshi (tr.) Noda Hideki (adpt. and dir.) [Tôhô Production]
	A Midsummer Night's Dream	Lindsay Kemp (dir.) [Lindsay Kemp Company]
August	*A Midsummer Night's Dream*	Odashima Yûshi (tr.) Deguchi Norio (dir.) [Shakespeare Theatre]
September	*The Taming of the Shrew*	Odashima Yûshi (tr.) Fukuda Yôichirô (dir.) [PARCO Gekijô Production]
	Romeo and Juliet	Fukuda Tsuneari (tr.) Bandô Tamasaburô (dir.) [Sunshine Gekijô and Shôchiku Joint Production]
	Macbeth	Odashima Yûshi (tr.) Endô Eizô (dir.) [Itabashi Engeki Centre]
	Macbeth	Fukuda Tsuneari (tr.) Fukuda Hayaru (dir.) [Gendai Engeki Kyokai Subaru]
	Kireiwa Kitanai: Macbeth ('Fair is Foul: *Macbeth*')	Odashima Yûshi (tr.) Takemura Rui (dir. and choreographer) [Super Company]
October	*Coriolanus*	Takahashi Masaya (adpt. and dir.) [PARCO Gekijô production]
	Makubesu Fujin ('Lady Macbeth': an adaptation of *Macbeth*; one-woman play)	Isoda Aki (adpt. and dir.) [Isoda Aki Hitori Shibai]
	Jajauma ha Naraseruka? ('Can a Shrew Be Tamed?': an adaptation of *The Taming of the Shrew*)	Abe Ryô (adpt. and dir.) [Zen Shakespeare]
November	*Shinkunaru Umini Inori wo: Antony and Cleopatra* ('With Prayer for the Red Sea')	Odashima Yûshi (tr.) Shibata Yukihiro (adpt. and dir.) [Takarazuka Kageki-dan]
	Much Ado About Nothing	Odashima Yûshi (tr.) Glen Walford (dir.) [Rhyming]
	Romeo and Juliet	Fukuda Tsuneari (tr.) Asari Keita (dir.) [Gekidan Shiki]

Date	Title	Translator/director [Theatre company]
	A Midsummer Night's Dream	Odashima Yûshi (tr.) Yoshizawa Takao (dir.) [Yoshizawa Engeki-juku]
	The Winter's Tale	Anzai Tetsuo (tr. and dir.) [Engeki Shûdan En]
1987 January	*King Richard the Third*	Odashima Yûshi (tr.) Deguchi Norio (dir.) [Shakespeare Theatre]
February	*The Merchant of Venice*	Odashima Yûshi (tr.) Isoda Aki (adpt. and dir.)
	Romeo and Juliet	Fukuda Tsuneari (tr.) Asari Keita (dir.) [Gekidan Shiki]
	Macbeth	Odashima Yûshi (tr.) Takemura Rui (dir.) [Super Company]
March	*The Tempest*	Odashima Yûshi (tr.) Ninagawa Yukio (dir.) [Tôhô Production]
	A Midsummer Night's Dream	Chinen Masafumi (adpt. and dir.) [Gekidan Chôjûgiga]
April	*Macbeth* (a production with actors/actresses and puppets)	Odashima Yûshi (tr.) Satô Makoto (dir.) [Yûki-za]
May	*King Lear*	Odashima Yûshi (tr.) Endô Eizô (dir.) [Itabashi Engeki Centre]
	The Comedy of Errors	Odashima Yûshi (tr.) Deguchi Norio (dir.) [Shakespeare Theatre]
	Twelfth Night	Fukuda Tsuneari (tr.) Fukuda Hayaru (dir.) [Gendai Engeki Kyôkai Subaru]
June	*The Winter's Tale*	Odashima Yûshi (tr.) Kimura Kôichi (dir.) [Spiral Theatre Production, No.4]
July	*The Taming of the Shrew*	Odashima Yûshi (tr.) Nishimura Makoto (dir.) [Gekidan Rutsubo]
August	*A Midsummer Night's Dream*	Lindsay Kemp (dir.) [Lindsay Kemp Company]
	Koino Mayoibitotachi ('People Lost in Love': an adaptation of *A Midsummer Night's Dream*)	Rick Besoyan (adpt.) Okumura Tatsuo (dir.) [Gekidan Sôen]

Date	Title	Translator/director [Theatre company]
September	*The Merchant of Venice*	Chinen Masafumi (adpt. and dir.) [Gekidan Chôjûgiga]
October	*Macbeth*	Odashima Yûshi (tr.) Deguchi Norio (dir.) [Shakespeare Theatre]
	King Lear	Anzai Tetsuo (tr. and dir.) [Engeki Shûdan En]
November	*Othello*	Fukuda Tsuneari (tr.) Murata Ganshi (dir.) [Gendai Engeki Kyôkai Subaru]
	Hamlet	Fukuda Tsuneari (tr.) Sueki Toshifumi (dir.) [Yamamoto Jimusho]
	King Richard the Third	Takahashi Masaya (adpt. and dir.) [PARCO Gekijô Production]
	Macbeth	Odashima Yûshi (tr.) Jiles Block (dir.) [Shôchiku and Sunshine Gekijô Joint Production]
	Twelfth Night	Odashima Yûshi (tr.) Adrian Noble (dir.) [Ginza Saison Gekijô Production]
December	*Ninagawa Macbeth*	Odashima Yûshi (tr.) Ninagawa Yukio (dir.) [Tôhô Production]
	The Comedy of Errors	Odashima Yûshi (tr.) Glen Walford (dir.) [Rhyming]
1988 January	*As You Like It*	Odashima Yûshi (tr.) Masumi Toshikiyo (dir.) [Haiyû-za]
April	*The Wars of the Roses:* *King Richard the Second* *King Henry the Fourth, Part One* *King Henry the Fourth, Part Two* *King Henry the Fifth* *King Henry the Sixth: the House of Lancaster* *King Henry the Sixth: the House of York* *King Richard the Third*	Michael Bogdanov (dir.) [English Shakespeare Company]
May	*The Comedy of Errors*	Odashima Yûshi (tr.) Deguchi Norio (dir.) [Shakespeare Theatre]

Date	Title	Translator/director [Theatre company]
	Unnatural and Unkind: Shakespeare Anthology (scenes from Shakespeare's plays)	Bill Buffery (dir.) [Royal Shakespeare Company]
	Ganso Hamuretto no Moto ('Materials of Original Hamlet')	Takeuchi Jûichiro (adpt. and dir.) [Hihô Rei-ban Kan]
	Hamlet	Odashima Yûshi (tr.) [Tokyo Engeki Shûdan Kaze]
May June	Hamlet	Tsubouchi Shôyô and Odashima Yûshi (trs.) Ninagawa Yukio (dir.) [Spiral Theatre Production, No.5]
June	Cymbeline The Winter's Tale The Tempest	Peter Hall (dir.) [Royal National Theatre]
July	Hamlet	Ingmar Bergman (dir.) [Swedish Royal Dramatic Theatre Company]
	A Midsummer Night's Dream	Fukuda Tsuneari (tr.) Terence Knapp (dir.) [PARCO Production]
August	Okanoueno Hamlet no Baka ('Hamlet, an Idiot, on a Hill: an adaptation of Hamlet')	Odashima Yûshi (tr.) Katô Tadashi (adpt. and dir.) [Move-on Production]
	As You Like It	Andrew Mulligan (dir.) [Oxford University Dramatic Society]
	Not As You Like It: Pillow Talk	Oxford University Dramatic Society (adpt.) Wes Williams (dir.) [Oxford University Dramatic Society]
September	Twelfth Night	Odashima Yûshi (tr.) Deguchi Norio (dir.) [Shakespeare Theatre]
	Okinimesumama Oshibai wo ('Enjoy the Play As You Like It': an adaptation of As You Like It)	Yamazaki Masakazu (adpt. and dir.) [Kinoshita Jimusho]
	Othello	Odashima Yûshi (tr.) Kuriyama Masayoshi (dir.) [Shôchiku Production]
	Romeo and Juliet	Fukuda Tsuneari (tr.) Bandô Tamasaburô (dir.) [Shôchiku Production]

Date	Title	Translator/director [Theatre company]
November	*Romeo and Juliet*	Fukuda Tsuneari (tr.) Murata Ganshi and Fukuda Hayaru (dirs.) [Gendai Engeki Kyôkai Subaru]
	The Taming of the Shrew	Mikami Isao (tr.) Senda Koreya (dir.) [Haiyû-za]
	Measure for Measure	Odashima Yûshi (tr.) Glen Walford (dir.) [Rhyming]
December	*The Tempest*	Odashima Yûshi (tr.) Ninagawa Yukio (dir.) [Tôhô Production]
	Macbeth	Ryûzanji Shô (adpt. and dir.) [Ryûzanji Jimusho]
1989 January	*Ito Ayatsuri Ningyô Shibai: Haru to Forusutaffu* ('A Puppet Play: Prince Hal and Falstaff': an adaptation of *King Henry the Fourth*)	Odashima Yûshi (tr.) Fukuda Yoshiyuki (adpt. and dir.) [Yûki-za]
	Romeo and Juliet	Kaneko Hiroshi (adpt. and dir.) [Mujintô]
	Ria-Ô no Shokutaku ('King Lear's Dining Table')	Miyoshi Yûdai(adpt. and dir.) [nafa]
February	*Noh Othello*	Munakata Kuniyoshi (tr. adpt. and dir.) [Noh Shakespeare Kenkyû-kai]
	Twelfth Night	Odashima Yûshi (tr.) Katô Tadashi (dir.) [Kon'nyaku-za]
March	*Twelfth Night*	Odashima Yûshi (tr.) Hodaka Minoru (dir.) [Gekidan Haikyô]
	Hamlet	Odashima Yûshi (tr.) Hara Tetsurô (dir.) [Move-on Production]
	The Tempest	Odashima Yûshi (tr.) Hirowatari Tsunetoshi (dir.) [Tokyo Engeki Ensemble]
	Much Ado About Nothing	Ogura Toshimasa (dir.) [Shakespeare Society]
April	*Kowai Hanashi* ('A Horrible Story': an adaptation of *Titus Andronicus*)	Abe Ryô (adpt. and dir.) [Zen Shakespeare]

Date	Title	Translator/director [Theatre company]
	A Midsummer Night's Dream	Uriu Masami (adpt.) Nakano Chiharu and Uriu Masami(dirs.) [Seinen Gekijô]
	King Lear	Odashima Yûshi (tr.) Suzuki Tadashi (dir.) [SCOT: Suzuki Company of Toga]
	Much Ado About Nothing	Odashima Yûshi (tr.) Miyamoto Amon (dir.)
	Twelfth Night	Takahashi Hideyuki (dir.) [Quixote]
May	*The Comedy of Errors*	Odashima Yûshi (tr.) Deguchi Norio (dir.) [Shakespeare Theatre]
	Hamlet	Odashima Yûshi (tr.) Endô Eizô (dir.) [Itabashi Engeki Centre]
	Julius Caesar	Anzai Tetsuo (tr. and dir.) [Engeki Shûdan En]
	The Taming of the Shrew	Odashima Yûshi (tr.) Deguchi Norio(dir.) [Shakespeare Theatre]
	Macbeth	Chiba Ken'ichi (adpt. and dir.) [Kaitenrô]
	King Lear	Odashima Yûshi (tr.) Itô Shirô (dir.) [Hitomi-za]
June	*Macbeth*	Odashima Yûshi (tr.) Jiles Block (dir.) [Shôchiku Production]
	Heisei God Caesar	Takabayashi Kôhei (adpt. and dir.) [Heisei Gan'nen]
July	*Macbeth*	Yamazaki Tsutomu (adpt.) Morita Yûzo (dir.) [Ginza Saison Gekijô Production]
	A Midsummer Night's Dream	Odashima Yûshi (tr.) Kino Hana (dir.) [Office the Third Stage Production]
	Hamlet	Fukuda Tsuneari (tr.) Sueki Toshifumi (dir.) [Kiyama Jimusho]
	King Lear	Anzai Tetsuo (tr. and dir.) [Engeki Shûdan En]

Date	Title	Translator/director [Theatre company]
August	*Yûjin-shô 1: Hamlet yori* ('Ode to Playboys 1: From *Hamlet*')	Odashima Yûshi (tr.) Suzuki Tadashi (adpt. and dir.) [SCOT]
September	*Macbeth*	Odashima Yûshi (tr.) Takemura Rui (dir.) [Super Company]
	Ryûzanji Macbeth	Odashima Yûshi (tr.) Ryûzanji Shô (dir.) [Ryûzanji Jimusho]
	Lady Macbeth (one-woman play)	Odashima Yûshi (tr.) Azuma Tadashi (adpt.) Isoda Aki (dir.)
	Love's Labour's Lost	Odashima Yûshi (tr.) Deguchi Norio (dir.) [Shakespeare Theatre]
	The Taming of the Shrew	Odashima Yûshi (tr.) Deguchi Norio (dir.) [Shakespeare Theatre]
October	*Shirohige no Lear* ('Lear with White Beard')	Suzuki Kenji (adpt. and dir.) [Tao]
	Uragiri ('Betrayal') (an adaptation of *The Two Gentlemen of Verona*)	Abe Ryô (adpt. and dir.) [Zen Shakespeare]
	Macbeth	[London Stage Company]
November	*Lady Macbeth* (one-woman play)	Isoda Aki (adpt. and dir.)
	King Richard the Third	Fukuda Tsuneari (tr.) Fukuda Hayaru (dir.) [Gendai Engeki Kyôkai Subaru]
	Twelfth Night	Tsubouchi Shôyô (tr.) Takase Toshiko (dir.) [Muruitobikiri]
	Twelfth Night	Odashima Yûshi (tr.) Endô Eizô (dir.) [Itabashi Engeki Centre]
	Hamlet	Richard Eyre (dir.) [Royal National Theatre]
December	*Twelfth Night*	Odashima Yûshi (tr.) Yasudo Yasuko (dir.) [Cosmos]
1990 January	*As You Like It*	Haraguchi Yome (tr.) Ishizaka Kôji (adpt. and dir.) [Ginza Saison Gekijô Production]

Date	Title	Translator/director [Theatre company]
February	*Hamlet*	Fukuda Tsuneari (tr.) Kimura Kôichi (dir.) [Shôchiku Production]
	Broken Hamlet	Uesugi Shôzô (adpt. and dir.) [Uesugi Shôzô Production]
March	*Fortinbras* (an adaptation of *Hamlet*)	Odashima Yûshi (tr.) Yokouchi Kensuke (adpt. and dir.) [Zen'nin Kaigi]
March April	*A Midsummer Night's Dream*	Kenneth Branagh (dir.) [Renaissance Theatre Company]
	King Lear	Kenneth Branagh (dir.) [Renaissance Theatre Company]
March April	*Hamlet*	Yuri Lyubimov (dir.) [Ginza Saison Gekijô Production]
April	*Macbeth*	Odashima Yûshi (tr.) Deguchi Norio (dir.) [Tokyo Globe Theatre Production]
	Moonlight (an adaptation of *A Midsummer Night's Dream*)	Takaizumi Junko (adpt.) Yoshizawa Kôichi (dir.) [YûKikai/Zenjidô Theatre]
	As You Like It	Odashima Yûshi (tr. and dir.) [Tokyo Globe Theatre Production]
	Hamlet	Naitô Hironori (adpt. and dir.) [Minami-Kawachi Banzai Ichiza]
	Romeo and Juliet	Odashima Yûshi (tr.) Shibata Yukihiro (adpt. and dir.) [Takarazuka Kageki-dan]
April May	*The Merchant of Venice*	Anzai Tetsuo (tr. and dir.) [Engeki Shûdan En]
May	*Berôna Watari Katteni Shitateta Shakespeare: Hanagumi Saô-geki Romio to Jurietto* ('A Free adaptation of a Shakespeare Play Which Originally came from Verona: Hanagumi's Shakespeare Play, *Romeo and Juliet*', a Kabuki adaptation of *Romeo and Juliet*)	Kanô Yukikazu (adpt. and dir.) [Hanagumi Shibai] (The Hanagumi Shibai Company is a young theatre company which stages modern Kabuki plays that they call 'neo Kabuki'.)

Date	Title	Translator/director [Theatre company]
	King Lear	Suzuki Tadashi (adpt. and dir.) [with actors from four American theatre companies]
	Hamlet	Watanabe Moriaki (tr. and dir.) [Tokyo Globe Theatre Production]
	Twelfth Night	Odashima Yûshi (tr.) Uyama Hitoshi (dir.) [Bungaku-za]
	Macbeth toiu Na no Otoko ('A Man Named Macbeth')	Kawamura Takeshi (adpt. and dir.) [Daisan Erotica]
	Hamlet no Jikan ('The Time of Hamlet': an opera)	Odashima Yûshi (tr.) Katô Tadashi (adpt. and dir.) Hayashi Hikaru and Hagi Kyôko (composers) [Kon'nyaku-za]
	King Lear	Suzuki Tadashi (adpt. and dir.) [SCOT]
	King Lear	Takatori Ei (adpt.) J.A. Caesar and Peter Stormare (dirs.) [Gekidan Ban'yû Inryoku]
	Ryûzanji Hamlet	Ryûzanji Shô (adpt. and dir.) [Ryûzanji Jimusho]
May June	*Hamlet*	Valerly Belyakovich (dir.) [Moscow Studio Theatre]
June	*The Taming of the Shrew*	Fukuda Tsuneari (tr.) Murata Ganshi and Kaseya Shin'ichi (dirs.) [Gendai Engeki Kyôkai Subaru]
	A Midsummer Night's Dream	Odashima Yûshi (tr.) Deguchi Norio (dir.) [Bunkamura Production]
	Macbeth toiu Na no Otoko	Kawamura Takeshi (adpt. and dir.) [Daisan Erotica]
	Moonlight	Takaizumi Junko (adpt.) Yoshizawa Kôichi (dir.) [YûKikai/Zenjidô Theatre]
	Romeo and Juliet	Odashima Yûshi (tr.) Endô Eizô (dir.) [Itabashi Engeki Centre]

Date	Title	Translator/director [Theatre company]
	A Midsummer Night's Dream	Odashima Yûshi (tr.) Endô Eizô (dir.) [Itabashi Engeki Centre]
July	*Berôna Watari Katteni Shitateta Shakespeare: Hanagumi Saô-geki Romio to Jurietto*	Kanô Yukikazu (adpt. and dir.) [Hanagumi Shibai]
	The Merchant of Venice	Neil Sissons (dir.) [Compass Theatre Company]
	Twelfth Night	Odashima Yûshi (tr.) Kino Hana (dir.) [Sakura Gumi and Katô Ken'ichi Jimusho Joint Production]
	Twelfth Night	Odashima Yûshi (tr.) Uyama Hitoshi (dir.) [Bungaku-za]
	Hamlet	Odashima Yûshi (tr.) Kataoka Takao (dir.) [Shôchiku Production]
	Much Ado About Nothing	Odashima Yûshi (tr.) Kaneko Hiroshi (dir.) [Mujintô]
August	*Noda Hideki no Much Ado About Nothing* ('Noda Hideki's *Much Ado About Nothing*)	Odashima Yûshi (tr.) Noda Hideki (adpt. and dir.) [Tôhô Production]
	Twelfth Night	Dominic Hill (dir.) [Oxford University Dramatic Society]
	A Midsummer Night's Dream	Fujibayashi Noriko and Kosuga Nobuko (adpts.) Fujibayashi Noriko (dir.) [Shakespeare Society]
	Falstaff (an adaptation of *King Henry the Fourth*)	Inoue Masaru (adpt. and dir.) [Fukurô-tô]
	Twelfth Night	Odashima Yûshi (tr.) Andô Suzuharu (adpt. and dir.) [Theatre 2+1]
August September	*Hamlet*	Andrzej Wajda (dir.) [Stary Theatre]
September	*King Lear*	Deborah Warner (dir.) [Royal National Theatre]
	King Richard the Third	Richard Eyre (dir.) [Royal National Theatre]

Date	Title	Translator/director [Theatre company]
	The Comedy of Errors	Odashima Yûshi (tr.) Deguchi Norio (dir.) [Shakespeare Theatre]
	The Taming of the Shrew (a Kyogen adaptation)	Miake Tôkurô and Izumi Motohide (adpts.) Izumi Motohide (dir.) [Izumi Sôke]
September October	*Hamlet*	Declan Donnellan (dir.) [Cheek by Jowl]
October	*The Winter's Tale*	Michael Bogdanov (dir.) [English Shakespeare Company]
	Coriolanus	Michael Bogdanov (dir.) [English Shakespeare Company]
	Hamlet	Odashima Yûshi (tr.) Miyagi Satoshi (dir.) [Miyagi Satoshi Production]
	Lady Macbeth (one-woman-play)	Odashima Yûshi (tr.) Isoda Aki (dir.)
	Heisei Rocky Hamlet	Takabayashi Kôhei (adpt. and dir.) [Heisei Gan'nen]
	The Merchant of Venice	Odashima Yûshi (tr.) Glen Walford (dir.) [Rhyming]
	Twelfth Night	Tsuchiya Sumie (adpt.) Suzuki Nobui (dir.) [Saisan Saishi]
	The Tragedy of Hamlet, Prince of Denmark	Hirota Hyô (adpt. and dir.) [Tenkano Tochigi-ya]
October December	*Sandaime Richard* ('Richard the Third')	Noda Hideki (adpt. and dir.) [Yume no Yûminsha]
November	*King Lear*	Odashima Yûshi (tr.) Nobuse Akira (adpt.) [Yasôkai]
	Macbeth	Odashima Yûshi (tr.) Satô Makoto (dir.) [Yûki-za]
	Chikyû Saizu no Hamlet ('*Hamlet* in the Size of the Globe')	Itô Yumiko (adpt. and dir.) [Ribureisen]
	A Midsummer Night's Dream	Lindsay Kemp (dir.) [Lindsay Kemp Company]
	Macbeth	Nakajima Jun'ichi (adpt. and dir.) [Nakajima Jun'ichi One-Man Play]

Date	Title	Translator/director [Theatre company]
	Othello	D. Chapman (dir.) [London Stage Company]
	The Taming of the Shrew (a Kyogen adaptation)	Miake Tôkurô and Izumi Motohide (adpts.) Izumi Motohide (dir.) [Izumi Sôke]
November December	Hamletmachine	Heiner Müller (adpt.) Federico Tiezzi (dir.) [I Magazzini]
December	The Taming of the Shrew (a Kyogen adaptation)	Miake Tôkurô and Izumi Motohide (adpts.) Izumi Motohide (dir.) [Izumi Sôke]
1991 January	Twelfth night	Odashima Yûshi (tr.) Endô Eizô (dir.) [Itabashi Engeki Centre]
	Macbeth: Sôshitsu no Yôshiki wo Megutte II: ('Macbeth: On the Style of Loss II')	Suzuki Tadashi (adpt. and dir.) [ACM: Acting Company of Mito]
	Romeo and Juliet	Shibata Yukihiro (adpt. and dir.) [Takarazuka Kageki-dan]
	The Taming of the Shrew (a Kyogen adaptation)	Miake Tôkurô and Izumi Motohide (adpts.) Izumi Motohide (dir.) [Izumi Sôke]
February	The Taming of the Shrew	Bill Alexander (dir.) [Royal Shakespeare Company]
	A Midsummer Night's Dream	Chinen Masafumi (adpt. and dir.) [Gekidan Chôjûgiga]
March	Troilus and Cressida	Eric Da Silva (dir.) [Emballage Theatre]
	A Midsummer Night's Dream	Suzuki Tadashi (adpt. and dir.) [ACM: Acting Company of Mito]
	The Merchant of Venice	Tim Luscombe (dir.) [English Shakespeare Company]
	Heisei Mad Macbeth	Takabayashi Kôhei (adpt. and dir.) [Heisei Gan'nen]
	The Winter's Tale	Kosuga Nobuko (tr. and dir.) [Shakespeare Society]

Date	Title	Translator/director [Theatre company]
March April	*La Tempête* ('*The Tempest*')	Jean-Claude Carrière (adpt.) Peter Brook (dir.) [Ginza Saison Gekijô Production]
April	*Othello* (an adaptation first performed by Kawakami Otojirô's company in 1903.)	Emi Suiin (adpt.) Ishizawa Shûji (dir.) [Seinen-za]
April May	*King Lear*	Odashima Yûshi (tr.) Ninagawa Yukio (dir.) [Point Tokyo Production]
May	*Hora Zamurai* ('Braggart Samurai or Falstaff': a Kyogen adaptation of *The Merry Wives of Windsor*)	Takahashi Yasunari (adpt.) Nomura Mansaku (dir.) [Mansaku no Kai]
	Hamlet	Odashima Yûshi (tr.) Itô Baku (adpt. and dir.) [Group Shizen]
	Measure for Measure	Neil Sissons (dir.) [Compass Theatre Company]
	Pericles	Odashima Yûshi (tr.) Takase Hisao (dir.) [Shakespeare Theatre]
	Jikken Ongaku Geki: Ria Ô ('An Experimental Musical Play: *King Lear*')	Tsubouchi Shôyô (tr.) J.A. Caesar (adpt. and dir.) [Ban'yû Inryoku]
	Twelfth Night	Komoda Naganori (adpt.) Gamagôri Heisuke (dir.) [Third Quarter]
	Hamlet no tameno Tokubetsu-seki ('A Special Seat for Hamlet')	Takubo Issei (adpt. and dir.) [Za Cupid Magic]
May June	*The Wars of the Roses*	Abe Ryô (adpt. and dir.) [Sakura Kai]
May June	*A Midsummer Night's Dream*	Fukuda Tsuneari (tr.) Kikuchi Jun (dir.) [Gendai Engeki Kyôkai Subaru]
June	*Hamuretto Yamato Nishikie* ('Japanese Coloured Woodblock Prints of *Hamlet*': This is the first performance of Robun's Kabuki adaptation of *Hamlet*, which was written in 1886.)	Kanagaki Robun (adpt.) Kawatake Toshio (supervisor) Oda Kôji (adpt. and dir.) [Shôchiku and Tokyo Globe Joint Production]
	A Midsummer Night's Dream	Katô Tadashi (adpt. and dir.) [Bunkamura Production]
	The Taming of the Shrew (a Kyogen adaptation)	Miake Tôkurô and Izumi Motohide (adpts.) Izumi Motohide (dir.) [Izumi Sôke]

Date	Title	Translator/director [Theatre company]
	Blindman's Bluff (a Kyogen adaptation of a scene from *King Lear* in English)	Don Kenny (adpt. and dir.) [Kenny and Ogawa Kyôgen Players]
	A Midsummer Night's Dream (a Kyogen adaptation in English)	Don Kenny (adpt. and dir.) [Kenny and Ogawa Kyôgen Players]
July	*The Merchant of Venice: Yokozawa's Version*	Odashima Yûshi (tr.) Taniguchi Shûichi (adpt.) Yokozawa Takashi (dir.) [Ginza Saison Gekijô Production]
	A Midsummer Night's Dream	Ôhashi Hiroshi (adpt. and dir.) [Proto Theatre]
	Heisei Rocky Hamlet	Takabayashi Kôhei (adpt. and dir.) [Heisei Gan'nen]
July August	*A Musical: A Midsummer Night's Dream*	Moriizumi Hiroyuki (adpt. and dir.) [Kiyama Jimusho]
July August	*Twelfth Night by Women* (in this production, all the roles were played by actresses)	Odashima Yûshi (tr.) Uyama Hitoshi (dir.) [Sunshine Gekijô Production]
August	*The Complete Works of Shakespeare*	[Reduced Shakespeare Company]
	Shakespeare dayo Zen'in Shûgô ('It's Shakespeare. Gather around Here!')	Kurai Hajime (adpt. and dir.) [WAHAHA Hompo]
	Ryûzanji Macbeth	Ryûzanji Shô (adpt. and dir.) [Ryûzanji Jimusho]
	Heisei Mad Macbeth	Takabayashi Kôhei (adpt. and dir.) [Heisei Gan'nen]
	Hora Zamurai	Takahashi Yasunari (adpt.) Nomura Mansaku (dir.) [Maṇsaku no Kai]
	Jikken Ongaku Geki: Ria Ô	Tsubouchi Shôyô (tr.) J.A. Caesar (dir.) [Ban'yû Inryoku]
	Noh Hamlet	Munakata Kuniyoshi (adpt. and dir.) [Noh Shakespeare Kenkyû-kai]
	A Love Letter (a Kyogen adaptation of *Twelfth Night* in English)	Arai Yoshio (adpt. and supervisor) [Izumi Sôke]

Date	Title	Translator/director [Theatre company]
	The Lovesick Man in Yellow (adaptation of *Twelfth Night* in English)	Arai Yoshio (adpt. and supervisor) Izumi Motohide (supervisor Kyogen acting) [Izumi Sôke]
	The Taming of the Shrew (a Kyogen adaptation)	Izumi Motohide (adpt. , dir. and supervisor) [Izumi Sôke]
	A Midsummer Night's Dream (a Kyogen adaptation)	Izumi Motohide (adpt. , dir. and supervisor) [Izumi Sôke]
	Twelfth Night (*Kiiroi Koi*) ('The Lovesick Man in Yellow': a Kyogen adaptation)	Izumi Motohide (adpt. , dir. and supervisor) [Izumi Sôke]
	Heimen no Hamlet ('*Hamlet* on a Flat Level')	Suganuma Naohiro (adpt. and dir.) [Loft and Theatre]
September	*Shirohige no Lear* ('Lear with White Beard')	Suzuki Kenji (adpt. and dir.) [Tao]
	Julius Caesar	Anzai Tetsuo (tr. and dir.) [Engeki Shûdan En]
	A Midsummer Night's Dream	Odashima Yûshi (tr.) Takamori Hideyuki and Harada Yoshinori (dirs.) [Quixote]
	Twelfth Night *Hamlet no Jikan* ('The Time of Hamlet') (opera adaptations)	Odashima Yûshi (tr.) Katô Tadashi (librettist and dir.) Hayashi Hikaru and Hagi Kyôko (composers) [Kon'nyaku-za]
	2022nen no Lear ('*Lear* in 2022')	Harada Hirofumi (adpt. and dir.) [Shishi-za]
	The Two Ladies of Verona (an adaptation of *The Two Gentlemen of Verona*)	Tsubouchi Shôyô (tr.) Edo Kaoru (adpt. and dir.) [Edo Yashiki Production]
September October	*The Winter's Tale*	Odashima Yûshi (tr.) Deguchi Norio (dir.) [Shakespeare Theatre]
October	*Lady Macbeth*	Hanayagi Toshisayuki (adpt.) [Toshisayuki no Kai]
	Arigachina Hanashi: Uwasano Juliet Hen ('The Same Old Story: The Rumour of Juliet'; an adaptation of *Romeo and Juliet*)	Odashima Yûshi (tr.) Iijima Sanae (adpt.) Suzuki Yumi (dir.) [Jitensha Kinqureat]
	The Tempest	John Retallack (dir.) [Oxford Stage Company]

Date	Title	Translator/director [Theatre company]
	As You Like It	Odashima Yûshi (tr.) Glen Walford (dir.) [Rhyming]
	A Midsummer Night's Dream	Lindsay Kemp (dir.) [Lindsay Kemp Company]
	A Midsummer Night's Dream	Odashima Yûshi (tr.) Takemura Rui (dir.) [Super Company]
	Macbeth	Fukuda Tsuneari (tr.) Hashimoto Izumi (adpt. and dir.) [Hashimoto Izumi Production]
	I Am Portia.	Odashima Yûshi (tr.) Suzuki Masamitsu (adpt. and dir.) [Tochinomi]
	The Two Gentlemen of Verona	Odashima Yûshi (tr.) Deguchi Norio (dir.) [Tokyo Globe Company]
	Pericles	Odashima Yûshi (tr.) Deguchi Norio (dir.) [Tokyo Globe Company]
	The Taming of the Shrew (a Kyogen adaptation)	Izumi Motohide (adpt. , dir and supervisor) [Izumi Sôke]
	A Midsummer Night's Dream (a Kyogen adaptation)	Izumi Motohide (adpt. , dir. and supervisor) [Izumi Sôke]
	Twelfth Night: Kiiroi Koi	Izumi Motohide (adpt. , dir. and supervisor) [Izumi Sôke]
November	*Macbeth*	Kinoshita Junji (tr.) Kanze Hideo (dir.) [Dengei Kikaku]
November December	*Heisei Othello*	Takabayashi Kôhei (adpt. and dir.) [Heisei Gan'nen]
December	*Antony and Cleopatra*	Odashima Yûshi (tr.) Nishikawa Nobuhiro (dir.) [Tokyo Globe Company]
	Julius Caesar	Odashima Yûshi (tr.) Nishikawa Nobuhiro (dir.) [Tokyo Globe Company]
	Broken Romeo and Juliet	Uesugi Shôzô (adpt. and dir.) [Uesugi Shôzô and Tokyo Globe Company Joint Production]

Date	Title	Translator/director [Theatre company]
	Puck (an adaptation of *A Midsummer Night's Dream*)	Misaki Tetsuya (adpt. and dir.) [Yokohama Pîtoru Carnival]
	Feste no Okurimono ('A Present from Feste': an adaptation of *Twelfth Night*)	Amaizumi Orie (adpt.) Gonda Kiyoshi (dir.) [Shakespeare Society]
	The Winter's Tale	Okuhara Katsuo (adpt. and dir.) [Okuhara Katsuo Jimusho]
	A Midsummer Night's Dream	Chûjô Yasuomi (dir.) [Ano]
1992 January	*As You Like It*	Declan Donnellan (dir.) [Cheek by Jowl]
	Othello	Kinoshita Junji (tr.) Fukuda Yoshiyuki (dir.) [Yûki-za]
	As You Like It	Odashima Yûshi (tr.) Endô Eizô (dir.) [Itabashi Engeki Centre]
	Hora Zamurai	Takahashi Yasunari (adpt.) Nomura Mansaku (dir.) [Mansaku no Kai]
February	*I Am Portia*	Odashima Yûshi (tr.) Suzuki Masamitsu (adpt. and dir.) [Tochinomi]
	Tempesuto Arashi Nochi Hare ('The Tempest: Stormy, and Later Fair': a Bunraku adaptation of *The Tempest*)	Tsubouchi Shôyô (tr.) Yamada Shôichi (adpt. and dir.) Tsurusawa Seiji (composer) [Committee of *Bunraku Tempest* Production]
	The Tempest	Odashima Yûshi (tr.) Okabe Haruka (dir.) [Errors]
March	*Broken Hamlet*	Uesugi Shôzô (adpt. and dir.) [Uesugi Shôzô Production]
	Twelfth Night	Michael Pennington (dir.) [English Shakespeare Company]
	Macbeth	Michael Bogdanov (dir.) [English Shakespeare Company]
	A Midsummer Night's Dream	Odashima Yûshi (tr.) Takagi Tôru (dir.) [Seinen-za]

Date	Title	Translator/director [Theatre company]
April	King Lear	Suzuki Tadashi (adpt. and dir.) [SCOT]
	King Lear	Kinoshita Junji (tr.) Yonekura Masakane (dir.) [Gekidan Mingei]
	The Taming of the Shrew	Odashima Yûshi (tr.) Deguchi Norio (dir.) [Shakespeare Theatre]
	Much Ado About Nothing	Odashima Yûshi (tr.) Deguchi Norio (dir.) [Shakespeare Theatre]
	The Winter's Tale	Odashima Yûshi (tr.) Kawasaki Hiroyuki (adpt. and dir.) [Ryûsei Butai]
	Twelfth Night	Odashima Yûshi (tr.) Takubo Issei (dir.) [Za Cupid Magic]
May	Titus Andronicus	Silviu Pucarete (dir.) [National Theatre of Craiova, Romania]
	Picaresque Iago (an adaptation of Othello)	Nakajima Takehiro (adpt.) Ryûzanji Shô (dir.) [Ryûzanji Jimusho]
	The Comedy of Errors	Odashima Yûshi (tr.) Deguchi Norio (dir.) [Shakespeare Theatre]
	Macbeth toiu Na No Otoko	Kawamura Takeshi (adpt. and dir.) [Daisan Erotica]
	Macbeth	Suzuki Tadashi (adpt. and dir.) [Playbox Theatre, Australia]
	A Midsummer Night's Dream	Iida Tetsuya (dir.) [Shakespeare Drama Society]
	Heisei Hamlet of Hamlets	Takabayashi Kôhei (adpt. and dir.) [Heisei Gan'nen]
June	Hamlet	Fukuda Tsuneari (tr.) Fukuda Hayaru (dir.) [Gendai Engeki Kyôkai Subaru]
	A Midsummer Night's Dream	Takahashi Yasunari (tr.) Ulla Åberg (adpt.) Peter Stormare (dir.) [Globe Theatre Company]

Date	Title	Translator/director [Theatre company]
	Romeo and Juliet	Odashima Yûshi (tr.) Nishikawa Nobuhiro (dir.) [Globe Theatre Company]
	A Midsummer Night's Dream: A Shakespeare Play Performed in the Manner of Balinese Mystery Play	Endô Tatsurô (adpt. and dir.) [Bunkamura Production]
	Kanadehon Hamlet (This play depicts the attempts that Kabuki actors in the Meiji era might have made to stage *Hamlet* for the first time in Japan.)	Tsutsumi Harue (playwright) Sueki Toshifumi (dir.) [Kiyama Jimusho]
July	*Hamlet King Lear*	Neil Sissons (dir.) [Compass Theatre Company]
	Puck	Koike Shûichirô (adpt. and dir.) [Takarazuka Kageki-dan]
	A Midsummer Night's Dream, 2: A Dream of A Midsummer Night's Dream	Ôhashi Hiroshi (adpt. and dir.) [Proto Theatre]
August	*Noda Hideki no A Midsummer Night's Dream* ('Noda Hideki's *A Midsummer Night's Dream*')	Odashima Yûshi (tr.) Noda Hideki (adpt. and dir.) [Nissei Gekijô Production]
	King Lear	Fukuda Tsuneari (tr.) Kosuga Hayato (dir.) [Shakespeare Society]
	Twelfth Night	Okuhara Katsuo (tr. and dir.) [Okuhara Katsuo Jimusho]
	A Midsummer Night's Dream	Odashima Yûshi (tr.) Ôtani Ryôsuke (adpt. and dir.) [Tokyo Ichigumi]
September	*Titus Andronicus*	Odashima Yûshi (tr.) Ron Daniels (dir.) [Ginza Saison Gekijô Production]
	Hamletmachine	Heiner Müller(adpt.) Iwabuchi Tatsuji and Tanikawa Michio (trs.) Joseph Sailer (dir.) [Tokyo Engeki Ensemble]
	Hamlet	Odashima Yûshi (tr.) Hirowatari Tsunetoshi (dir.) [Tokyo Engeki Ensemble]
	Broken Macbeth	Uesugi Shôzô (adpt. and dir.) [Uesugi Shôzô Production with Globe Theatre Company]

Date	Title	Translator/director [Theatre company]
September	Hamlet	Odashima Yûshi (tr.) Kadota Kimio (dir.) [Rôze no Kai]
October	Macbeth	Odashima Yûshi (tr.) Endô Eizô (dir.) [Itabashi Engeki Centre]
	King Lear	Kinoshita Junji (tr.) Yonekura Masakane (dir.) [Gekidan Mingei]
	As You Like It	Odashima Yûshi (tr.) Glen Walford (dir.) [Rhyming]
	Aoi Tori no Hamlet ('Aoi Tori's Hamlet)	Odashima Yûshi (tr.) Serikawa Ai (dir.) [Aoi Tori]
	Macbeth	Euan Smith (dir.) [Watermill Theatre Company]
	King Lear	Takabayashi Kôhei (adpt. and dir.) [Heisei Gan'nen]
	Hamlet no Jikan (an opera adaptation)	Odashima Yûshi (tr.) Katô Tadashi (dir.) Hayashi Hikaru and Hagi Kyôko (composers) [Kon'nyaku-za]
	King Richard the Third	Kawasaki Hiroyuki (adpt. and dir.) [Ryûsei Butai]
November	Twelfth Night	Anzai Tetsuo (tr. and dir.) [Globe Theatre Company and Engeki Shûdan En]
	Much Ado About Nothing	Alexandru Darie (dir.) [Oxford Stage Company]
	Hamlet	Takahashi Yasunari (tr.) Ulla Åberg (adpt.) Peter Stormare (dir.) [Globe Theatre Company]
December	The Merry Wives of Windsor	Anzai Tetsuo (tr. and dir.) [Globe Theatre Company]
December January	Hamlet Dream	Takatsu Sumio (adpt. and dir.) [Kikansha]
1993 January	King Lear	Odashima Yûshi (tr.) Jiles Block (dir.) [Ginza Saison Gekijô and Shôchiku Joint Production]

Date	Title	Translator/director [Theatre company]
	Much Ado About Nothing	Odashima Yûshi (tr.) Endô Eizô (dir.) [Itabashi Engeki Centre]
	Broken Hamlet '93	Uesugi Shôzô (adpt. and dir.) [Uesugi Shôzô Production with Globe Theatre Company]
	Twelfth Night	Ozu Jirô (tr.) Gonda Kiyoshi (dir.) [Shakespeare Society]
February	King Richard the Third	Sam Mendes (dir.) [Royal Shakespeare Company]
	Macbeth	Inoue Takuhisa (adpt. and dir.) [Serious Barbarian]
March	A Midsummer Night's Dream	Odashima Yûshi (tr.) Itô Shirô (dir.) [Hitomi-za]
	Helena and Hermia (an adaptation of A Midsummer Night's Dream)	Ikuta Yorozu and Katagiri Hairi (adpts.) Ikuta Yorozu (dir.) [Buriki no Jihatsu-dan]
	Titus no Nikuya ('Titus, a Butcher') (an adaptation of Titus Andronicus)	Kawamura Takeshi (adpt. and dir.) [Daisan Erotica]
	Ai toiu Na no Byôki ('Sickness Called Love': an adaptation of Twelfth Night)	Odashima Yûshi (tr.) Tamura Ren (adpt. and dir.) [Super Company]
	A Midsummer Night's Dream	Odashima Yûshi (tr.) Hirowatari Tsunetoshi (dir.) [Tokyo Engeki Ensemble]
	The Merchant of Venice vs. The Merchant of Osaka	Odashima Yûshi (tr.) Takubo Issei (adpt. and dir.) [Za Cupid Magic]
	Berôna Hensôkyoku ('Verona Variation': an adaptation of The Two Gentlemen of Verona)	Chûjô Masao (adpt. and dir.) [Shin-Geijutsu]
	Sawada Kenji ACT Shakespeare	Katô Tadashi (adpt. and dir.) [Kokoro]
April	The Tempest	Michael Bogdanov (dir.) [English Shakespeare Company]
	Hamlet	Odashima Yûshi (tr.) Satô Makoto (dir.) [Theatre Cocoon Production]

Date	Title	Translator/director [Theatre company]
	The Merchant of Venice	Motohashi Tetsuya and Motohashi Tamaki (trs.) Gerald Murphy (dir.) [Globe Theatre Company]
	Gensô no Romeo to Juliet ('A Vision of Romeo and Juliet')	Uriu Masami (adpt.) Nakano Chiharu (dir.) [Seinen Gekijô]
May	King Lear	Odashima Yûshi (tr.) Endô Eizô (dir.) [Itabashi Engeki Centre]
	Buriki no Machi no Natsu no Yo no Yume ('A Midsummer Night's Dream in a Tinny Town')	Ikuta Yorozu (adpt. and dir.) [Buriki no Jihatsu-dan]
	A Midsummer Night's Dream	Odashima Yûshi (tr.) Deguchi Norio (dir.) [Shakespeare Theatre]
	King Richard the Third	Odashima Yûshi (tr.) Fukuda Yoshiyuki (dir.) [Ito-Ayatsuri Ningyô Yûki-za]
	The Comedy of Errors	Odashima Yûshi (tr.) Deguchi Norio (dir.) [Shakespeare Theatre]
June	As You Like It	Fukuda Tsuneari (tr.) Richard White and Christin Sampsion (dirs.) [Gendai Engeki Kyôkai Subaru]
	A Midsummer Night's Dream	Odashima Yûshi (tr.) Hayashi Makiko (adpt. and dir.) [Romantica]
July	Gansaku: Venice no Shônin ('Fake: The Merchant of Venice')	Nakajima Atsuhiko (adpt. and dir.) [Honky-Tonk Theatre]
	A Midsummer Night's Dream	Gotô Shôin (adpt. and dir.) [Mugen Hôyô]
	Hamlet no Hitorigoto ('Hamlet's Soliloquy')	Kawasaki Hiroyuki (adpt. and dir.) [Kawasaki Hiroyuki Recital Theatre]
	A Midsummer Night's Dream	Yoneuchiyama Akihiro (adpt.) Yoneuchiyama Akihiro and Shôzaki Takashi (dirs.) [Deaf Puppet Theatre and Hitomo-za Joint Production]

Date	Title	Translator/director [Theatre company]
	Okini Mesumama Jajauma Naraseba ('If You Tame the Shrew as You Like': an adaptation of *The Taming of the Shrew*)	Katsura Yumiko (adpt. and dir.) [Shinra Banshô]
	Horatio no Yûutsu: Hamlet ('Horatio's Melancholy: *Hamlet* ')	Takabayashi Kôhei (adpt. and dir.) [Heisei Gan'nen]
	A Midsummer Night's Dream	Takahashi Yasunari (tr.) Ulla Åberg(adpt.) Peter Stormare (dir.) [Globe Theatre Company]
	A Midsummer Night's Dream, 3: Hadakano Yume ('Naked Dream')	Ôhashi Hiroshi (adpt. and dir.) [Proto Theatre]
	A Midsummer Night's Dream	Mito Yagaigeki Jôen Iinkai ('Mito Open-air Production Committee': adpt. and dir.) [Mito Geijutsu-kan]
	Lady Macbeth	Ikkai Kazuaki (adpt. and dir.) [Off Off Tokyo]
July August	*Romeo and Juliet* (In this production, the Montagues are played by Russian actors in Russian and the Capulets are played by Japanese actors in Japanese.)	Tsuzuka Yuriko (tr.) Valerly Belyakovich (dir.) [Tôen and Yugo-Zapade Theatre (Russia) Joint Production]
August	*A Midsummer Night's Dream*	Odashima Yûshi (tr.) Fujimori Ichirô (dir.) [Muraku-za]
	A Midsummer Night's Dream	Lindsay Kemp (adpt. and dir.) [Lindsay Kemp Company]
	A Midsummer Night's Dream	Komura Tetsuo (adpt. and dir.) [Yume-makura]
	A Midsummer Night's Dream	Kojima Nobuko (adpt. and dir.) [Shakespeare Society]
	Twelfth Night	Harold Sugawara (adpt. and dir.) [Garancho Brothers]
	King John	Odashima Yûshi (tr.) Deguchi Norio (dir.) [Shakespeare Theatre]
	Juliet: Sekaino Hate kara Konnichiwa 3 ('Waiting for Juliet: Greetings from the End of the World, 3')	Odashima Yûshi (tr.) Suzuki Tadashi (adpt. and dir.) [SCOT]

Date	Title	Translator/director [Theatre company]
	King Richard the Third	Mikami Isao (tr.) Ryû Tomoe (dir.) [Mumei-juku]
September	*King Henry the Eighth*	Odashima Yûshi (tr.) Deguchi Norio (dir.) [Shakespeare Theatre]
	2022nen no Lear	Harada Hirofumi (adpt. and dir.) [Shishi-za]
	Cymbeline	Neil Sissons (dir.) [Compass Theatre Company]
	Twelfth Night	Hirota Hyô (adpt. and dir.) [Tenkano Tochigi-ya]
	Ninagawa Tempest	Odashima Yûshi (tr.) Ninagawa Yukio (dir.) [Kawaguchi Riria Hall Production]
	Twelfth Night	Mikami Isao (tr.) Michael Pennington (dir.) [Haiyû-za]
	Koibitotachi ('Lovers': an adaptation of *A Midsummer Night's Dream*)	Abe Ryô (adpt. and dir.) [Abe Ryô and Jean Jean Joint Production]
October	*Hamlet*	Fukuda Tsuneari (tr.) Asari Keita (dir.) [Gekidan Shiki]
	The Comedy of Errors	Odashima Yûshi (tr.) Deguchi Norio (dir.) [Shakespeare Theatre]
	Pericles	John Retallack (dir.) [Oxford Stage Company]
	The Comedy of Errors	John Retallack (dir.) [Oxford Stage Company]
	Twelfth Night	Nonaka Shigi (adpt. and dir.) [Shibaigoya Edo Yashiki]
	Shirohige no Lear	Suzuki Kenji (adpt. and dir.) [Tao]
	Hamlet	Kawasaki Hiroyuki (adpt. and dir.) [Ryûsei Butai]
November	*Macbeth*	Michel Garneau (tr.) Robert Lepage (dir.) [Théâtre Repère / Le Maège]
	La Tempête	Michel Garneau (tr.) Robert Lepage (dir.) [Théâtre Repère / Le Maège]

Date	Title	Translator/director [Theatre company]
	Coriolan	Michel Garneau (tr.) Robert Lepage (dir.) [Théâtre Repère / Le Maège]
	Rock Opera Hamlet	Matsumoto Kazuki (adpt.) Satô Hirofumi(dir.) [Nakano Sun Plaza Production]
	King Lear	Leck Mackiewicz (dir.) [Playbox Theatre]
	King Richard the Third	Mikami Isao (tr.) Ryû Tomoe (dir.) [Mumei-juku]
	Twelfth Night	Kino Hana (adpt. and dir.) [Kino Hana Drama Studio]
December	Macbeth	Mori Ôgai (tr.) Robert Lepage (dir.) [Globe Theatre Company]
	The Tempest	Takahashi Yasunari (tr.) Robert Lepage (dir.) [Globe Theatre Company]
	Twelfth Night by Women	Odashima Yûshi (tr.) Uyama Hitoshi (dir.) [Sunshine Gekijô Production]
	Macbeth	Kinoshita Junji (tr.) Kanze Hideo (adpt. and dir.) [Mu no Kai]
	A Midsummer Night's Dream in Christmas	Odashima Yûshi (tr.) Takamori Hideyuki (dir.) [Quixote]
	The Merchant of Venice	Okuhara Katsuo (tr. and dir.) [Okuhara Katsuo Jimusho]
December January	Hanagumi Saô-geki Tempest: Tempesuto Arashi Nochi Hare (Originally a Bunraku adaptation of The Tempest, first performed in February, 1992, but re-adapted by the director for this Kabuki-style production.)	Tsubouchi Shôyô (tr.) Yamada Shôichi (adpt.) Tsurusawa Seiji (composer) Kanô Yukikazu (dir.) [Hanagumi Shibai]
1994 January	The Merchant of Venice	Odashima Yûshi (tr.) Endô Eizô (dir.) [Itabashi Engeki Centre]
	Juliet, According to Prokofiev: Sôshitsuno Yoshiki wo Megutte ('On the Style of Loss')	Odashima Yûshi (tr.) Suzuki Tadashi (adpt. and dir.) [SCOT with Mito Geijutsu-kan]

Date	Title	Translator/director [Theatre company]
	Troilus and Cressida	Jatinder Verma (dir.) [Tara Arts]
February	The Winter's Tale	Odashima Yûshi (tr.) Deguchi Norio (dir.) [Shakespeare Theatre in association with the Panasonic Globe Theatre]
	Julius Caesar	David Thacker (dir.) [Royal Shakespeare Company]
	The Tempest	Odashima Yûshi (tr.) Satô Makoto (dir.) [Yûki-za]
	The Winter's Tale (in Romanian)	Alexandru Darie (dir.) [Teatrul Bulandra (Romania)]
	Measure for Measure	Declan Donnellan (dir.) [Cheek by Jowl]
March April	The Winter's Tale	Adrian Noble (dir.) [Royal Shakespeare Company]
April	The Comedy of Errors	Matsuoka Kazuko (tr.) Peter Stormare (dir.) [Globe Theatre Company]
	Hora Zamurai–A Kyôgen Falstaff: The Braggart Samurai	Takahashi Yasunari (adpt.) Nomura Mansaku (dir.) [Mansaku no Kai]
	Acharaka Shônin ('Showy and Farcical Merchants': an adaptation of The Merchant of Venice]	Yamamoto Kiyokazu (adpt.) Katô Tadashi (dir.) [Kuro Tent]
	Romeo and Juliet	Michael Bogdanov (dir.) [English Shakespeare Company]
May	The Merchant of Venice	Odashima Yûshi (tr.) Glen Walford (dir.) [Sunshine Gekijô Production]
	A Midsummer Night's Dream	Matsuoka Kazuko (tr.) Kushida Kazuyoshi (dir.) [Theatre Cocoon Production]
	Akkan Richard ('Richard the Villain': an adaptation of King Richard the Third)	Odashima Yûshi (tr.) Yamamoto Kiyokazu (adpt.) Ryûzanji Shô (dir.) [Ryûzanji Jimusho]
June	As You Like It	Motohashi Tetsuya and Motohashi Tamaki (trs.) Gerald Murphy (dir.) [Globe Theatre Company]

Date	Title	Translator/director [Theatre company]
	A Midsummer Night's Dream	Odashima Yûshi (tr.) Ninagawa Yukio (dir.) [T.P.T.(Theatre Project Tokyo)]
	As You Like It: A Musical Play	Fukuda Tsuneari (tr.) Kikuchi Jun (dir.) [Shôchiku Production]
July	*Kanadehon Hamlet*	Tsutsumi Harue (playwright) Sueki Toshifumi (dir.) [Kiyama Jimusho]
August	*Hamlet*	J. A. Caesar (adpt. and dir.) [Ban'yû Inryoku]
	Hamlet (With this production, Hira Mikijirô began his project of performing the protagonists of all the Shakespeare plays.)	Odashima Yûshi (tr.) Ron Daniels (dir.) [Globe Theatre Company in association with Hira/Globe 37 Production]
	Kyôso Richard ('Richard, the Founder of Religion': an adaptation of *King Richard the Third*)	Takabayashi Kôhei (adpt. and dir.) [Heisei Gan'nen]
September	*Othello* (The title role was played by a Kabuki actor, Matsumoto Kôshirô .)	Odashima Yûshi (tr.) Ninagawa Yukio (dir.) [Shôchiku Production]
	Richard the Third: Roses, a Fool and the Crown	Dômoto Masaki (adpt.) Mizuta Haruyasu (dir.) [Théâtre Écho]
	A Midsummer Night's Dream (Deguchi's three different directorial versions of *A Midsummer Night's Dream* were staged: 'School Version', 'Mask Version' and 'Bar Version'.)	Odashima Yûshi (tr.) Deguchi Norio (dir.) [Shakespeare Theatre]
	King Richard the Second	Fukuda Tsuneari (tr.) Murata Ganshi (dir.) [Gendai Engeki Kyôkai Subaru]
October	*A Tale of Lear*	Odashima Yûshi (tr.) Suzuki Tadashi (dir.) [SCOT]
November	*Lady Macbeth*	Odashima Yûshi (tr.) Azuma Tadashi (adpt. and dir.) [Isoda Aki Jimusho]
	Macbeth	Odashima Yûshi (tr.) Glen Walford (dir.) [Rhyming]

Date	Title	Translator/director [Theatre company]
	Romeo and Juliet	John Retallack (dir.) [Oxford Stage Company]
	Romeo and Juliet	Matsuoka Kazuko (tr.) John Retallack (dir.) [Globe Shakespeare Company]
	(John Retallack directed Japanese actors and British actors respectively in these productions of *Romeo and Juliet*.)	
December	*The Winter's Tale*	Okuhara Katsuo(tr. and dir.) [Okuhara Katsuo Jimusho]

Notes

NOTES TO CHAPTER I

1. From the Message at the close of UK90 sent by Sir John Whitehead, the British ambassador, to British Embassy and British Council staff.
2. For further information, see Ryuta Minami's chronology of performances printed in this book, pp. 257–331.
3. Sir Peter Parker, writing in the Official Programme of the Festival, p. 3.
4. Kenneth Rea, review of Banyu Inryoku's *King Lear*, *Japan Digest*, 2, 3 (Jan. 1992).
5. Sir Richard Eyre, in the programme for the Grand Kabuki at the Royal National Theatre.
6. For more detailed discussion of Robert Wilson's debt to Japanese theatre, see Christel Weiler, 'Japanese Traces in Robert Wilson's Productions', in Patrice Pavis, ed., *The Intercultural Performance Reader* (London and New York: Routledge, 1996), pp. 105–13.
7. I owe these points to Takashi Sasayama.
8. The production was designed by Vicki Mortimer.
9. Richard Schechner, 'Interculturalism and the Culture of Choice' in Pavis, ed., *Intercultural Performance Reader*, p. 45.

NOTES TO CHAPTER 2

1. Hideki Noda, *Mawashi wo shimeta Shakespeare* (Tokyo: Shinchosha, 1994). *Mawashi* is a sumo wrestler's belly band, which is folded, looped over the groin, and wrapped tightly around the waist.
2. Hisashi Inoue, *Tempo Juninen no Shakespeare* (Tokyo: Shinchosha, 1973), p. 7.
3. Shuichi Kato, *Zasshu Bunka* [A Hybrid Culture] (Tokyo: Kodansha, 1974).
4. SCOT: Suzuki Company of Toga.
5. *The Asahi*, 15 October 1973.
6. 'A Table Talk with Trevor Nunn', *The Asahi*, 23 January 1970.
7. 'Shakespeare – The Directors' Age', in *Gekijo Geijutsu* (Theatre Arts), 4 (May 1989). A conversation between Yukio Ninagawa and Kazuko Matsuoka.
8. 'Shakespeare – The Director's Age'.
9. Yukio Ninagawa, *Sen-no Naifu, Sen-no Me* [A Thousand Knives, A Thousand Eyes] (Tokyo: Kinokuniya Shoten, 1993), p. 107.
10. *Sen-no Naifu*, p. 107.
11. Motojiro Kajii, *Sakura no Ki no shitani wa* [Under a Cherry Tree] (1928).

12. Tamotsu Watanabe, *Sembon Zakura – Hana no Nai Shinwa* [A Thousand Cherry Trees: A Myth without Flowers] (Tokyo: Tokyo Shoseki, 1990), p. 300.
13. Yukio Ninagawa, *Note 1969–1988* (Tokyo: Kawade Shobo Shinsha, 1989), pp. 294–5.
14. Shozo Uesugi, an ex-chief member of 'Yume no Yuminsha', wrote, directed and played the title role of *Broken Hamlet*.
15. *Broken Hamlet* was published in a monthly theatre magazine, *Shingeki* (March 1990).
16. The Chinese characters for 'Asuka' can mean 'flying birds'. The trade mark of Japan Air Lines representing a flying crane is used here as a symbol of the Asuka dynasty.
17. The company's name is not easy to translate. Its three main Chinese characters mean 'dreams', 'sports/play' and 'sleep' respectively. The name can be roughly translated as 'Dreaming Players' or 'Sleep of Playful Dreams'.
18. Noda's adaptations of *Much Ado About Nothing, A Midsummer Night's Dream* and *Richard III* are printed in *Mawashi wo Shimeta Shakespeare*.
19. Juichiro Takeuchi, *Himawari* (Tokyo: Jiritsu Shobo, 1991).
20. Harue Tsutsumi, *Kanadehon Hamlet* (Tokyo: Bungei Shunju, 1993).
21. The plan of presenting *Hamlet* in translation at the Shintomi-za is a fiction created by the playwright. According to Toshio Kawatake's *Nippon no Hamlet* [Japanese *Hamlet*] (Tokyo: Nansosha, 1972), *Hamlet* was first staged in adaptation by Otojiro Kawakami's Company in 1903, and then in Tsubouchi's translation by Bungei Kyokai (The Literary Arts Society) in 1907.

NOTES TO CHAPTER 3

1. Toshio Kawatake, *Nihon no Hamuretto* (Tokyo: Nansosha, 1972), p. 25.
2. *Ibid.*, p. 305.
3. Yoshio Ozasa, *Nihon Gendai Engeki-Shi, Meiji Taisho-hen* (Tokyo: Hakusuisha, 1985), p. 56.
4. Shoyo Tsubouchi, '*Hamuretto* no koen ni sakidachite', *Tsubouchi Shoyo Senshu*, XII (Tokyo: Shun'yodo, 1927), pp. 590–1.
5. Information on *Rodoku* is taken from Shigetoshi Kawatake, *Shingeki Undo no Reimeiki* (Tokyo: Yuzankaku, 1947), pp. 56–64.
6. Kappei Matsumoto, *Nihon Shingeki-shi* (Tokyo: Chikuma Shobo, 1967), pp. 23–6.
7. Kawatake, *Shingeki*, p. 62.
8. *Ibid.*, pp. 192–3.
9. See Kawatake, *Nihon no Hamuretto*, pp. 273ff.
10. Daisui Sugitani (1874–1915).
11. Shoyo Tsubouchi, 'Nihon de enzuru *Hamuretto*', in Tsubouchi, *Tsubouchi Shoyo Senshu*, p. 657.
12. *Ibid.*, p. 655.
13. See Kawatake, *Nihon no Hamuretto*, p. 280.
14. See *ibid.*, pp. 320–2.
15. Shoyo Tsubouchi, 'Teikoku gekijo nite enzuru *Hamuretto* ni tsuite', *Waseda Bungaku*, 66, 5 (May 1911), p. 5.

16. *Ibid.*, p. 6.
17. See Brian Powell, 'Matsui Sumako, Actress and Woman', in W. G. Beasley, ed., *Modern Japan, Aspects of History, Literature and Society* (London: Allen and Unwin, 1975).
18. Ozasa, *Nihon Gendai Engeki-shi* p. 78.
19. Taro Akiba, *Nihon Shingeki-shi* II (Risosha, 1971), II, p. 102.
20. '*Hamuretto* shokan', *Nichinichi Shinbun* (Tokyo), 22 May 1911, p. 4.
21. Tanaka ('a student'), '*Hamuretto* no insho', *Shin Koron*, 26, 6 (June 1911), p. 70.
22. Furuhito Kurihara, '*Hamuretto*', *Nichinichi Shinbun* (Tokyo), 31 May 1911, p. 7.
23. Quoted in Akiba, *Nihon Shingeki-shi*, p. 104.
24. Quoted in Shinko Matsumoto, *Meiji Engekiron-shi* (Tokyo: Engeki Shuppansha, 1980), p. 1022.
25. *Ibid.*, pp. 1026–7.
26. Cho-haku-san, 'Shibai mita mama, *Hamuretto*', *Engei Gaho*, 5, 7 (July 1911).
27. Quoted in Matsumoto, *Meiji Engekiron-shi*, pp. 1018–9.
28. Toyotaka Komiya, *Engeki Ronso* (Tokyo: Seibunkaku, 1937), p. 299.
29. Biyo Mizuguchi, '*Hamuretto* o mite', *Engei Gaho*, 5, 7 (July 1911), p. 123.
30. Tanaka,'*Hamuretto* no insho', p. 69.
31. Shoyo Tsubouchi, '*Hamuretto* no koen ni sakidachite' addressed to his students in March 1911; later printed in Tsubouchi, *Tsubouchi Shago Senchu* XII p. 591.
32. Tanaka, '*Hamuretto* no insho', p. 69.

NOTES TO CHAPTER 4

1. For the complete text and the background of this incident, see Donald T. Roden, *Schooldays in Imperial Japan* (Berkeley: University of California Press, 1980), pp. 165–73.
2. Kiyokazu Yamamoto, Kazuko F. Goodman, and David Goodman, 'Senda Koreya: An Interview', conducted at the Actor's Theatre in Tokyo, 10 January and 5 February 1970, published in *Concerned Theatre Japan*, 1, 2 (Summer 1970), 56. Hereafter referenced in the text as Yamamoto-Goodman.
3. Sano and Y. Hidjikata [or Hijikata], 'Stage Directors and Playwrights: Korea [*sic*] Senda', *International Theatre*, 2 (1934), 48.
4. For Senda's reflections on the production of *The Beggar's Opera*, see his *Mo hitotsu no shingeki shi – Senda Koreya jiden* [Another History of Shingeki – The Autobiography of Senda Koreya] (Tokyo: Chikuma Shobo, 1975), pp. 237–40.
5. Koreya Senda, '*Hamuretto* enshutsu koki' [A Postscript to Directing *Hamlet*], a lengthy essay originally published in *Teatro* magazine (Tokyo) in three instalments, August, September, and October 1964. Reprinted in Senda, *Engeki hyoron shu* [Collected Theatre Criticism] (Tokyo: Miraisha, 1980), V, pp. 239–308. The comment on Osaka is on p. 287.
6. Akimasa Minamitani, '*Hamlet* in Japan', *Japan Quarterly*, 37, 2 (April–June 1990), 188.
7. Senda, *Engeki hyoron shu*, II, p. 230.

8. Peter Brook, *The Shifting Point, 1946–1987* (New York: Harper and Row, 1987), p. 44. For a further discussion of the major traditions of postwar European Shakespeare performance, see Dennis Kennedy's 'Shakespeare without His Language', the introduction to *Foreign Shakespeare: Contemporary Performance*, ed. Kennedy (Cambridge: Cambridge University Press, 1993).

9. The translation of Kott into Japanese was prepared by Tetsuo Kishi (whose essay is included in this volume), with the assistance of his colleague, Akio Hachiya, who knew the Polish language.

10. Senda, *Engeki hyoron shu*, V, pp. 327, 329.

11. Senda, '*Hamuretto* enshutsu oboegaki' [A Memo on Directing *Hamlet*], *ibid.*, p. 234–5.

12. Senda, 'Koki', *ibid.*, pp. 272–3.

13. Senda, 'Oboegaki', *ibid.*, pp. 236–7.

14. Senda, 'Koki', *ibid.*, pp. 241, 276.

15. *Ibid.*, pp. 240, 252.

16. *Ibid.*, p. 244.

17. All three reviews were published in the evening editions of the newspapers on 16 June 1964. Copies of these reviews, and other research materials for this essay, were kindly provided by Akihiko Senda and Shinko Matsumoto of Tokyo.

18. *Shingeki*, 134 (July 1964), 31. In an article on recent productions of Shakespeare by Japanese troupes, published in *Asahi* on 25 June 1964 (p. 26), the critic Yoshio Nakano remarked that the limited number of Shakespeare productions in Japan has a dire affect on native acting of the European classics. Actors such as Nakadai show considerable raw talent, he noted, but their rare opportunities to play Shakespeare impede the development of their craft.

NOTES TO CHAPTER 5

1. Patrice Pavis, *Theatre at the Crossroads of Culture*, trans. Loren Kruger, (London and New York: Routledge, 1992), p. 1.

2. *Ibid.*, p. 2.

3. Rustom Bharucha, *Theatre and the World* (London and New York: Routledge, 1993; first published by Manohar Publications, India, 1990), p. 8.

4. Richard Schechner, *The Future of Ritual: Writings on Culture and Performance* (London and New York: Routledge, 1993), p.1.

5. *Ibid.*, p. 4.

6. *Ibid.*, p. 4.

7. *Ibid.*, p. 251.

8. *Ibid.*, p. 257.

9. Bharucha, *Theatre and the World*, pp. 1–2.

10. *Ibid.*, p. 2.

11. *Ibid.*, p. 4.

12. *Ibid.*, p. 7.

13. *Ibid.*, p. 67.

14. *Ibid.*, p. 241.

15. *Ibid.*, p. 243.

16. *Ibid.*, p. 8.

17. It should be said that Bharucha has made his position a good deal more flexible in his most recent writing. His 'Under the Sign of the Onion: Intracultural Negotiations in Theatre' (*NTQ*, 12, 46 (May, 1996), 116–29) stresses the aesthetic and even moral benefits that accrue from the disciplined translation processes entailed by intercultural work. In moving away from the rigidities of his earlier stance, he writes:

> a more nuanced position on the intellectual scenario would move beyond the strictures of domination to highlight the series of complicities between systems of power, which are ultimately determined by the state and increasingly by the market … Whatever autonomy an intercultural encounter may assume, therefore, is invariably circumscribed by this larger scenario, and interculturalists (however altruistic and anti-state) have no other option but to work through the mechanisms, languages, rules and regulations, politics, complicities, and formalities of larger power groups. (p. 117)

Recognising as keenly as ever the pitfalls of interculturalism, Bharucha now turns these into virtues (however strenuously accomplished) as in his own Indian production (in Kannada) of *Peer Gynt.*

18. Richard Schechner, *Asian Theatre Journal*, 1, 2 (Fall, 1984), p. 24.
19. Schechner, *Asian Theatre Journal*, p. 24.
20. Eugenio Barba, *The Paper Canoe: A Guide to Theatre Anthropology*, trans. Richard Fowler (London and New York: Routledge, 1995; first published as *La Canoa di Carta*, Bologna: Società editrice il Mulino, 1993), p. 42.
21. Barba, *The Paper Canoe*, p. 44.
22. *Ibid.*, p. 46.
23. Richard Schechner, *The End of Humanism:Writings in Performance* (New York: Performing Arts Journal Publications, 1982), p. 19.
24. Schechner, *The End of Humanism*, p. 70.
25. Richard Schechner, *The Future of Ritual* (London and New York: Routledge, 1993), p. 17.
26. Schechner, *The Future of Ritual*, p. 17.
27. Patrice Pavis, ed., *The Intercultural Performance Reader* (London and New York: Routledge, 1996).
28. *Le laboratoire de Grotowski* (Varsoire: Editions Interpress, n.d.), p. 19; quoted in Pavis, ed., *Intercultural Reader*, p. 231.
29. See Roland Barthes, *The Empire of Signs*, trans. Richard Howard (London: Jonathan Cape, 1983; first published as *L'Empire des Signes*, Geneva: Editions d'Art Albert Skira S.A., 1970).
30. Pavis, ed., *Intercultural Reader*, pp. 45, 80.
31. Richard Schechner, 'Interculturalism and the Culture of Choice' in Pavis, ed., *Intercultural Reader*, pp. 42–50.
32. Clive Barker, 'The Possibilities and Politics of Intercultural Penetration and Exchange' in Pavis, ed., *Intercultural Reader*, pp. 248–56.
33. As played at the Royal National Theatre, London, September/October 1996.
34. James Clifford, *The Predicament of Culture: Twentieth-Century Ethnography, Literature and Art* (Cambridge, Mass.: Harvard University Press, 1988), quoted in Philip B. Zarilli, 'For whom is the King a King? Issues of Intercultural Production, Perception and Reception in a *Kathakali King*

Lear', in Janelle G. Reinelt and Joseph R. Roach, eds., *Critical Theory and Performance* (Ann Arbor: University of Michigan Press, 1992), pp. 16–40.

35. See A. Horrie-Webber, 'Modernisation of the Japanese Theatre: The Shingeki Movement', in W. G. Beasley, ed., *Modern Japan: Aspects of History, Literature and Society* (London: Allen and Unwin, 1975), pp. 147–65.

36. See the chapters in this volume by Brian Powell and Akihiko Senda, pp. 38–52 and 15–37.

37. J. Thomas Rimer, *Towards a Modern Japanese Theatre: Kishida Kunio* (Princeton: Princeton University Press, 1974), p. 5.

38. *SCOT: Suzuki Company of Toga*, Publication for the 25th Anniversary of SCOT and the 10th Anniversary of the Toga Festival, Souvenir Brochure, 1992, p. 79.

39. Interview at The Pit, Barbican Theatre, London, 11 November 1994.

40. Tadashi Suzuki, *The Way of Acting*, trans. J. Thomas Rimer (New York: Theatre Communications Group, 1986), p. 12.

41. See, for example, *The Paper Canoe, passim*.

42. Suzuki, *The Way of Acting*, p. 90.

43. *Ibid.*, p. 91.

44. *Ibid.*, p. 91.

45. *Ibid.*, p. 9.

46. Interview with Tadashi Suzuki, 11 November 1994.

47. *The New Republic*, June 1988.

48. *Time*, May 1988.

49. 'Talks with Mr. Tadashi Suzuki', 6 April 1995, trans. Kayoko Hashimoto, Ian Carruthers and Yasunari Takahashi, unpublished typescript, pp. 4–5.

50. 'Shakespeare our Foreign Contemporary', unpublished paper, World Shakespeare Congress, Los Angeles, 1996, p. 5

51. Quoted in Ian Carruthers and Patricia Mitchell, 'Theatre East and West: Problems of Difference or Problems of Perception? Suzuki Tadashi's Australian *Macbeth*, 1992', *Asian Studies Papers, Research Series Five* (La Trobe University, Australia, August 1995).

52. Tadashi Suzuki, in *SCOT: Suzuki Company of Toga*.

53. *The New Republic*, June 1988.

54. Yasunari Takahashi, 'Tadashi Suzuki's *The Tale of Lear*', unpublished paper, World Shakespeare Congress, Los Angeles, 1996, pp. 1–2.

55. *Ibid.*, p. 3.

56. Michael Billington, 'King of Rages', *The Guardian*, 10 November 1994.

57. 'Talks with Mr. Tadashi Suzuki', trans. Kayoko Hashimoto, Ian Carruthers and Yasunari Takahashi, unpublished typescript, April 1995.

58. Takahashi (World Shakespeare Congress paper, p. 4) remarks on 'the ironical gap between the auditory signifier and the visual-situational signified' in the performance.

NOTES TO CHAPTER 6

1. Edited by Yume no Yuminsha, photos by Daisaburo Harada (Tokyo, 1986).

2. Sue Henny in the Edinburgh Festival Programme for *Descent of the Brutes* (1987) and *Half Gods* (1990).

3. Hideki Noda in the Edinburgh Festival Programmes for *Descent of the Brutes* and *Half Gods*.
4. Samuel L. Leiter, *The Great Stage Directors: 100 Distinguished Careers of the Theatre* (New York: Facts on File, 1994).
5. My thanks for access to these recordings, and to recordings of the Toho Company's *Much Ado About Nothing* and *A Midsummer Night's Dream* (both directed by Noda) go to Ryuta Minami.
6. Jeanette Amano, *The Tokyo Journal*, 1985.
7. See Sue Henny's discussion of Yume no Yuminsha in the Edinburgh Festival Programmes for *Descent of the Brutes* and *Half Gods*; also Susan Chira, *The New York Times*, 7 July 1988.
8. Hideki Noda in the Edinburgh Festival Programmes for *Descent of the Brutes* and *Half Gods*.
9. The Edinburgh Festival Programme for *Half Gods*.
10. *The New York Times*, 9 July 1988.
11. *Ibid.*
12. Staged in Paris in 1921 by the Ballets Suedois.
13. Noda played the part of Princess Twelve-Layers. Her name reflects the elaborate layers of Kabuki-style costumes.
14. See Luigi Pirandello, *Six Characters in Search of an Author* (1921) and *Tonight We Improvise* (1929).
15. Sue Henny, Edinburgh Festival Programme (1990).
16. Taken from Noda's 'Synopsis' contained in the Programme for *Descent of the Brutes*.
17. Perhaps this should be set alongside the influence of Ango Sakaguchi acknowledged in Noda's tongue-in-cheek autobiography printed in the programmes for at least the Western productions of his plays.
18. See Akihiko Senda, p.32 above.
19. See Emrys Jones, *Scenic Form in Shakespeare* (Oxford: Oxford University Press, 1971), *passim*.
20. From an unpublished interview with Hideki Noda conducted by Kazuko Matsuoka, Ryuta Minami, John Gillies and Masae Suzuki at the Cocoon Theatre, Shibuya, Tokyo, translated into English by Masae Suzuki.
21. See for example Dennis Kennedy ed., *Foreign Shakespeare* (Cambridge: Cambridge University Press, 1993) in which Kennedy argues that 'what Mnouchkine did was to take a style, or rather a series of styles, and detach them from their origins and cultures' (p. 296).
22. From an unpublished interview with Hideki Noda in which Noda explains that 'the two faces were based on the story of Oedipus and the Sphinx'.
23. Michael Billington, writing in *The Guardian* (13 July 1994), reviewed the Takarazuka Company performing at the London Coliseum:

> The stage foams with feathers, tuxedos, kimonos, falling cherry-blossom and dancing androgynes, but the overall effect, while ravishing for the retina, is curiously sexless . . . In fact, the fascination of Takarazuka is as much sociological as artistic. What it suggests is that Japanese women yearn to escape from their dominant menfolk into a world of colour and romance and spectacle, where relations between the idealised sexes are unimpeded by anything as threatening as carnal contact.

24. Akihiko Senda, p.34 above.
25. My thanks to Ms Nabuko Kawashima for her translation of these lyrics.
26. David Johnston, ed., *Stages of Translation* (Bath: Absolute Classics Books, 1996), Introduction, p. 9.
27. Joseph Farrell, 'Servant of Many Masters', in Johnston, ed., *Stages of Translation*, p. 51.
28. Andrea J Nouryeh, 'Shakespeare and the Japanese Stage', in Kennedy, ed., *Foreign Shakespeare*, p. 254, n. 21.
29. From a translation by Ryuta Minami of Professor Odashima's comments in *The Sankei*, 15 December 1990.
30. From an unpublished interview with Hideki Noda.
31. Tsuno Kaitaro, 'Shakespeare in Tokyo', in *Concerned Theatre Japan*, 1, 1 (Spring, 1970), 14–16 (p. 15).
32. *Ibid.*, p. 15.
33. *Ibid.*, p. 16.
34. Peter Brook, *The Empty Space* (London: McGibbon & Kee, 1968; Harmondsworth: Penguin Books, 1972), p. 52. Noda saw Brook's *A Midsummer Night's Dream* when he was sixteen.
35. My thanks to Ms Nabuko Kawashima for translating this voice-over.
36. From an unpublished interview with Noda.
37. Yushi Odashima in *The Sankei*, 15 December 1990, translated by Ryuta Minami.
38. Akihiko Senda, p.34 above.
39. Odashima in *The Sankei*.
40. Kazuko Matsuoka in *The Asahi*, 11 August 1992, translated by Ryuta Minami.
41. *Ibid.*
42. From the Edinburgh Festival Programme for *Descent of the Brutes*.
43. Jean Cocteau, 'Preface de 1922', for *Les Mariés de la Tour Eiffel*, in *Théâtre 1* (Paris: Gallimard, 1922), p. 45.
44. Comte de Lautréamont (Isadore Ducass), quoted in Robert Hughes, *The Shock of the New* (London: BBC Books, 1980), p. 221.

NOTES TO CHAPTER 7

1. Peter Brook, *There Are No Secrets* (London: Methuen, 1993), p. 106.
2. *The Quarterly Journal of the Japanese Centre of the OISTAT and AICT*, 4 (March 1989), 23.

NOTES TO CHAPTER 10

All quotations from Shakespeare are from *The Riverside Shakespeare* (Boston: Houghton Mifflin, 1974).
1. The present essay is based on the plenary session lecture at the Fifth World Shakespeare Congress held in Tokyo in summer 1991.
2. Cf. Asataro Miyamori, *Chikamatsu to Shekusupiya* [Chikamatsu and Shakespeare] (Tokyo: Dobunsha, 1929).
3. Asataro Miyamori, *Masterpieces of Chikamatsu, The Japanese Shakespeare* (London: Kegan Paul, 1926).

4. Asataro Miyamori, *Chikamatsu to Shekusupiya*, pp. 108–13.
5. Among popular Noh plays is *Kagekiyo*, based on a story that is a sequel to that of the puppet play I am dealing with; the relation of the former to the latter is somewhat similar to that of *Oedipus at Colonus* to *Oedipus Tyrannus*, that is, the story of the self-blinded hero in exile to the story of his tragic life leading to his self-blinding.
6. Paul Claudel, 'Lettre au Professeur Miyajima' (1926), *Oeuvres completes* (Paris: Gallimard, 1952), V, p. 230.
7. Cf. E. H. Gombrich, *Art and Illusion: A Study in the Psychology of Pictorial Representation* (Princeton: Princeton University Press, 1960), pp. 103–9, 207–8, *passim*.
8. Cf. Francis Berry, *The Shakespeare Inset:Word and Picture* (London: Routledge and Kegan Paul, 1965).
9. F. R. Leavis, 'Diabolic Intellect and the Noble Hero', *Scrutiny*, 6, 3 (1937) (rept. in *The Common Pursuit* (Harmondsworth: Penguin Books, 1962)).
10. T. S. Eliot, 'Shakespeare and the Stoicism of Seneca', *Selected Essays* (London: Faber and Faber, 1932; new edn, New York: Harcourt, 1950), p. 111.
11. Ikan Hozumi reports in *Naniwa Miyage* [Souvenir of Naniwa] that Chikamatsu used this expression in his talk on his art.
12. A. C. Bradley, *Shakespearean Tragedy* (London: Macmillan, 1904), p. 60.
13. Introduction to *The Bacchae*, *The Complete Greek Tragedies*, ed. David Grene and Richmond Lattimore (Chicago: Chicago University Press, 1958), IV, pp. 540–1.

NOTES TO CHAPTER 11

1. In this argument, I follow the analyses of Elaine Showalter, 'Toward a Feminist Poetics', and Lillian Robinson, 'Treason Our Text: Feminist Challenges to the Literary Canon', both in Showalter, ed., *The New Feminist Criticism* (New York: Pantheon, 1985), who advocate the need for a continuing feminist critique of the traditional androcentric canon in addition to the need for greater scholarly attention to the literary productions of women writers.
2. Cf. Bourdieu, *Language and Symbolic Power*, ed. John B. Thompson, tr. Gino Raymond and Matthew Adamson (Cambridge: Cambridge University Press, 1991).
3. For reasons that will be explained in greater detail below (in the sections on 'Character' and 'Language'), it is misleading to speak of Japanese deities as either male or female, either masculine or feminine. In this essay, I use the terms 'male/female deity' only to refer to deities who have a consistent tradition of being perceived as anthropomorphically singular and sexed (such as deified humans), and 'masculine/feminine manifestation/form of the deity' to refer to a gendered manifestation of a deity who has a known tradition of being perceived as possessing multiple sexual aspects. It might seem simpler to use the term 'masculine/feminine deity', but in my view this term is too reductive, seeming to refer to the dominant trait of a singular entity with a fixed identity, thus obscuring a complex and crucial issue.
4. An English translation of *Takasago* may be found in the Penguin

Classics edition, *Japanese Nō Dramas* (London, 1992), ed. and trans. by Royall Tyler.

5. Akira Omote, *Nogakushi shinko* (Tokyo, 1979), divides Zeami's *oeuvre* into four groups according to the degree of certainty of authorship (cf. Thomas Blenman Hare, *Zeami's Style: The Noh Plays of Zeami Motokiyo* (Stanford, CA: Stanford University Press, 1986). Here I refer only to canonical works; neither Omote nor Hare makes this distinction in his figures.

6. The various scholarly conjectures about the significance of these events are summarised in Hare, *Zeami's Style*.

7. Details about the various Japanese literary genres and works mentioned in this essay may be found in *The Princeton Companion to Classical Japanese Literature*, ed. Earl Miner *et al.* (Princeton: Princeton University Press, 1985).

8. Cf. Akio Nagao, 'Gobandate no seiritsu', *Geinoshi kenkyu*, 80 (January 1983). Detailed English-language introductions to all Japanese scholarship cited in this essay, excepting Omote, *Nogakushi shinko*, may be found in Gerry Yokota-Murakami, *The Formation of the Canon of No: The Literary Tradition of Divine Authority* (Osaka: Osaka University Press, 1997). *On the Art of No Drama: The Major Treatises of Zeami*, ed. and trans. J. Thomas Rimer and Masakazu Yamazaki (Princeton: Princeton University Press, 1984).

9. Cf. Akira Omote and Fumio Amano, *No no rekishi. Iwanami koza no kyogen* (Tokyo, 1987), I. 1987.

10. Yokota-Murakami, *Formation*.

11. This conventional hierarchy is reflected in the organisation of standard anthologies such as Toyoichiro Nogami, ed., *Kaichu yokyoku zenshu*, 6 vols. (Tokyo; 1935–6).

12. An English-language introduction to the standard Japanese scholarship on this historical trend may be found in Yokota-Murakami, *Formation*.

13. Cf. Sachiko Oda, 'Zeami no shugen no', *Geinoshi kenkyu*, 80 (January 1983), and Yokota-Murakami, *Formation*.

14. Cf. Mikio Takemoto, 'Tennyomai no kenkyu', *Nogaku Kenkyu*, 4 (July 1978), and Yokota-Murakami, *Formation*.

15. Examples of canonical plays subjected to such revision (evidenced by old stage manuals and other textual evidence clearly indicating the presence of additional characters in the original plays) include *Yuya*, *Awaji*, *Iwafune*, *Oimatsu*, and *Kasuga Ryujin*. Cf. Yokota-Murakami, *Formation*.

16. Cf. Akira Omote, 'No no do (on) to ji(utai)', *Tokyo Daigaku Kokugo to Kokubungaku*, 62, 4 (April 1985), and Yokota-Murakami, *Formation*.

17. For my analysis of this effect I am indebted to feminist theorists of cinema, most notably Laura Mulvey and Teresa de Lauretis.

18. Stage manuals for the production of plays such as *Ukon* and *Yoshino Tennin* provide clear evidence of these changing trends in masking and costuming of feminine deities. Cf. Yokota-Murakami, *Formation*.

19. Examples of plays for which stage manuals (and comparison of older and newer compositions) clearly indicate this trend include *Himuro* and *Oyashiro*. Cf. Yokota-Murakami, *Formation*.

20. Plays exhibiting this trend include *Kusenoto*, *Enoshima*, and *Nezame*. Cf. Yokota-Murakami, *Formation*.

21. The wide-ranging differences in the staging of this play are charted in Yokota-Murakami, *Formation*.

22. Janet Goff has clearly demonstrated how true this is for the plays adapted from *Genji Monogatari* in her *Noh Drama and The Tale of Genji* (Princeton, NJ, 1991).

23. Masayoshi Ito (ed.), *Yokyokushu* (Tokyo, 1986), I, 290 n.2.

24. I find Michel Foucault's analysis in *Discipline and Punish* (Harmondsworth: Penguin, 1979) of the self-policing by the prison inmate appropriate to this discussion.

25. Royall Tyler (ed. and trans.), *Japanese Nō Dramas*, pp. 290–91. The suggestion of the fertility ritual might be evoked more effectively if the line which this translator poetically renders as 'Our light craft under all sail' were translated more literally as 'Raising the mast in this inlet vessel'.

26. *Flowing Traces* (1992), a collection of essays on the expression of this dualistic principle in a range of traditional Japanese arts, includes a chapter on Buddhism in Noh by Royall Tyler entitled 'The Path of My Mountain'.

27. The Meiwa Edition is an infamous collection of revisions of the Kanze repertoire directed by Motoakira Kanze (1722–74), the troupe leader in the Meiwa era (1764–71) of the Tokugawa shogunate, in collaboration with nativist scholars. It was abandoned immediately after Motoakira's death. Cf. Omote and Amano, *No no rekishi*; Yokota-Murakami, *Formation*.

28. One famous example of such a revision is the non-canonical *Unoha*, which was revived on the Noh stage in 1991 after a hiatus of three centuries. The *waki* in the original version of this play was a Buddhist priest, but was later changed to a courtier in the service of the *tenno*, who was believed to be descended from the *kami*. Cf. Ito (ed.), *Yokyokushu* (Tokyo, 1986), I; Kenji Kobayashi, '*Unoha* no sozai to Eshin sozu', in *Fukkyoku Unoha* (Osaka, 1991); Yokota-Murakami, *Formation*.

29. Readers more familiar with Shakespeare may be reminded of *A Midsummer Night's Dream*, where the very seasons are disrupted by the conflict between Oberon and Titania (II.i).

30. Readers more familiar with the Elizabethan tradition may in this case find a parallel in Shakespeare's use of archaic metre and singsong rhyme to establish an aura of timelessness in plays such as *Pericles*, where the unity of the man's virtue with the natural order is symbolised by his ability (and his alone) to hear heavenly music (V.i).

31. Masayoshi Ito, ed., *Yokyokushu* (Tokyo, 1986), p. 289 n.18. Also see note 3 of this essay.

32. Similar dynamics in Shakespearean drama are analyzed in depth by Jeanne Addison Roberts in *The Shakespearean Wild* (Lincoln: University of Nebraska Press, 1991).

33. I argue that it is not Eurocentric to characterise this logic as metaphysical. The worldview expounded here is clearly based on a common concept of the transcendental. On the contrary, the characterisation of Eastern ways of thinking as irrational in contrast to rational Western logic is an Orientalist dichotomy. Zeami's theoretical treatises are full of such metaphysical pairs as form and content, being and non-being. See *On the Art of the No Drama*.

33. For a detailed introduction of extensive textual evidence of such mythmaking techniques, see Yokota-Murakami, *Formation*.

34. Tyler, ed. and trans., *Japanese Nō Dramas*, p. 291.

35. This trend is noted by Maurice Charney in *All of Shakespeare* (New York: Columbia University Press, 1993), p. 140.

36. Catherine Belsey, 'Afterword: A Future for Materialist Feminist Criticism', in Valerie Wayne, ed., *The Matter of Difference* (Ithaca, NY: Cornell University Press, 1991), p. 265.

37. Stephen Greenblatt, *Renaissance Self-fashioning from More to Shakespeare* (Chicago: University of Chicago Press, 1980), p. 254.

NOTES TO CHAPTER 12

1. Dr Frances Yates told me in March 1976 that in the late 1960s she watched a performance by a touring troupe of Japanese Noh professionals on the stage of the Teatro Olympico in Vicenza. She was deeply impressed by the way in which the building's inner structure, with its symbolic meanings, closely fitted almost every phase of the performance. This, Dr Yates thought, was because the Noh was another 'Theatre of the World' in close, though historically unconnected, parallel with the kind of theatrical performance at which the original Teatro Olympico aimed, on the basis of Neo-Platonic philosophy. In *Theatre of the World* (Chicago: University of Chicago Press, 1969), Dr Yates argued that the idea and ground plan of the Teatro Olympico may have reached James Burbage through the Magus philosopher, John Dee, and influenced him in his construction (1576) of The Theatre, the predecessor of Shakespeare's Globe. Dr Yates's work drew on Bernard Beckerman's *Shakespeare at the Globe* (New York: The Macmillan Company, 1962). In 1983, I asked Professor Beckerman whether he had any guiding idea or inspiration in conceiving his own book. His reply was: 'Yes, I had one. It was Japanese Noh Theatre.'

2. The topos can be traced back to classical antiquity, but was most actively canvassed in the Renaissance period. In the Middle Ages, it was sanctioned by Catholicism and pervaded the theatre of the mysteries and miracle plays. In the modern period it has lost its religious force, but remains a complex feature of the implicit understanding of theatrical performance. Compare Howard D. Pearce, 'A Phenomenonological Approach to the *Theatrum Mundi* Metaphor', *PMLA*, 95 (1980), 42–57.

3. Philip Stubbes, *The Anatomie of Abuses. Containing A Discoverie, or Briefe Summarie of such Notable Vices and Imperfections, as now raign in many Countryes of the World, but (especiallie) in a famous ILANDE called AILGNA* (London, 1583), p. 94.

4. Shimpei Matsuoka, *Utage no Shintai – Basara kara Zeami e* [Corpus of Festive Rituals: From *basara*-Lords to Zeami] (Tokyo: Iwanami-shoten, 1991), pp. 7–112.

5. Victor Turner, *From Ritual to Theatre: The Human Seriousness of Play* (New York: PAJ Publications, 1982), p. 47.

6. For the festive, ritual elements in Shakespeare's work, see C. L. Barber, *Shakespeare's Festive Comedy : A Study of Dramatic Form and its Relation to Social Custom* (Princeton: Princeton University Press, 1955). My analysis of *A Midsummer Night's Dream* could also be applied in the case of three other

plays for which there is no extensive source-material: *Love's Labour's Lost, The Merry Wives of Windsor* and *The Tempest*.

7. Zeami himself says, in one of his major treatises, *Sarugaku dangi* [An Account of Zeami's Reflections on Art], written *c.* 1430: '*Izutsu* can be said to be on the highest level, that of the Flower of Peerless Charm'. See J. Thomas Rimer and Masakazu Yamazaki, trans., *On the Art of the Nō Drama: The Major Treatises of Zeami* (Princeton: Princeton University Press, 1984), p. 214.

8. Royall Tyler, ed. and trans., *Japanese Nō Dramas* (Harmondsworth: Penguin Books, 1992) p. 131.

9. For Zeami's definition of *yugen*, see e.g. *Fushikaden* [Teachings on Style and the Flower], ch. 6; *Kakyo* [Mirror Held to the Flower], ch. 12. Rimer and Yamazaki, trans., *On the Art of the Nō Drama*, pp. 43–52, 92–5.

10. See Francis Macdonald Cornford, *The Origin of Attic Comedy* (Cambridge: Cambridge University Press, 1934), pp. 115–33.

11. Cf. Francis Hugh Mares, 'The Origin of the Figure Called "the Vice" in Tudor Drama', *HLQ* 22 (1958), pp. 11–29; Wylie Sypher, *Comedy* (1956; Baltimore: The Johns Hopkins University Press, 1980), pp. 214–30; Sandra Billington, *A Social History of the Fool* (Brighton: The Harvester Press, 1984), p. 39; David Wiles, *Shakespeare's Clown: Actor and Text in the Elizabethan Playhouse* (Cambridge: Cambridge University Press, 1987), pp. 162–3.

12. All quotations from the play are taken from The New Cambridge Shakespeare edition, edited by R. A. Foakes (1984).

13. See Frank Kermode, 'Shakespeare's Best Comedy', in John Russell Brown and Bernard Harris, eds., *Early Shakespeare* (London: Edward Arnold, 1961), p. 219; Jan Kott, *The Bottom Translation* (Chicago: Northwestern University Press, 1987), p. 31; Annabel Patterson, *Shakespeare and the Popular Voice* (Oxford: Basil Blackwell, 1989), pp. 68–9.

14. Kermode, 'Shakespeare's Best Comedy'.

15. C. G. Jung, *The Archetypes and the Collective Unconscious*, trans. R. F. C. Hull, *Collected Works*, IX.i., ed. Sir Herbert Read *et al.* (London: Routledge and Kegan Paul, 1968 [1957]), p. 36.

16. *Shakespeare and the Popular Voice*, p. 62.

17. John D. Jones, trans., *Pseudo-Dionysius Areopagite: The Divine Names and Mystical Theology* (Milwaukee: Marquette University Press, 1980), p. 175. See also C. E. Rolt, trans., *Dionysius the Areopagite on the Divine Names and Mystical Theology* (London: The Macmillan Company, 1920), p. 147. I owe to Dr Charles Burnett of the Warburg Institute my knowledge of the existence and importance of the former text.

18. Rolt, *Dionysius*, p. 178. Also cf. Jones, *Pseudo-Dionysius*, p. 197.

19. See Wiles, *Shakespeare's Clown*, pp. 112–15, 179–81.

20. Zeami, *Kakyo* [Mirror Held to the Flower], ch. 6; Rimer and Yamazaki, *On the Art of the Nō Drama*, p. 81.

21. *Kakyo*, ch. 14, p. 98.

22. *Ibid.*, p. 97.

23. William Butler Yeats, 'Introduction' to Ezra Pound and Ernest Fenellosa, *The Classic Noh Theatre of Japan* (New York: New Directions Books, 1959 [1917]), p. 158. Other quotations from Yeats are from pp. 153–5.

24. *Shikado* [True Path to the Flower], ch. 4 (literal translation mine). For a more

elegant translation, see Rimer and Yamazaki, trans., *On the Art of the Nō Drama*, p. 70: 'a level where the artist moves beyond his means of expression to produce a performance of profound ease'.

25. Dogen, *Shobo Genzo* [Storehouse of True Enlightenment], 2 vols., 'Genealogy of Great Books of Thought', nos. 12 and 13, Toru Terada and Naoko Mizuno edd. (Tokyo: Iwanami-shoten, 1970, 1972), II, ch. 53, pp. 122–3. The translation is by Toshihiko Izutsu, quoted in 'The Nexus of Ontological Events: A Buddhist View of Reality', in Adolf Partmann and Rudolf Ritsema, eds., *Eranos Jahrbuch*, vol. 49 [1980] (Frankfurt-on-Main: Insel Verlag, 1981), p. 384.

NOTES TO CHAPTER 13

1. In the Bunraku version of *The Tempest* the characters were, of course, all given their adapted names such as *Gonzaemon* for Gonzalo and *Erihiko* for Ariel. In this essay, however, I use the original names solely for the sake of convenience.

2. Interview with Shoichi Yamada in *The Globe* XVI (The Tokyo Globe, 1991), p. 10.

3. Cf. Barbara C. Adachi, *Backstage at Bunraku* (London: Weatherhall, 1985), p. 57.

4. See chapter 1 in this volume, p. 8.

5. *Sugawara and the Secrets of Calligraphy*, ed. and trans. Stanleigh H. Jones, Jr. (New York: Columbia University Press, 1984), s.d. to IV.i, p. 199.

6. Jones, *Sugawara*, p. 212.

7. C. Andrew Gerstle *et al.*, *Theatre as Music: The Bunraku Play 'Mt. Imo and Mt. Se: An Exemplary Tale of Womanly Virtue'* (Ann Arbor: University of Michigan Press, 1990), p. 11.

8. Adachi, *Backstage*, p. 66.

9. Patrice Pavis, *Theatre at the Crossroads of Culture*, trans. L. Kruger (London: Routledge, 1992), p. 34.

NOTES TO CHAPTER 14

1. Jacques Derrida, 'The Law of Genre', trans. Avital Ronell, *Glyph: Textual Studies*, 7 (1980), 203–4. French permits an ambiguity which is not available in English: *genre* means both genre and gender.

2. Tamotsu Hirosue, *Henkai no Aku-sho* (Tokyo: Heibonsha, 1973), p. 13.

3. Kyoko Ogasawara, *Toshi to Gekijo: Chu-Kinsei no Chinkon, Yugaku, Kenryoku* (Tokyo: Heibonsha, 1992), pp. 221–4.

4. Yukio Hattori, *Oinaru Koya: Kinsei Toshi no Shukusai Kukan* (Tokyo: Heibonsha, 1986), pp. 50–5.

5. Ogasawara, *Toshi to Gekijo*, pp. 235–59.

6. For further discussion on the contradictory implications of the Kabuki player and the *onnagata* as the marginal others in the *aku-sho*, and their subversive power, see Yoko Takakuwa, 'Performing Marginality: The Place of the Player and of "Woman" in Early Modern Japanese Culture', *New Literary History*, 27 (1996), 213–25.

7. Steven Mullaney, *The Place of the Stage: License, Play, and Power in Renaissance England* (Chicago: University of Chicago Press, 1988), pp. 30–1.

8. Kyoko Ogasawara, *Izumo no Okuni* (Tokyo: Chuokoronsha, 1984), pp. 17–18.

9. Meanwhile, Ogasawara suggests that female entertainers still performed at least until 1645 (*Toshi to Gekijo*, pp. 196–200).

10. Quoted in Yukio Hattori, *Edo Kabuki* (Tokyo: Iwanami Shoten, 1993), pp. 20–1.

11. References to *Antony and Cleopatra* are to the Arden Shakespeare, ed. John Wilders (London and New York: Routledge, 1995).

12. For discussions on the theatricality of Cleopatra's speech, see, for example, Phyllis Rackin, 'Shakespeare's Boy Cleopatra, the Decorum of Nature and the Golden World of Poetry', *PMLA*, 87 (1972), 201–12, reprinted in *Antony and Cleopatra*, ed. John Drakakis (London: Macmillan, 1994), pp. 78–100, and Michael Shapiro 'Boying Her Greatness: Shakespeare's Use of Coterie Drama in *Antony and Cleopatra*', *Modern Language Review*, 77,1 (1982), 1–15.

13. Stephen Orgel, *Impersonations: The Performance of Gender in Shakespeare's England* (Cambridge: Cambridge University Press, 1996), p. 70.

14. Joan Riviere, 'Womanliness as a Masquerade', in *Formations of Fantasy*, ed. Victor Burgin, James Donald and Cora Kaplan (London: Methuen, 1986), p. 38.

15. Marjorie Garber, *Vested Interests: Cross-Dressing and Cultural Anxiety* (New York: Routledge, 1992), p. 355.

16. Judith Butler, *Gender Trouble: Feminism and the Subversion of Identity* (New York: Routledge, 1990), p. 139.

17. Once 'the subversion of identity' is achieved as a kind of utopian emancipation from 'the convergent power regimes of masculine and heterosexist oppression', for example, is it perhaps too easy for Butler to institute and relinquish identities alternately 'according to the purposes at hand', regardless of the contexts – as an autonomous subject – as the origin of meaning? (*Gender Trouble*, pp. 33, 16).

18. Ayame Yoshizawa, 'The Words of Ayame', in *The Actors' Analects* (*Yakusha Rongo*), ed. and trans. Charles J. Dunn and Bunzo Torigoe (Tokyo: University of Tokyo Press, 1969), pp. 49–50.

19. For a more detailed discussion of these issues, see Yoko Takakuwa, 'Masquerading Womanliness: The *Onnagata*'s Theatrical Performance of Femininity in Kabuki', *Women: A Cultural Review*, 5, 2 (1994), 154–6.

20. Tamotsu Watanabe, *Onnagata no Unmei* (Tokyo: Kinokuniya Shoten, 1974), pp. 118–19.

21. *Ibid.*, pp. 124–46.

22. Kunitaro Kawarazaki, *Onnagata Geidan* (Tokyo: Miraisha, 1972), p. 192. *Kyoganoko Musume Dojoji*, according to Tamotsu Watanabe, contains every artistic genre synthetically like *bricolage*. A woman represented in this dance sometimes looks like a maiden and sometimes like a courtesan, but such a discrepancy itself makes the polyhedral illusion of 'woman' possible. For this reason, the grand illusion of 'woman' produced in *Kyoganoko Musume Dojoji* has fascinated the Japanese audience for a long time (*Musume Dojoji* (Tokyo: Shinshindo Shuppan, 1986), pp. 476–7, 485). However, this grand illusion of 'woman' is not universal. In the Kabuki overseas performances, the audience

tend to find drama more understandable than dancing (a mere configuration of the signifiers 'woman'): for example, they prefer the tragedy of the priest Shunkan, abandoned alone on a desert island, to *Musume Dojoji* (Toshio Kawatake, *Kabuki Biron* (Tokyo: Tokyo University Press, 1989), pp. 57–61). Perhaps it is the contexts that help the foreign audience to understand 'the unknown language' of the other (Roland Barthes) based on the cultural convention of writing and reading.

23. Watanabe, *Onnagata no Unmei*, pp. 114–16.

24. *Ibid.*, pp. 110–23, 158.

25. Catherine Belsey, 'Cleopatra's Seduction', in *Alternative Shakespeares* 2, ed. Terence Hawkes (London: Routledge, 1996), pp. 48–62.

26. Jacques Derrida, *Of Grammatology*, trans. Gayatri Chakravorty Spivak, (Baltimore: Johns Hopkins University Press, 1976), p. 311.

27. Jacques Derrida, 'Differance', *Speech and Phenomena and Other Essays on Husserl's Theory of Signs*, trans. David B. Allison (Evanston: Northwestern University Press, 1973), pp. 129–60.

28. In *Sukeroku Yukari no Edozakura* (1713), the theatre turns into the brothel-town in Shin-Yoshiwara. The *keisei* Agemaki, the highest-ranking courtesan of the famous Miura-ya brothel, appears on the stage, attended by many beauti-fully-dressed courtesans and menials. Defiantly refusing Ikyu, the wealthy, weighty customer, Agemaki ignores Ikyu's threat to kill her and proudly affirms her love to Sukeroku: 'Black is the courtesan's life bereft of her beloved, but even in the blackest night, how could she mistake Sukeroku for Ikyu?'. She wears the gorgeously gilded and embroidered *keisei*'s costume showing festival designs, which is (and this is often given as the *raison d'être* of the *onnagata*) too heavy for an actress to wear. With this outfit, she cloaks Sukeroku in order first to conceal him from his antagonist Ikyu and, at the end of the play, in order to protect Sukeroku, who killed Ikyu, from the pursuers. Agemaki certainly incarnates the idea(l) of the eternal (maternal) feminine, beautified with the aesthetics of Kabuki. At the same time, as her high-spir-ited, straightforward speech shows, Agemaki is a resolute, *active* woman of Edo, different from the idea(l) of silent, submissive woman (legendary female passivity). The meaning of the ideal eternal feminine itself is ambiguous.

29. Thomas Laqueur, 'Orgasm, Generation, and the Politics of Reproductive Biology', *Representations*, 14 (1986), 1–41. According to Laqueur, the Renaissance understood effeminacy as 'a condition of instability, a state of men who through excessive devotion to women became more like them' (*Making Sex: Body and Gender from the Greeks to Freud* (Cambridge, MA: Harvard University Press, 1990), p. 123).

30. Stephen Orgel, 'Nobody's Perfect: Or Why Did the English Stage Take Boys for Women?', *South Atlantic Quarterly*, 88, 1 (1989) 7–29.

31. Laura Levine, *Men in Women's Clothing: Anti-Theatricality and Effeminisation from 1579 to 1642* (Cambridge: Cambridge University Press, 1994), pp. 57, 64, 66. Levine writes that 'there is no such a thing as an essential gender' (p. 19) or 'a masculine self' (p. 24). I have modified her terminology to clarify the problem of gender in distinction from that of the self.

32. Jacques Lacan, *The Four Fundamental Concepts of Psychoanalysis*, trans. Alan Sheridan (Harmondsworth: Penguin, 1979), p. 107.

33. Jacques Lacan, *Écrits: A Selection*, trans. Alan Sheridan (London: Tavistock, 1977), p. 291.
34. Lacan, *The Four Fundamental Concepts of Psychoanalysis*, p. 151.
35. Jacques Lacan, 'Of Structure as an Inmixing of an Otherness Prerequisite to Any Subject Whatever', *The Structuralist Controversy*, eds. Richard Macksey and Eugenio Donato (Baltimore: Johns Hopkins University Press, 1970), p. 194. Lacan, *The Four Fundamental Concepts of Psychoanalysis*, p. 176.
36. Slavoj Žižek, *The Sublime Object of Ideology* (London: Verso, 1989), p. 118.
37. Jacques Lacan, *Television: A Challenge to the Psychoanalytic Establishment*, ed. Joan Copjek, trans. Denis Hollier, Rosalind Krauss and Annette Michelson (New York: W. W. Norton, 1990), p. 38.

NOTES TO CHAPTER 15

1. E.g. Tokuro Miyake's 12-minute-long *The Taming of the Shrew*. More successful, though un-Shakespearean, are Tadashi Iizawa's *Susugigawa* (Washing in the River) adapted from a French medieval farce, and Junji Kinoshita's *Hikoichi-banashi* (Stories of Hikoichi) based on a Japanese folk-tale.
2. Quotations from *The Merry Wives of Windsor* and other Shakespeare plays are from the Alexander Text of the *Complete Works of William Shakespeare* (London and Glasgow: Collins, 1951).
3. These lines are written with full confidence in the great talent of Mansai (formerly Takeshi) Nomura who created the part of Taro Kaja.
4. *Kambara* (Sickle and Harakiri).
5. *Ishigakmi* (The Stone-God).
6. *Higeyagura* (The Beard-Citadel).
7. See R. S. White, *The Merry Wives of Windsor: Harvester New Critical Introductions to Shakespeare* (London: Harvester Wheatsheaf, 1991), p. xxix.
8. The one dubious case is *Okosoko*, in which a man makes an insinuation about his wife's adultery with his friend, incurring a sound beating from her.
9. The song he sings as he leads the finale quotes the all-too-familiar folksong of 'the Fool Dance of Awa' (Awa refers to an area in Shikoku Island), which goes something like, 'We are fools whether we dance or watch, / If we are all fools, / We had better be dancing fools, hadn't we?' And the refrain, 'Dou, dou, kero-kero, dou-jaina', which, though rendered here into Feste's 'hey, nonny-no', in the original Japanese could suggest anything from a shout (*dou*) to a fool (*douke*) to a croaking frog (*kero-kero*) to a defiant gesture (*dou-jaina*).
10. A tribute to Mansaku Nomura's performance as a Japanese Falstaff was published by Ronnie Mulryne in the *Festschrift* compiled for Nomura's sixtieth birthday (Tokyo, 1992).

NOTES TO CHAPTER 17

1. Certain ideas and details in this essay were first expressed in my article 'The Japanese Example: Five Meditations on Classic Drama Today in Japan, England, and the United States', *Osaka University Journal*, 5 (1979), 1–17, written after my first year in Japan in 1977. Permission to rework this material is gratefully acknowledged. Also included here are comments on Japanese

productions seen during the second year of my stay and a later visit in the spring and summer of 1992, plus touring productions in London and New York.

2. Although Zeami wrote for and starred in his own repertory company, his writings in performance theory reveal a constant readiness to improvise interpretive adjustments to suit the particular circumstances of performance and the moods of his audience of nobles. See Motokiyo Zeami, *On the Art of the Nō Drama: The Major Treatises of Zeami*. trans. J. Thomas Rimer and Masakazu Yamazaki (Princeton: Princeton University Press, 1984).

3. S. Aubrey and Giovanna M. Halford, *The Kabuki Handbook* (Rutland, Vermont and Tokyo: Tuttle, 1956), p. 260.

Index

The Index includes play titles and the names of authors, as well as other proper names, but not the names of characters in plays. Authors or adapters of plays and operas, and other writers and composers (except Shakespeare) are given in round brackets after the titles. Play types and other literary or musical forms are indicated where appropriate. Japanese as well as Western names are listed by family name. Entries in the Chronology are not included, nor is the text of *The Braggart Samurai*. R.M.